W9-CKQ-519

NAZI BILLIONAIRES

NAZI BILLIONAIRES

THE DARK HISTORY OF GERMANY'S
WEALTHIEST DYNASTIES

DAVID DE JONG

MARINER BOOKS

Boston   New York

Maps of Berlin and Nazi Germany © Pharus-Plan. Used by permission.
Design of map locations by Mapping Specialists, Ltd.

Family trees by Mapping Specialists, Ltd.

HarperCollins books may be purchased for educational, business, or
sales promotional use. For information, please email the Special
Markets Department at SPsales@harpercollins.com.

FIRST EDITION

Library of Congress Cataloging-in-Publication Data has been applied for.

ISBN 978-1-328-49788-8

Designed by Chloe Foster

22 23 24 25 26 LSC 10 9 8 7 6 5 4 3 2 1

In loving memory of my grandparents
Alice and Hans,
Hannie and John,
for they resisted, survived, and thrived,
giving their families the best life possible

"They have plundered the world, stripping naked the land in their hunger ... They are driven by greed, if their enemy be rich; by ambition, if poor ... They ravage, they seize by false pretenses, and all of this they hail as the construction of empire. And when in their wake nothing remains but a desert, they call that peace."

—Tacitus, *Agricola*

CONTENTS

Maps   x

Cast of Characters   xv

PROLOGUE: THE MEETING   1

INTRODUCTION   6

PART I: "PERFECTLY AVERAGE"   13

PART II: "THE NATIONAL SOCIALIST HAUNT WILL SOON PASS"   73

PART III: "THE CHILDREN HAVE NOW ALREADY BECOME MEN"   133

PART IV: "YOU WILL LIVE ON"   179

PART V: "NINE ZEROS"   239

PART VI: THE RECKONING   273

EPILOGUE: THE MUSEUM   311

Appendix: Family Trees   313

Acknowledgments   316

A Note on Sources   319

Notes   326

Photo Credits   362

Index   363

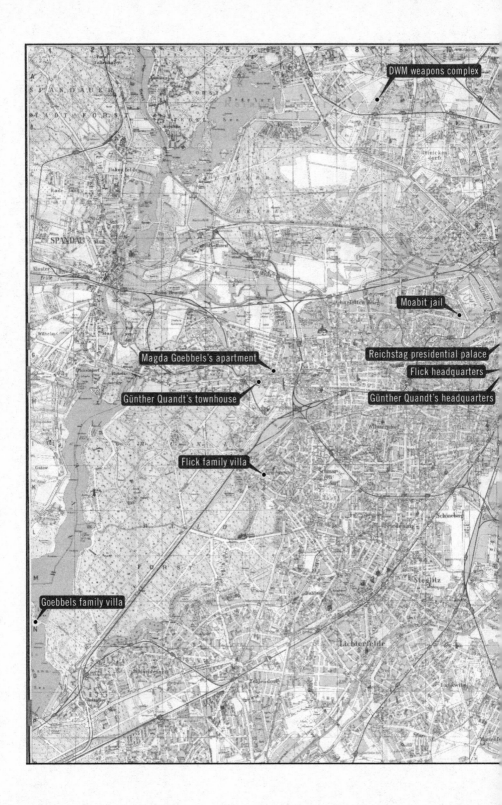

DWM weapons complex

Moabit jail

Reichstag presidential palace

Flick headquarters

Magda Goebbels's apartment

Günther Quandt's headquarters

Günther Quandt's townhouse

Flick family villa

Goebbels family villa

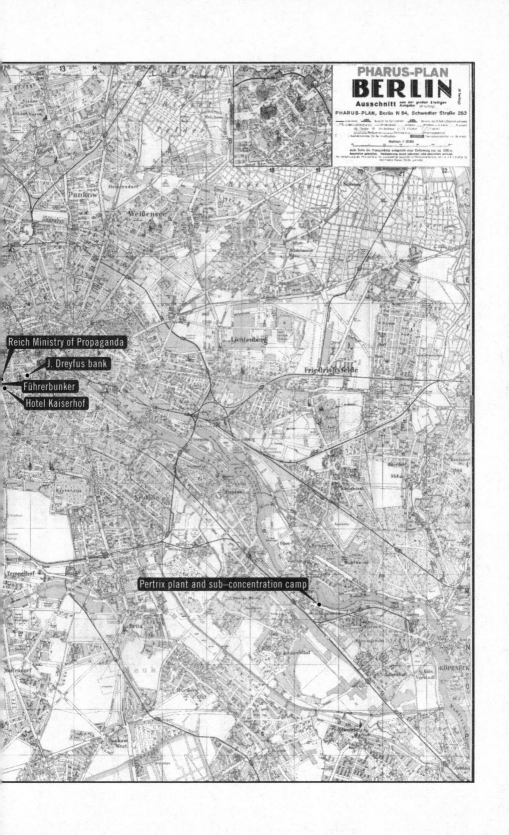

PHARUS-PLAN
BERLIN
Ausschnitt aus der großen 3 teiligen Ausgabe

PHARUS-PLAN, Berlin N 54, Schwedter Straße 263

Reich Ministry of Propaganda

J. Dreyfus bank

Führerbunker

Hotel Kaiserhof

Pertrix plant and sub—concentration camp

Pharus-Reisekarte
von
DEUTSCHLAND

Pharus-Plan Berlin N 54, Schwedter Str. 263

Maßstab 1 : 2300000

1 cm — 23 km

Hauptbahnen .... Nebenbahnen
—— Chausseen

Kleine Ausgabe

Hamburg
Neuengamme concentration camp

Fallersleben
Volkswagen factory complex and camps

Bielefeld
Dr. Oetker headquarters

Hannover
AFA battery plant and
sub−concentration camp

Ruhr area
Flick coal mines

Lorraine
Rombach steel complex

Stuttgart
Porsche car design company

Munich
Merck Finck bank

Severin
Günther Quandt's country estate

Masurian forest
Hitler's and Himmler's war lairs

Poznan
DWM weapons complex

Niewerle
Herbert Quandt's country estate

Saxony
Flick arms and steel factories

Vienna
S.M. von Rothschild bank

Zell am See
Porsche-Piëch estate

CAST OF CHARACTERS

THE QUANDTS

Günther Quandt: Patriarch. Industrialist.

Horst Pavel: Günther's right-hand man.

Toni Quandt: Günther's first wife. Herbert's mother.

Magda Goebbels: Günther's second wife. Harald's mother.

Ello Quandt: Günther's sister-in-law. Magda's best friend. Harald's god-mother.

Harald Quandt: Only child from Magda and Günther's marriage.

Gabriele Quandt: Harald's daughter.

Herbert Quandt: Günther's eldest son. BMW's savior.

Susanne Klatten: Herbert's youngest daughter. BMW heiress.

Stefan Quandt: Herbert's youngest son. BMW heir.

THE FLICKS

Friedrich Flick: Patriarch. Industrialist.

Otto Steinbrinck: Friedrich's right-hand man.

Otto-Ernst Flick: Friedrich's eldest son.

Muck, Mick, and Dagmar Flick: Otto-Ernst's children.

Friedrich Karl Flick: Friedrich's youngest son.

Eberhard von Brauchitsch: Friedrich Karl's best friend.

Ingrid Flick: Friedrich Karl's widow.

THE VON FINCKS

August von Finck Sr.: Patriarch. Private banker.

Kurt Schmitt: Allianz CEO. Reich minister of economic affairs.

August "Gustl" von Finck Jr.: Investor.

Ernst Knut Stahl: Gustl's right-hand man.

THE PORSCHE-PIËCHS

Ferdinand Porsche: Patriarch. Creator of Volkswagen and Porsche.

Anton Piëch: Ferdinand's son-in-law. Married to Louise.

Ferry Porsche: Ferdinand's son. SS officer.

Louise Piëch: Ferdinand's daughter. Married to Anton.

THE OETKERS

Richard Kaselowsky: Patriarch. CEO of Dr. Oetker.

Rudolf-August Oetker: Kaselowsky's stepson. Waffen-SS officer.

Rudolf von Ribbentrop: Rudolf-August's best friend. Waffen-SS officer.

THE TOP NAZIS

Adolf Hitler: The führer.

Joseph Goebbels: Reich minister of propaganda. Magda's spouse. Harald's stepfather.

Hermann Göring: *Reichsmarschall.* Main decision maker in Nazi economic policy.

Heinrich Himmler: *Reichsführer SS.* Principal organizer of the Holocaust.

Hjalmar Schacht: Reichsbank president and Reich minister of economic affairs.

Walther Funk: Reich minister of economic affairs and Reichsbank president.

Otto Wagener: Hitler's economic adviser.

Wilhelm Keppler: Hitler's economic adviser. Kranefuss's uncle.

Fritz Kranefuss: Organizer of Himmler's Circle of Friends. Keppler's nephew.

THE PERSECUTED

Adolf Rosenberger: Cofounder of Porsche.

Johanna and Fritz Heine: Business owners.

Hahn family: Business owners.

Heirs of Julius and Ignaz Petschek: Business owners.

Willy Dreyfus: Private banker.

Louis von Rothschild: Private banker.

THE AMERICANS

Telford Taylor: Chief prosecutor of the Nuremberg Military Tribunals.

John J. McCloy: US high commissioner for occupied Germany.

THE REIMANNS

Albert Reimann: Patriarch. CEO of Joh. A. Benckiser (JAB).

Peter Harf: Chairman of JAB. Family confidant.

Wolfgang Reimann: Albert's eldest son.

PROLOGUE: THE MEETING

"And there they stand, affectless,
like twenty-four calculating machines at the gates of Hell."
— Éric Vuillard, *The Order of the Day*

The invitations, sent by telegram four days earlier, left no doubt. The capital was calling. On Monday, February 20, 1933, at 6 p.m., about two dozen of Nazi Germany's wealthiest and most influential businessmen arrived, on foot or by chauffeured car, to attend a meeting at the official residence of the Reichstag president, Hermann Göring, in the heart of Berlin's government and business district. The attendees included Günther Quandt, a textile producer turned arms-and-battery tycoon; Friedrich Flick, a steel magnate; Baron August von Finck, a Bavarian finance mogul; Kurt Schmitt, CEO of the insurance behemoth Allianz; executives from the chemicals conglomerate IG Farben and the potash giant Wintershall; and Gustav Krupp von Bohlen und Halbach, chairman-through-marriage of the Krupp steel empire.

Three weeks earlier, Adolf Hitler had seized power in Germany after concluding a backroom deal that led the Reich president, Paul von Hindenburg, to appoint Hitler as chancellor. Now the leader of the Nazi Party wanted to "explain his policies" to the group of industrialists, financiers, executives, and heirs, or at least that's what he'd led them to believe. The businessmen were hoping for reassurance concerning the direction of Germany's economy under this new government. They would not get it. Hitler had his own plans for the meeting, and the country.

The businessmen arrived on time at Göring's palatial sand-red residence on the south bank of Berlin's Spree River, next door to the Reichstag. But they were kept waiting — not something that the impatient tycoons were particularly used to or fond of. Göring, their host, didn't greet them until fifteen minutes after the scheduled start time. In tow was Walther Funk, the dumpy and balding chief press officer for Hitler's government. The new chancellor arrived even later, accompanied by Otto Wagener, his main economic adviser. The master of ceremonies was Hjalmar Schacht, formerly president of the Reichsbank, Germany's central bank. (As it turned out, Funk, Schacht, Göring, and Allianz CEO Schmitt, four of Hitler's future ministers of economic affairs, were all present.) The meeting was the culmination of years of careful groundwork laid by Hitler's officials — years of cultivating relationships with the tycoons to build up enthusiasm for the Nazi cause.

After shaking hands with the businessmen, Hitler launched into a rambling ninety-minute speech, delivered without notes or pauses. But instead of the policy talk that had been promised, Hitler gave a sweeping diagnosis of the current political moment. The year 1918 had been a catastrophic turning point in German history, with the defeat of the German Empire in World War I and the revolution in Russia, during which the Communists came to power. In Hitler's eyes, the time had come to settle the struggle between the right and the left once and for all.

Hitler argued that, in supporting his rise as führer, the moguls would in effect be supporting themselves, their firms, and their fortunes. "Private enterprise cannot be maintained in the age of democracy," the forty-three-year-old chancellor said. "It is conceivable only if the people have a sound idea of authority and personality. Everything positive, good and valuable, which has been achieved in the world in the field of economics and culture, is solely attributable to the importance of personality." Hitler didn't speak about abolishing labor unions, rearmament, war, or the removal of Jews from German life. But he did provide a glimpse of what was to come: "We must first gain complete power if we want to crush the other side completely."

Near the end of his speech, Hitler laid out how that would happen. In only two weeks, on March 5, 1933, the people of Germany would determine the country's future by casting their votes in the national election — "the last election," according to Hitler. One way or another, democracy would fall. Germany's new chancellor intended to dissolve it entirely and replace it with a dictatorship. "Regardless of the outcome," he warned, "there would be no retreat ... There are only two possibilities, either to crowd back the opponent on constitutional grounds ... or a struggle will be conducted with other weapons, which may demand greater sacrifices." If the election didn't bring Hitler's party into control, a civil war between the right and the left would certainly erupt, he intimated. Hitler waxed poetic: "I hope the German people recognize the greatness of the hour. It shall decide the next ten or probably even hundred years."

The arms and steel tycoon Gustav Krupp, as chairman of the Reich Association of German Industry, was first among equals in the group of businessmen and its designated spokesperson. The sixty-two-year-old industrialist had prepared an extensive memo on economic policy for this meeting, his first encounter with Hitler. But given that the new chancellor had just called for the dissolution of Germany's democracy, Krupp thought it best not to initiate a dialogue on the boring details of policy. Instead, he meekly thanked the chancellor on behalf of the gathered men "for having given us such a clear picture of the conception" of his ideas. Krupp wrapped up with anodyne general remarks about the need for a swift remedy to Germany's political troubles and for a strong state, which would help the "economy and business develop and flourish."

After listening to Krupp's remarks, the Austrian-born chancellor didn't take any questions from his audience, nor did he reveal the true purpose of the meeting. He left that to the host, Göring. Hitler departed.

Göring opened the topic with a welcome promise of stability. He assured the giants of industry and finance "that with political pacification, [the] domestic economy would also quiet down." No economic "experiments" would be conducted, he said. But to guarantee a favorable climate for business, Hitler's new coalition had to emerge victorious in the coming election. The Reichstag president got to the main point: the Nazi Party needed money for the election campaign. Because taxpayers' money and state funds couldn't be used for political ends, "other circles not taking part in this political battle should at least make the financial sacrifices so necessary at this time."

Göring's conclusion echoed Hitler's: it was more than reasonable to request "financial sacrifices" of these business titans, given that "the election of March 5th would surely be the last one for the next ten years, probably even for the next hundred years." After these remarks, Göring exited the room, leaving his guests stunned, with much to ponder.

Then the mustachioed economist Hjalmar Schacht took the floor. Unlike the previous two speakers, Schacht got right down to business and suggested raising an election campaign fund of three million reichsmarks (about $20 million in today's money) for the benefit of the Nazi Party and its nationalist coalition partner, the German National People's Party, which it still needed, in order to rule the country. But not for much longer.

Right on the spot the businessmen allocated the sums among themselves. One million reichsmarks were to be paid by the black coal and iron industries from the Ruhr area, and 500,000 reichsmarks each by the potash mining and chemicals industries. The remaining million would be drawn from the brown coal industry, carmakers, and mechanical and electrical engineering firms. The men agreed that 75 percent of the money would go to the Nazi Party. The remaining quarter would proceed to its coalition partner. In conclusion, Schacht uttered the shortest and most expensive line of the evening: "And now, gentlemen, to the cash register!"

Hitler's invitation to a discussion of economic policy had been, in truth, little more than a pretext for requesting millions to build up an election campaign slush fund. Hitler and Göring had conveniently left out an important detail: the dire financial state of the Nazi Party. It was more than twelve million reichsmarks in debt, and the little cash on hand was far from enough to stage a national election campaign. But this issue would be quickly resolved. In the days and weeks following the meeting, many of its attendees, through their companies and industry associations, wired large amounts to a trust account that Schacht had opened at a private bank, Delbrück Schickler, in Berlin. The tycoons clearly had no qualms about funding the demise of their democracy. The largest donations to the Nazis came from the mining industry association (600,000 reichsmarks) and IG Farben (400,000 reichsmarks).

The day after the meeting, February 21, 1933, thirty-five-year-old Joseph Goebbels, who led the Nazi propaganda machine from Berlin as the capital's *Gauleiter* (regional leader), wrote in his diary: "Göring brings the joyful news that 3 million is available for the election. Great thing! I immediately alert the whole propaganda department. And one hour later, the machines rattle. Now we will turn on an election campaign . . . Today the work is fun. The money is there." Goebbels had started this very diary entry the day before, describing the depressed mood at his Berlin headquarters because of the lack of funds. What a difference twenty-four hours could make.

INTRODUCTION

On May 8, 2019, Verena Bahlsen, the twenty-six-year-old heiress to Germany's famous maker of cookies, the Bahlsen company, walked onto the stage at a digital marketing conference in Hamburg to give a livestreamed keynote speech about sustainable food production. She was wearing blue denim overalls and a black turtleneck, topped with a black suit jacket; the muted colors were a striking contrast to her wavy red hair and bright freckles. She confidently took the microphone. Minutes into her speech, however, she veered off topic, responding to a socialist politician who had spoken earlier about the idea of common ownership of Germany's largest companies, such as BMW. "I am a capitalist," Verena declared. "I own a quarter of Bahlsen and I am happy about it too. It should continue to belong to me. I want to make money and buy sailing yachts from my dividend and stuff."

Her offhand remarks immediately drew furious reactions on social media. How dare she brag about her wealth, especially when her family firm was known to have used forced labor during World War II? A few days later, Verena brushed the criticism aside in comments to *Bild,* Germany's largest tabloid: "That was before my time and we paid the forced laborers exactly the same as the Germans and treated them well." She added: "Bahlsen has nothing to feel guilty about."

A scandal erupted. Verena had committed what is considered perhaps the greatest moral offense in Germany today: displaying ignorance about the Nazi era. It was no secret that her family firm, like most other German companies, had benefited from Nazi Germany's system of forced labor during World War II, wherein millions of foreigners were taken from their homelands and compelled to work in German factories, often for paltry wages under abominable conditions. In Bahlsen's case, some seven hundred coerced workers, most of them Polish and Ukrainian women, were deported to the cookie factory in Hannover, where they were underpaid and abused. Verena's comments generated headlines worldwide, and the fallout was swift. Historians and politicians condemned her remarks. Calls for a boycott of Bahlsen cookies followed.

Within days, a line of black Mercedes limousines pulled up to Verena's apartment building in Berlin's Prenzlauer Berg neighborhood, to whisk her and her possessions home to Hannover. Verena then, through her family firm, issued a public apology. But reporters at *Der Spiegel* magazine dug in. They revealed that Verena's grandfather and great-uncles, the men who ran Bahlsen during the Third Reich, had been members of Hitler's Nazi Party (the National Socialist German Workers' Party, or NSDAP) and had donated money to the SS, Nazi Germany's all-powerful paramilitary organization. Many of the Ukrainian women were deported to the plant in Hannover from an expropriated cookie factory in Kyiv that Bahlsen had taken over, the reporters discovered. After the war, like millions of Germans, the Bahlsen men denied all charges of complicity with the Nazis and got off scot-free.

As public outrage grew, the Bahlsen family used a tried-and-true method to deal with the fury: they announced, through their company, that they had hired a prominent German historian to independently investigate the history of the entire firm and family, including their actions during the Nazi era. The findings were to be published in a study for anyone to read, once the research was concluded. The announcement worked, and the controversy faded. But I knew where this story was headed.

I had joined *Bloomberg News* years earlier, in late November 2011, as a reporter on a new team investigating hidden wealth, billionaires, and family-owned companies many times bigger than Bahlsen. I began in the New York office the week after the NYPD had violently removed members of the Occupy Wall Street movement from Zucotti Park, in the heart of Manhattan's financial district. In the wake of the previous years' financial crisis, the tension between the 1 percent and the 99 percent was palpable around the globe. Though I was hired to cover American business dynasties such as the Kochs and the Waltons (who control Walmart), I was soon asked to add the German-speaking nations to my beat, since I am Dutch.

I accepted the additional beat grudgingly. Germany's brutal occupation of my native Netherlands from May 1940 through May 1945 had left a deep scar among the generations before me and in our national consciousness. Back then, "they" had occupied and pillaged our country. As a kid growing up in Amsterdam in the 1990s, I saw the Germans "invade" our nearby beaches during the spring and summer holidays, and worse, they often beat us at soccer (and still do).

My playful antagonism toward Germans was compounded by my family's experiences during the war. In 1941, my maternal grandfather, a Protestant and not yet married, attempted to flee the Netherlands by sailing to England with his best friend. Their plan was to join the Royal Air Force, but their boat was blown back to shore. German soldiers arrested them, and they were sentenced as political prisoners. My grandfather spent almost two years in captivity, forced to work in a steel factory in Bochum. He contracted tuberculosis there and was emaciated, near death, at the time of his release.

My father's parents, who were Jewish, were separated during the war. My paternal grandfather owned and ran lace and stocking factories near the Dutch-German border. He managed to hide in the center of Amsterdam after his firm was expropriated. My grandmother, a native of Switzerland, tried to flee with my three-year-old aunt and a companion to her country of birth in 1942. They were arrested by the Gestapo (Nazi Germany's secret police) at the French-Swiss border. A Gestapo officer took pity on my grandmother and her young child, and he let them go. They made it over the border to Switzerland. Their companion in this attempted escape, a well-known painter, was not so fortunate. He was put on a train to Sobibor, the extermination camp in Nazi-occupied Poland, where he was murdered.

My grandparents, despite their suffering in the war, were exceptionally lucky. My Jewish grandfather was reunited with his wife and young daughter after the liberation of Europe, and he got his stocking factories back, but tragically, his father had died in a concentration camp, Bergen-Belsen. My Jewish grandparents were never bitter about the ones they loved and lost, murdered by the Nazis. Nor was my maternal grandfather bitter about the time he spent in German captivity. Before he was robbed of his freedom, he had fallen in love with the girl next door. He recovered from tuberculosis at a Swiss sanatorium; my grandmother remained at his bedside the entire time. They married shortly after he recovered.

My parents were born a few years after the war. All told, my grandparents made a good life for themselves, for their children, and for me.

Yet my maternal grandfather had a way of taking some gentle "revenge" on the Germans: he constantly made jokes about them. He was my hero growing up, a proud Dutch patriot. My grandparents lived on a farming estate in a tiny Dutch village with three hundred inhabitants, near the German-favored beaches. "Another incoming invasion," he quipped every spring. He would ask me to promise never to take the Germans seriously because they took themselves so seriously. I earnestly swore to him that I would not. "Humor is the best revenge," he said.

But on my new beat, I came to take the Germans very seriously — particularly those in big business and finance. In summer 2012, as part of a reporting assignment, I stumbled on an inconspicuous website. "Harald Quandt Holding," read the homepage of this company, which listed the assets of its various investment firms at $18 billion. How did an obscure German family office with a bare-bones, one-page website manage to invest such staggering amounts of money? That question became the loose thread that led me to this history.

It turned out that this branch of the Quandt business dynasty descended from one Magda Goebbels, the unofficial First Lady of the Third Reich and wife of the Nazi propaganda minister, Joseph Goebbels. Magda's son Harald was the only one of her seven children to survive the war. Harald, sole offspring of Magda's first marriage to the industrialist Günther Quandt, grew up in the Goebbels household but never joined the Nazi Party. Harald did have an older half brother, Herbert Quandt, who would save BMW from bankruptcy years after the war. By 2012, Herbert's youngest heirs remained Germany's wealthiest family, with a near-majority control of BMW, whereas Harald's heirs oversaw a "smaller" holding in a leafy spa town outside Frankfurt.

In 2007, the Quandt dynasty, in a move not unlike the Bahlsens', commissioned a German history professor to investigate the family's Nazi past. This move came on the heels of a critical TV documentary that threw light on some of the dynasty's involvement in the Third Reich, focusing on its mass production of weapons, its use of forced and slave labor, and its seizure of firms owned by Jews. Günther and Herbert Quandt led the family firms involved in these activities.

What struck me during my reporting was the continuing lack of historical transparency among members of the Quandt dynasty's richer branch, the one that owns BMW, even after the family-commissioned study — with the professed goal of "openness" — was published in 2011. The study revealed that the family patriarchs committed many more brutal crimes during the Nazi era. As I soon discovered, the Quandts were not alone. Other German business dynasties flourished during the Third Reich and went on to control enormous global fortunes, all the while struggling, or outright failing, to reckon with a dark lineage.

These histories have never been told to an audience outside Germany. Meanwhile, these families still control billions of euros and dollars. Some of the heirs no longer own a business; they simply manage their inherited wealth. But many own well-known brands, whose products blanket the globe — from the cars we drive, to the coffee and beer we drink, to the houses we rent, the land we live on, and the hotels we book for vacations and business trips. My articles focused mainly on these families' finances. It was *Bloomberg*, after all. But that angle left the most compelling questions unanswered. How did the patriarchs of these families rise to greater heights of power under Hitler's rule? Why were almost all of them allowed to walk free after Nazi Germany fell? And why, after so many decades, are many of the heirs still doing so little to acknowledge their forebears' crimes, projecting a view of history that keeps these matters opaque? Why are their charitable foundations, media prizes, and corporate headquarters still named for their Nazi-collaborator patriarchs?

The answer to those questions, or at least a piece of it, lies in these pages — in the origin stories of some of Germany's wealthiest reigning dynasties, who continue to control swaths of the global economy. More specifically, the answer lies in the stories of those dynasties' patriarchs, who amassed untold money and power by abetting the atrocities of the Third Reich. Born in or near imperial Germany, these men joined the ranks of the business elite during the volatile period after World War I. By the start of the Nazi era, in 1933, they were well-established industrialists, financiers, food producers, or car designers, though some were just starting a career as the designated heir to an imperious father. These men collaborated with Hitler's regime in the years leading up to and including World War II, enriching themselves and their firms through weapons production, the use of forced and slave labor, and the seizure of companies owned by Jews and non-Jews alike in Germany and Nazi-occupied territories.

Some of these tycoons were ardent Nazis, who unquestioningly embraced Hitler's ideology. But most were simply calculating, unscrupulous opportunists looking to expand their business empires at any cost. All of them became members of the Nazi Party or the SS, or both, during the Third Reich. Such is the dark history of the Quandts of BMW; the Flicks, former owners of Daimler-Benz; the von Fincks, a financier family who cofounded Allianz and Munich Re; the Porsche-Piëch clan, who control Volkswagen and Porsche; and the Oetkers, who own global empires of baking ingredients, prepared foods, beer, and luxury hotels. Their patriarchs are the Nazi billionaires. This book details the Third Reich histories and reckoning of those German business dynasties that continue to have worldwide influence and relevance today.

But this book isn't just about the sins of Germany's titans of industry and finance. Here too is the story of how, after the war, it fell to the victorious Allies to decide the fate of these Nazi profiteers. But for the sake of political expediency, and for fear of the looming threat of Communism, the United States and the United Kingdom quietly handed most of these tycoons back over to Germany, which in turn allowed most of the guilty moguls to walk free, with little more than a slap on the wrist. In the decades that followed, the western part of a divided Germany developed one of the world's most prosperous economies, and those same Nazi businessmen amassed billions of dollars, joining the ranks of the world's wealthiest tycoons. All the while they kept silent, or outright lied, about their ties to genocide.

As of today, a small few of these men's heirs have truly reckoned with the family past. Others still refuse to do so, with little negative effect. Verena Bahlsen escaped any professional consequences for her comments. In fact, her father soon promoted her. In mid-March 2020, Bahlsen announced that Verena, instead of her three siblings, would become the company's primary active shareholder and represent the next generation at the family firm.

The Germany that rose out of defeat in World War II matured into a tolerant society, one that educated its people, in remembrance and remorse, about its past mistakes. As many of today's great global powers have fallen prey to dictators, far-right populists, and demagogues, Germany has remained the moral backbone of the West. Much of that delicate equilibrium stems from its continuous public reckoning with the Nazi past and the mass atrocities that occurred under Hitler's regime. Over the past fifty years, German political leaders haven't shied away from taking moral responsibility and acknowledging the sins of the past. But more recently, Germany has begun a transformation in a different direction. As the last witnesses to the Nazi era die and the memory of the Third Reich fades, an increasingly mainstream and brazen reactionary right is brutalizing the progressive ideals of postwar Germany.

At a time when disinformation is omnipresent and the far right is rising globally, historical transparency and the subsequent reckoning become even more important, as we can see in the United States and in the United Kingdom, where statues of Confederate generals, slave traders, and Christopher Columbus are being torn down and colleges named after racist presidents are being rechristened. Yet this movement toward facing the past is somehow bypassing many of Germany's legendary businessmen. Their dark legacy remains hidden in plain sight. This book, in some small way, tries to right that wrong.

PART I

"PERFECTLY AVERAGE"

1.

The Quandt family had profited for decades from war and upheaval. But when Günther Quandt permanently moved to Berlin amid the flu pandemic in October 1918, war and upheaval were about to take the thirty-seven-year-old textile magnate's country from him. Günther witnessed the demise of his beloved German Empire firsthand when it lost World War I, along with millions of its men in the trenches. Despite the imperial state's crushing defeat, the Quandts made millions from the war. The family textile factories that Günther led in rural Brandenburg, a few hours north of the capital, had churned out thousands of uniforms a week for their longtime imperial client. Waves of young German soldiers were sent to the trenches and front lines, and each one needed a new uniform to replace the shredded fatigues of their fallen comrades. So it went, week in, week out, for four seemingly endless years.

Yet Germany's loss was Günther's gain. By the time the war had ended, the money Quandt had pocketed from it was enough to bankroll his permanent move to Berlin. During the war, Günther had managed to avoid military service, initially because he was found to be unfit physically, but later because he had become a leading figure in the empire's war economy. From Berlin, he oversaw a government department that supplied the army and the navy with wool. At the same time, Günther managed his family factories, providing daily instructions via letter, while his two younger brothers and brother-in-law were fighting at the front. When they returned alive from battle, Günther told them that he was moving to Berlin for good. He would continue to oversee the textile factories from the raucous German capital. But he also aspired to operate on a bigger stage, explore new business ventures, and branch out to other industries.

Günther loved Berlin. He was born on July 28, 1881, in rural Pritzwalk, some eighty miles northwest of the imperial capital. As the firstborn son of a prominent textile family, and thus automatically his father's heir apparent, he was sent to Berlin for a proper education at fifteen; he lived there with his English teacher. The German Empire had become a leading industrialized nation at the turn of the century, and Berlin its beating heart. Günther used his free time to explore the sprawling, bustling metropolis, where he witnessed the building of the elevated railway and the underground metro. Günther recalled his Berlin school days as "happy years." He would have preferred going on to study architecture, but that was out of the question. Günther was called home to learn the textile trade from his sickly father, Emil, a tall, burly man with a thick mustache. This proud Prussian Protestant held to strict tenets of frugality, piety, and hard work.

But this time, Günther wasn't moving to Berlin alone. His wife, Toni, and their two young sons, Hellmut and Herbert, were joining him. Günther had been married to Toni for twelve years, and Hellmut and Herbert were ten and eight years old, respectively. Toni, a pretty brunette, was the love of Günther's life. He had almost been barred from marrying her, as his parents considered her family nouveau riche. Their attempts to end the relationship made Günther seriously contemplate immigrating to the United States. He even went so far as to find the cheapest route there, via boat to Baltimore, in order to look for work in Chicago. But Günther stayed put. In the end, love and persistence prevailed, and his parents gave their blessing.

On October 15, 1918, during the fall holiday, Toni and the two boys traveled to Berlin to visit Günther and the new family home. The family of four stayed at the luxurious Hotel Fürstenhof on Potsdamer Platz. Günther was eager to show them the mansion he had bought some fifteen miles southwest from the city center, in the leafy suburb of Neubabelsberg, a colony of villas that was home to many of Berlin's bankers, industrialists, and moneyed intelligentsia. The house stood directly on a lake, Griebnitzsee, and at the edge of Babelsberg Palace Park, the site of the emperor's summer residence; the grounds were filled with ancient trees. Toni had yet to fully recover from the operation that had followed Herbert's complicated birth. She was hoping to regain her health at the house, with its pleasant setting: a lake, a park, and a street lined with lush sycamore, lime, and maple trees.

"This is where I will become completely well," Toni told Günther, after he showed her and the two boys around.

It was not to be. The day after their visit, Toni and her sons traveled back to Pritzwalk. That night Günther received a phone call from an employee: Toni had returned from Berlin with light flu symptoms. The boys had been brought to stay with a family member, in order to avoid infection. In a pandemic, you had to take every precaution — the Spanish flu spread so easily. Within two days, Toni's flu developed into double pneumonia. Desperate, Günther drove to a doctor he knew, but the man couldn't offer immediate help: he had almost a dozen patients suffering from the same illness. Toni died that cold October night. She was only thirty-four. The frail woman, who had longed for a fresh start, was no match for the second global wave of the Spanish flu, which was leaving millions of deaths in its wake.

In an instant, Günther became a widower, alone in the frantic capital of a defeated empire on the verge of extinction. What's more, soon his two young sons, who had just lost their mother, would be moving in with him; they needed far more care than he could ever give. Günther had little time for them. He had to build an empire. After Toni's funeral in Pritzwalk, on a sunny fall day, Günther stood at her grave and felt that he had lost "something irretrievable." "I believed that people are capable of giving and receiving true love only once in their lives," he later wrote.

But six months later, Günther fell in love again. It was an attachment that haunts the Quandts to this day. He became smitten with Magda Friedländer, who later would become well known as Magda Goebbels, "the First Lady of the Third Reich."

2.

On the warm spring evening of April 21, 1919, Günther Quandt boarded a packed night train in Berlin. It was Easter Monday, and he was all set to travel first class, with two associates, to Kassel in central Germany, to attend a business meeting. Shortly before departure, a mother posited her teenage daughter outside the businessmen's private compartment; the girl was weighed down with luggage and boxes. Her mother had searched the entire train for a free seat. Her parting instructions: "Magda, this is where you'll stay put." Günther waited two, three minutes before getting up and casually inviting the young girl to sit with them. It took many more minutes, and a few more invitations from Günther, before the timid Magda opened the compartment door and joined the trio of much older men.

After Günther helped her stow her things, Magda sank down into a plush upholstered seat. Once the two began to talk, Günther discovered just how attractive the girl was: "I had invited in an exceptionally beautiful apparition: light blue eyes, beautiful full blond hair, a well-cut, regular face, a slender figure," he later wrote. Magda was only seventeen, twenty years younger than Günther and only six years older than his eldest son, Hellmut. Magda had just spent Easter holiday with her mother and stepfather in Berlin and was returning to her boarding school in Goslar, at the mountainous center of Germany. Günther and Magda talked throughout the entire train ride, discussing travel and Berlin's theaters. He was infatuated with her. Around 1 a.m., the train stopped at Goslar station. Günther helped Magda get her belongings off the train; as inconspicuously as possible, he stole a glance at a luggage label and noted her boarding school's address.

As soon as Günther arrived in Kassel, he sent Magda a letter, asking if he could visit her the following afternoon at the boarding school. He would pretend to be a friend of her father's in order to get permission from the headmistress to take her out. Magda replied, giving her assent. The next day, Günther showed up at the school with a bouquet of roses — not for Magda, but rather to charm her headmistress into allowing Magda to take a stroll with him. A courtship began. On just their third date, during a scenic drive through the Harz mountains, Günther proposed to Magda in the back of his chauffeured car. Stunned, she asked him for three days to consider. The marriages she had witnessed over her seventeen years had been far from good.

Magda was born out of wedlock in Berlin on November 11, 1901. Her parents, the engineer Oskar Ritschel and the maid Auguste Behrend, eventually married. But Magda's mother divorced Ritschel after discovering that he was having an affair. Auguste then remarried; her second husband, Richard Friedländer, was a German Jewish businessman. Now they too were about to get a divorce. Magda grew up an only child in a cosmopolitan, upper-middle-class household, moving with her mother and stepfather between Berlin and Brussels, where she attended a strict Catholic boarding school run by nuns. Her Jewish ties extended beyond her stepfather. When Magda met Günther, she had just split up with a boyfriend, Victor Chaim Arlosoroff, an ambitious Jewish émigré from Russia. He studied economics at Berlin's prestigious Humboldt University. But as a shiksa, a non-Jewish woman, Magda felt that she would never truly belong in the Jewish community.

After three days of thought, Magda accepted Günther's marriage proposal. She was bemused that this stout, older man, who wore double-breasted suits, starched collars, and golden cuff links and exuded money and power, took such an interest in her. A tall man with piercing blue eyes, a round, balding head, and a bad comb-over, Günther looked imposing — but not necessarily attractive. Yet the choice to marry someone two decades older wasn't driven by romantic love; fascination and ambition played their part. Magda was impressed by Günther, who always wore a mischievous grin, as if he knew something that others did not. Magda longed to leave boarding school and become the wife of someone with great financial resources and esteem in the business world. She fantasized about running a large household and organizing social events for his friends and business partners. Günther, however, insisted that Magda meet two conditions before they married. She had to give up Catholicism and reconvert to Protestantism; she also had to reassume her original surname, Ritschel. Friedländer, her stepfather's Jewish surname, was a no-go for Günther and his conservative Lutheran family. Magda dutifully obliged. She told her mother: "Religion doesn't matter to me, I have my God in my heart."

In early January 1921, Günther and Magda married in a spa hotel on the west bank of the Rhine, just outside Bonn. The bride wore a gown of Brussels lace. But the harmony between them didn't last. The newlyweds' differences in age and character quickly became painfully clear when the work-

Günther Quandt.

aholic Günther abruptly ended their ten-day honeymoon in Italy to attend
an "unmissable conference." Even before this sudden departure, the trip
had not been a success. While the couple was driving through the Italian
countryside in a chauffeured Mercedes limousine, Magda discovered that
her husband didn't care much for the "real" Italy. As her mother, Auguste,
later recalled, Magda realized that "fundamentally he was a man lacking
all aesthetic sensibilities, a thorough-going pragmatist to whom art and
beauty meant little. Nature, too, left him quite unmoved. As they traveled
through Umbria, through the landscape of classical beauty and historical
significance . . . Quandt was explaining to his wife the geological structure
of the soil and calculating its possibilities for industrial exploitation." The
trip wasn't a total flop, though. On November 1, 1921, a little more than
nine months after their honeymoon, Magda gave birth to the one child
they would have together, a son named Harald.

Magda Friedländer.

She gave birth to him alone in the hospital. Günther was working, of course. Now that they were back home in Berlin, for him there was only business; he did not cultivate a personal life. When he took a trip with his wife and sons, visits to companies or factories were the main focus. He always worked twelve-hour days, arriving at his desk at 7:30 a.m. and returning home at 7:30 p.m., "tired and battered," Magda's mother later recalled. "After dinner, he would sit in his chair, open Berlin's financial newspaper, and fall asleep three minutes later." Günther was chronically exhausted. He complained that he had no time to read books or think up new ideas. Social life barely interested him — he might attend an affair if it was business-related, but it "was only arranged if unavoidable." This pained Magda. Events at home provided the only moments when she, housewife and hostess, could be the center of attention. But there was barely any space for married life in Günther's world. Magda had no choice but to adapt.

3.

In the early 1920s, as Günther and Magda Quandt were already growing apart, the new postwar German state, known as the Weimar Republic, was devolving into chaos. Many businessmen kept their distance from its volatile parliamentary politics, as one constitutional crisis followed another. Instead, they turned to another playing field for leverage and profit: the stock market.

Hyperinflation and the flight of capital out of Germany accelerated in summer 1922, following the assassination of the minister of foreign affairs, the Jewish industrialist Walter Rathenau, and the threat of defaulting on gargantuan reparation payments imposed on Germany under the Treaty of Versailles. After Rathenau's murder in Berlin, any last shred of confidence in Germany's currency evaporated. The nation's inflation rate rose by 1,300 percent, and the Reichsbank began printing trillion-mark bills. Only the few wealthy Germans who had invested in tangible assets, such as real estate and factories, profited from this situation; any debt they held promptly evaporated. But most of Germany's middle class had put its money in savings or in worthless bonds that had been used to finance World War I. Millions of Germans were ruined.

Stocks, however, floated somewhere between tangible and liquid, in a financial no-man's-land where only the most audacious speculators dared tread. Günther Quandt was one of those speculators. In search of an opportunity to diversify the money he had made during the war, Günther turned to currency trading and stock market speculation. As prices fell, small investors began to sell off their shares, leaving those few firms backed by tangible assets to trade at bargain prices. It was a speculator's dream — but a dangerous one. The unsteady German currency made for volatile price swings, and a rookie trader could easily get caught out, betting against big investors who were trying to snap up large packages of shares and using cheap debt to speculate.

After a particularly risky trade on a wool firm netted Günther forty-five million marks in fall 1921, he commissioned a dozen banks to buy up shares in a dozen industrial companies. One firm he invested in was Germany's massive producer of potash, Wintershall. Although Günther had already joined its mining board, he lacked overall control. This bothered him deeply. "I had nothing to say anywhere," he later recalled. It was an unpleasant and unfamiliar role for the textile mogul, who, while leading his family factories from a distance, was determined to become a major player in a different industry. He had just turned forty, and time was ticking by. The prospect of using his fortune solely to speculate on stocks during "the evil period of inflation" repulsed him, Günther wrote. Yet for someone who proclaimed to have such an aversion to speculation, he was managing to overcome his professed disgust with great success. Even after his stock-buying spree, he still had thirty-five million marks left. He was ready to buy a firm of his own.

In spring 1922, Günther identified his prey: the Berlin-based business Accumulatoren-Fabrik AG (AFA). This company had become one of the world's biggest producers of batteries. When Günther set his sights on AFA, electrification was in full swing around the globe. The firm also had deep ties to the arms industry, having supplied batteries to German submarines during World War I. However, AFA's intrinsic value wasn't reflected in its stock price. Its ownership was spread wide, and it lacked proper mechanisms, such as preferential shares, to protect it from a takeover.

As Günther began to make daily purchases of AFA shares, he used a web of shell companies, banks, and straw men, including family members, to avoid attention, remain anonymous, and raise more money. But he was forced to go public in September 1922, when the AFA board announced a capital increase, accompanied by an issuance of preferential shares. By then, Günther had amassed only a quarter stake in AFA. Acquiring a majority would be next to impossible if the share increase went through.

The day after the announcement, Günther was reading Berlin's financial newspaper at his office desk when he came across an anonymous ad calling for fellow AFA shareholders to vote against the board's proposals. Günther called Walther Funk, the newspaper's editor in chief. Funk knew everyone of any business stature in Germany, and he revealed that a man named Paul Hamel had placed the ad; Günther arranged a meeting with him that night. Hamel was a partner at the private bank Sponholz and specialized in corporate takeovers. He and Günther decided to join forces.

After a month of strenuous negotiations with the board of AFA, the corporate raiders emerged victorious. No preferential shares were issued, and Günther received four supervisory seats on the board. Meanwhile, in secret he kept buying AFA shares, financed by his textile factories. In June 1923, Günther became supervisory board chairman, with his group controlling some 75 percent of the shares.

The hostile takeover of AFA was complete. Günther had gained control of a world-renowned firm in a new industry. He had made a swift transformation, from textile merchant to shrewd speculator to full-fledged industrialist. Plus, thanks to Funk, he had gained a business partner in Paul Hamel. After an AFA executive died in January 1925, Günther took over the late businessman's office at company headquarters, at Askanischer Platz 3. It lay next to Berlin's main railroad station, in the heart of the government and business district, close to money and power. From there, sitting behind a big, dark double desk in a large office suite with high, wood-paneled walls, Günther ruled over the nascent Quandt empire.

Three years later, Günther conquered a second company: Deutsche Waffen- und Munitionsfabriken (DWM). During World War I, the business had been one of the most important makers of arms and ammo for Germany's imperial army. Its subsidiaries had produced the famous Mauser rifles and Luger pistols, plus millions of bullets and parts for fighter planes. Günther fondly thought of DWM as "a little Krupp," referring to the infamous Krupp steel firm, Germany's largest producer of arms.

But the once-mighty DWM was in dire shape when Günther and his business partners made a move for it in summer 1928. The Berlin-based firm had been forced to retool as part of Germany's agreement to disarm after losing the war, and it now produced only kitchen appliances and sewing machines, among other harmless items. The only weapons DWM was allowed to make were sporting and hunting rifles. The company's share price had plummeted, plagued by rumors of insolvency and an antiquated management team.

DWM's sorry state made it a much easier, and cheaper, target for takeover than AFA had been. In his 1946 memoir, published in the wake of World War II, Günther desperately attempted to create the impression that he had never been deeply involved in the arms business. He alleged that it was Paul Hamel who brought him the opportunity to expand into the weapons industry. (The duo had added another Paul — Paul Rohde, a steel tycoon — to form a takeover trio for DWM.) According to Günther, Hamel mobilized investors so successfully at the next DWM shareholders' meeting that the entire executive board resigned in July 1928. Revisionist history aside, it was ultimately Günther who, again, was named supervisory board chairman, due to his reputation for capably restructuring companies, whatever the industry.

4.

As the era of hyperinflation peaked and ended in late 1923, Friedrich Flick, a forty-year-old steel mogul, moved with his wife, Marie, and their sons to Berlin. They settled in a villa tucked away in the upscale Grunewald neighborhood, in the forested western part of the capital. Flick too had been profiting enormously from the heady years of speculation and inflation, which enabled him to leave his native Siegerland, a rural region southeast of the Ruhr area, and settle in the capital. Now Flick paced the well-kept gravel path around his new villa, chomping on cheap cigars and plotting his next audacious move.

To mark his arrival, Flick bought a stately office building at Bellevuestrasse 12, from which to rule his growing empire of industrial interests. It lay on a quiet street, right between the Tiergarten and Potsdamer Platz. Berlin's bustling center was just down the road, and Günther Quandt's headquarters on Askanischer Platz were only a three-minute drive south. With his dour determination, ruthlessness, and knack for numbers and

subterfuge, Flick was rapidly becoming one of Germany's most successful
and influential steel tycoons. He rarely seemed to enjoy it. No hint of glee
lit up Flick's blue eyes, nor did any faint smile pass over his features. His
squat build, gaunt face, focused stare, and full head of rapidly graying hair
gave him an intimidating and stern look that befit the man who would
become Nazi Germany's most notorious industrialist.

Two years younger than Günther Quandt, Flick was born on July 10,
1883, in Ernsdorf, a sleepy village in imperial Germany's burgeoning industrial heartland. The son of a timber merchant who held stakes in several ore mines, Flick studied business and economics in Cologne before
parlaying his apprenticeship at a struggling Siegerland steel firm into a di-
rectorship at age twenty-four. He then joined the board of another local
steel firm that was also in a financial bother. The move to the boardroom
enabled Flick to marry Marie Schuss, daughter of a respected Siegen city
councilor and textile producer, in 1913. Before long the couple had three
sons: Otto-Ernst, Rudolf, and the latecomer Friedrich Karl. The Flick dynasty was beginning to take shape.

Friedrich Flick.

Flick had an uncanny gift for memorizing numbers and analyzing balance sheets. Back to back, he restructured the two struggling steel firms before seizing an opportunity presented by the outbreak of World War I. In 1915, Flick was appointed to the board of Charlottenhütte as its commercial director. The financially sound firm was the largest producer of steel in Siegerland, but it was still small compared to its many competitors across the German Empire. Flick's fellow board members allowed him to embark on an ambitious spree of takeovers, quadrupling the balance-sheet total over the course of the war. The company profited handily from the army's increased demand for weapons-grade steel.

As demand for weapons rose in the final two years of World War I, the prices of steel, ore, and scrap metal exploded along with it. Flick used Charlottenhütte's exorbitant wartime profits to finance the company's takeover strategy. At the same time, he implemented his own scheme: Flick began secretly buying up stock in Charlottenhütte, which had no dominant shareholder. He financed a stealthy takeover through a profitable side business in scrap metal, his father's money, and his wife's dowry. What's more, he twice convinced his board and the state to issue preferred stock to ward off takeover threats, both realistic ones and those he exaggerated, so that no one else would end up gaining control of Charlottenhütte.

After fending off a real takeover threat by the legendary Ruhr steel mogul August Thyssen and after striking a deal with him in early 1920, Flick became Charlottenhütte's controlling shareholder. He then transformed the firm into his personal holding company for a rapidly changing array of shares in steel, mining, and other heavy industry firms, often purchasing stocks through straw men and shell companies to hide his identity and intentions, much as Günther Quandt was doing at the same time. Flick's menacing pace of share acquisitions, sales, and swaps brought him into fierce competition and occasional collaboration with established industrialists such as Thyssen, Krupp, and others.

After making a pact with Thyssen, Flick agreed to stay out of the Ruhr area, temporarily abandoning his ultimate aim. Instead, he started doing steel deals in Upper Silesia, a heavily contested region that went back and forth between German and Polish control. Its volatility was fertile ground for cheap buying opportunities. Flick's Upper Silesian steel deals brought him national attention for the first time. A business journalist at the *Berliner Tageblatt*, the capital's largest newspaper, was the first to profile Flick. In 1924, the reporter wrote that Flick was "seized with the spirit of the times and felt himself equally called upon. He jumped with both feet into the cauldron of the reshuffling process, dived under a few times and resurfaced as the new conglomerate king of heavy industry . . . Friedrich Flick —whose name is unknown to the public, but whom mining colleagues and big bank directors (who can't stand him, because he shuts them out) acknowledge as one of the most powerful, successful, and skillful." Flick hated any form of media attention and began bribing journalists to kill the articles they were writing about him.

Through his incursion into Silesia, Flick finally gained a foothold in the industrial region he coveted most: the Ruhr area. Over 1923–24, he swapped a large part of his Upper Silesian interests for stakes in Ruhr steel firms controlled by a competitor. The swap included shares in Gelsenberg, a mining firm. Flick's next move was his boldest yet. In 1926, a group of Ruhr industrialists established the Vereinigte Stahlwerke (VSt), a conglomerate that regulated steel production and pricing, in Düsseldorf. Largely financed by American bonds, it became the world's second-largest steel firm, bested in size only by US Steel. Flick received a sizable stake in the VSt because of his Silesian share swap and moved many of his business interests into the new Ruhr conglomerate. But it wasn't enough. He wanted to control the entire VSt. When a few of its controlling companies merged, and Gelsenberg surfaced as the VSt's largest shareholder, Flick seized the opportunity. He began buying up Gelsenberg shares in hopes of acquiring a majority stake. After making a series of stock swaps and trades, mainly with a former rival, Flick became the VSt's majority shareholder, gaining control of one of the world's largest industrial conglomerates. By 1929, at only forty-five years of age, he effectively ascended to the rank of Germany's most powerful industrialist.

5.

The sky was also the limit for Günther Quandt in the late 1920s. Although his brothers were increasingly taking over the running of the textile factories back in Brandenburg, he continued to set the strategy for the family business. He was a major shareholder in Wintershall, Germany's largest potash firm. And, most important, he had conquered two big industrial businesses that sold their goods around the world. A DWM executive wrote that Günther had converted to a new faith: "He belongs to those men whose strength only lies in their belief in the invincible power of money. His success only serves to strengthen this, again and again. This belief has turned into a religion for him, albeit one that doesn't necessarily contain a faith in God."

With the new money came the typical trappings of the parvenu. For years, Günther had been looking for a suitable pied-à-terre in central Berlin, so that he didn't have to travel home after leaving the office late or going to the theater with Magda. One day in 1926, his real estate broker contacted him: a businessman needed to sell his townhouse immediately, to avoid bankruptcy. Günther bought the place, and all its contents, after haggling with the desperate owner to bring the price down. The townhouse, located in Berlin's sophisticated Westend, came expensively furnished, with its entire inventory intact, down to the last wine bottle, artwork, and piece of cutlery. It was decorated far more stylishly than his own mansion — the centerpiece of its living room was a large organ. After buying the townhouse, Günther quipped to Magda: "See, dear, how wrong you were when you said that culture cannot be bought. I *have* bought it!"

But as his belongings steadily increased, Günther's family life was falling apart once again. Disaster struck in early July 1927. His firstborn son and heir apparent, Hellmut, had just started a year-long work-study program abroad when he died in Paris, after a botched operation for appendicitis. He was only nineteen. Hellmut's last words were addressed to Günther: "I would have so gladly helped you with your great work, my dear father."

Günther was devastated. He wrote: "I lost my dear, sweet boy, who I was always so proud of, for whom I had built everything." Magda, who had stayed at Hellmut's bedside for days, was deeply shaken by her son-in-law's death. Hellmut was only six years younger than she was, and the two had been very close — so much so that some suspected that the two shared romantic feelings. Hellmut was buried next to his mother, Toni, at Pritzwalk's cemetery, in the family mausoleum that Günther had built. "Everything he was destined to carry in life now has to be taken over by his brother Herbert, the seventeen-year-old," Günther wrote.

Günther's second-born son, Herbert, seemed woefully ill-equipped to succeed his brother. A moody introvert, slender and shy, he was the opposite of his gifted, handsome, and empathetic older brother. What's more, Herbert was born with a visual disability so severe, he had to be homeschooled from age ten. As he was barely able to read, Herbert was forced to memorize all his lessons, learning information by means of his private teachers' oral explanations.

Herbert's doctor predicted that he could find a professional future only in agriculture, working with his hands. Günther therefore bought Herbert the grand Severin estate in the northern state of Mecklenburg. The center of the estate was a neo-Renaissance brick manor, dating from the 1880s, which was surrounded by about twenty-five hundred acres of land, ranging from farmland to forest. Its fields, meadows, and woodlands rested on a gentle ridge. Günther appointed his former brother-in-law, Walter Granzow, as Severin's caretaker, and a profitable agricultural business soon developed. Before long, the estate would serve a much darker purpose.

Hellmut's death speeded the unraveling of Günther and Magda's marriage. They were mismatched from the start, and whatever romantic feelings Magda retained for Günther vanished after her stepson's death. On his deathbed at the hospital on Paris's rue de Clichy, Hellmut had begged his constantly fighting father and stepmother to "always be kind to each other." Hellmut's words pierced Günther's heart "like a stab," he wrote. "I felt that if Hellmut died, our marriage would break up. He was the strong support that, unconsciously perhaps, had always led us to each other."

Günther was right, and the problem was of his own making. For six years, Günther had neglected Magda emotionally, socially, and financially.

He had been stingy with her, initially giving her an allowance that was a third of what the maids received in pay. She had to keep a record of all household expenses, and whenever Magda showed the record book to her husband, he would leaf wordlessly through it page by page, finally writing, in red ink: "Read and approved, Günther Quandt." Her whole life consisted of looking after children and managing a household staff of five in a Berlin suburb. But Magda was made for adventure, not domesticity. She was well-educated, spoke many languages, and loved the fine arts. She wanted more from life, preferably the limelight, and had expected, in vain, that being married to a rich industrialist would give her a socially prominent place in Berlin's roaring 1920s.

In fall 1927, a few months after Hellmut's death, the couple went on a trip to the United States. Günther hoped it would revive their marriage. He even shipped over a luxury motorcar, his red Maybach cabriolet, for the occasion. Despite his efforts, the road didn't rekindle their love. But a different kind of spark did ignite. In Midtown Manhattan, of all places, Günther and Magda received their first overtures from the Nazi Party. Kurt Lüdecke, a jet-setting playboy and an early member of the NSDAP, was based in New York for the time being and was hoping to sell the Nazi cause to wealthy Americans. Lüdecke had just failed to raise funds from Henry Ford, the virulently anti-Semitic automobile tycoon from Detroit. Maybe, Lüdecke thought, he would have more luck with a rich German like Günther, who happened to be the older brother of a friend.

The couple met Lüdecke at the Plaza Hotel, where they were staying during their visit to New York. "I lunched with him and his charming young wife," Lüdecke wrote in his memoir, *I Knew Hitler.* "He was now one of the richest men in Germany, with the mentality typical of internationally and economically minded business machines who have little or no imagination left for other things. Of course he had become at once another object for speculation for me — I wanted to get him and his money interested in our cause. But he was skeptical."

Günther didn't take the bait, so Lüdecke changed his focus. Magda seemed "much more open to suggestion," he wrote. "Her eyes sparkled when I told her about Hitler and the Nazi heroics. By the time I said good-bye to them on the ship which carried them home to Germany, Frau Quandt had become my ally. She promised to read the Nazi books I had given her and to work on her husband, and warmly invited me to visit them in Berlin. We became close friends during my visit in Germany in the summer of 1930, and I made a fervent Nazi out of her."

They became far more intimate than that. It wasn't Magda's first affair, nor would it be her last. After returning to Berlin from their American trip in early 1928, Günther gave Magda more freedom and more money. The tycoon, consumed with the DWM takeover, upped her allowance and stopped criticizing her clothing, her daily plans, and her spending. Magda was finally allowed to engage distinguished fashion designers to upgrade her wardrobe and to attend society balls on grand estates. Still, she wasn't happy. Her feelings for Günther were gone. She repeatedly asked him for a divorce, but Günther wouldn't have it.

At one of these balls, Magda met a young student from a wealthy family, and the two started an affair. She had no qualms about taking trips with her new lover. When Günther became suspicious, it wasn't because of Magda's frequent absences but rather her mood, which had changed from sulking to radiant. He had a private detective shadow her, and soon it was documented that Magda and her lover were staying at a hotel in the same Rhine River town where she and Günther got married. When Günther confronted her, she admitted to everything.

The ramifications were severe. Magda was to leave the house immediately. Günther initiated divorce proceedings. Suddenly, young Magda found herself in an unenviable position: the industrialist's wife was to become penniless overnight. Having admitted to the affair, Magda stood to lose everything in court: her marriage, her son, Harald, and any prospect of alimony. But she wasn't helpless after all — she had her own dirt on Günther. Years earlier, she had discovered in his writing desk a pack of love letters from other women. Now she was prepared to use them to bring Günther back to the negotiation table.

Her plan worked. Günther and Magda's marriage was dissolved on July 6, 1929, in Berlin's regional court. Her lawyers, Katz, Goldberg, and others, got her a good deal. Magda had to assume the blame for the divorce and the legal costs because she had "forsaken her marital duty" by refusing to sleep with her husband for over a year. And the once frugal Günther would have to provide generously for his ex-wife. She was to receive a monthly alimony of almost four thousand reichsmarks, twenty thousand reichsmarks in case of any illness, plus fifty thousand reichsmarks to finance the purchase of a new home. Magda also got custody of Harald until he turned fourteen. Then he would return to Günther, to be groomed by him so that he could one day take over half of the Quandt business empire. This custody arrangement rested on one condition: if Magda were to remarry, Harald would return to his father immediately. Günther didn't want his son to be influenced by another father figure. In addition to this custody clause, Günther granted Magda the right to use his Severin estate without any restrictions. These provisions would have major consequences for the former spouses and their son.

While Günther devoted tens of pages in his memoir to describe his life with Magda, he spent only one terse paragraph documenting their divorce, which he considered amicable: "In summer 1929, I separated from Magda . . . Since then, we were on friendly terms with each other." Günther at first took responsibility for the failed marriage, blaming his workload, but then he switched to absolving himself: "With all the stress, I didn't look after Magda as she needed and deserved. I have often blamed myself bitterly for this. But how often do we humans blame ourselves, without actually being guilty." Still, Günther kept a soft spot for his ex-wife: "Even when our ways parted, I always thought of her with admiration."

After the divorce papers were signed, Günther sent Magda a bouquet of flowers and took her to dinner at Restaurant Horcher, one of Berlin's most exclusive dining spots and Göring's favorite. Initially, the occasional family gatherings that followed the divorce were "in greatest harmony," Günther's elder son, Herbert, later declared. Magda was a free woman and well provided for. She rented a seven-room apartment on Reichskanzlerplatz 2 in Berlin's Westend, around the corner from Günther's townhouse. She could finally be the host that Günther had never allowed her to be. She had to look after her young son, but since she could afford to hire a maid and a cook, Magda had more free time than she knew what to do with. Although

she was still seeing the young student, she was looking for a more ma-
ture man. She had other suitors, including a rich nephew of the American
president, Herbert Hoover, but when he proposed marriage, she declined.
Magda was restless, searching for new meaning in life. She soon found it —
in the burgeoning Nazi Party and its most vocal proponent besides Hitler:
Dr. Joseph Paul Goebbels.

6.

The Nazi playboy Kurt Lüdecke first introduced twenty-eight-year-old
Magda Quandt to the more refined circles of the National Socialist movement in the summer of 1930. As Lüdecke put it: "With nothing to do and
a good income to do it on, she became an active Nazi supporter." The
wealthy divorcée made her entry through the Nordic Ring, an elite racial
debating club in Berlin. It counted among its ranks many German aristocrats, equally bored and wealthy. The group advocated a "Northerning" of
the German people, as they considered "the Nordic race" superior to all
others. One evening "after consuming considerable quantities of alcohol,"
Magda complained to the intoxicated clique that "her life repelled her and
that she thought she was going to die of boredom." Prince Auwi, a son of
the abdicated emperor, Wilhelm II, was sitting at her table and leaned toward Magda with a conspiratorial smile: "Bored, my dear? Let me make a
suggestion: come and join us! Come work for the Party."

Magda immediately took Prince Auwi's advice. On a stifling hot summer evening in late August 1930, Magda visited a Nazi Party election rally
in Schöneberg's Sportpalast, Berlin's largest convention hall. It was her first
encounter with that night's main speaker — Joseph Goebbels — Herr Dok-
tor, as he had obtained a PhD in literature from the University of Heidelberg. Goebbels had failed as a fiction writer, playwright, and journalist
before joining the nascent Nazi Party in 1924. With his gift for rhetoric
and bombast and his slavish devotion to Hitler, he rapidly rose through the
ranks. Hitler had promoted his trusted friend to Berlin Gauleiter in 1926.
Now, four years later, the thirty-two-year-old Goebbels had risen even

higher. He was now a member of the Reichstag, the Nazis' chief of propaganda, and the architect of the party's national election campaign. Votes would be cast in just two weeks, and Goebbels was only getting warmed up.

Goebbels had a long nose, a pale face, a high forehead, and swept-back dark-brown hair. He rarely smiled. His large head was an awkward contrast to his height (only five feet five) and his scrawniness. He walked with a limp because of a clubfoot, and he wore ill-fitting shirts and suits. Why would an attractive, rich divorcée who attended a debating club that preached the virtues of Nordic superiority notice him at all? And yet that night, as Goebbels began to address the crowd of thousands, Magda was hooked. He had a deep, booming voice; he could sneer and screech; his tone veered from sadness to sarcasm. He hurled fast insults at his enemies: the Jews, the Communists, and even the capitalists. Magda's mother later described her daughter's first experience of hearing Goebbels as near-erotic: "Magda was inflamed. She felt addressed by this man as a woman, not as a supporter of the 'party,' which she hardly knew. She had to get to know this man, who from second to second could make you boiling hot and freezing cold."

A few days later, on September 1, 1930, Magda joined the Nazi Party. She bought Hitler's *Mein Kampf*, his autobiographical manifesto, and read it from cover to cover; she studied the work of Alfred Rosenberg, the Nazi theorist who was a rival of Goebbels. After a failed stint leading the NSDAP's working-class women's committee in her tony neighborhood, Magda went in search of another job. She had to get close to Goebbels. One gray day in late October, she chanced it. She traveled to Berlin's city center, showed up unannounced at the fortresslike regional headquarters of the Nazi Party, and offered her services. When she highlighted her knowledge of foreign languages, she received a warm welcome. Three days later, she took the post of secretary to Goebbels's deputy.

After a few days in the office, Magda was descending the stairs when a short man in a trench coat came up in a hurry. It was Goebbels. When they passed in the stairwell, they briefly exchanged glances. Magda, cool as ever, walked on and didn't look back. Goebbels immediately turned to his adjutant and asked: "Who was that amazing woman?" The next day Magda was summoned to Goebbels's office. He told her that he was looking for a reliable person to make a private archive for him and asked her if she could do it. The archive was to consist of domestic and international news clippings about the Nazi Party, Hitler, and, above all, Goebbels himself. Goebbels knew the power of information. He handpicked news items to use in his deceptive propaganda campaigns. Newsgathering also gave him an advantage in navigating the NSDAP's bloody palace intrigues. Goebbels was always looking for the competitive edge. He wasn't a celebrated aviation war hero like Hermann Göring or the leader of the SS like Heinrich Himmler. Goebbels had only his wits and his devotion to Hitler to rely on.

Magda accepted the job. She first appears in Goebbels's diary on November 7, 1930: "A beautiful woman named Quandt is making me a new private archive." As Magda came under the spell of Nazism and Goebbels, her relationship with Günther changed. The former spouses still kept in frequent contact. Harald lived with her, so Günther and Herbert often visited the two at their apartment on Reichskanzlerplatz. She even joined them for family holidays. Magda was at Günther's side in Florence for Christmas 1930, after he suffered a hip injury. They traveled to St. Moritz together, where Günther recuperated in the mountain air.

But something had come over Magda. Their conversations now focused on politics alone. Magda had tried to convert Günther to the Nazi cause after attending her first rally. "It was supposedly absolutely necessary to join this movement, it would be the only salvation from communism, which Germany would otherwise face given its difficult economic situation," Günther later recalled her saying. On subsequent visits, he noticed "that Magda became an ever more zealous propagandist for the new cause and that she was wholeheartedly involved." Günther initially thought that Magda merely had an "infatuation" with Goebbels's oratorical gifts, but when she kept repeating the same message, he limited the visits.

During that Christmas holiday, Magda went further, and tried to proselytize both father and son, urging them to join her new cause. "She became the most fervent advocate of National Socialist ideas and tried to convert my son and me for the party. That we should at least provide money for this cause. The arguments seemed so fanciful; it wasn't easy to go against them. When we saw from our further conversations that only the party was being talked about, and no longer . . . beautiful things, my son Herbert and I decided to stop our visits to her," Günther later testified in court. He said that he stopped seeing her altogether after their time in St. Moritz.

Herbert confirmed his father's recollection under oath. Despite all the "admiration and gratitude" he felt toward his former stepmother, he had been so startled about "this development of views and fanaticism" that it seemed pointless to keep in touch with Magda, "since she had become too stubborn to be told otherwise." But Günther and Herbert lied. Their visits did not stop, and father and son Quandt were far more interested in fascist thought than they ever did admit.

7.

Although the period of the Weimar Republic was profitable for Günther Quandt, he was no fan of the new, more liberal Germany. There was too much political turmoil and economic volatility. He missed the days of the stricter German Empire. Günther had witnessed its demise firsthand. On October 5, 1918, ten days before Toni died, he attended the Reichstag session in which imperial Germany's last chancellor acquiesced to US president Woodrow Wilson's demands for peace by asking for an immediate ceasefire and an end to World War I. It was the first and last time Günther went to the Reichstag. "A picture of misfortune is all I remember," he later wrote. "Our fatherland was facing chaos." Over the years, Günther developed an interest in authoritarian ways of ruling. Whereas Magda entered the Nordic Circle, Günther joined the Society for the Study of Fascism in Berlin. The invitation-only study and debate group of about two hundred members explored fascism as practiced by the Italian dictator Benito Mussolini. The group, established in 1931, aimed to bring ideological unity to Germany's disparate far-right factions, and it examined how the fascist system might work as an alternative to the democratic Weimar Republic.

The group's head and driving force was Waldemar Pabst, the ardent

anti-Bolshevist who had ordered the executions of the German Communist leaders Rosa Luxemburg and Karl Liebknecht in 1919. The club's mix
of elites included conservative academic theorists who studied Italian fascism, aristocratic landowners, the trio of future Nazi ministers of economic
affairs (Hjalmar Schacht, Walther Funk, and Hermann Göring), Günther's
business partners (the two Pauls), and Fritz Thyssen, a steel industrialist
who was an early supporter of the Nazi Party.

At the club, Günther led a study group that drew up guidelines for the
reduction of unemployment in Germany. The club organized evening lectures, readings of pamphlets on fascism, and discussions of alternative
ways of ruling. The wealthy members of the group were essentially the fascist counterpart of "salon socialists." Interest in the group, however, proved
short-lived. Its members found ideological unification closer to home, opt-
ing to support a homegrown brand of fascism: Nazism.

Initially, most business tycoons viewed Hitler and his Nazis as loud, vi-
olent, boorish, brutish uniformed curiosities from the uneducated and impoverished hinterlands — just some outlandish figures to joke about. That
changed in the wake of the worst global slump in the stock market, culmi-
nating in the collapse of share prices on the New York Stock Exchange on
October 29, 1929. Plummeting stock prices wiped out most investors and
firms, many of them leveraged on credit. Demand for goods and services
was shattered. The Great Depression took a devastating toll on Germany.
By late 1930, the stock market had lost two-thirds of its value, industrial
production had halved, and millions of Germans were unemployed.

In mid-September 1930, Hitler's Nazi Party rode a wave of economic
and political discontent to become the second-largest party in the Reichstag, receiving 6.4 million votes. The Goebbels-led election campaign —
which blamed Jews and Communists for the financial crisis — was a resounding success. That winter, Hitler began trying to make inroads among
Germany's wealthiest businessmen. Economic malaise opened the door for
him; many moguls feared political upheaval from the left while the financial system was teetering. Günther and his fellow tycoons soon received a
call inviting them to Hitler's corner suite at Berlin's Hotel Kaiserhof.

8.

On Sunday morning, February 1, 1931, Hitler was at his home base in Munich and went to see Otto Wagener, his chief economic adviser. The leader of the Nazi Party had money on his mind. Hitler and Wagener began considering ways to get hold of millions of reichsmarks to arm the Sturm-abteilung (SA), the Nazi Party's paramilitary wing, in case a putsch from the left turned into civil war. They settled on the business community, but there was one problem: neither of them had any good contacts there. That needed to change, and fast. Wagener immediately called Walther Funk at his home in Berlin. The newspaper editor was eager to set up meetings with industrialists and financiers for the Nazi leader, and he recommended that Hitler and his entourage set up shop at the capital's chic Hotel Kaiser-hof. Funk told Wagener that this place, Berlin's first grand hotel, was the only suitable location if Hitler wanted to make a good first impression on the tycoons and if he wanted a serious chance at getting some money from them. The building was situated opposite the Reich Chancellery, around the corner from the offices of Günther Quandt and Friedrich Flick. Funk would reserve the appropriate rooms.

The next morning, Hitler, Wagener, and their entourage left Munich by car. It took more than a day to drive to Berlin. Wagener prepared Hit-ler, urging him to first discuss economic issues with the men, ease them into conversation, and then ask them for money to acquire weapons for the SA. They finally arrived at the hotel at 2 p.m. on Tuesday, February 3. Funk awaited them in the lobby and showed them their rooms: a large corner suite on the third floor. Hitler had his own bedroom, with a private bath. The rest were quartered together. The Nazi leader would receive his guests in the suite's richly decorated sitting room, overlooking the Reich Chancellery park. Funk had moved quickly. In two hours, at 4 p.m., Hit-ler's first introduction of the week was due to arrive: Baron August von Finck.

The thirty-two-year-old aristocratic financier from Munich was Bavaria's richest man. His father had left him a business empire, including control of Merck Finck, one of Germany's major private banks, and the largest stakes in two global insurance giants, Allianz and Munich Re.

August von Finck was tall and regal in bearing, with a cool expression and a full head of immaculately swept back brown hair. He was to the manor born. Von Finck's father, Wilhelm, was a cofounder of both Allianz and Munich Re. And insurance wasn't even his main profession. Wilhelm was a financier who built his own private bank, Merck Finck. His entrepreneurial spirit was boundless. Wilhelm started beer breweries, helped expand the railway network, cofounded a venture with the inventor of diesel, and helped build the first hydroelectric power station in the German Empire. In recognition of his many efforts, he was ennobled: Wilhelm Finck became Baron Wilhelm *von* Finck in 1911. He bought thousands of acres of land and became one of the largest landowners in Bavaria. All in all, he was a tremendously successful man, especially for a pious Protestant living in a devoutly Catholic part of Bavaria.

But disaster struck the family during World War I, when August's older brother was killed at the front in 1916. Wilhelm had planned on leaving his eldest son his bank, business interests, and board positions; the land and its agricultural enterprises were intended for August. At eighteen years of age August entered the army — on the same day that his older brother was killed in action. August served for two years in a forage unit in the Balkans, searching for food and other provisions. He was injured, but not badly — his right knee was hurt.

After his eldest son's death, a grieving Wilhelm decided that his bank should be liquidated when he passed away. But on his deathbed in 1924, he reconsidered. Wilhelm changed his will, appointing August to succeed him as principal partner at Merck Finck and as proprietor of all his other business interests, from insurers to breweries. August also inherited an enormous amount of land.

Thus, at age twenty-five, August took up about two dozen board positions, including two of the most important ones in global finance: supervisory board chairman of both Allianz and Munich Re. After all, this was no meritocracy. August also inherited his fathers' devout Protestantism and famed thriftiness. The young heir became known in his circle as the richest *and* stingiest man in Bavaria, with a frugality that made him appear cruel and distant. A die-hard conservative, August withdrew to the reactionary aristocratic salons of Munich during the dying years of the Weimar Republic, when a bored and listless Magda was doing the same in Berlin. But now the time had come for him to emerge from that insular far-right clique. August too was feeling more ambitious than ever and ready to get to work on something new and radical.

On that freezing, cloudy Tuesday afternoon in early February 1931, August von Finck, accompanied by Kurt Schmitt, the opportunistic and well-connected CEO of Allianz, was to meet Hitler for the first time. Allianz's headquarters were across the street from the Hotel Kaiserhof. At 4 p.m., the two men arrived at the suite. Walter Funk took them to the sitting room where Hitler was waiting. Over the next half hour, Hitler sketched a capitalist's nightmare to the financier duo; he "conjured up the specter of unemployed masses rising in a leftist revolt." Von Finck and Schmitt agreed with Hitler's view. The two were displeased with the political situation and the hopelessness of providing millions with jobs. They were "absolutely convinced . . . of the eventual eruption of riots and a major shift to the left," they told Hitler. After the meeting, Funk walked the two out. He soon returned to the suite with big news: von Finck and Schmitt had pledged to make five million reichsmarks available via Allianz to arm the SA as a stay against a putsch, which might devolve into civil war.

Hitler was speechless. After Funk left, Hitler marveled to Otto Wagener at "the kind of power big business wields." It was as if the monetary strength of capitalism had revealed itself to the Nazi leader for the first time. But his economic adviser warned him about the businessmen: "They want to earn money, nothing but money, filthy money—and they don't even realize that they are chasing a satanic phantom."

Hitler did not care. Many more millions were about to be pledged. Funk had invited Günther Quandt to visit the Kaiserhof the next morning.

9.

The next day, Wednesday, February 4, 1931, the ex-spouses Günther and Magda Quandt each met Hitler for the first time and in the same place — but unbeknownst to each other. That morning, Günther and two Wintershall executives spoke with Hitler in his hotel suite. By the time they left, the amount pledged to arm the SA had reached thirteen million reichsmarks. (The fundraising ended the following afternoon, at twenty-five million reichsmarks, after Funk had summoned four more businessmen to the suite. But in the end, none of the tycoons had to pay up, as the leftist putsch never occurred.) Günther's impression of Hitler, eight years his junior, was underwhelming: "I can't say that Hitler made a significant or meaningless, a sympathetic or repulsive impression on me. He struck me as perfectly average," the mogul later wrote.

Günther left the Kaiserhof by noon. At 4 p.m., one of Hitler's bodyguards entered the suite and announced that a boy was waiting outside the door, wanting to speak to the Nazi leader. Hitler told the bodyguard to let him in. A slender, handsome, and confident-looking nine-year-old strode into the suite. He was wearing a blue uniform, with a dagger on one side and a forage cap over his blond hair. It was Harald Quandt, Günther's younger son. Magda had sent Harald up from the lobby, unannounced. Harald gave the men the Nazi salute and introduced himself: "The youngest Hitler Youth in Germany is reporting to his Führer!"

An amused Hitler asked Harald for his name and age, and posed another question: "Who made you this beautiful uniform?"

"My mother," Harald replied.

"And how does the uniform make you feel?"

"Twice as strong!"

Hitler told Harald to visit again soon and to send regards to his mother, this mysterious woman who was having tea in the lobby. Minutes after Harald left, Goebbels arrived. The romance between him and Magda was developing, but slowly. Goebbels first had to let another fling fizzle. But he was about to have some romantic competition for Magda, and from the man he revered like nobody else: Hitler himself.

Goebbels had reserved a corner table for Hitler's group in the hotel lobby for high tea. Hitler, unaware of the budding romance between Magda and Goebbels, asked if he could invite mother and son to the table. Goebbels obliged and left the suite. Moments later Hermann Göring arrived. When Hitler told him they'd be meeting "a Frau Quandt" for tea soon, Göring exclaimed: "Oh Goebbels' Madame Pompadour!" He was comparing Magda to the chief courtesan of the French king Louis XV.

Otto Wagener's eyewitness report of the five-o'clock tea could have come straight out of a pulp romance: "Even at first glance, Frau Quandt made an excellent impression, which only increased in the course of our conversation ... She was dressed well but not excessively, calm in her movements, assured, self-confident, with a winning smile — I am tempted to say: enchanting. I noticed the pleasure Hitler took in her innocent high spirits. I also noticed how her large eyes were hanging on Hitler's gaze. And whenever the conversation ground to a self-conscious halt, young Harald always served as the catalyst to restore contact." Wagener had to tear his boss away from Magda to get him ready for the opera. Nevertheless, the economic adviser had "no doubt that a closer tie of friendship and veneration between Hitler and Mrs. Quandt had begun to take shape." Hitler was devastated when, later that night, he was told that Goebbels already had a key to Magda's apartment. But the new lovers had yet to consummate their relationship.

That happened ten days later, on Valentine's Day, 1931. "Magda Quandt comes in the evening. And stays very long. And blossoms into a ravishing blonde sweetness. How you are my queen! (1) ... Today I walk almost as if in a dream," Goebbels wrote in his diary. Throughout March he indicated in parentheses when the couple had sex: "Magda ... goes home late. (2.3.)" Five days later: "Magda, the lovely ... Some more learning about me and about her, and we'll be a perfect match. (4.5.)" One week later, on March 22: "Magda ... shoos all my worries away. I love her very much (6.7.)" The final (sex) diary parentheses coincided with the night of their first fight and makeup sex. The two clearly entered couplehood on March 26: "A lot of work done until the evening. Then came Magda, there was love, a fight, and again love (8.9.). She's a fabulous child. But I mustn't lose myself in her. The work is too big and momentous for that."

Harald also began to appear in Goebbels's diaries. "In the afternoon Magda came with her boy Harald. He is 9 years old and a lovely chap. All blond and a bit cheeky. But I like that," the top Nazi wrote on March 12, 1931. Goebbels was immediately taken with Harald, an Aryan poster child indeed: tall for his age, with big blue eyes and long, light-blond hair. He was handsome, with almost girlishly delicate features. In countless diary entries Goebbels gushed at how "sweet" Harald was. He soon began bringing Harald to school, writing that he would make "a useful boy out of him."

And Goebbels wasn't Harald's only fan. Hitler loved Harald "idolatrously." That fall, shortly before Harald's tenth birthday, the two top Nazis began using the boy as a prop in their propaganda campaigns. In mid-October 1931, Hitler and Goebbels took Harald to a two-day SA march in Braunschweig, in central Germany. Impressed by Harald's dress performance at the Hotel Kaiserhof, Hitler had ordered members of the entire Nazi organization to wear their uniforms in public at all times. More than 100,000 people, including tens of thousands of SA and SS men, took part in the rally, the largest paramilitary march ever held in the Weimar Republic. In his diary Goebbels described Harald at the event: "Harald looks so sweet in his new SA uniform. His long yellow boots. He's all man now. We leave together with boss . . . Torchlight procession! Harald's in the car with boss. He's all man. Ovation of thousands. A rush of enthusiasm. Boss is completely overjoyed. He picks up Harald's arm. The sweet boy has stood brave beside me all day."

Magda, meanwhile, was like a mad groupie, following Goebbels around on his work travels across Germany. The rich divorcée would surprise Goebbels by waiting for him in his hotel room or by showing up in whichever city he was giving a speech or attending a Nazi Party function. Magda spoiled Goebbels, who had little money, showering him with flowers and taking him to the Berlin zoo. Unlike Günther, the top Nazi let Magda be a part of his life. Goebbels was grateful for her support. "She stood by me

A young Harald Quandt, with his mother,
Magda, and Joseph Goebbels, 1931.

during the hard days: I won't forget that," he wrote in April 1931. Goebbels also could be possessive and jealous. "Small quarrel with Magda, who at 8 in the evening receives her ex-husband at home. That's so careless and only fuels gossip. She has now cut off all ties there and belongs only to me," he wrote in late June 1931.

But Günther's largesse toward his ex-wife was a key element in strengthening the relationship between Magda and Goebbels. In the divorce agreement, Günther had granted her the right to use his Severin estate without restrictions. From the start, Magda had no problems with bringing her new lover to her ex-husband's country estate. It became the couple's favorite getaway, a mere three hours' drive north from Berlin; they spent an entire week there over Pentecost in 1931. Hitler also started spending weekends on Günther's estate with his entourage. Rural Severin and its surroundings were an NSDAP stronghold. Walter Granzow, the estate's caretaker, welcomed them all. An ambitious Nazi, he had set his sights on public office.

At Severin over Pentecost, the couple decided on their future together. "Now we are clear on everything. We have made a solemn promise: when we conquer the Reich, we will become man and wife," Goebbels wrote in his diary on May 31, 1931. They didn't wait for that to happen, however, and announced their engagement later that summer. Magda broke the news to Günther and Hitler on the same day. The men didn't take it well. "Magda . . . had a talk with G. Quandt on Saturday. Told him we are getting married. He was devastated. Magda took revenge for all the harm he did to her. Then with boss. Told him the same thing. He was also devastated. He loves her. But he's loyal to me. And Magda too . . . Hitler is gloomy. He's very lonely. Has no luck with women. Because he is too soft with them. Women don't like that. They have to feel the master over them . . . Poor Hitler! I'm almost ashamed to be so happy. I hope this doesn't cloud our friendship," Goebbels wrote in his diary on September 14, 1931. To his massive dissatisfaction, Hitler and Magda kept on flirting whenever they met, often when Goebbels wasn't around. There was nothing the jealousy-stricken Goebbels could do about that. This was Hitler, after all.

Hitler envisioned an important role for Magda. He told Otto Wagener that "she could represent the feminine counterpart to my single-mindedly male instincts." Wagener came up with a peculiar proposition, which became known as "the arrangement." Hitler had renounced marriage: his "bride" was the German people. (He was, at the time, just getting to know Eva Braun.) Wagener therefore suggested a triangular relationship that would be platonic where Hitler was concerned. Through her marriage to Goebbels, Magda would serve as the unofficial First Lady of the Third Reich. Hitler was practically already a family member. He and his entourage spent many a night at Magda's apartment on Reichskanzlerplatz, dining on special meals that her cook prepared for the vegetarian Nazi leader and talking until the early hours of the morning. Magda and Goebbels accepted this pact with the man they worshipped, and they decided to move their wedding up to December.

By sheer coincidence, Günther and Hitler met for a second time, two days before Magda broke the news of the engagement. "Nausea: Mr. Günther Quandt has been to the boss," Goebbels wrote in his diary on September 12, 1931. "Of course he posed and tried to make an impression. Boss fell for it. Loved him. When I tell Magda, she turns white with anger and rage. I can understand that. But maybe that's what it takes for her to be cured for good." As it turned out, there was no reason for the engaged couple to be suspicious about what transpired between Günther and Hitler. The two had simply talked about dry economic policy.

According to Günther's postwar description of the encounter, he had been invited to this second meeting at Hitler's Kaiserhof suite by his own business partners, the two Pauls. Hitler wanted to hear the three moguls' ideas on how Germany's economic crisis could be remedied. Günther advised the Nazi leader that workdays should be reduced from eight to six hours, to deal with the high unemployment. Furthermore, he suggested cutting wages by 25 percent, prohibiting consumer credit payments, and eliminating unemployment benefits. The money saved could then be spent on state infrastructure, while the construction industry was stimulated by tax breaks. It was conventional wisdom, Günther explained to Hitler, that the economy improves when the construction industry flourishes.

In turn, Hitler thanked the three businessmen and told them that he wanted to fight unemployment with large state contracts. Above all, he aimed to boost the economy through rearmament of the military. This was very welcome news for the trio of weapons producers. The conversation between Hitler and the men, scheduled to last for fifteen minutes, had taken three times as long, as Günther later proudly noted. But though he was under the impression that Hitler considered his proposals "impressive," and had even asked Otto Wagener to write down his name so the two could speak again, Günther never again heard directly from the Nazi leader. Years later, on the stand in a courtroom, he remembered his meetings with Hitler a little differently: "Our views were so different that we never understood each other. Hitler didn't let me speak at all in the two conversations I had with him."

10.

Günther Quandt and Joseph Goebbels finally met in person at Magda's thirtieth birthday party, which took place on November 11, 1931, at the apartment on Reichskanzlerplatz that she had rented since the windfall of her divorce. Goebbels was about to move in with her. Günther "instinctively felt that we didn't match," he later recalled about that night. The feeling was mutual. When the mogul visited his own estate a few weeks later to see Harald, who was staying at Severin with Magda and Goebbels, the Nazi politician vented in his diary about the intrusion, calling the industrialist "a tactless lout. The typical capitalist. A citizen of the worst kind." This, while Goebbels was living off Magda's royal alimony, in her massive apartment, enjoying the hospitality of the Quandt estate, all paid for by Günther.

Despite the two men's immediate aversion to each other, Günther would drop in on his ex-wife and her husband-to-be from time to time, to hear them out on politics and to donate money to the Nazi Party—later he would lie about both these activities. On December 11, 1931, Goebbels documented one such visit: "Günther Quandt came in the evening. He wants to give money to the party. Magda takes him to task. She's our best advocate . . . I talk politics. He's completely taken. An old man. But the smart, energetic, brutal capitalist has come over to us completely. As he should—and give money, too. I get 2,000 [marks]. That's for the prisoners and wounded. For my people, I'll take it. With a heavy heart." However, Goebbels added: "The conversation wasn't as cold as I thought." The atmosphere was much improved by Günther's donation as well as his praise for Goebbels's new book, *Battle for Berlin,* which Günther was reading, or so he told the Nazi.

Goebbels could not refuse Günther's money. The Nazi Party was constantly broke and needed all the funds it could get. Goebbels lived off a meager salary, supplemented by his wife's massive alimony—and that support was about to run dry. With their wedding only eight days away, Magda and Goebbels were about to lose her alimony as a source of income, as stipulated in the divorce agreement. Worse, they would lose Harald too. He would have to return to Günther. The tycoon didn't want his youngest son to be raised and influenced by another man—let alone by the Nazi Party's master of propaganda.

Magda and Goebbels's wedding ceremony took place on December 19, 1931. A biographer of Magda later called the wedding "from start to finish unequalled for its lack of taste." Magda Quandt became Magda Goebbels on her ex-husband's Severin estate, of all places—and without his permission. The wedding had been planned by Günther's estate manager and for-

Magda and Joseph Goebbels arm in arm at their wedding, with Harald Quandt, 1931. The best man, Hitler, is in the background.

mer brother-in-law, Walter Granzow, who agreed to keep it a secret from his boss. Granzow was keen on making a swift career pivot to the NSDAP. He had already been offering up Günther's estate to host secret meetings between Hitler, Goebbels, and other Nazi leaders. Severin, which Günther had bought to secure a future for his near-blind son Herbert, had been turned into Mecklenburg's de facto Nazi headquarters. Günther suspected it, but his repeated requests to Magda not to turn Severin into the local nerve center of the party fell on deaf ears. There was little Günther could do about it, since he had granted her unrestricted use of the estate, including the right to receive guests. Thus the wedding breakfast was held around Günther's dining table. Toasts to the couple's health were raised with his glasses at the reception, which was held in his manor.

The Protestant wedding ceremony took place in Severin's small village church; Hitler served as Goebbels's second witness. For the occasion, the church altar had been adorned with the flag of the Nazi Party, draped around a crucifix. The eighteen members of the wedding party walked from Günther's manor to the church for the ceremony, through the woods of Severin, and back again for the reception. Magda, who was secretly pregnant, and Goebbels walked arm in arm through the snow-covered forest. They were both dressed entirely in black, except for the white shawl of Brussels lace draped around Magda's shoulders — a piece of the gown she had worn for her first wedding, to Günther. It was the last glimmer of the precocious young woman she had been.

Ten-year-old Harald, wearing a costume modeled on the SA uniform, with shank boots, breeches, a brown shirt, and a belt with shoulder strap, walked beside his stepfather. Directly behind the couple walked Magda's mother, Auguste. Next to her, his arm in hers, strode Hitler. His face was almost obscured by his wide-brimmed hat, and his body was shielded from the cold by a double-breasted coat. Along the route, SA men wearing white shirts and ties stood between the trees, ramrod straight and performing the Nazi salute, paying homage to the newlyweds.

Günther later wrote that he might easily have visited Severin that December day and unwittingly barged right into his ex-wife's wedding. He blamed Hitler, who apparently pushed for the event to take place in an obscure rural location, and Granzow, who put his Nazi career interests above those of his employer. Günther fired Granzow, but the estate manager's planning paid off. He made a swift ascent within the Nazi Party.

In the weeks after the wedding, Günther enforced his legal custody of Harald, and a battle between him and the newlyweds erupted. Whatever détente had existed among the three adults turned into all-out war. Goebbels flew into a rage when Magda told him Günther was taking Harald back. Magda too was "furious like a lioness for her cub. I will help her. This hypocrite's mask must be torn off his face," Goebbels wrote in his diary on December 29, 1931. "Up late with Magda . . . planning revenge. Poor Günther Quandt! I wouldn't want to have Magda as an enemy." The date of the entry was no coincidence. Three days later, on New Year's Day, 1932, Harald officially moved back into his father's townhouse, although Günther often allowed him to visit his mother around the corner on Reichs-kanzlerplatz.

Despite the strife over Harald, Günther did attend a two-hour speech Goebbels made in February. While, according to Goebbels, Günther was "over the moon" with what he heard and saw, it didn't bring the men any closer in the custody conflict. Günther later claimed that he went to this Nazi rally in Berlin only to get "an idea of the public speaking and popular sentiment" after his meetings with Hitler; after attending the rally he "never cared for this movement again."

Apart from young Harald, Goebbels came to have a low opinion of the Quandt men. When he met Günther's elder son, Herbert, for the first time, in April 1932, Goebbels thought that the near-blind future savior of BMW was "slightly retarded." Upon later hearing that Magda's best friend, Ello, had left her husband, Werner Quandt, Günther's younger brother, Goebbels called him "a real prole." After Magda and Goebbels told Hitler about "the capitalist" Werner, the German chancellor flew into a rage and promised to do something about him. Despite the threat, Günther's younger brother was left untouched. Even so, Goebbels clearly had it in for most of the Quandt men, and his power was growing.

11.

Another Berlin capitalist was in much bigger trouble by spring 1932. Friedrich Flick had finalized his takeover of the Düsseldorf-based VSt steel conglomerate, and right between the global rout of the stock market and the start of the Great Depression, no less. He had been able to finance a majority stake in Europe's largest industrial conglomerate only by taking out massive loans and bonds. The debt was secured by his shares in the VSt through Gelsenberg, both of which Flick had put up as bank collateral. However, given the stock market's collapse, the value of these shares had plummeted, and Flick owned few other tangible assets that could serve as further collateral. Flick's holding company and Gelsenberg were on the brink of insolvency; he was about to be wiped out.

In early 1932, Flick needed to make a quick financial exit from Gelsen-berg. At the same time, Hitler too needed money, yet again. He wanted financial backing for the upcoming presidential election. Walther Funk arranged an introduction to Flick, again at the Hotel Kaiserhof, on an icy February morning, a year after Günther Quandt and August von Finck had visited Hitler's suite at the invitation of the cunning newspaperman. In the year since that first meeting, Funk had left Berlin's financial newspaper and started editing the NSDAP's economic newsletter. He had also become acquainted with Otto Steinbrinck, Flick's ruthless right-hand man.

Steinbrinck was a highly decorated navy veteran who had sunk more than two hundred merchant ships as an enterprising submarine com-mander during World War I. Flick had spotted his business talent when Steinbrinck prepared an investing memo for him. He had quickly risen to

Flick's right-hand man, Otto Steinbrinck,
in his SS uniform, 1934.

become Flick's most trusted confidant. Flick, who cultivated a public image of abstinence from politics, made Steinbrinck his liaison with the Nazis after he proved himself very capable in backroom dealing in business *and* politics.

Funk relayed Flick's Kaiserhof invitation through Steinbrinck. Flick was keen to get to know the man who had started to play such a major role in German politics. But their one-hour meeting in late February 1932 was a disaster. As Steinbrinck waited outside the suite, Hitler mistook Flick for the naval hero and talked endlessly about his plans for a confrontation with the Polish navy. As the two men walked back from the hotel to their office nearby, Flick told his top aide that he had not been able to get a word in with Hitler. The Nazi leader too was disappointed with the one-sidedness of the conversation. Miffed, Flick decided to throw his financial might behind Paul von Hindenburg, the sitting president and the conservative establishment's candidate; he donated almost a million reichsmarks to his reelection campaign.

Flick badly needed some clout with the government. The state was the only liquid buyer for his Gelsenberg stake and had no clue about the sorry state of his finances. He had only just started negotiating a deal when he first met Hitler. Talks dragged on for months, but Flick at last succeeded. In a stunning act of gamesmanship, he managed to sell his Gelsenberg stake to the government for more than ninety million reichsmarks, about three times its market value, in late May 1932. Flick strong-armed the state at the negotiating table by alleging that his fellow VSt shareholder Fritz Thyssen was willing to buy out his majority stake with financial backing from French lenders. A takeover of Germany's largest conglomerate with French money was unthinkable. It had been only a few years since France had co-occupied the Ruhr area in response to Germany's failure to continue reparation payments. When the government bailed out Flick at an enormous premium, he was able to pay off his debts. The deal left him flush with cash.

When news of Flick's backroom deal with the government broke in mid-June 1932, it caused a national scandal. At the height of the Great Depression, with more than six million Germans unemployed, the state had used taxpayer millions to unwittingly bail out a speculating industrialist and his private holding company. But in a matter of weeks, the Gelsenberg affair was eclipsed by bigger news: the parliamentary elections of July 31, which for the first time made the NSDAP Germany's largest party in the Reichstag. By late summer 1932, as the public and the politicians moved on from the financial scandal, Flick began to prepare for Nazi Party rule.

Although the Gelsenberg affair had made Flick even richer, the PR disaster associated with it had tainted his name. Flick had also spurned Hitler's initial advances, and now the magnate was convinced he needed political protection; he was happy to pay handsomely for it. In early fall, Walther Funk dropped by Flick's headquarters on Berlin's Bellevuestrasse with a new request from the NSDAP: money was needed for yet another election campaign cycle. Funk left with some thirty thousand reichsmarks. Soon, a procession of Nazis soliciting for funds found their way to Flick's office door. The SA needed new boots for another torchlight parade: two to three thousand reichsmarks. Flick's handlers wanted positive coverage of their boss in the press: a few thousand reichsmarks to Nazi newspaper and magazine editors. As Flick and Steinbrinck discovered, "Giving money to Nazis was rather like shedding blood while swimming in the presence of sharks."

Then the SS came knocking. On a somber gray day in late fall 1932, the chicken farmer turned SS leader, Heinrich Himmler, visited Flick's headquarters. He had come to make a deal. To put an end to the requests for Flick's money that were emanating from every corner of the Nazi universe, Himmler proposed that the steel tycoon's future donations go solely to the SS. Flick quickly agreed. It was a devil's pact. The rising paramilitary organization offered the ultimate political protection, but at what price? Flick would soon find out.

Steinbrinck and Himmler's aide Fritz Kranefuss helped broker the agreement between their bosses. The ambitious Kranefuss was a nephew of Wilhelm Keppler, a failed businessman who was quickly becoming Hitler's favored economic adviser. Earlier that year, Hitler had told Keppler to establish a council comprising industrialists and financiers who could advise him on economic policies and "who will be at our disposal when we come into power." He enlisted his nephew to help recruit members and establish the Keppler Circle, as it soon became known. One of their first recruits was Otto Steinbrinck. He joined the group as Flick's representative just as the Gelsenberg affair erupted. His beleaguered boss instructed him to find out which way "the wind was blowing" in the Nazi elite. Flick was eager to use that information to ready himself for rearmament.

12.

As the rainy summer of 1932 wound down in Berlin, tensions between the Goebbels and Quandt households continued to rise. In late September, Magda and Goebbels hid Harald at a friend's place after the couple got into a fight with Günther over the phone. It took Günther's threat of legal action to convince the couple to return Harald. Günther later said that Goebbels never forgave him for his dogged fight for the boy: "Goebbels . . . got it into his head that Harald . . . whom he dragged along to all sorts of party events and who was therefore in the public eye naturally considered as his son, was his to keep. The boy was tall and blond, so a good showpiece for a Nazi leader, who himself didn't exactly have the appearance of a Nazi German."

In early November 1932, around Harald's eleventh birthday, tensions between the two men somewhat eased. Goebbels wrote in his diary that he "talked to G. Quandt. He's not entirely unreasonable. Not even in social matters." Günther agreed to let Harald spend Christmas break with the Goebbelses. But when Harald arrived at their apartment on Christmas Eve, his mother wasn't there. It was only Goebbels. Magda had just been committed to the hospital with severe stomach pains, he told Harald; the boy then burst into tears. Goebbels consoled Harald over Christmas by taking him to the cinema and opera. They visited Magda in the hospital and brought her a lit-up Christmas tree adorned with presents. The day after Christmas, Hitler invited Goebbels and Harald to spend New Year's Eve at the small chalet Hitler rented on Bavaria's Obersalzberg, near the border with Austria. Goebbels and Harald drove over. On the last day of the year, Hitler, Goebbels, and Harald wrote a letter to Magda with their best wishes for her health. Magda remained in the hospital, riddled with fever. She was recuperating from a miscarriage. They didn't know it yet, but 1933 would change the course of their lives and transform Germany and the world.

On December 29, 1932, Hitler received a message at the chalet: the former chancellor, Franz von Papen, wanted to meet. A week later, the men gathered at dusk in Cologne at the mansion of Baron Kurt von Schröder, a virulently anti-Semitic private banker. Hitler and von Papen brokered a backroom deal at the financier's villa that night. Von Papen was plotting a return to power and believed that he could use the more popular Hitler as an instrument to that end. Convinced that he could control Hitler, he persuaded Reich president von Hindenburg to appoint the Nazi leader as chancellor and himself as vice chancellor. This would turn out to be one of the most catastrophic miscalculations in human history. Instead of reducing the Nazi leader to a figurehead, von Papen enabled Hitler to seize power.

On the evening of January 30, 1933, members of the SA celebrated their führer's ascent to the position of chancellor with a torchlight parade through the center of Berlin, marching over Unter den Linden, under the Brandenburg Gate, and past the Reichstag and the Tiergarten to hear Hitler speak from the balcony of the Reich Chancellery, his new home. Parliamentary elections were scheduled five weeks out, for March 5. Democratic rule was on the horizon again, so it seemed. Few understood that Hitler actually had seized power that night — that the Third Reich had begun, that the Weimar Republic had been transformed into Nazi Germany, and that it would remain so for more than twelve long, dark, bloody years.

With Hitler in charge, the balance of power between Günther and Goebbels shifted decisively. Six days after Hitler's power grab, Günther visited Goebbels at Magda's apartment to congratulate him. After he left, Goebbels triumphantly wrote: "Mr. Quandt came to visit. Overflowing with devotion. That makes the victory."

13.

On the day that Adolf Hitler seized the most powerful post in the country, an entirely different Adolf quit his job. On January 30, 1933, the thirty-two-year-old Adolf Rosenberger gathered the staff of nineteen at the office of the Porsche automobile design firm in central Stuttgart's Kronenstrasse and told them he was resigning as their commercial director. Rosenberger had cofounded the company two years earlier with two partners: the mercurial but brilliant car designer Ferdinand Porsche and his son-in-law, Anton Piëch, a pugnacious Viennese lawyer. Rosenberger was the firm's financial backer and fundraiser, but he had grown tired of spending his own money and raising funds from family and friends for the Porsche firm, which was burning through cash and nearing insolvency. Rosenberger had arranged a successor: Baron Hans von Veyder-Malberg, a retired race-car driver and an acquaintance of both Rosenberger and Porsche. The firm was in such dire straits that the Austrian aristocrat had to bring in forty thousand reichsmarks as a bridge loan. Despite the financial situation, Rosenberger left his job on good terms. He would stay on as a shareholder and focus on peddling Porsche patents to foreign markets in more of a freelance role.

Adolf Rosenberger could not have been more different from the new chancellor, despite the shared first name. The handsome, tech-savvy German Jew had been a race-car driver for Mercedes. Some of his race cars were designed by Ferdinand Porsche. Rosenberger's racing career ended abruptly in 1926, after a serious accident at the Grand Prix in Berlin left three people dead; he was severely injured. He instead began investing in real estate in his hometown, then partnered with Porsche to help finance their race-car designs and turn them into drivable prototypes.

When Ferdinand Porsche started his namesake firm in Stuttgart at the height of the Great Depression, it was the first time that the fifty-five-year-old mustachioed autodidact had struck out on his own as an entrepreneur. Previously, he had been terminated twice as chief technical designer, most recently at Austria's Steyr Automobiles, where he was laid off after a few

*Porsche's Jewish cofounder,
Adolf Rosenberger.*

months because of the economic crisis. Before that, his executive contract
at Daimler-Benz wasn't renewed because his designs were exceedingly expensive and the personal debt that he owed to the carmaker was mounting;
he had taken loans from Daimler to finance the building of a vast family
villa on a hill in Stuttgart.

Porsche moved back to Stuttgart from Austria with his family in 1930.
Finding a job during the worst economic crisis in modern times was tough,
especially for a man in his midfifties operating in a niche industry and
expecting a good salary. Plus, Porsche had a reputation for being difficult. Those in the automotive industry viewed him as an "unemployable
perfectionist" because of his lack of financial discipline and volatile tem-
per. So Porsche started his own company. He hired veteran engineers and
partnered with cofounders who could lend balance where he lacked it. But
Porsche could not overcome his worst impulses. He still threw tantrums,
often grabbing the wide-brimmed hat he always wore, throwing it on the
ground, and stomping on it like a petulant child. What's more, his designs

continued to be too costly. They would never be approved for production during a depression. He found himself facing bankruptcy.

When Hitler seized power, Porsche had just turned down a job to head up vehicle production for Joseph Stalin's Soviet regime in Moscow. After careful consideration, Porsche declined this lifeline. He deemed himself too old, and besides, he didn't speak Russian. Politics didn't matter to Porsche; he cared only about his car designs. When the dictator back home threw Porsche another lifeline, he grabbed it with both hands.

At 10 a.m. on February 11, 1933, twelve days after Adolf Rosenberger quit his job, Hitler gave his first opening speech at Berlin's International Motor Show. In his upbeat address, the chancellor announced tax relief for motorists and a modern road-construction plan to revive the ailing car industry, which was still reeling from the economic crisis. Hitler, a car nut who had never even obtained a driver's license, praised Germany's automotive designers and engineers "whose genius creates these marvels of human ingenuity. It's sad that our people hardly ever get to know these nameless men." The führer was, however, about to get to know one particular car designer exceptionally well.

Hitler's message was met with cheers back at the Porsche office in Stuttgart, where the whole team was listening to the speech on the radio. After Hitler finished speaking, Ferdinand Porsche sent him a telegram, providing a brief résumé and offering his services: "As the creator of many renowned constructions in the field of German and Austrian motor and aviation and as a co-fighter for more than 30 years for today's success, I congratulate Your Excellency on the profound opening speech." Porsche and his staff were ready to put their "will and ability at the disposal of the German people," he cabled to Berlin. In an accompanying telegram, Porsche wrote: "We express the hope that in our endeavors we will receive Your Excellency's attention and encouragement." His telegrams weren't just acknowledged by Hitler's state secretary. They were received graciously, and Porsche promptly was sent words of encouragement.

Porsche's first contact with Hitler had been indirect, and a sheer coincidence. In 1925, the Mercedes limousine that was used to chauffeur Hitler was brought to Daimler's body shop in Berlin for repair. Porsche, then

Daimler's technical director, happened to be visiting the garage and diag-
nosed the problem: heavily contaminated lubricating oil. He had no idea
whose shiny black limo it was. A year later, the two men were properly
introduced on the sidelines of a racing event in Stuttgart. Now, seven years
later, Ferdinand Porsche was about to become Hitler's favorite engineer.

On May 10, 1933, Hitler and Porsche met again, this time at the Reich
Chancellery in Berlin. During their thirty-five-minute meeting, Porsche
convinced Hitler to allocate state subsidies for the development of a race
car that Porsche and Rosenberger had designed, regaling the car-crazy
führer with tales of technical innovation. Hitler's decision helped Porsche
turn things around financially. And when the time came for Hitler to look
for a man capable of realizing his prestige car project — the Volkswagen
— he knew just where to find him: at his drawing desk in Stuttgart.

14.

On the cold, pitch-black evening of February 20, 1933, Günther Quandt,
Friedrich Flick, and Baron August von Finck met with the führer and his
economic advisers once again in Berlin. Only this time, the location had
been upgraded — instead of a discreet suite at the nearby Hotel Kaiserhof, they entered the palatial domicile of the parliamentary president, and
more than twenty other tycoons and executives joined them there. Von
Finck was again accompanied by Allianz's CEO, Kurt Schmitt, one of the
four future Nazi ministers of economic affairs in attendance. The other
three — Walther Funk, Hjalmar Schacht, and Hermann Göring — were on
hand to convince these two dozen titans of German industry and finance,
one final time, to donate to a Nazi election campaign.

After Hitler's and Göring's speeches and Schacht's call to pony up, it was
up to the tycoons to make the next move, a delicate one. In keeping with
his legendary thriftiness, August von Finck made a beeline for the exit
"at the first possible moment" after realizing that Schacht was coming to
extract a personal pledge from him on the spot. Friedrich Flick donated
royally. As was his custom, he hedged his bets and gave to all parties in-

volved — as much as 120,000 reichsmarks each to the Nazi Party and its nationalist coalition partner. The smallest contribution that evening came from Günther Quandt. He wired 25,000 reichsmarks to the Nazi slush fund via his battery firm AFA, weeks later. The gift paled in comparison to the six-figure donations made by IG Farben and Flick. But Günther recognized a cheap opportunity when he saw one. This ability, after all, was what had made him rich.

Of course, Günther had a far more pressing personal reason to stay on the good side of the Nazis. Goebbels was about to get a promotion. Just days after Günther's donation, Hitler appointed Goebbels as Reich minister of public enlightenment and propaganda. He was now one of the most powerful men in Nazi Germany, controlling every aspect of the press, cultural life, and political promotion. In the end, the outcome of the March 5, 1933, elections had not mattered. Six days before it, the Reichstag burned down, under mysterious circumstances, exactly one week after the secretive meeting at Göring's residence next door. The rule of law was suspended, and democracy in Germany was dead. Hitler was in control.

15.

On May 1, 1933, the Nazi regime celebrated Labor Day, a national holiday in Germany for the first time. As many as 1.5 million people gathered at dusk on Berlin's Tempelhof airfield to hear Hitler give a speech about the German work ethic. The chancellor was positioned high above the crowd, flanked by massive swastika flags; from an immense grandstand he thundered on about workers' rights. The next day, he would bust and ban all labor unions.

Günther Quandt joined the Nazi Party that Labor Day, receiving membership number 2,636,406. He and hundreds of thousands of other Germans, including August von Finck, had joined just in time, as Hitler imposed a membership ban the next day. Some 1.6 million Germans had joined the NSDAP since his power grab in January, bringing the total to 2.5 million within just a few months. Hitler worried that these rapidly climbing numbers were diluting the value of party membership. He kept the ban in place for four years; Friedrich Flick and Ferdinand Porsche had to wait until May 1937 to join.

After the war had ended, Günther concealed his Nazi Party membership and prided himself on his "disapproving attitude to the party." He was, however, soon enough forced to explain himself when documentation surfaced about his entry into the party. He claimed that Goebbels had coerced him. On a warm spring day in late April 1933, according to Günther, he was summoned to a meeting at the propaganda minister's office in the Ordenspalais, just off Wilhelmsplatz, a ten-minute walk from his own headquarters. When he sat down, Goebbels coolly sized up Günther and asked him whether he had joined the party yet. Günther responded no; as a businessman he had "never belonged to a political party." He vividly described how Goebbels began to blackmail him on the spot: "His face changed color. Brutally and extortionately, he said in a threatening voice that I had to become a party member immediately. Otherwise, the party would take over my son's education." In Günther's telling, Goebbels threatened him with "insane disadvantages" if he didn't enter the NSDAP and donate more money: "Goebbels kneeled on my soul, reminding me of the death of my eldest son in Paris, and that I had the choice of keeping my second son or not. I said that I didn't mind the penny contribution to the party and I joined."

In his diary, Goebbels noted that he had received Günther at his office on Friday, April 28, 1933, but suggested a scenario that was the complete opposite of Günther's story: Quandt was eager to join the NSDAP and wanted to tell the top Nazi in person before signing up. "Received Dr. Quandt," Goebbels wrote the next day. "He's so insignificant now. Wants to enter the party."

Günther's NSDAP membership did nothing to protect him. On May 3, 1933, two days after joining the party, he was attending a meeting of the Deutsche Bank supervisory board in Berlin when the police stormed in. Günther was handcuffed, driven to police headquarters on Alexanderplatz, and put in a basement cell. The next day, he was transferred to a jail in the capital's working-class Moabit neighborhood, where he was held in solitary confinement on undisclosed charges. His houses were searched, and his business headquarters on Askanischer Platz and one of his AFA factories were occupied.

One week after his arrest, Nazi Party officials publicly announced that Günther had been detained because he had shifted money abroad and wanted to relocate factories to foreign countries. His arrest allegedly "prevented" both. Günther, meanwhile, still had no idea why he had been arrested. One evening he was taken from his cramped, musty isolation cell to a cold, gray interrogation room, where two high-ranking members of the Justice Department awaited him. According to Günther, his inquisitors began playing "good cop, bad cop" and finally revealed the reason for his arrest: an anonymous complaint had supposedly come in, vaguely accusing him of violating German commercial law. The duo, who had set up an anticorruption unit, told Günther "in a courtly manner" that he would be released if he signed over AFA to one of his executives, an early member of the NSDAP. Günther laughed at them, refused, and was taken back to his cell immediately, where a written charge of embezzlement awaited him.

On June 13, 1933, after almost six weeks in solitary confinement and countless nightly interrogations, Günther paid four million reichsmarks in bail, a gargantuan sum, and was released from jail. "$1,144,000 Bail Furnished by a German Industrialist," the *New York Times* reported the next day. Under the conditions of his release, Günther wasn't allowed to visit his headquarters on Askanischer Platz or any of his Berlin residences. Instead, he set up shop in a suite at the Hotel Kaiserhof.

In the weeks after his release, Günther donated about forty-three thousand reichsmarks to a new Nazi fund: Voluntary Donations for the Promotion of National Labor. Whereas the initiative was meant to help reduce unemployment by providing money to German businesses, the funds were sometimes used to "buy impunity from prosecution" in certain legal proceedings. Günther's house arrest was lifted in early September 1933, soon after he started donating the money. The charge of embezzlement, however, wasn't dismissed until two years later.

16.

Günther Quandt later lamented that "the year 1933 formed a sudden and abrupt barrier for me everywhere." But following his release from solitary confinement, he vigorously capitalized on Nazi Germany's newly codified anti-Semitism. The month after his house arrest was lifted, he demanded the removal of membership and voting rights for Jewish members of Berlin's Association of Merchants and Industrialists. And that was after he had already, "lightheartedly and shamefully early," ousted four Jewish executives serving on his own firms' supervisory boards, a historian later discovered.

Günther opportunistically claimed that the arbitrariness of his arrest and his time in jail remained a defining trauma for him. "It became clear to me that a hitherto unknown state of legal insecurity had commenced," he wrote in his memoir. "This was a shocking experience for me, since I was raised to be unconditionally loyal to the state. The reasons for my arrest were never disclosed to me." But they had been. His two interrogators at the jail had revealed to him that one of his AFA executives, the early member of the Nazi Party, had orchestrated the corporate coup against him. After the war, however, Günther handily used his time in jail to portray himself as a victim of the vindictive Goebbels, claiming that Goebbels had masterminded his arrest and imprisonment. This too was a lie.

On May 5, 1933, two days after Günther's arrest, Goebbels wrote in his diary: "Günther Quandt arrested. Why? Tax matter. With Hitler. He's outraged that the economy isn't allowed to settle down. Göring is to investigate the Quandt case. I don't feel sorry for him, just for dear Harald." One day later, Goebbels discussed the "G. Quandt case" with Hitler again, alone. Industrialists and their firms were essential to the chancellor's soon-to-be-initiated rearmament policy. So he was troubled by rebellious factions within the Nazi Party who attacked businessmen and tried to seize their companies. These upstarts threatened to destroy the goodwill that Hitler had so carefully cultivated with the tycoons.

Goebbels was immediately informed when Günther got out of jail. "Detention warrant against Günther Quandt," Goebbels wrote on June 14,

1933. "Released for about 4 million. That's how it goes. I'm not interfering in any way. If he messed up, he should pay." Günther's former sister-in-law, Ello, followed the affair at the side of her best friend, Magda. "Goebbels said he knew nothing about it, but that it was just as well," Ello later declared. "He welcomed the arrest. Goebbels said upon his release that, unfortunately, no one could touch the guy anymore."

The same couldn't be said of Magda's childhood boyfriend from Berlin, Victor Chaim Arlosoroff. Three days after Günther's release, Arlosoroff was assassinated by two gunmen while taking an evening stroll with his wife on a beach in Tel Aviv. The Zionist leader had returned from Germany two days earlier, where he had brokered an agreement with Hitler's regime, allowing about sixty thousand German Jews to immigrate, with their possessions, to the British Mandate for Palestine. Arlosoroff's murder remains unsolved to this day.

17.

In May 1933, Günther Quandt's elder son, Herbert, returned to a Germany that was unrecognizable to him. His home city, Berlin, was now the capital of a new state. His former stepmother was now considered the First Lady of the Third Reich, and her new husband was the Nazi minister for propaganda. Meanwhile, his father was sitting in a cell in a Moabit jail, on unknown charges, while a corporate coup was being engineered against him at AFA.

The twenty-two-year-old Herbert had spent much of the past four years outside Germany, after barely finishing his "downright torturous" schoolwork for good. For better or for worse, he was, after Hellmut's death, his father's heir apparent. Herbert relished the opportunity despite his visual impairment. (His sight had remarkably improved over the years due to medical treatment.) The Great Depression also had no negative effect on him. Herbert had learned English and French in London and Paris, traveled around the world with his father, and received vocational training at an AFA battery factory in Germany and at firms in Belgium, England, and the United States.

He especially enjoyed his time in America and told his family repeatedly over Christmas in 1932 that he planned to move there if Communism drove the Quandts from Europe. "That danger wasn't small," Herbert later wrote, in fall 1979. "Why did Hitler come to power at the time? Because, I'm not afraid to say this here, he had declared war on communism in Germany again and again in a very impressive and pithy way." While Herbert said he was "a blank page politically," by January 1933 he saw Communism, not Nazism, as the great German peril. "The looming red communist danger, which had already been brought to my attention by the press in America, I now experienced firsthand as a threatening, ever-growing monster," he later recalled.

Still, Herbert kept his head down until his father was released from jail and had returned to the office. Herbert then married his fiancée, Ursula; moved to the villa his father bought for him near the family mansion in Babelsberg; and began a four-year stint as a management trainee at AFA in Berlin. Not until two years after Hitler seized power did Herbert sign up as a supporting member of the SS.

18.

On June 30, 1933, two weeks after Günther Quandt's release, Hitler appointed Allianz CEO Kurt Schmitt as his Reich minister of economic affairs. Schmitt beat out Hitler's economic adviser Otto Wagener, who jockeyed too hard for the position and fell entirely out of favor with the Nazi leader. Baron August von Finck had fervently advocated for Schmitt as the best candidate for the job. Von Finck "was anxious for business to have a strong voice in the new regime and felt [that the appointment of Schmitt] would be helpful to Allianz and to his bank," according to a fellow Allianz executive. Hitler and Göring, who was looking to become the de facto leader of the Nazi economy, agreed with von Finck, but for a different reason. In the eyes of the two Nazi leaders, the business community had to be placated as the Nazis consolidated power and jump-started rearmament.

The consummate corporate insider, Schmitt seemed to be the perfect point man for this task, but he quickly resigned his post after collapsing from stress during a speech. Another establishment figure, Hjalmar Schacht, succeeded him. Meanwhile, von Finck's devotion to Hitler deepened. Schmitt, far more an opportunist than a believer, found von Finck's "outlook on the world . . . rather provincial. He had little first-hand knowledge of the countries outside of Germany and had never . . . traveled in foreign countries. Hence . . . his inner faith in Nazism and particularly in Hitler never faltered," Schmitt told an American interrogator after the war.

Von Finck's devotion to the führer stood out to all his colleagues and friends. Hitler "exercised on him a great fascination" and "a hypnotic influence," according to Hans Schmidt-Polex, a longtime friend of the aristocrat. Hans Hess, who succeeded Schmitt as CEO of Allianz but refused to ever join the Nazi Party, revealed after the war that von Finck had told him on several occasions "that he believed that Hitler was sent by God, to become Führer of the German people."

Nonetheless, von Finck's zealotry stopped at his wallet. The banker's stinginess didn't endear him to NSDAP officials. They "felt that his contributions to the Party were not in keeping with his wealth," Allianz's press chief, Baron Edgar von Uexküll, declared after the war. The Nazis had to find a way to capitalize on the devotion, clout, and connections of Bavaria's wealthiest man, but without making him spend a penny of his own fortune. Around the time of Schmitt's appointment, Hitler came up with an idea: he would give von Finck the opportunity to spend other people's money. After the ceremony at the Reich Chancellery, Hitler took von Finck aside, looked him in the eye, and said: "You are my man. You must build me a house of German art."

In July 1933, Hitler, once a dilettante painter himself, appointed von Finck as chairman of the board of trustees for the Haus der Deutschen Kunst, an art museum to be built in Munich. It was Hitler's pet project. The führer envisioned it as a prime example of Nazi architecture, where artworks that he considered quintessentially German would be placed on display. The museum was to be built on Prinzregentenstrasse, on the southern edge of Englischer Garten and near Hitler's luxurious apartment.

On October 15, 1933, Hitler was to lay the cornerstone of the building in an elaborate ceremony. At its conclusion, Hitler struck the cornerstone three times with a specially designed silver hammer. But the tool broke, and its parts scattered across the ground. Von Finck looked on somberly from behind. Enraged, Hitler forbade any mention of the mishap in the German press. Despite the bumpy start, a von Finck–führer synergy soon developed. To begin a museum-related event, the two men would stand side by side before the audience, their posture stiff, the right arm of each man suspended in the air, with the hand held straight. Von Finck would give a three-minute speech to introduce Hitler, and the führer would then

Hitler striking the museum's foundation stone with August von Finck, in suit, standing directly behind him. Moments later, the silver hammer broke.

ramble on for an hour. Going forward, von Finck would be Hitler's museum guide, enjoying the distinct honor of sitting at the chancellor's right side during ceremonies and dinners. He had secured proximity to his beloved führer.

19.

On March 7, 1934, Hitler returned to Berlin's International Motor Show for another opening speech. This time he wasn't happy. The chancellor berated the carmakers for focusing only on luxury vehicles and accused them of peddling the idea that the automobile was only for the rich. Hitler felt bitter about the "millions of decent, industrious, and hardworking fellow citizens" who could not even contemplate buying a car. It was high time, the führer thundered, for the vehicle to lose its "class-based and, as a sad consequence, class-dividing character." His voice boomed through Berlin's largest exhibition hall as executives from Daimler-Benz grimly looked on, chastened and terrified. Ferdinand Porsche, on the other hand, found that he and the führer shared the same view. He had recently added something new to his repertoire: designing small, affordable cars. Earlier that year, on January 17, Porsche's design office had sent a twelve-page memo from Stuttgart to the Reich Ministry of Transport on Berlin's Wilhelmplatz; it outlined plans for the construction of a Volkswagen, a "people's car."

Porsche's unsolicited memo had not made it to Hitler's desk, though. The führer had apparently taken inspiration from the designs of Josef Ganz, a Jewish car engineer. Of course, a Jew would never get to design the car for the people of Nazi Germany. A Daimler car salesman turned confidant of Hitler, however, did read Porsche's memo after the speech and alerted the chancellor to it. A week later, early on a spring day, Hitler summoned Porsche to the Hotel Kaiserhof. Hitler had retained the suite for off-the-record conversations. In the Reich Chancellery, opposite the hotel, every word he uttered was recorded in writing. And after a year in power, Hitler knew the value of privacy. He had become accustomed to bypassing the bureaucracy and awarding political contracts to people he trusted — and Porsche was about to become one of them.

Ferdinand Porsche didn't know exactly why he had been summoned to the Kaiserhof, but he fondly recalled the conversation with Hitler from the previous May, when he saved his company by wowing the führer with racing stories. Porsche expected much of the same this time around. He was wrong. As soon as Porsche entered the suite, the Nazi chancellor began barking orders at him: the Volkswagen had to be a four-seater with a diesel-powered, air-cooled engine that could be converted for military purposes. Hitler didn't have just "the people" on his mind. Rearmament was the real priority.

Porsche absorbed the demands of the autodidact car nut in silence. Then came the kicker. Hitler had read somewhere that Henry Ford, a man he revered, was building a car in Detroit that cost a thousand dollars. The Volkswagen, therefore, could not cost more than a thousand reichsmarks, Hitler declared. Porsche looked at him incredulously but did not dare talk back. Finally, the issue of Porsche's citizenship arose. The fifty-eight-year-old designer had been born in North Bohemia, then part of the Austro-Hungarian Empire; now, in 1934, it was a region of Czechoslovakia. Porsche had chosen Czech citizenship after the empire had collapsed. But to Hitler, a citizen of a despised Slavic country could never design the German people's car. Two weeks later, Porsche and his family discovered that they were suddenly citizens of Nazi Germany, though they had done little to effect this change. Back home in Stuttgart, in his vast villa on the hill, Porsche shrugged and told a relative: "I really don't see what we can do about it." He had bigger problems to solve anyway.

20.

After his release from jail, Günther Quandt soon discovered that his newfound untouchability did not extend to keeping custody of his twelve-year-old son, Harald. The Goebbelses remained hell-bent on getting Magda's firstborn for themselves. In spring 1934 they finally succeeded. On Friday, April 13 — the day Magda gave birth to her second daughter, Hilde — Goebbels complained in his diary that Günther had refused to hand over Harald days earlier to spend time with the growing family over Easter. In addition to Hilde, Harald now had a one-year-old half sister, Helga. The next child, Goebbels's only biological son, was named Helmut, after Günther's dead son, to whom Magda had been so attached. Three more H-named siblings would follow, all sharing the first letter of their first name with Harald and his brothers — and with the surname Hitler.

Goebbels had reached the breaking point with Günther. "We'll now bring out the big guns. I'm not giving in to this anymore," Goebbels wrote. Three days later, he told Hitler about the couple's "fight for Harald." According to Goebbels, the chancellor was "completely on our side. Magda will get her Harald." The propaganda minister then discussed the "Harald matter" with Göring and the leader of the SA, Ernst Röhm, on April 18, 1934. "They both support me a lot," Goebbels wrote. (Ten weeks later, Röhm and most of his allies in the SA were executed on Hitler's orders, with urging from Göring and Himmler, during the Night of the Long Knives massacre.)

Goebbels also spoke with Günther on April 18. The propaganda minister wrote in his diary that he was "tough on [Günther's] sentimentality." Apparently, the strategy worked. "He gives in," Goebbels wrote. "Magda gets her Harald back. She's overjoyed!" Günther expected the couple to return Harald after Easter break, but that didn't happen. In early May, Günther hired a prominent Berlin litigator to force Harald's release. He was one of the few remaining attorneys in Germany still bold enough to file a kidnapping claim against Goebbels and his wife, now the most powerful couple in the country. It made no difference. A week later the lawyer returned to Günther empty-handed. No court in the capital dared to accept the lawsuit.

Goebbels was furious when Magda told him that Günther had hired a lawyer to sue them. "I won't put up with this rude treatment any longer," the propaganda minister wrote. "We won't give Harald back . . . I tell Quandt. He's furious." On May 8, 1934, the couple visited Magda's lawyer to sign a new custody agreement with a revised plan for visitation. "She's happy. Now Günther Qu. has to agree," Goebbels wrote. Günther had no choice but to accept the new arrangement. Harald belonged to Magda and Goebbels now. The boy was allowed to visit Günther twice a month.

Goebbels's final diary entry featuring Günther would be written four years later, in early June 1938. On that balmy spring day in Berlin, Harald told his stepfather that his biological father was getting married again. "Old fool!" Goebbels wrote after he heard the news. The rumor turned out to be false. Günther never remarried. With Toni's death and Magda's troubles, Günther had experienced enough marital distress to last him a lifetime. He chose the safer confines of business and the single life.

With the custody battle over, Günther no longer weighed on Goebbels's mind. But the two men, with their intertwined personal histories, still had to coexist. At least now they had space for the things that made them tick. Goebbels was beginning to exert power. There was a country to be led into battle, and a part of its population to be alienated and disenfranchised — and exterminated. Plus, there was a continent, then a world, to be conquered.

Günther, meanwhile, had a different empire to expand, and he fully dedicated himself to the task. Despite the rough start, he had established himself as a prominent participant in Hitler's new Germany. The country was climbing out of the Great Depression, and rearmament was about to take off. With all the financial opportunities that the Third Reich provided, things were finally looking up for Günther. There was business to do, and money to be made. The world spun on.

PART II

"THE NATIONAL SOCIALIST HAUNT WILL SOON PASS"

1.

On July 28, 1941, Günther Quandt celebrated his sixtieth birthday with a grand dinner for 130 men at the Hotel Esplanade, one of Berlin's famed luxury hotels. With its belle epoque sandstone façade and its neo-Rococo and neo-Baroque interior, the hotel towered over Potsdamer Platz in the bustling heart of the capital. Günther's dinner likely took place in the Kaisersaal, where the German emperor Wilhelm II used to host lavish banquets. Parties befitting a kaiser usually followed in the hall next door, where, during Berlin's hedonistic Golden Twenties, the movie stars Greta Garbo and Charlie Chaplin drank and danced the night away.

All those carefree, heady days were long gone, though. A vicious new war was raging in Europe and threatened to engulf the rest of the world. Hitler was at the peak of his power that summer. He and his allies controlled much of the continent. That same evening, Hitler's armed forces, the Wehrmacht, were closing in on Leningrad and Kyiv as part of Operation Barbarossa, the invasion of the Soviet Union.

A different kind of headiness pervaded the hall where Günther's dinner took place that sweltering summer evening. Günther and his male guests laughed and perspired the night away. They had all grown financially fat on war and conquest. They had been gorging on forced labor, on Jewish companies that they seized with impunity; many, like Hermann Göring, had become literally obese. Fulfilling the endless demand for artillery and tank shells kept the cash pouring in. Yet few had succeeded like Günther.

The Reichsbank president and minister of economic affairs, Walther Funk, began the evening with a "brilliant speech." Funk was feeling sentimental; he and Günther had come a long way together. Twenty years earlier, Funk had merely been a well-connected editor of a financial newspaper, and Günther a rich stock speculator from the provinces. Now Günther had "accomplished something that is written with golden letters in the history of the German war economy," Funk said. He wasn't wrong. Through his arms, battery, and textile firms, Günther had established himself as one of the Third Reich's leading industrialists. Göring had awarded him a phony title, *Wehrwirtschaftsführer*, "military economy leader," and Günther reciprocated the gratitude. Thanks to the regime's rearmament policies and expropriation decrees, he was benefiting massively.

Günther's weapons firm, DWM, was manufacturing millions of bullets, rifles, and Luger pistols for the Wehrmacht. Its stock price would soon skyrocket by 300 percent because of the war and the insatiable demand for arms. Overall, business was going so well that he could afford to buy more shares and would finally become DWM's majority shareholder. His firm AFA was churning out thousands of batteries for Nazi submarines, torpedoes, and rockets. His textile companies made so many millions of uniforms for the Wehrmacht, the NSDAP, the SS, and the SA that, if lined up, the cloth could have spanned more than half the country, from east to west. Günther was keeping up his old ways too, secretly buying up shares in Germany's largest construction firm and mounting a hostile takeover. His greatest coup had occurred just two months earlier, when he entered two of Germany's largest industries by buying a 60 percent stake in Byk Gulden, a pharmaceuticals and chemicals company formerly owned by Jews. Günther's new 60 percent majority interest nicely corresponded to another milestone, his sixtieth birthday.

Even *Das Reich*, the weekly newspaper founded by Goebbels, published a birthday tribute to Günther: "Military cloth, accumulators, dry batteries, firearms, ammunition, light metal — whoever produces all this is rightly called *Wehrwirtschaftsführer*." Günther had, in fact, been agonizing over whether to invite Goebbels to the evening's festivities. Their feud was years behind them, but their relationship had stayed chilly, at best. Three weeks before the dinner, in a letter from his holiday address in the mountains, Günther fretted to an aide about what to do: "He almost certainly won't come, but if he hears that Funk and Milch were there and that he wasn't invited, he may take offense." Günther couldn't risk incurring Goebbels's wrath again. He was convinced that his arms factories had caught Goebbels's attention for a personal reason: nineteen-year-old Harald had developed an interest in mechanical engineering.

Günther ended up inviting Goebbels. And, as expected, Goebbels declined. In his place, Goebbels sent his new deputy, Leopold Gutterer, who earned a seat at Günther's table, the largest one, in the middle of the Hotel Esplanade's hall. Two months earlier, Gutterer had replaced Karl Hanke, Goebbels's most trusted aide over the past decade, as the propaganda minister's state secretary. Hanke's dismissal involved Magda, and intimately. Now Gutterer was just weeks away from introducing a new policy affecting the entire German Reich: the mandatory labeling of Jews with the yellow Star of David.

Günther had fashioned his birthday bash as a networking event, and the party had started early. That morning in late July he held a reception at his newly acquired, extensively renovated four-story townhouse next to the Tiergarten, overlooking Berlin's Landwehr Canal. At the former Hungarian delegation, they lined up to shake his hand: Günther's executives and business partners, along with representatives of the regime, the Nazi Party, and the Wehrmacht. Above these middle-aged men, in their double-breasted suits and uniforms, hung paintings by the Italian Renaissance masters Tintoretto and Bonifacio Veronese. Günther had started to collect art. Impressionist paintings by Claude Monet, Alfred Sisley, and Camille Pissarro graced the dining room of his Babelsberg villa. He still thought culture could be bought. It was later said that Günther had obtained about ten paintings from the collection of the Dutch Jewish art dealer Jacques Goudstikker, which the Nazis had looted in the Netherlands.

At the Esplanade dinner, Günther arranged his executives across fourteen tables, seating each next to a Nazi bureaucrat or general to discuss arms deals and Aryanizations. Naturally, the men who financed these transactions — the leading executives of Commerzbank, Dresdner Bank, and Deutsche Bank — were present. These financiers of the Third Reich competed bitterly to serve the deep-pocketed Nazi regime and to satiate their private clients' ravenous appetite for credit. Nazi Germany's endless drive to expand arms companies, establish concentration camps and death camps, and extend conglomerates at home and in occupied territories was bringing in millions for the banks.

Günther maintained a close relationship to his biggest creditor, Deutsche Bank; he still served on its supervisory board. As a birthday present, one Deutsche Bank executive gifted Günther a seat on Daimler-Benz's supervisory board. It was the official start of the Quandts' lucrative relationship with Germany's largest carmaker. The aloof, mustachioed Hermann Josef Abs, another Deutsche Bank executive at Günther's table, represented the bank on the supervisory boards of DWM, AFA, and forty-four other companies. The pious Catholic was a towering business figure in Nazi Germany and "the lynchpin of the continent-wide plunder." At the end of the dinner, the future Deutsche Bank chairman tapped his glass, got up, and toasted Günther's health. "You were able to make the successful transition to the new era in 1933 as a result of your skillful tactics and your special abilities," Abs said. "But your most outstanding characteristic is your faith in Germany and the Führer." When Abs sat down again, Günther remained standing. As he surveyed the crowd of powerful, gluttonous men, his eyes glazed over and his thoughts wandered back to the past.

2.

Almost eight years earlier, on June 8, 1933, two miles southeast of where Günther Quandt was sitting in solitary confinement in Berlin's Moabit jail, the Reichsbank president, Hjalmar Schacht, approved a gargantuan financial stimulus package to initiate the first phase of Nazi Germany's rearmament. The decision was probably made in a discreet meeting with the new aviation minister, Hermann Göring; his deputy, Erhard Milch; and the defense minister, Werner von Blomberg. They decided that over the next eight years, almost 4.4 billion reichsmarks annually would be spent on rearming the military, totaling a massive 35 billion reichsmarks, some 5 to 10 percent of Germany's annual GDP.

This had to be done in secret. Barring a few notable exceptions, Germany was strictly forbidden to produce weapons under conditions of the Versailles Treaty, a matter Hitler constantly railed against. So Schacht came up with an off-budget financing system for the military, setting up a shell company to pay arms producers in IOUs. A few months after the ministers' meeting, Hitler withdrew from the League of Nations and international disarmament talks. Soon enough, billions were flowing to German industrialists and their arms companies.

Following his release from jail, Günther was exceptionally well positioned for the rearmament boom. Not only did he, in DWM, rule one of Germany's largest potential weapons producers, but he also controlled AFA, the battery behemoth with historical ties to the defense and automobile industries. He began pursuing a dual strategy, servicing military and civilian clients while being careful not to rely too much on either.

Günther reactivated DWM's Berlin facilities right after Hitler seized power. In the years leading up to 1933, from behind his massive, dark double desk overlooking Askanischer Platz, he had planned meticulously for rearmament. "It took no small effort to maintain the company's intellectual, economic, and financial capacities undiminished during the years of decline," Günther wrote in DWM's anniversary publication on May 8, 1939, four months before the start of World War II. "But it was possible at the moment of the seizure of power to place plants at the disposal of the Führer in which the production of army equipment could be resumed immediately on a large scale." For what followed, Günther credited Hitler, "who with indomitable will carried out the rehabilitation and rearmament of the German people."

DWM's arms complex, located in Berlin's blue-collar Wittenau neighborhood, had stood largely empty since the start of the Great Depression. Its facilities were rented out to General Motors. But the weapons manufacturing machinery, parts of which had been dismantled and secretly stashed at scrap metal dealerships, were swiftly bought back, upgraded, and reinstalled. The entire complex was expanded, all paid for by the regime after an order from the Army Weapons Agency (HWA). It quickly became one of Berlin's largest arms-manufacturing complexes, divided across three plots of land. DWM kept one plot, focusing on the production of gun parts and tank shells.

That same year, the HWA commissioned DWM to build a production facility for infantry ammunition in Lübeck. The thousand-acre site, camouflaged by trees, became the most important weapons complex in the Hanseatic port city. DWM's research institute served as Nazi Germany's nerve center for ammunition innovation, and it included a 6,234-foot shooting range for ballistic experiments. Günther's firm hired a group of mathematicians to assist with ammo experiments, improve shell production and ballistics quality, and manufacture hand grenades and explosives. The cities in which Günther built his weapons factories started naming streets after the mogul.

The two other plots of land at Günther's arms complex in Berlin were leased to Mauser and Dürener, DWM's largest subsidiaries. On the verge of bankruptcy during the Great Depression, Mauser, renowned for its rifles and pistols, was "freed" from the "shackles of Versailles" after Hitler's power grab. Mauser also received massive subsidies from the army and soon started cranking out the Karabiner 98k, the Wehrmacht's service rifle, in the millions. Mauser also brought the Luger P08, one of the German army's most-used pistols during World War I, back into production. To this day, the iconic black sidearm is easily recognizable as the weapon of choice for Nazi villains in movies. Allied officers came to call Mauser's arms research facilities a "dream come true."

However, it was Dürener, the other DWM subsidiary to lease a plot at Günther's Berlin arms complex, that truly made the mogul a household name in military and government circles. Dürener was renowned in the aviation world for making Duralumin, a light aluminum with steel-like qualities. Defense aviation was quickly becoming Nazi Germany's fastest-growing and most innovative industry, with Göring and Milch spending billions on the technological sector. As a result of this shelling out of cash, Günther's Dürener became a key supplier to the Luftwaffe, Nazi Germany's air force. Duralumin was an indispensable part of not only the Luftwaffe's fighter jets, but also transport and civilian aircraft made by fa-

mous German aviation companies such as Junkers, Messerschmitt, Hein-
kel, Dornier, and Arado. A new aviation firm that came to rely on Dürener's prized innovation as well was ATG, controlled by Friedrich Flick, who
hadn't been as well prepared for rearmament as Günther Quandt had been.
But the austere industrialist was making up for lost time.

3.

As the Gelsenberg affair blew over, Friedrich Flick was eager to start capitalizing on his regained political clout and excess cash. His ability to sweep
aside sentiment and adapt with the times, making his firms indispensable
to whichever political regime was in power, defined him. A ruthless tac-
tician, Flick bested even an indefatigable networker like Günther Quandt
when it came to tenacious plotting and dealmaking. Aided by lieutenants
like Otto Steinbrinck, Flick paid lobbyists, bureaucrats, and journalists to
receive intel or suppress information. Nazi Germany was particularly sus-
ceptible to his brand of aggressive, under-the-radar politicking. But despite
his massive industrial interests, Flick did have a weakness — he was still a
relative newcomer to arms production, unlike his competitors Krupp and
Thyssen. He developed a strategy to make his steel conglomerate essential
to rearmament and break the traditional dominance of the Ruhr moguls
in the weapons business. And he had ample resources at his disposal to do
just that.

Flush with an added ninety million reichsmarks from the Gelsenberg
deal, Flick was busy building his own steel, coal, and machinery conglomerate from Berlin's Bellevuestrasse in spring 1933. The core of Flick's new
industrial empire consisted of two major steel firms in central and southern Germany: Mittelstahl, active in Brandenburg and Saxony, and Maxhütte, operating in Bavaria and Thuringia. In buying a majority in Harpener and Essener mining, Flick added hard coal from the Ruhr area to
his conglomerate. In January 1933, he added Leipzig-based ATG to the
train-, tractor-, and truck-making firms he already owned. With these new
industrial and political connections, Flick was perfectly positioned for the

rearmament era. He had only one thing left to do: convince Hitler's regime to bring him in.

After the Reichsbank president, Hjalmar Schacht, approved Germany's secret arms budget in June 1933, Flick and his aides went to work preparing an aggressive marketing blitz to pitch the conglomerate as an arms producer for the German government. In September, his office sent a memo to the relevant Nazi ministries across Berlin; parts of it sounded like a weapons catalog. It laid out what Flick's firms could offer the regime: a massive steel-production capacity that could quickly be recalibrated to make guns, ammunition, missiles, bombs, tanks, or aircraft parts; a wealth of raw materials; and factories located across central Germany.

To get a leg up on the competition, Flick walked from his office on Berlin's Bellevuestrasse to the nearby Reichsbank in late November 1933 to personally pitch and lobby Schacht, whom he had known for over a decade. The Reichsbank president directly introduced Flick to the defense minister, von Blomberg, and the usually secretive Flick invited von Blomberg to personally tour three of Flick's steel factories near Dresden. During the tour, on December 5, Flick explained to the defense minister and his clique of officials why his factories were the best choice to produce arms for Germany: they were independent of the Ruhr area and foreign countries for sources of energy, and better protected from air strikes due to their relatively obscure locations and distance from the country's borders. Flick had written Schacht to thank him: the defense minister had been "extraordinarily kind" and showed "very great interest" in his presentation and factories, which, von Blomberg admitted, were not familiar to him.

Now, Flick thought, the arms orders would come flowing in. But nothing happened.

A few months earlier, Flick had instructed Otto Steinbrinck to use his naval credentials and connections as leverage to secure arms deals. Flick's lieutenant had already signaled a renewed interest in all things lethal by joining the SS that year. Over the summer of 1933, Steinbrinck's contacts paid off immediately; he convinced the navy to finance Flick's acquisition of new machines that made artillery casings. But no other orders followed. Unlike the navy, the HWA wasn't convinced that abandoning the tycoons of the Ruhr area was a good idea. Plus, the HWA viewed Steinbrinck as too closely aligned with the navy and refused to place any orders for arms with Flick's factories. Flick, stuck between two parties, complained vehemently to von Blomberg, who intervened directly with the HWA on the mogul's behalf. The defense minister stated that he was "extremely agitated" by the lack of orders for Flick.

Soon after this intervention, the army placed its first series of orders at Flick's plants for millions of grenades and artillery shells. Moreover, in August 1934, Kurt Liese, the general who was heading the HWA, told Steinbrinck that managers at Flick's steel factories "should not hesitate to prepare themselves for a continuous flow of big orders for a number of years." Flick was in, but not before a little quid pro quo.

4.

Over the spring and summer of 1934, Friedrich Flick did the HWA, and himself, a massive favor by facilitating the expropriation of Donauwörth, a Bavarian arms firm on the Danube River that produced artillery ammo. Unfortunately for the company's owner, Emil Loeffellad of Stuttgart, the HWA had labeled his factory indispensable to the rearmament effort. But since the Allies still strictly prohibited military weapons production in Germany, the army had to find a way to seize Donauwörth secretly and operate it under the guise of a normal business. Flick entered the picture through a former employee. One of Flick's steel firms provided the HWA with a shell company called Montan (German for "mining"), which served as a front through which a legitimate transaction could take place. In May 1934, Loeffellad was arrested by the Gestapo, accused of corporate espionage, classified a "state pest," and forced to sell his business to Montan. The HWA kept most of the purchase price as an "atonement sum" for Loeffellad's alleged improper use of government funds.

In July 1934, the HWA-controlled Montan leased Donauwörth back to Flick's steel firm, where it continued to produce artillery ammo. The so-called Montan scheme was beneficial to both parties. It enabled the HWA to buy arms firms in secret, invest in them, and ensure competent business leadership. At the same time, it let Flick secure a major customer with no costs involved. The solution was so convenient that Montan became a secret holding company for all army-owned weapons firms collaborating with German industry. When the war started, Montan controlled more than a hundred arms firms and employed some thirty-five thousand people. Flick soon joined its supervisory board.

The Montan scheme was a turning point in Flick's tense relationship with the HWA. He now became one of the preferred partners for the army. Like Günther Quandt, who financed one of his weapons facilities through Montan, Flick could now build new factories, expand old ones, shift the costs to the army, and make his arms plants as modern as those of his Ruhr competitors, Krupp and Thyssen. It was a dream come true for the industrialist.

But Flick didn't yet seize every opportunity to expand his business empire at the expense of others. In October 1934, the HWA general Kurt Liese asked Otto Steinbrinck whether his boss was interested in buying Simson, a machine-gun factory in Suhl, a city in Thuringia. The Simson family had a remarkable monopoly. At the time, they owned the only firm in Germany that the Allies allowed to produce light machine guns. But the Simsons were Jewish. Their arms monopoly was grist for the mill for the Nazi Party. The family had become a target of vitriolic anti-Semitic propaganda, particularly from Fritz Sauckel, Thuringia's ambitious *Gauleiter,* a short, bald man with a Hitleresque mustache and a heavy rural accent. He wanted to expropriate the Simsons, bring their firm under his control, and turn it into an NSDAP-run weapons company.

The HWA generals had no problem with seizing a Jewish-owned firm. However, they wanted competent business leaders, not some Nazi hack with no entrepreneurial experience running a company in which the HWA had invested twenty-one million reichsmarks. And they were particularly concerned with the "smooth cooperation" of the factory owner, Arthur Simson. Steinbrinck euphemistically relayed Flick's interest in the idea, "if for general national-political reasons the takeover of Simson by our group should be required." But the initial negotiations quickly fell apart.

Seven months later, in early May 1935, Hitler's economic adviser Wilhelm Keppler, backed by the SS leader Heinrich Himmler, offered the Simson firm to Flick once again. A few days later, Arthur Simson was arrested on Sauckel's instructions; he was accused of "excess profits," a practice of extortion; such accusations soon became commonplace as a means of forcing Jewish entrepreneurs to sell their companies. With his back against the wall, Simson signaled his "willingness" to sell his family's firm. Steinbrinck reiterated Flick's interest but now offered a lower price. "We as a private group can only buy, if Simson can meet us without coercion and in complete freedom. We would have to refuse an expropriation in favor of the Flick/Mittelstahl group," Steinbrinck wrote in a memo in late May, coyly covering his boss's hide. It was a textbook feint by Flick's right-hand man. Steinbrinck did share Flick's willingness to buy the Simson firm, but under one condition: the HWA had to first seize the arms business and then sell it on to the mogul. An expropriation was fine as long as Flick and his conglomerate did not directly have to dirty their hands. They wanted an intermediary to do the grunt work for them. Plus, Flick wasn't planning on indiscriminately seizing companies. A takeover target had to add something of significant value to his conglomerate.

Sauckel soon prevailed over the HWA. The *Gauleiter* expropriated the Simson factory and made it a part of a Nazi-run conglomerate consisting of companies stolen from Jews. The Simson family, meanwhile, fled to America via Switzerland. Flick didn't mind the outcome. The final negotiations for Simson took place just months before the Nuremberg Race Laws were enacted, in September 1935; they provided a legal basis for the expulsion of German Jews from their own society, along with the expropriation of their properties. The laws stripped them of citizenship and professional standing, and forbade them sex with and marriage to those deemed to be "of German blood." But at this time, expropriations of Jewish firms were still rare. For the moment, Flick remained concerned about negative optics associated with buying such a factory, which might have consequences for his financial obligations abroad. He also did not want to make a powerful enemy of Sauckel, who would come to provide him with tens of thousands of people to do forced labor. Meanwhile, Flick and Steinbrinck were drawing closer to the man who would become the architect of the Holocaust. The duo had, quite literally, entered Himmler's Circle of Friends.

5.

In early September 1934, Friedrich Flick and Otto Steinbrinck attended the annual Nazi Party convention in Nuremberg at Himmler's invitation. Like many other guests of honor, they were put up at the city's only grand hotel, at the entrance to Nuremberg's old town, a short drive from the party festivities. One gloomy morning, guests made their way downstairs for breakfast only to find a sign hanging outside the small dining room. It read: RESERVED FOR THE GUESTS OF THE REICHSFÜHRER SS. This was Himmler's official title. His thirty-three-year-old aide, Fritz Kranefuss, had placed the sign there.

That drab morning, Kranefuss took the reins of his uncle's group, the Keppler Circle, and turned it into Himmler's Circle of Friends. As Hitler's economic adviser, Wilhelm Keppler was too busy negotiating between the regime and German businesses — arranging a weapons deal here or an expropriation there — to devote time to his circle. Plus, the group had made no impact on Hitler's economic policies, which was its original purpose. Kranefuss had helped his uncle establish the circle and recruit its members. Now he could do with it what he wanted. He was like any good Nazi — what pleased his boss pleased Kranefuss even more. So he decided to turn the circle into an invitation-only networking group for big business and the SS.

The circle's rebranding implied that it had an amicable connection with Himmler. But Himmler didn't have any friends. He could not have cared less about these rich men. He was interested only in what they represented and what he could gain from them — and they had the same attitude toward him. Himmler knew the moguls were interested in the ultimate insurance: a relationship with the SS leader, the Third Reich's chief of police. But even he was always competing for influence. Now that Göring was emerging as the most powerful man in the Nazi economy, Himmler wanted his own ties to big business to benefit the SS. First he would lure the tycoons in. Then he would take their money.

When Flick and Steinbrinck entered the reserved room that morning, they saw many familiar faces among those whom Kranefuss had invited: Keppler, who was present for the handover and was named an honorary member; executives from Commerzbank and Dresdner Bank, nicknamed "SS-Bank," on whose supervisory board Flick served; Göring's corrupt half brother Herbert; and the CEO and chairman of Wintershall. For whatever reason, Wintershall's major shareholder, Günther Quandt, wasn't invited. Kurt Schmitt was there too, this time without August von Finck, who wasn't included because he was known to be excessively frugal. Himmler had just promoted Schmitt to honorary SS general, only months after Schmitt had resigned as minister of economic affairs due to burnout. The "physically impressive" Schmitt loved parading around in his black SS uniform. Himmler hadn't come to greet his "friends." He would see them later, at dinner.

6.

Friedrich Flick came to praise Himmler's Circle of Friends as a "mirror image" of German business. But at the next Nazi Party convention, a new member joined who didn't quite fit that description. Richard Kaselowsky was a pudding executive from the provinces, far removed from Berlin and the Ruhr area and the mighty moguls who exercised power there. He hailed from Bielefeld, a sleepy city in the region of East Westphalia, not far from the Dutch border. Kaselowsky, a stout man with oily brown-gray hair and a meaty face, was determined to put Bielefeld on the map. The forty-seven-year-old was the CEO of Dr. August Oetker, a food company whose namesake founder had pioneered packaged cake and pudding mixes and ingredients like baking powder in Germany. Kaselowsky had married into the family business through Ida Oetker, the widow of his best friend. His main task, besides serving as CEO, was to prepare Rudolf-August Oetker,

Kaselowsky with his Nazi Party badge.

his teenage stepson and the designated company heir, to one day succeed him.

What Kaselowsky lacked in business stature, he made up in zeal for Hitler. He handed out signed copies of *Mein Kampf* to new employees and hung a portrait of the führer in his office suite. Moreover, Kaselowsky and Himmler shared a common background as poultry farmers. Kaselowsky and the SS leader were both intrigued by the agrarian aspects of Nazism, specifically its (re)settlement of people to the countryside. The idea went hand in hand with Hitler's desire to gain more *Lebensraum* (living space) for the German people; Himmler and his acolytes propagated the concept of *Blut und Boden* (blood and soil) — a "racially pure Nordic" people would leave the decadent and depraved cities to settle and work as peasant farmers in grounded rural communities.

Kaselowsky's dedication to Nazism often came at the expense of the firm he led. Between 1933 and 1935, he spent hundreds of thousands of reichsmarks in company money on settlement projects in the east of Germany, which failed. And he clearly learned nothing from those experiences. In the summer of 1935, he merged a profitable regional newspaper, owned by an Oetker-controlled publisher, with a local Nazi Party publication that was losing money.

Bad business decisions aside, Kaselowsky's financial devotion to hopeless Nazi causes put him in excellent standing with Westphalia's *Gauleiter,* who invited him to the Nazi Party convention that September. As second-tier guests of honor, Kaselowsky and his wife were put up at Nuremberg's Hotel Bamberger, where Hitler's secret girlfriend, Eva Braun, and the movie director Leni Riefenstahl were also staying. Word of Kaselowsky's spending had somehow made its way to the grand hotel, and Fritz Kranefuss soon invited the provincial pudding boss to join Himmler's inner circle.

Kaselowsky readily accepted. He was hooked from the start. Present at every meeting, he loved the perks and elite access that came with membership. Every second Wednesday of the month, Kaselowsky traveled from Bielefeld to Berlin to meet up with Himmler's Circle of Friends at the Aero Club. In the heart of the capital, Göring had repurposed Prussia's majestic parliament as a lavish clubhouse with a round-the-clock bar, a beer room, and a famous restaurant, all next door to the Ministry of Aviation and opposite the headquarters of Himmler's security apparatus. After a drink to welcome them, the forty men would dine lavishly, in a seating order that rotated from meeting to meeting. Afterward, they withdrew to clubrooms to talk shop but never politics.

Himmler came to collect his dues just before Kaselowsky joined. On a bright, cold morning in January 1936, Flick, Steinbrinck, and the rest of the circle met the SS leader at Munich's Regina Palace Hotel on Maximilianstrasse, from which they embarked on a day trip. A bus waited outside the luxury hotel to take them to a destination northwest of town: Dachau concentration camp. When they arrived, Himmler walked the men into the camp, passing a group of inmates in prison uniform. The SS leader's personally guided tour of Dachau was "very carefully prepared and dressed up," one member later declared. He first showed the men to the camp barracks and workshops, where imprisoned tailors, carpenters, and shoemakers plied their trades. The tycoons had lunch in the camp canteen, after visiting the kitchen to taste the food that was being prepared. Himmler even led the men into a passage of cells, unlocking one to personally check on a prisoner. Afterward the group visited a nearby SS-run porcelain factory before returning to Munich, where they dined together.

After dinner, Himmler stood to make a short speech. Now that he had showed the men that concentration camps weren't as bad as the rumors made them out to be, he had something to ask of his wealthy friends. Himmler said, in a humble tone, "For the SS and my other tasks, I need no money and want no money, but for some cultural tasks and for doing away with certain states of emergency for which I have no funds at all, if you want to place funds at my disposal for that purpose, then I would be most grateful to you." His pet projects included the *Lebensborn,* a human-breeding association in whose maternity homes children were bred for the "master race."

Of course, none of the businessmen dared say no. Kranefuss suggested an annual membership contribution of at least 10,000 reichsmarks. He had already lined up Baron Kurt von Schröder, the financier at whose villa Hitler and von Papen had sealed Germany's fate, to serve as group treasurer. To collect the fees, von Schröder opened "special account S" at his private bank in Cologne. Steinbrinck would be in charge of fundraising. Millions soon flowed in. Flick started giving 100,000 reichsmarks a year to the circle. Kaselowsky gave 40,000 reichsmarks. Although he had missed the Dachau excursion, Kaselowsky was present for Himmler's personally guided tour of another concentration camp, Sachsenhausen, north of Berlin. Different camp, same spiel.

7.

In late June 1934, Ferdinand Porsche signed a contract with the skeptical, reluctant Reich Association of the German Automotive Industry to develop the Volkswagen. The carmakers' organization had accepted financial responsibility for the project, and its members were dismayed that Hitler had picked the volatile designer Porsche over more established names to create the first car for the masses. Of course, the executives didn't dare contest the führer's will, but they also didn't believe Porsche could actually, in a matter of months, pull off the task of developing a small car that would cost only a thousand reichsmarks. At the contract-signing ceremony in Berlin, one executive sneered at Porsche, saying, "If . . . you can't turn out such a car at the expected price, don't worry. Just tell Hitler it can't be done and that the man in the street should just go by bus!" In making sure the profligate Porsche didn't spend too much of the association's money, he was allowed to charge them only as much as twenty thousand reichsmarks a month to develop the car; plus, the first prototype had to be finished in ten months. It was a herculean task. Ultimately, it would take Porsche 1.75 million reichsmarks, two years, three versions of the design, and much political pandering to Hitler to complete a suitable prototype of the Volkswagen.

In the meantime, Porsche and his son-in-law, Anton Piëch, tightened the family grip on the car design office in Stuttgart. On September 5, 1935, ten days before the Nuremberg Race Laws were enacted, the cofounder of Porsche, Adolf Rosenberger, was arrested by the Gestapo in his hometown near Stuttgart, charged with "race defilement," and put in remand prison in Karlsruhe. His "crime" was dating a gentile girl. Given his prominence as a Jewish entrepreneur and a former race-car driver, Rosenberger had been warned that he was a target of the Gestapo. He ignored the writing on the wall.

The signs had been clear. Five weeks earlier, on July 30, 1935, Rosenberger had transferred his 10 percent stake in the car design firm to Porsche's twenty-five-year-old son, Ferry. The young man had been working for his father's firm for almost five years, under the tutelage of Porsche and veteran engineers. The once struggling firm had finally become profitable through Porsche's Volkswagen contract and a race-car design that he and Rosenberger had developed. Company profits that year neared 170,000 reichsmarks. So, Porsche and Piëch started to buy out the two shareholders who were not part of the family: Adolf Rosenberger and Baron Hans von Veyder-Malberg.

They bought out their Jewish cofounder at a fraction of the value of his

Father and son Porsche in the 1930s.

shares. In fact, the duo bought out Rosenberger for the exact same nominal amount he had paid for his founding stake in Porsche in 1930: just
three thousand reichsmarks. Despite all that Rosenberger had done for the
company, the price severely undervalued his shares in Porsche. "It was held
against me that a pennant or the like as a Jew-free company would not be
given as long as I was a shareholder . . . I don't accuse Mr. Porsche and Mr.
Piëch at any rate of personal anti-Semitism," Rosenberger later contended.
"But . . . they used my membership as a Jew to get rid of me cheaply."

    Porsche and Piëch denied the allegation. Still, regardless of motive, the
duo's acquisition of Rosenberger's Porsche stake was an "Aryanization,"

plain as day. An asset was considered Aryanized in the Third Reich when the Jewish "element" of ownership had been removed. Aryanizations could involve paying less than the actual value for firms, houses, land, jewelry, gold, art, or shares owned by Jews, as had been the case with Rosenberger; it could extend to the outright theft of possessions. Because of Nazi Germany's penchant for formal legal procedure, Aryanizations often had the veneer of a normal business transaction. But eventually that nicety was discarded.

On September 23, 1935, after almost three weeks in the Gestapo prison, Rosenberger was transferred to Kislau, a concentration camp south of Heidelberg. After four days of beatings, he was suddenly let go. Baron von Veyder-Malberg, Rosenberger's successor at Porsche, had intervened with the Gestapo in Karlsruhe, successfully lobbying for his release. But Rosenberger still had to pay the Gestapo fifty-three reichsmarks and forty pennies for his time in "protective custody," as the euphemism went. Despite later claims to the contrary, Ferdinand Porsche and Anton Piëch did nothing to secure their cofounder's freedom. Via his lawyer, Rosenberger begged Porsche to help save his life, but Porsche was too busy hobnobbing at the Spanish Grand Prix, outside Bilbao.

Rosenberger left Germany a month later and moved to Paris in November 1935. Following his departure as Porsche's commercial director in early 1933, he had been working on a contractual basis for the design firm. Even after his imprisonment, the thirty-five-year-old remained a foreign representative for the company, licensing Porsche patents in France, England, and America. Rosenberger could keep 30 percent of sales provisions with a contract running until 1940, or so he thought. Porsche and Piëch weren't quite finished with demeaning their persecuted cofounder, but they had to contain their cruelty for now. First, Porsche needed to introduce the führer to his long-awaited masterpiece: the Volkswagen.

On a blisteringly hot afternoon in early July 1936, Porsche presented two test cars to Hitler, Göring, and their entourage at the chancellor's Bavarian mountain retreat on the Obersalzberg. The top Nazis were sweating in their jackboots and uniforms, which were decked out in rows of medals and ribbons — awards for sycophancy. Hitler wore just one such decoration: his Iron Cross First Class, given to him as a lance corporal in the Bavarian army in World War I. He didn't need to flaunt any other awards. He was the führer, after all. Porsche sold Hitler on the design firsthand. Years later, in the midst of the war, with his end drawing near, Hitler would reminisce to a journalist about that sunny July day: "The way these Volkswagens whizzed up Obersalzberg, buzzing around and over-taking . . . big Mercedes cars like bumblebees, was enough to impress any-one." After Porsche's presentation, Hitler gave a tour of the Eagle's Nest, the teahouse that was being built for him, overlooking the quiet mountain town of Berchtesgaden. Hitler had already decided that he would have Eu-rope's largest car factory built in the center of Germany, just to make the Volkswagen. Now they had to find the right location for it.

8.

Rudolf-August Oetker, the "pudding prince," knew he had a special posi-tion in life. Named after a father and a grandfather he never knew, he grew up with a sense of purpose and entitlement in the family villa on the Jo-hannisberg in Bielefeld. As the sole male heir, destined to carry on the fam-ily food company and surname, Rudolf-August realized early on that "the most valuable thing I inherited is the Oetker name." His stepfather, Richard Kaselowsky, whom he considered his real father and always addressed him as such, diligently prepared him for the task of taking over Dr. Oetker. Yet Rudolf-August was a bad student. He preferred riding horses, much like Kaselowsky, who was an avid rider and breeder himself. Whereas his thrifty mother disliked her husband's expensive hobbies, Rudolf-August's grandmother had no such reservations. She spoiled the boy rotten, gifting him a BMW convertible for Christmas in 1933. When he later had to sell his BMW motorbike, as a consolation she gave him a horse.

Rudolf-August began riding horses when he was twelve. When his local riding school was incorporated into the Reiter-SA in 1933, the sixteen-

*Rudolf-August Oetker standing between his grandmother (right)
and her chauffeur (left), 1933.*

year-old Oetker was automatically enrolled as a member of the paramilitary organization's horse-riding division. It was hardly a political statement on his part. But another membership was. Rudolf-August's stepfather
joined the Nazi Party in May 1933. His mother followed, and then his older
sister. Rudolf-August was the last one to do so. They were a Nazi family,
through and through.

When Rudolf-August finished high school in September 1936, he took
part in six months of Nazi-mandated labor service. For the labor service's
graduation ceremony, he bused in two hundred female employees from
Dr. Oetker in Bielefeld as dance partners for his comrades. He would remember it as "a fun party." After dropping out of military service because
of health problems, he moved to Hamburg in 1937 to complete a bank
apprenticeship. Hardly your average apprentice, Rudolf-August first lived
in the Four Seasons Hotel on central Hamburg's Inner Alster Lake, but
soon he started searching for a suitable residence on the banks of the Outer
Alster, Hamburg's priciest location.

He quickly found a property at Bellevue 15. There, Rudolf-August bought an Aryanized lake villa with a large plot of land previously owned by Kurt Heldern, a Jewish tobacco executive who had fled Nazi Germany for Sydney, Australia. Rudolf-August was aware of the acquisition's dubious provenance; even his Nazi stepfather was initially against the purchase. "It's out of the question," Kaselowsky told him. "Tears stick to this house." Undeterred, Rudolf-August bought the villa and the land through Dr. Oetker, at far below their market value. His new neighbors included Hamburg's Nazi mayor, whom his stepfather knew from Himmler's Circle of Friends. Rudolf-August then Aryanized a plot of land behind his new villa from a different neighbor: the Lipmanns, a Jewish couple. They were forced to sell their land, among other belongings, to finance their "desperate emigration efforts." The land was worth at least 119,000 reichsmarks. "After lengthy negotiations," Rudolf-August stated that he was willing to pay just half. The local Nazi authorities, who had to approve the sale of any Jewish-owned asset, lowered the final price to 45,500 reichsmarks. The Lipmanns eventually managed to flee to Uruguay.

Rudolf-August, meanwhile, was making the most of his move to Hamburg. He often spent weekends with friends along the Baltic Sea, in fashionable beach towns like Heiligendamm. There, he ran into Joseph Goebbels, who was on a family holiday. Rudolf-August approached the propaganda minister and introduced himself, and they exchanged a few "friendly words." At the town's racecourse, Hermann Göring awarded Rudolf-August the prize when a stud from his stepfather's stable won a race. The Oetker heir's group of friends in Hamburg included Jews, who "must have suffered from the reprisals," but like so many other Germans, Rudolf-August was indifferent to their plight. He also knew about the concentration camps but accepted the regime's line that the camps held only enemies of the state. "We thought nothing more of it. After all, those who came out of the concentration camp said nothing," Rudolf-August later recalled. But the heir had gotten to know concentration camps much better than he let on. After all, the SS had trained him in one.

9.

In the summer of 1936, Günther Quandt was helping a Jewish arms executive in order to benefit both men. That past November, Frankfurt's Goethe University had sent Georg Sachs, a professor of metallurgy, on leave soon after the Nuremberg Race Laws came into effect. Just a few months earlier, Günther had installed Sachs on Dürener's executive board as head of its research department. In Nazi Germany, whom you knew and how useful you were could mean the difference between life and death. Few understood that better than Erhard Milch, Hermann Göring's deputy and the son of a Jewish pharmacist. Although Milch had a combative relationship with his boss, Göring shielded him from persecution, squelching a Gestapo investigation as rumors about Milch's heritage swirled around the Ministry of Aviation in Berlin. "I'll decide who's a Jew!" Göring allegedly said. Milch's value to the regime and to business lay in his authority over the Luftwaffe and its billions; Hitler would soon provide the Luftwaffe at least 40 percent of the entire war budget. Hence, Günther gave Milch a particularly warm welcome at Dürener's showy anniversary party in 1935.

That same opportunism is what made Sachs, with all his expertise in metallurgy, almost as important to Günther. In April 1936, Goebbels's Berlin district got wind that Günther had appointed a Jew to the board of one of his arms companies. Günther was forced to suspend Sachs, but Milch decided that Sachs could continue to be employed in a lower-profile role, despite his "dark spot." After all, Milch knew about those all too well. However, in mid-July 1936, Sachs wrote a letter to Günther, asking to be let go "in the interest of both parties." Günther initially refused his request, keen to keep the man because of his expertise, but he grudgingly acquiesced weeks later. Sachs was leaving Nazi Germany while he still could. Günther gave Sachs about thirty-six thousand reichsmarks to help him settle his emigration bill — Sachs had to pay a Reich "flight tax" of twenty-three thousand reichsmarks. Days before Sachs left for America, in early fall 1936, Günther visited him at his home to say farewell. Sachs quickly found a position as a professor of physical metallurgy at Case Western

Reserve University in Cleveland, Ohio, where his family joined him soon after. Sachs's wife later said that "old Quandt" proved to be "an upstanding helper." And Sachs came to return the favor, after the war.

A problem had been solved for both parties. Dürener soon proudly reported that no "foreign or Jewish capital" had a stake in the firm. In late 1937, Göring rewarded Günther for his mass arms production with the title of *Wehrwirtschaftsführer* (military economy leader), awarded to those business owners and executives whose firms were deemed crucial to rearmament. Friedrich Flick and Ferdinand Porsche received the title soon after. The benefits it bestowed were limited to an ornate gold badge and good standing with the regime, as long as one remained useful. Günther later said that the Ministry of Aviation had awarded him the title because of his work with Dürener. He figured the firm's lavish anniversary bash had clinched the decision. The benefits of throwing a good party were certainly clear to Günther. But when he invited Milch to his sixtieth-birthday dinner, planning to seat the half-Jewish Nazi by his side, at the last moment the state secretary decided not to attend.

10.

While Berlin was hot with Olympic fever in late summer 1936, Magda Goebbels had something to confess. On August 1, during the opening ceremony at Berlin's Olympic Stadium, the Nazi theorist Alfred Rosenberg told Joseph Goebbels about "an unpleasant thing" that had transpired years earlier between Magda and Kurt Lüdecke, who had introduced her to the NSDAP. That evening, at their new villa, Goebbels confronted Magda with the story. Magda started crying and at first denied everything, but eventually she came clean to her husband: she'd had an affair with Lüdecke in the first years of their marriage. After her confession, Goebbels wrote in his diary the next day: "I'm very depressed about this. She lied to me constantly. Huge loss of trust. It's all so terrible . . . It will take me a long time to recover from this." Since Lüdecke had long ago fled back to America, after falling out with other top Nazis, Goebbels had to find a different way to exact revenge. Nearby, an opportunity beckoned.

Two months earlier, on the muggy evening of June 2, 1936, Goebbels and his three-year-old daughter, Helga, were taking a stroll on Schwanenwerder Island. Goebbels, Magda, and their three children, plus Harald, had just moved to the exclusive residential enclave in Berlin's southwestern corner. Father and daughter were almost home when they ran into a neighbor, a famous actor. The thespian was accompanied by his twenty-one-year-old girlfriend, Lida Baarová, a Czech movie star. The beautiful brunette had recently started acting in German films. Baarová had been cast in femme fatale roles by Berlin's prominent movie production company, UFA, whose studios were in nearby Babelsberg. At Goebbels's request, Baarová and her boyfriend showed him and Helga around their house that night. Baarová didn't know it yet, but Goebbels was about to consume UFA and her personal life.

After Magda confessed to her affair with Lüdecke, Goebbels decided to get to know Baarová better. He arranged for her latest UFA movie, appropriately named *Traitor*, to have its grand premiere at Nuremberg's Nazi Party convention in early September 1936. Back in Berlin, Goebbels invited Baarová and her boyfriend to his box at the opera and organized a screening of the boyfriend's latest movie at the villa on Schwanenwerder. Soon Goebbels and Baarová started meeting more often, and alone, often at the minister's lakeside timber cottage north of Berlin. As fall turned into winter, the two started an affair. They quickly took their tryst public, and Goebbels began to take Baarová as his date to movie premieres. Her actor boyfriend sent her packing. Magda, preoccupied with health issues and birthing more children for the Reich, seemed to care little at first. Hitler, on the other hand, was still deeply invested in the Third Reich's most famous marriage.

11.

Prominence had its perks, Richard Kaselowsky soon discovered. On May 1, 1937, Dr. Oetker was one of thirty German businesses to be awarded the honorary title of "national-socialistic model company." During the award ceremony at Berlin's Aero Club, Hitler gave Kaselowsky a golden flag. The food firm garnered the prize for taking such good care of its employees and, decisively, for its dedication to Nazi ideals concerning labor. As for Kaselowsky, he wore the mantle of Nazi CEO with pride and jumped at the opportunity for Dr. Oetker, its subsidiaries, the Oetker family, and the other firms they controlled to Aryanize assets.

After Kaselowsky forced the Oetker-controlled publisher Gundlach to merge its profitable newspaper with the unprofitable Nazi Party publication in 1935, the firm tried to offset the considerable loss by looking to the magazine market. Once "non-Aryan" publishers and those who opposed the regime were censored and then forbidden to own and distribute paper media by Goebbels's Reich Press Chamber, the rights to their magazines and publications could be bought on the cheap. Over the course of 1935, a Berlin magazine publisher and its office on Potsdamer Strasse were Aryanized by Gundlach, as were the rights to a magazine previously owned by a Jewish distributor. In Austria, Gundlach Aryanized Oskar Fischer, a Viennese publishing house that owned six magazines. In January 1936, Kaselowsky approved an Aryanization by a subsidiary of Dr. Oetker in the Nazi-ruled "Free City of Danzig" (Gdansk). In the Baltic Sea port city, a majority stake in a packaging business was Aryanized by the firm at an "extremely favorable" price, some 60 percent below actual market value, after its Jewish majority shareholders announced their withdrawal from the company.

The Kaselowsky/Oetker family also bought stakes in three companies that had previously been Aryanized by other parties. Most prominent among them was a firm owned by the Berlin beer brewer Ignatz Nacher, whose companies had been brutally Aryanized by Dresdner Bank and, separately, by a consortium led by private bankers from Munich. Around the same time that Friedrich Flick acquired Nacher's Bavarian estate in 1937, the Oetker family acquired a one-third stake in Groterjan malt beer, one of the breweries Aryanized from Nacher by the bankers' consortium. The brewery marked the Oetker dynasty's entry into the alcoholic beverage industry, still a major part of the family empires today. But the Aryanizations by Kaselowsky, Oetker, and Porsche-Piëch paled in comparison to the size and scope of those carried out by Günther Quandt, Friedrich Flick, and August von Finck.

12.

In late spring 1937, while deeply entangled with Lida Baarová, Joseph Goebbels was busy planning art exhibitions. He had Baron August von Finck to thank for that. What the frugal financier lacked in generosity, he made up for by inspiring it in others. In four years' time, von Finck had raised twelve million reichsmarks for Hitler's new museum in Munich, enough money to cover the building's continual cost overruns. Bavarians were mockingly calling the massive building "the white sausage temple." The Nazi Party had to contribute only 100,000 reichsmarks to its construction; von Finck did the rest. The banker combined business trips with his fundraising mission, visiting other tycoons at their villas and estates. As rearmament millions flowed from the regime into industrialists' pockets, von Finck convinced some of the biggest names in German business to give back and become founding members of the museum — and all this for just 100,000 reichsmarks. Friedrich Flick, Gustav Krupp, Carl Friedrich von Siemens, and Robert Bosch were among the munificent moguls who got their checkbooks out.

In early June 1937, Hitler and Goebbels flew to Munich to inspect the museum and its jury-picked inaugural show, called "The Great German Art Exhibition." Von Finck personally led the tour. The duo, however, were appalled: "They have hung works here that make your flesh creep," Goebbels wrote in his diary. "The Führer is seething with rage." The walls were mostly lined with grisly historical scenes depicting German conquests. Apparently, those planning the exhibition had focused on the Nazi theme of "blood and soil," interpreting the concept quite literally. The resulting show didn't quite live up to the chancellor's artistic vision of National Socialism. Hitler considered postponing it for a year rather than "display such muck," and he appointed his personal photographer to curate the show going forward. But the high-profile exhibition couldn't be dismantled at a moment's notice without causing the chancellor some minor embarrassment. The show had to go on.

When Hitler and Goebbels returned a month later for the opening, the chancellor was happier. Nothing had been changed thematically; the number of gory paintings had simply been reduced. On July 18, 1937, the führer opened the Haus der Deutschen Kunst and its premier exhibition, with von Finck standing at his side. At the vernissage, Magda and Goebbels spent fifty thousand reichsmarks on Nazi art for their homes. Goebbels had staged another show, just a few blocks away in the Hofgarten Arcades, which was intended to run at the same time. Goebbels had come up with the idea of displaying confiscated works by mostly German modern artists, and some foreign ones; together they were meant to represent art that had no place in the Third Reich, at least in Goebbels's opinion. The exhibition of "degenerate art" displayed six hundred works by artists such as Max Beckmann, Marc Chagall, Max Ernst, Otto Dix, Paul Klee, George Grosz, and Wassily Kandinsky. The show quickly drew over two million visitors, twice as many as attended the exhibition at the Haus der Deutschen Kunst.

Overall, the regime was pleased with von Finck and his efforts to raise funds for Hitler's museum. The banker would soon be rewarded for his service.

Months later, Goebbels gave his feedback on another prized Nazi innovation. In early September 1937, Goebbels visited Stuttgart to join Ferdinand Porsche for a test ride in the Volkswagen. "The car has fabulous pulling power, climbs well and has excellent suspension. But does it have to be so unadorned on the outside? I give Porsche some advice on that. He takes it readily," Goebbels wrote in his diary. He preferred to ride in fancy limousines. The propaganda minister inspected the Volkswagen again three months later and was happy with the improvements. "Dr. Porsche delivers a masterpiece here," Goebbels wrote, pleased as he always was when someone obeyed him. He soon awarded Porsche the National Prize of Art and Science. Even bigger rewards awaited Porsche down the road.

13.

Months after helping one Jewish family flee Germany, Günther Quandt robbed another. On June 9, 1937, his weapons firm DWM published a one-sentence statement in Berlin's financial newspaper, noting that it had taken over a new business: Henry Pels, a state-of-the-art toolmaker that produced hole punches and iron cutters at its factory in Erfurt, Thuringia's largest city. What wasn't explained in the terse announcement was how Günther had viciously Aryanized the business eleven days earlier. On the morning of May 29, 1937, the Berlin surgeon Fritz Heine had been forced to sell his wife's majority stake in her family firm at far below market value, and to resign his supervisory board seat. It all took place during a tense shareholders' meeting at Günther's office on Askanischer Platz. Heine had been the only "non-Aryan" supervisory board member, representing his wife, Johanna. She had inherited the stake after her father, the firm's founder, Henry Pels, and her mother died, in 1931. Her only brother had already died a "heroic death for his fatherland" as a German officer in World War I. The Heines and their two children had been baptized Protestant, but that would not save them under the Nuremberg Race Laws, as their parents were Jewish.

Günther bought the Heines out of their stake with hard-to-sell treasury notes worth about 500,000 reichsmarks, cheating the Heines out of at least 1.5 million reichsmarks. The nominal value of Johanna's stake was about two million reichsmarks, but its actual value was likely much higher. Günther valued the company's machinery alone at three million reichsmarks, soon after the Aryanization. Günther became Henry Pels's supervisory board chairman, filled the board with his business partners and executives, and retooled the company into a productive weapons business. By 1938, the firm had already turned a gross profit of six million reichsmarks, producing gun mountings, cannons, and anti-aircraft artillery for submarines. Günther also Aryanized the company name, removing the name of Johanna's father (Henry Pels) and rechristening the company Berlin-Erfurter Maschinenwerken. Yet business correspondence was frequently carried out using stationery stamped with the old "non-Aryan" name.

Things didn't end well for the Heines. Their son had already moved to America after finishing his engineering studies, and their daughter soon fled to England, aided by a pastor in Berlin. But the couple stayed in Germany. They were confident that "the National Socialist haunt will soon pass." It did not. Johanna and Fritz Heine were forced to move out of their villa in Berlin's Westend; they scrambled to sublet two rooms. On October 24, 1941, they were deported by train from Berlin to Lodz in the Warthegau, a Nazi-named area in occupied Poland where Günther's acquaintance, the cruel *Gauleiter* Arthur Greiser, ruled over millions — including those in Lodz's Jewish ghetto, which was the main collection point for Chelmno, the extermination camp. The Heines were likely murdered in Chelmno in mid-November 1941, although their death certificates said Litzmannstadt, the Nazis' new name for Lodz. Back home, the couple's remaining possessions were confiscated as an exit tax for "fleeing" Reich territory. For Günther, the Heines were merely the start of his juggernaut of plunder, which would stretch across Germany and other parts of Europe.

And he wouldn't be working alone. Günther had discovered a young talent to help him expand his empire. On a rainy morning in September 1937, Günther sat behind his double desk in his office on Askanischer Platz 3, interviewing the dashing lawyer who sat opposite him. Günther carefully wrote down the man's answers to his questions. He had met the twenty-nine-year-old Horst Pavel at a business reception and sensed the man's gift for dealmaking. At noon, Günther offered Pavel the role of head of AFA's legal department. Pavel had three hours to consider the offer; he accepted it at 3 p.m. Günther thought that his elder son and heir apparent, Herbert, could do with a little competition. Herbert had finished his four-year management training at AFA in May 1937 and had started to work as a director at Pertrix, a subsidiary of AFA in Berlin, which produced flashlights and batteries. Pavel was two years older than Herbert, and just as ambitious. He would do his utmost to best the boss's son.

Günther, thinking in Darwinian terms, encouraged the competition. He wrote about his son's "struggle for life." Günther gave Pavel the office next to his own, and shortly after hiring him, he took his new protégé on a cruise, lasting almost four months, to South America. Writing from the cruise ship *Cap Arcona*, Günther shared some personal observations about Latin Americans in a letter to his executives back in Germany: "The principle of the pure race is impossible [in Brazil] since the whole country consists of Italians, Spaniards, Germans interbred with Indians," he wrote. "In addition to Negroes, with whom one also mixed indiscriminately. This has given rise to a race that is resistant to the murderous climate with enough intellectual impact from the white and red skinned. Hostile to this stands the white country of Argentina. It has the higher intelligence." During the cruise, Günther made Pavel a sweeping offer: the entire commercial management of AFA and an executive board position, provided he stayed with the Quandt group. Just like that, Günther made Pavel his right-hand man, and Herbert would once again have to fight to get his father's attention.

14.

In the fall of 1937, Friedrich Flick was preparing for plunder. On November 4, Flick's lieutenant, Otto Steinbrinck, had written in a memo to his boss that Wilhelm Keppler, Hitler's ubiquitous intermediary between regime and business, had informed him that "for some time Jewish assets in Germany have been seized by a new wave of sales." Even Jewish owners "from whom one wouldn't have expected it before" were striving to "get rid of their possessions in Germany," Steinbrinck wrote. Flick promptly seized the opportunity. Some of the first Jewish-owned assets that he purchased were for his own private use. He loved buying grand properties. This time, Flick bought three estates: one in Bavaria, one near Berlin, and one, a hunting property, in Austria. All came from Jewish business families who needed to sell while they still had the option of doing so. (The Bavarian estate and the Austrian hunting grounds are still owned by some of Flick's grandchildren.)

By November 1937, Flick's first Aryanization had been underway for months. Late that summer, he had started pursuing the Lübeck blast furnaces, a major pig-iron plant in the Hanseatic port town and one of the few larger firms in German heavy industry owned by Jews. Lübeck's shareholders were mostly German Jewish business families, as well as companies and banks affiliated with them. Flick had eyed the firm for almost a decade. Now it was time to strike.

Earlier that year Flick had come to see acquisition of the Lübeck blast furnaces as acutely important. They could supply his steel firms with pig iron; there was a major shortage of this metal. What's more, Lübeck had a Nazi CEO, who was eager to help Aryanize the firm he led. He saw his Jewish shareholders as the main reason why the company was being passed over for weapons contracts from the HWA. Flick now swung into action. First, he successfully staged a hostile takeover of Lübeck's second-largest shareholder, an iron-ore trading firm classified as a Jewish company. When some of the firm's shareholders tried to pool their shares and move their stock abroad, Flick invoked the threat of regime sanctions to force Jewish shareholders to sell. He did not, however, attend the final takeover meeting at his headquarters on Berlin Bellevuestrasse in early December 1937. Its aim was to convince the final holdouts, a group of foreign shareholders and the Warburg bank, to sell their stock. Flick explained his absence to Walther Oldewage, the regime's enforcer on the deal: "The discussion with this committee is a renewed Jewish trick, which I'm not willing to fall for after my bad experiences so far." In the end, the shareholders sold.

In the days after that deal was struck, Flick approached Lübeck's largest shareholders, the Hahns, a Jewish family. They agreed to sell their stake to him in two parts almost immediately, and for millions below market value, but on one condition. To protect their own family firm, a steel mill in the Ruhr area, the Hahns insisted on receiving a written statement to the effect that a sale of their Lübeck shares would be interpreted by the authorities as a sign of their goodwill, and that their steel mill would be spared any coercive measures. But Oldewage refused; instead he gave only an oral statement to that effect. The Hahns still went ahead with the deal, selling the first part of their Lübeck shares to Flick in December 1937. Weeks later, Flick poached Oldewage from the government. As a reward for his help, Flick stashed him away in a middle-management job on a generous salary at one of his steel firms. As Oldewage was about to assume his new role, Steinbrinck gave him some parting feedback: "[Oldewage] seems to be a little too soft in human terms; I personally advised him to give in less to Jewry."

In the weeks after the Hahns' first sale of shares to Flick, the Nazis put even more pressure on the Jewish family. They were threatened with arrest and internment in a concentration camp. When the Hahns went to the Aryanization department of the Ministry of Economic Affairs in Berlin to make good on the assurance that their firm would be left alone, a Nazi official told them he couldn't believe they had been foolish enough "to accept a bill of exchange for which there is no cover." The Hahns saw only one option at that point: to sell their steel mill to a major competitor and immigrate to England. The family sold the last part of its Lübeck shares to Flick, once again for millions under market value; they needed the money to get out. Flick now had his majority in Lübeck, and he was already busy with his next Aryanization project.

On their one-way flight to London, the Hahns ran into Otto Steinbrinck. Flick's lieutenant was on a business trip. He sneered at the Jewish family: "You're lucky to get out at all."

15.

Friedrich Flick's next and much bigger Aryanization was already taking shape during his assault on Lübeck. In early November 1937, Wilhelm Keppler told Otto Steinbrinck that a number of other firms were also slated for Aryanization. These included German assets owned by the Julius and Ignaz Petschek conglomerates, which were originally established by the eponymous Petschek brothers, who were Czech Jews. By the time the two conglomerates caught Flick's eye, they had long been separately owned and operated by the siblings' sons, who weren't on good terms with each other. The Nazi regime took an enormous interest in the Petschek heirs. Taken together, the cousins controlled about 65 percent of the brown coal reserves in eastern and central Germany, making them responsible for 18 percent of raw coal production in the entire German Reich. And this was just a small part of the Petscheks' operations. The larger part was a range of coal mines in Bohemia and Moravia, Czech regions on which Hitler had already set his sights.

When Keppler told Steinbrinck that the Petscheks' German interests were slated to be Aryanized, he confirmed something that Flick and Steinbrinck had heard from other sources: the Prague-based Julius Petschek group, the smaller of the two conglomerates, was already in talks with two companies to sell its majority stakes in two big German brown-coal firms. And these weren't just any two companies vying for control of the Petschek's German assets: they were Wintershall, the potash and oil giant that Günther Quandt owned a quarter of, and IG Farben, the world's largest chemicals firm. If Flick could just get his hands on the Petschek brown coal interests in Germany, he could secure a fuel base for his main steel firm for decades to come. This was a "matter of life," Steinbrinck told Keppler on November 3, 1937. Two weeks later, Steinbrinck reiterated to Keppler that the Flick conglomerate, "under all circumstances," wanted to participate in the "liquidation of P.'s property." The duo agreed on "making trouble for the Jewish element," as Keppler called it.

The "Petschek or P. problem," as Flick and his aides euphemistically called their Aryanization effort, became top priority. Flick and Steinbrinck began to lobby the Nazi regime and Petschek contacts in order to enter the negotiations in pole position. Many of these contacts were fellow members of Himmler's Circle of Friends. Most notable among them was Herbert Göring, the *Reichsmarschall* Hermann's half brother. Simply because of this family relationship, Herbert had gained a position as general secretary in the Ministry of Economic Affairs and then got appointed to various executive positions at major German firms. As one historian put it, Herbert

Göring "created an outright parasitic position in the Third Reich by turning direct access to his powerful half-brother into cash." Flick and Steinbrinck bought into the ploy, promising Herbert a big payout "in case of a solution to the P. problem."

In a meeting with Steinbrinck, Herbert Göring said the Petscheks had the full attention of his half brother. Hermann Göring was in the midst of executing his "Four Year Plan" for Nazi Germany's economy. His grandiose design aimed at the further rearmament of the country, but, most important, at making Germany an autarky: a self-sufficient state in all respects, no longer dependent on imports from foreign countries. The Petscheks' brown coal reserves, owned by Jewish foreigners no less, would form a natural part of that. In a follow-up meeting with Flick, Herbert Göring confirmed that whereas the Julius Petschek heirs wanted to sell, the Ignaz Petschek group rejected all overtures. They would have to be dealt with later.

With backing from both Görings, Flick established a leading position at the negotiating table. In mid-December 1937, Flick informed Wintershall's CEO, who was also Günther Quandt's business partner and yet another member of Himmler's Circle of Friends, that he was making a claim to Julius Petschek's German brown-coal firms. The CEO responded with "angry silence." Simultaneously, Herbert Göring told a Julius Petschek board member that the negotiations were to be handed over to a consortium under Flick's leadership. The information was relayed to one of Julius Petschek's sons, who promptly broke off negotiations with Wintershall and IG Farben, signaling their willingness to talk with Flick. But the process stalled. Julius Petschek's sons, Czech citizens, had created a complicated ownership structure. They had long ago moved the main holding company for their German shares safely overseas. The shares now sat with the United Continental Corporation (UCC) in New York; its former chairman was John Foster Dulles, the future US secretary of state. Furthermore, Julius Petschek's heirs wanted to be paid in American dollars, but Hermann Göring and the Nazi authorities didn't allow this currency to be used for the purchase of German companies.

In mid-January 1938, Steinbrinck wrote an extensive memo that Flick would use one week later in a presentation on how to solve the "Petschek problem." On January 21, Flick spoke to an audience of one in Berlin: Hermann Göring. Flick suggested to the *Reichsmarschall* that a two-pronged Aryanization be undertaken. Flick alone would negotiate a deal with Julius Petschek's sons, but a compromise on the issue of foreign currency would be necessary, the mogul said. Flick argued that he should be given the sole mandate to negotiate on this matter; multiple bidders would drive up the price and give the Petscheks a choice of the best offer. In turn, a voluntary sale would weaken the holdout position of the Ignaz Petschek heirs. Flick's presentation was a major success. Hermann Göring signed a prepared document providing Flick with the exclusive negotiating mandate for both Petschek groups, albeit a nonbinding one with no commitment on the issue of foreign currency.

The representatives of the Julius Petschek heirs arrived in Berlin the next day. Their chief negotiator was George Murnane, a well-connected New York investment banker who had succeeded his friend Dulles as UCC chairman. Murnane wanted to create a "calming atmosphere," but Flick directly drew a hard line in their first meeting, saying that he alone had been authorized to negotiate on "orders from top quarters [*sic*]." Dollar payments for German resources were out of the question. Without quick concessions from the Petscheks, Flick threatened that an involuntary takeover would be likely. But Murnane refused to budge on foreign currency and an asking price of about $15 million. Although not before expressing his sympathy for what he called the "German problem, namely the rearmament question and the Jewish question."

After two more fruitless meetings, Flick abruptly broke off negotiations at the start of a new round on January 31, 1938. He lied, saying that his mandate to negotiate had expired that day. In the final passage from a statement that Flick cryptically read aloud in the meeting room, he made it clear that the Petschek heirs would be expropriated without a deal. The impervious Murnane, whom Flick had put under constant surveillance, called his bluff and said that he had already received an offer of $11 million from Günther Quandt's Wintershall. Murnane then upped the ante: German companies in America could be "threatened . . . by the same problems as those that now preoccupied him in Germany."

Murnane's response set off alarm bells at the highest levels of Nazi economic leadership. Faced with this threat to German assets abroad, particularly IG Farben's American subsidiaries, Hermann Göring and his lackeys gave up their opposition to a dollar payment. Flick, however, was in no rush to resume the negotiations. Hitler's annexation of Austria was imminent, and Flick wanted to wait and see how it would affect his bargaining position. As it turned out, it had a very positive effect.

After Hitler annexed his home country, Austria, in mid-March 1938, and threatened that Czechoslovakia would be next, the Julius Petschek heirs were willing to lower their asking price significantly. More political pressure soon followed. In late April 1938, Hermann Göring issued several decrees intensifying the persecution of Jews. All sales or leases of an asset were now subject to state authorization if a Jew, German or foreign, was involved, and foreign Jews now also had to declare all their property in Germany to the authorities. Göring also outlined the possibility of state expropriation if it was in the interest of the German economy.

On May 10, 1938, Flick and the UCC, now represented by Murnane's British associate Viscount Strathallan, resumed their negotiations in Baden-Baden, a chic spa town near the French border. In follow-up meetings in Berlin a week later, they hashed out a deal for $6.3 million, less than half of the shares' market value and almost $5 million less than Wintershall's offer and $9 million less than Murnane's initial asking price three months earlier. The mood and the balance of power had shifted in Flick's favor. Strathallan thanked Flick and praised "the spirit of all our talks." Murnane cabled Flick from New York: "Wish express my admiration your ability and fairness in carrying out transaction and your skill in negotiating." Flick responded in kind, attributing the success to "working together in mutual loyalty and we encountered on your side a broad understanding of German conditions." (US investigators later accused Murnane of badly representing "the interests of his customers." The Americans thought that "he played the Petschek-property into the hands of the nazis by giving way . . . in all points and by showing weakness.") The Julius Petschek heirs managed to sell their remaining assets in Sudetenland to a Czech consortium just weeks before Hitler occupied the area. Then they immigrated to the United States and Canada.

Flick wasn't done yet. He proceeded to sell some of the Julius Petschek brown coal mines to Wintershall and IG Farben. Flick ended up making a profit of almost $600,000 on the entire Aryanization, in addition to securing a fuel base for his steel firms free of charge. As a broker's fee, Flick temporarily transferred one million Lübeck shares to Herbert Göring. The *Reichsmarschall's* corrupt half brother could keep them until the shares yielded a dividend. Flick also gave him a loan to buy into a shipping conglomerate. According to Flick, Herbert Göring repaid the loan after making a "rather good deal" by selling the majority stake to Flick's arms and steel competitor, the Krupp dynasty. Wintershall ultimately lost out in the Julius Petschek Aryanization, but Günther Quandt wasn't deterred. He would have plenty opportunities in shady deals to come. And anyway, you win some, you lose some. Flick was about to learn that same lesson.

16.

The Haus der Deutschen Kunst opened in July 1937, just as the Aryanizations began to take off, and Baron August von Finck was ready to capitalize on all his hard work for Hitler. Nazi Party luminaries, like the führer's personal lawyer Hans Frank and Munich's corrupt chief Christian Weber, already held NSDAP and personal accounts at the aristocrat's private bank, Merck Finck. Now it was time for von Finck to expand his financial institution and get rid of his Jewish rivals. He first attacked a competitor in Munich: Martin Aufhäuser, senior partner at H. Aufhäuser, one of Germany's largest private banks. The financier had protested against the Nuremberg Race Laws, under which he was classified as Jewish. Aufhäuser applied for an exemption in order to have his personal rights reinstated and to save his family bank, a procedure that required Hitler's personal permission. Unsurprisingly, the führer rejected the application.

*August von Finck and Hitler giving the Nazi salute
at the Haus der Deutschen Kunst.*

Von Finck seized the chance to escalate the matter. In a letter to Munich's Chamber of Commerce on November 11, 1937, he laid out a proposal on how to eliminate the H. Aufhäuser bank, concluding: "Today, the German private banking sector is still largely made up of non-Aryan firms. The gradual cleansing of this trade, which is so strongly influenced by the Jewish element, must not be halted by the granting of applications for exemptions but must . . . be promoted by all means." The H. Aufhäuser bank was seized during Kristallnacht, the notorious pogrom against Jews that occurred throughout Nazi Germany on November 9 and 10, 1938, and swiftly Aryanized. After spending weeks in "protective custody" at Dachau concentration camp, Martin Aufhäuser and his brother fled Germany and ended up in America. Their other bank partner and his wife committed suicide after Kristallnacht. Von Finck, as state representative for Bavaria's private banks, was responsible for the liquidation of Martin Aufhäuser's private portfolio of shares. The proceeds were used to pay Aufhäuser's "flight tax" after he managed to escape the country.

Von Finck's first Aryanization presented itself while he was ramping up attacks against his Jewish colleagues at Aufhäuser. Otto Christian Fischer, a prominent Nazi banker who served on the museum board of trustees with von Finck, was a key figure in finance Aryanizations as head of the Reich banking authority. In fall 1937, Fischer put von Finck in touch with Willy Dreyfus, the owner of the prominent German private bank J. Dreyfus, and Paul Wallich, a partner at Dreyfus's Berlin branch.

Willy Dreyfus had decided to sell his family bank because of the pressure to agree to an Aryanization. He had already closed his Frankfurt branch, after one of his partners was threatened with deportation to a concentration camp. At the same time, Dreyfus started to look for a buyer for the bigger Berlin branch. Adding an office in the capital was a rare opportunity for von Finck. His private bank still had only a Munich branch, but all the action was in Berlin. Naturally, he wanted in.

The negotiations between Willy Dreyfus and von Finck's deputy began in December 1937. Julius Kaufmann, a half-Jewish Dreyfus director, witnessed the three-month talks in Berlin. He later detailed how von Finck coerced Dreyfus to lower the sale price of his bank branch. For starters, von Finck refused to take over the bank's pension obligations, worth 450,000 reichsmarks, to its Jewish employees and pensioners. After Willy Dreyfus submitted a balance sheet that already included provisions and depreciations that lowered the value of his bank branch by another 400,000 reichsmarks, von Finck pressured the man for further reductions, including undervaluing his real estate. These adjustments took another 700,000 reichsmarks off the sale price, which came out to about two million reichsmarks. All in all, Julius Kaufmann estimated that von Finck forced Willy Dreyfus to sell his Berlin branch for at least 1.65 million reichsmarks (about $1.5 million at the time) below its actual value. But Merck Finck would later assert that "friendly negotiations" had led to the Dreyfus "takeover."

Paul Wallich, the Berlin branch's former partner, signed a contract to stay on for a decade as a consultant. This, despite Merck Finck's having issued a company rule stating that the bank could employ only individuals of "pure German blood"; "proof of Aryan origin" for an employee's spouse was also required. Wallich and Julius Kaufmann were both classified as Jewish under the Nuremberg Race Laws, but they had married gentiles. Both men were allowed to transition from Dreyfus to Merck Finck, but the arrangement lasted only as long as the two Jewish men, in "privileged mixed marriages" that predated Hitler's power grab, were deemed useful to Merck Finck.

Baron Egon von Ritter, a close friend of von Finck, became the leading partner at Merck Finck's Berlin branch. Von Ritter quickly fired Kaufmann for being "non-Aryan" but forced him to stay on for the remaining six months of his employment contract to help with the reorganization. Kaufmann at least survived. Paul Wallich fared far worse. His contract was terminated once Merck Finck no longer required his services, but only after taking advantage of his help in reallocating client accounts. Wallich committed suicide on a business trip to Cologne, just days after Kristallnacht.

The Dreyfus Aryanization gave von Finck's bank instant notoriety in Berlin, where it became known as the "bank of the Führer." It was the greatest compliment one could give to a Hitler-obsessed zealot like von Finck. The Aryanization was also lauded in German financial circles as a blueprint for the further "dejewification" of the private banking industry, triggering a run on smaller Jewish-owned banks across the country. After the Aryanization was finalized and published on March 5, 1938, Willy Dreyfus immigrated to Basel, Switzerland. But he hadn't seen the last of von Finck.

17.

The most spectacular private banking Aryanization landed in August von Finck's lap one week after the conclusion of the Dreyfus takeover. On March 12, 1938, the German army drove into Austria and incorporated the country into the Reich. Thousands of Austrians lined the roads and streets to welcome the troops. The persecution of the nation's Jewish population, by both Germans and Austrians alike, began while the Anschluss, as the takeover was called, was still in progress. Von Finck was soon offered the chance to Aryanize S.M. von Rothschild, the country's largest private bank, which belonged to the Austrian branch of the famed Rothschild dynasty. Baron Louis von Rothschild led the Vienna-based bank founded by his great-grandfather. Louis was arrested during the annexation and imprisoned at the former luxury Hotel Metropole, the Gestapo's new headquarters in Vienna's old town. The Rothschilds' family bank was seized. All their other personal belongings, including their art and palaces, were looted. Adolf Eichmann's notorious Central Office for Jewish Emigration was quickly established at one of the Rothschilds' palaces.

Emil Puhl, vice president of the Reichsbank under Walther Funk, later recalled that Funk's Ministry of Economic Affairs preferred having a private bank Aryanize S.M. von Rothschild. Funk wanted to prevent the major commercial banks, like Deutsche and Dresdner, from increasing their influence in Austria. Puhl said that many German private banks wanted to Aryanize S.M. von Rothschild, but that Merck Finck's selection "undoubtedly goes back to the influence Mr. Fink [sic] had on party and state." Von Finck, among his many positions under the Nazi regime, served on the Reichsbank's advisory board.

Von Finck's father and Louis von Rothschild's father had been good friends. The younger von Finck was therefore invited to Zurich by a representative of the Rothschilds in early May 1938 "to discuss possible solutions" for the seized bank. Afterward, von Finck traveled on to Vienna, where he met with Josef Bürckel, the capital's corrupt *Gauleiter* and Austria's Reich commissioner following the Anschluss. Von Finck told Bürckel that he wanted to expand his bank to southeast Europe and asked him for help "in obtaining for that purpose a Jewish-owned bank in Vienna."

In a bigger meeting the next day, von Finck was told that the S.M. von Rothschild bank would be best suited to his needs, and Merck Finck was appointed as its trustee. But the SS refused to transfer trusteeship of such a valuable asset. Von Finck then traveled to Berlin to ask Hermann Göring to intervene. Only after Göring signed and sent a telegram to Austria's ranking SS chief, with the assurance that von Finck was "up to tackling difficult jobs" and had "excellent party connections," did the SS recognize his bank's trusteeship. Administration of S.M. von Rothschild was transferred to Merck Finck in early July 1938 — just in time for the baron's fortieth-birthday bash, coming up in two weeks.

Weeks before concluding his second Aryanization, von Finck refused another one. On June 3, 1938, he received a letter from Nuremberg's Nazi mayor. In it, the mayor asked von Finck if he was still interested in Aryanizing the private bank Anton Kohn, citing preliminary talks they had held on the matter. The financial institution, owned by the Jewish Kohn brothers, had been Bavaria's premier private bank alongside Merck Finck, but it had fallen on hard times under Hitler. On June 11, 1938, von Finck wrote back to the mayor, stating that he was no longer interested in Aryanizing Anton Kohn because of the bank's bad financial state and its limited "Jewish clientele." In von Finck's eyes, the lack of Jewish customers meant there were fewer assets up for grabs. With less to steal, it just wasn't an attractive business proposition for the anti-Semitic aristocrat.

Later that summer, von Finck and Friedrich Flick actually teamed up for a banking Aryanization. In September 1938, they provided capital in the Aryanization of Simon Hirschland, a prominent Jewish-owned private bank in the Ruhr area. In this transaction, led by Deutsche Bank, they received assistance from the Aryanization expert Hugo Ratzmann, the banker whom Günther Quandt used in his seizure of Henry Pels one summer earlier. The moguls all knew one another well by now. Von Finck served on the supervisory boards of a steel firm and a coal company of Flick's. The two also served on Allianz's supervisory board together and at AEG, a producer of electrical equipment, with Günther.

Like Flick, von Finck had developed a mutually beneficial bond with Hermann Göring. Merck Finck soon bought S.M. von Rothschild out of trusteeship for about 6.3 million reichsmarks, some forty-two million below the bank's estimated value. The acquisition was partly financed with securities stolen from the Rothschilds' private bank accounts. After the sale, Göring again intervened at von Finck's request. This time, it was Funk's Ministry of Economic Affairs that refused to release the S.M. von

Rothschild assets to Merck Finck. After Göring once again intervened, the ministry directly transferred the assets to von Finck's private bank.

The Aryanizations brought von Finck and Flick even closer to Göring. All avid hunters, von Finck and Flick attended Göring's birthday gatherings at Carinhall, his country estate north of Berlin, numerous times. Von Finck gave Göring birthday presents, worth as much as ten thousand reichsmarks, as thanks for his aid in getting the Rothschild bank. Flick went even bigger, gifting to Göring some Old Master paintings he had bought at auction. Bribes were a staple of the Göring family.

They were a staple of the Nazi regime too. After thirteen months of imprisonment, Louis von Rothschild was released from Gestapo custody after having been forced to sign over his family bank and personal possessions. Von Finck later claimed that he used his own contact with Göring to secure Rothschild's release, when in truth it was Rothschild's two siblings who paid some $21 million for the release of the bank executive. It remains the largest known ransom paid in modern history, totaling about $385 million in current value. Rothschild immigrated to America.

The Aryanized S.M. von Rothschild was reestablished as the Eduard von Nicolai bank, named after the new principal partner in Vienna. Von Finck provided most of the capital and retained a majority stake in the bank. The other partner in Vienna was Baron Edmund von Ritter. He was recommended to von Finck by his brother Egon, the principal partner at Merck Finck's Aryanized Berlin branch. Two baron brothers, two different Aryanizations. Eduard von Nicolai didn't endear himself to the Viennese business community at all. His "aggressive and elbowing tactics in the acquisition of new business for his banking house were of such a nature that they gave a bad name abroad to German businessmen," according to Allianz's director in Austria. Managing to stand out for bad business behavior was quite an achievement; in the Third Reich it was a particularly crowded and competitive field.

Von Finck's fundraising efforts for Hitler's pet project had paid off massively. Within one year of the museum's opening, he had Aryanized two major private banks. Merck Finck's assets quickly quadrupled, from 22.5 million to 99.2 million reichsmarks. Despite his famed stinginess, von

Finck shared the spoils with his friends. The baron had started by making his fellow aristocrats, the von Ritter brothers, partners at his Aryanized banks. Then he rewarded his fellow museum trustee Otto Christian Fischer for his Aryanization referral by making the top Nazi banker a partner and shareholder at Merck Finck. With those shrewd moves, one historian concluded, Merck Finck "established itself as the most successful private bank in the National Socialist era." It was an expansion built on business savvy, some good old-fashioned networking, and of course, the spoils of virulent anti-Semitism.

18.

On May 26, 1938, Hitler stood at a podium in a forest clearing, his visor cap shielding him from the sweltering sun, and snarled at an audience of more than fifty thousand people: "I hate the word impossible!" He was about to lay the foundation stone for the Volkswagen factory. The building site was located in Nazi Germany's geographic center, in the municipality of Fallersleben, near an estate called Wolfsburg. It was perfectly positioned next to the highway from Berlin to Hannover, the railroad from Berlin to the Ruhr area, and a shipping canal. One year earlier, Hitler had moved the responsibility for building Europe's largest factory away from the car industry to the German Labor Front (DAF), the Nazi organization that had replaced trade unions. He deemed the DAF better equipped to handle a project of such national importance and huge expense; earlier estimated to cost ninety million reichsmarks, it was already nearing two hundred million. The DAF's corrupt and alcoholic leader, Robert Ley, had issued Ferdinand Porsche a blank check for the project, financed by membership fees and assets seized from the unions. For the factory site, the DAF had bought thirty-seven hundred acres of meadowland from a count. As far as the impoverished aristocrat was concerned, the loss of his estate's hundred-year-old oaks paled in comparison to a potential expropriation. So he succumbed to the lure of Nazi millions.

On the morning of the ceremony, thousands of people were transported

Laying the foundation stone at the Volkswagen factory, May 26, 1938.

to the countryside in specially reserved trains. They lined the road to the construction site, where Hitler arrived in an open car amid the sounding of trumpets and shouts of "*Sieg Heil!*" The SS had difficulty controlling the crowd. Everyone pushed ahead to get a glimpse of the führer and the shiny new cabriolet in which he rode. "In the cordoned-off area reserved for Hitler and his entourage, three models of the 'people's car' . . . gleamed in the sunlight, strategically placed in front of the wooden grandstand draped with fresh forest green," a chronicler wrote. From there, the German chancellor delivered his speech. Toward the end of the hour-long event, broadcast live on national radio, Hitler made a surprise announcement: the new car would not be called the Volkswagen, but rather the Kraft durch

Freude-Wagen (Strength Through Joy–Car), after the DAF's tourism organization. Ferdinand Porsche, horrified, looked on. Its impracticality aside, the name was far removed from the one Porsche desired: his own.

The previous summer, Porsche had met his longtime hero Henry Ford at Ford's River Rouge factory complex in Detroit. Ferdinand Porsche wanted to be for Germany what Ford was for the United States. The Volkswagen plant would be modeled after Ford's. And just like Ford, with his eponymous creation, Porsche hoped the Volkswagen would be named for him. Yet this wasn't meant to be. After the ceremony, Porsche's twenty-eight-year-old son, Ferry, driving the cabriolet, took Hitler back to his private train. His father, disappointed, sat in the back.

Nevertheless, the ceremony was good publicity for the Volkswagen. A correspondent for the New York Times excitedly wrote about the prospect of European highways filled with "thousands and thousands of shiny little beetles," thereby unwittingly coining the car's nickname, which endured when the vehicle became a global phenomenon years later. Pictures of Ferry, driving the führer to his train, circulated all over the world. The Porsche design office in Stuttgart was inundated with love letters, racy pictures, and marriage proposals addressed to Hitler's handsome impromptu chauffeur.

Now that his father had become director of the Volkswagen factory, Ferry would take control of the design office back in Stuttgart. Porsche was in the midst of an expansion, to be financed by the DAF's millions. One month after the ceremony, the car design firm moved from its office in central Stuttgart's Kronenstrasse to a major plot of land in the city's Zuffenhausen district. A factory had been built on the site, where cars could be constructed. The land, still part of the site where Porsche's headquarters stand today, had been Aryanized from a Jewish family, the Wolfs, that previous spring, at a price below market value. It was business as usual for Porsche. Another matter involving the firm's Jewish cofounder, whose shares Ferry had received, needed to be handled immediately.

In early June 1938, Adolf Rosenberger received a letter at his Paris apartment on avenue Marceau, around the corner from the Arc de Triomphe. The message from Stuttgart contained bad news. Baron Hans von Veyder-Malberg informed his predecessor that Porsche was no longer able to maintain its patent licensing contract with him "on higher authority." The man who had freed Rosenberger from a concentration camp was now cutting off all professional and personal contact because of "certain aggravations in the internal situation." The letter was dated June 2, one week after Hitler had laid the foundation stone for the Volkswagen factory. Ferdinand Porsche and Anton Piëch were severing their last ties with the firm's Jewish cofounder.

On July 23, 1938, Rosenberger wrote to Piëch, who was also the company's tough legal counsel, suggesting two ways to part amicably: $12,000 to start over in the United States or a transfer of Porsche's American patent license to Rosenberger. But Piëch did not merely go along with the Nazis as a necessity for doing business; he shared their ideology and had just become a party member for the second time. As an Austrian native, he first entered the NSDAP's sister party in his home country in May 1933, only to apply for membership in the German Nazi Party on June 2, 1938. Later, Piëch sought to gain admission to the SS and was accepted.

In a separate letter, Rosenberger made a personal appeal to the firm he cofounded: "Dr. Porsche has told me on several occasions that, in view of our many years of cooperation and the risk that I have assumed for the company at all times, I can count on him at any time, and I believe that the modest claims for compensation that I'm making will meet with his full approval and that he too will use all his influence to bring our eight-year relationship to an amicable end." Rosenberger acknowledged "that it may be difficult for you to continue to work with me as a non-Aryan in the old way."

But, adding insult to Aryanization, Anton Piëch coldly rejected the proposal. "My company does not recognize your claims under any circumstance and rejects them for a lack of legal basis," Piëch responded on August 24, 1938, on the grounds that Rosenberger hadn't succeeded in selling any patent licenses abroad in recent years. That same month, the Gestapo began the process of revoking Rosenberger's German citizenship. It was time for him to leave Europe.

19.

Things between Joseph and Magda Goebbels ruptured on a sweltering Sunday in mid-August 1938. For the past two years there had been three in their marriage. Now the couple thought they had found a solution. That day, Goebbels invited his lover, Lida Baarová, to join him, Magda, and some friends on his yacht, *Baldur.* They would go on a trip on the Havel River, which flowed by their villa on Berlin's Schwanenwerder Island. The couple had something important to ask the Czech actress. Over lunch, Goebbels and Magda proposed a ménage à trois: Magda would remain the wife who would look after the house, the children, and Reich duties, and Baarová would be Goebbels's official mistress. Perplexed, Baarová asked for time to think it over. Magda immediately had second thoughts, and the next evening she poured her heart out to Hitler. The führer retained a deep-seated affection for Magda. Plus, he'd had a particular platonic arrangement with the married couple since 1931: Magda and Goebbels were supposed to be his role models for matrimony.

Hitler ordered Goebbels to the Reich Chancellery and demanded that he end the affair. The next day Goebbels wrote in his diary, "I've come to some very difficult decisions. But they are final. I drive around in the car for an hour. Quite a long way, without going anywhere in particular. I'm living almost as if in a dream. Life is so hard and cruel . . . But duty comes before everything else." He then had "a very long and very sad telephone conversation" with Baarová. "But I remain firm, even though my heart threatens to break. And now a new life begins. A hard, tough life dedicated to nothing but duty. My youth is over," he wrote on August 16, 1938. But in truth, he continued his affair with Baarová. Magda began to consider a divorce.

Goebbels and Magda agreed to a truce, postponing any decision on their marriage until the end of September. Bigger things were at hand. War was nearing; Hitler had threatened to invade and occupy Czechoslovakia's Sudetenland, a region whose population largely consisted of ethnic

Germans. When the couple's truce ran out at the height of the Sudetenland crisis, Goebbels asked his longtime deputy, Karl Hanke, to mediate
in the marital mess, happy to have someone to confide in. After Hanke
spoke to all parties involved, Goebbels asked him to put the matter before
Hitler again. "Everything depends on his decision," he wrote in his diary
on October 11, 1938, a day after Hitler completed the annexation of Sudetenland.

Hitler hadn't changed his position. He was tired of the "divorce mania"
among the ranks of Nazi leaders. Goebbels finally acquiesced. He developed "terrible heart pains" and went to see Baarová's most recent film, aptly
titled *Prussian Love Story*, to catch a final glimpse of her. Because Goebbels lacked the courage to break up with her himself a second time, he
had his close friend Count Helldorf, Berlin's chief of police, "carry out my
difficult task." Adding insult to injury, Helldorf told Baarová that she was
no longer allowed to work as an actress in Germany. She immediately left
Berlin for Prague, which fell under German occupation just a few months
later.

Goebbels, however, wasn't happy with Hanke's performance as a mediator. "I'm not talking to Hanke anymore. He is my cruelest disappointment,"
Goebbels wrote in his diary just before Hitler reaffirmed his decision. As
one biographer of Goebbels delicately put it: "It appears that he had traded
upon his position of mediator to offer more than kind words of comfort"
to Magda. She confessed her affair with Hanke to her husband the next
summer. "Hanke has proven to be a first-class rogue. My mistrust of him
was fully justified," Goebbels wrote on July 23, 1939.

This time, it was Magda who brought her affair before Hitler. Once
again, the führer would decide the fate of the Third Reich's most high-profile marriage. His decision was the same: they were to stay together. After
all, their marriage was a matter of state. Goebbels sent Hanke on permanent leave from the Ministry of Propaganda. Hanke had fallen madly in
love with Magda and wanted to marry her. Instead, he went to fight on the
front. The Goebbelses reconciled, and Magda soon gave birth to Heidrun,
their sixth and last child.

20.

After the Julius Petschek German brown-coal firms had been Aryanized, by early June 1938, the Ignaz Petschek heirs still retained control of their own family conglomerate, which was larger. But Friedrich Flick was ready to make a move on that too, and by any means necessary. However, from the company's headquarters in Sudetenland's Aussig on the Elbe, a twenty-minute drive from the German border, the message remained the same: a resounding no. The Petschek family refused to negotiate about the assets that Flick was eyeing, a vast range of brown-coal mining, production, and trading operations in central Germany valued at as much as a quarter billion reichsmarks. Karl Petschek, one of Ignaz's sons, oversaw the family's German brown-coal assets. "These people want to slaughter me . . . well they will not succeed," he mused combatively. Karl argued that he wasn't able to sell the family assets because his father had already "sold" them by securing stakes across holding companies in the tax havens of Monaco, Switzerland, and Luxembourg.

However, even foreign residency or business ownership no longer guaranteed safety from Nazi greed. With the Sudetenland crisis beginning to brew, Flick decided to turn up the heat on the Ignaz Petschek heirs. Over the course of June 1938, Flick's legal counsel, Hugo Dietrich, dug up heaps of information on the Ignaz Petschek ownership interests in corporate registries, which Otto Steinbrinck provided to the relevant Nazi authorities. Steinbrinck complained to one Nazi bureaucrat that the Petscheks' "attitude is completely indifferent." But he considered the rumor that "J. P. Morgan [Jr.] is behind the Ignaz Petschek group improbable. Morgan has always been an anti-Semite, and even tempted by excellent business, will hardly be prepared to camouflage Jews." Steinbrinck had Dietrich write a legal opinion arguing that the Petschek heirs actually ran their businesses from Berlin; therefore the companies could be taken over through "regular" Aryanization procedures. Dietrich also drafted a decree that provided for the state to appoint a trustee at any company that was classified as Jewish-owned. According to the draft, that trustee could then sell the business against the will of its owners. These ideas were subsequently fed to Walther Funk's Ministry of Economic Affairs and Göring's Four Year Plan office, in hopes that they would be adopted as official party policy. It was all that Flick could do. The Ignaz Petschek heirs still refused to negotiate with anyone, and all hopes of acquiring their German interests through the private sector had been dashed. Now it was the regime's turn to step in.

In late July 1938, an interministerial working group was formed in Berlin, solely dedicated to "solving" the Ignaz Petschek "problem." The Nazi bureaucrats soon landed on what had become a tried-and-true method of Aryanization: they imposed a gargantuan fictitious back tax on the conglomerate, allowing the regime to seize the Petschek coal assets as payment. Starting at 30 million reichsmarks in September, the claim eventually grew to 670 million, about three times higher than the actual value of the Petscheks' German brown-coal assets. The heirs lost their leverage.

So had Flick. With the Aryanization preparations now firmly in the hands of the Reich Ministry of Finance, the tycoon suddenly faced stiff competition for the coal interests. Germany's industrial firms were lining up to pick the conglomerate clean. Most prominent among these new players was the Nazi regime itself, via Reichswerke Hermann Göring, a state-owned industrial conglomerate upon which the megalomaniac minister had conferred his own name. Flick also had a powerful new adversary in Paul Pleiger, the state complex's CEO and one of the Third Reich's most important economic functionaries.

Pleiger had a problem to solve. The Reichswerke lacked a major source of energy. In late June 1938, he told Flick he was "very displeased" at having been left out of the spoils from the Aryanization of Julius Petschek's German assets, which Flick had captured from Julius's branch of the embattled family only weeks earlier. Flick's advice to the director of the Reichswerke was to hop into the ring this time. Pleiger coyly responded that he could envision a swap of brown coal for hard coal. Pleiger desperately needed to secure a hard coal base for the Reichswerke in central Germany, which, unlike firms in the Ruhr area, didn't have its own coal mines for making coke. Massive quantities of coke were needed to smelt ore and produce iron competitively. Having its own supply would lower the Reichswerke's costs and free it from its current dependency on the Ruhr moguls for this source of energy.

As it happened, Flick had much more hard coal than he could process through his Harpener and Essener coal mines in the Ruhr area, and he wanted more brown coal. Pleiger was well aware of this. Whereas hard coal had a much greater value for heating, brown coal was more profitable. Pleiger needed energy; Flick wanted to corner a lucrative market.

Hitler occupied Sudetenland in early October 1938, and over the course of ten days the territory was ceded to Germany. On the first day of the invasion, the Nazis raided the offices of the Ignaz Petschek conglomerate. Documents that remained there were confiscated. At the same time, Pleiger returned to Flick with his idea for a coal swap, just after Göring promised him that the Reichswerke would have a stake in the Aryanization of the Petschek conglomerate. But Flick was in no hurry to settle. He knew a trustee would soon be appointed at Ignaz Petschek.

On December 3, 1938, just three weeks after Kristallnacht, Hermann Göring issued the "Decree Concerning the Utilization of Jewish Assets." It had a premise similar to Hugo Dietrich's draft law. Going forward, the state would appoint a trustee to any company classified as Jewish, and this trustee would be able to sell the business against the will of its owners. However, the decree would eventually expand in scope. The Nazi regime would use it to deprive Jews living within the territory of the Reich of all belongings of relative value: firms, houses, land, shares, art, jewelry, and gold. It robbed them of almost everything they owned, except for possessions that served their most basic needs. Theft of those items was still to come.

A trustee was appointed at the Ignaz Petschek conglomerate in January 1939. Although Flick's mandate to serve as sole negotiator for all Petschek assets remained valid, it was losing its value. With competition mounting and the regime veering toward an outright expropriation of the assets, Flick saw that his best chance at getting any of the loot was to cut a deal with Pleiger. So he agreed to Pleiger's proposition. The Reichswerke would receive its share of the Ignaz Petschek brown coal assets and then swap them for some of Flick's hard coal mines. The regime soon signed off on the plan.

However, the negotiations between Flick and Pleiger in Berlin were contentious and protracted, lasting a year. The main issue was quantifying the valuations and volumes of the coal. In addition, Pleiger wanted much more hard coal than Flick was willing to give up. Neither side was initially willing to compromise. Pleiger, who was staking his position in the Reich on this deal, turned out to be a fickle negotiator. When Flick thought they had reached an agreement in early June 1939, Pleiger changed the terms. Flick then angrily withdrew from the negotiations. It was only in early December that both sides came to an agreement, but the execution of it would drag on until the end of the war.

Flick drew the short straw in the negotiations with the state conglomerate. He forced his prized Harpener mines in the Ruhr area to give up more than one-third of their employees, coke, and coal production. Pleiger secured 1.8 billion tons of hard coal, plus some potentially productive mines. Flick could manage the losses, but he would have to do some costly reinvestments. In return, Flick gained 890 million tons of lignite, making him the most powerful player in Nazi Germany's brown coal industry.

Of course, the only people who truly lost out were the Ignaz Petschek heirs. Whereas their cousins had managed to sell their companies in the nick of time, Karl Petschek and his siblings received nothing for their family interests. The gargantuan tax claims against them were offset against their assets, and the family was ruthlessly expropriated by the Nazi regime, aided and abetted by Friedrich Flick.

21.

On April 20, 1939, Ferdinand Porsche gifted the first finished Volkswagen, a black Beetle convertible, to a delighted Hitler at the führer's fiftieth-birthday party in Berlin. Göring received the second, and Goebbels the fourth. The "people's car" was not, in fact, delivered to the people. Only 630 of them were built during the Third Reich, and they all went to the Nazi elite. The 340,000 Germans who signed up for the DAF's program to save for the purchase of the car were bilked of around 280 million reichsmarks. Meanwhile, the Volkswagen factory complex in Fallersleben was nowhere near finished; soon work was underway to retool it for arms production. Aided by his son, Ferry, and his son-in-law, Anton Piëch, Volkswagen's factory chief, Ferdinand Porsche, had to abruptly change gears. The designer of civilian automobiles and race cars became a maker of weapons, tanks, and army cars.

But to produce anything, there first had to be a factory that was fully functional. When Hitler visited the plant in early June 1939, Porsche dared show him only the pressing shop, because it was the most developed part of the complex. The factory's massive red-brick façade, measuring eight tenths of a mile in length, obscured the largely empty inner halls. What was supposed to be the world's largest automobile plant, capable of churning out 1.5 million cars per year, still lacked much basic machinery. Fallersleben was little more than a dusty barracks camp, mostly filled with the three thousand Italian construction workers that Hitler's ally Mussolini had sent over to help finish construction. German men were barely available, as most had been called to military service. By the time the brutally cold winter of 1939 arrived, Volkswagen's main factory halls remained unheated, and its stairwells were missing window glass. Many more workers were needed to finish the job and keep the place running. Ferdinand Porsche did not care whether they came voluntarily or by force.

22.

On the evening of Friday, December 29, 1939, Otto Steinbrinck sat down at his desk at home in Berlin's lush Dahlem neighborhood and wrote a letter to Friedrich Flick, his boss of fifteen years, who was spending the

Christmas holidays at his estate in Bavaria. Steinbrinck was resigning. He had found a new job. The regime was appointing him to oversee the expropriated steel empire of Fritz Thyssen. The first mogul to openly back Hitler, Thyssen had now turned against the führer. As a member of the Reichstag, Thyssen had refused to consent to the declaration of war and fled Germany.

Steinbrinck too was under a pall; he was leaving the Flick conglomerate on terrible terms. His relationship with Flick had been deteriorating for years. The workload was stifling, the men's wives didn't get along, and Steinbrinck had fallen out with Flick's elder son, Otto-Ernst, who was being groomed to succeed his father. Steinbrinck's professional ambitions were going unfulfilled, and he wanted a more prominent position. The Flick family conglomerate would never give it to him — he would never be part of the dynasty. "The effort of a forced cooperation has destroyed in us more than the worth of the superficial profit achieved. Several times you expressed the opinion that I did my work with too much ambition and personal zeal. Today I know that your criticism of my work, within your sphere of interests, is right," the fanatical SS officer wrote bitterly to his boss. "I have remained in the first line a soldier and therefore I have not always been able to share the opinion of a merchant who merely calculates and risks much." Flick dictated an angry response to his secretary, reproaching Steinbrinck for what he saw as duplicity. But he didn't send the letter. Instead, Flick accepted the resignation and promoted two relatives to take Steinbrinck's place.

By then, World War II had started. The peaceful years of rearmament and Aryanizations had been exceptionally good to Flick. He was now Nazi Germany's third-largest steel producer, overseeing about 100,000 employees, up fivefold from 1933. Flick's taxable income from 1937 to 1939 alone had been sixty-five million reichsmarks, some $320 million in today's money. And the territorial conquests achieved by Hitler's army across Europe were about to provide Flick with far more opportunities to expand his industrial empire. Now he had to train his successor and embark on a new mission of plunder — although without the help of his trusted lieutenant. But that did not in the least slow down the enterprising tycoon.

23.

Though he had become one of Nazi Germany's largest producers of arms, Günther Quandt didn't want war. "Most disturbing news," he wrote at the time of the Sudetenland crisis. He was glad when it seemed that war had been avoided: "Things are looking up again!" Günther had always considered German rearmament a defensive measure. "I didn't believe they would let it come to war," he wrote after the Third Reich had fallen. But when Germany invaded Poland, on September 1, 1939, he quickly adapted to the new reality. "The German people are fighting for their life rights. Full of confidence we look to our Führer and his Wehrmacht, which has already achieved unprecedented successes in a short time and fills us with pride and admiration," Günther wrote to the employees at his AFA battery firm two weeks after the invasion.

War was good for his business. Günther projected that annual sales at AFA would grow to 150 million reichsmarks, a record revenue figure and a threefold increase from sales during the years of peace. And his weapons firm DWM soon surpassed that benchmark — even doubled it. A few days after the war began, Günther told one of his executives: "If there's war, there's war and then we must act as if it never ends. Let us be happily surprised by peace." Günther's elder son, Herbert, deemed his father's stance a "sober corporate strategy." Whereas his half brother, Harald, was about to volunteer on the front, Herbert had to prove himself to his imperious father on the equally merciless battleground of business succession. Neither field of conflict rewarded moral character.

PART III

"THE CHILDREN HAVE NOW ALREADY BECOME MEN"

1.

In late October 1939, Harald Quandt came home to Berlin, taking a short break from his six-month mandated labor service as a motor courier in occupied Poland. The country had been conquered and divided between Hitler's Germany and Stalin's Soviet Union earlier that month, following the terms of a nonaggression pact made by the two dictators. Günther's younger son was on the precipice of adulthood, just a few days shy of turning eighteen. He had finished high school just before the war erupted. At his graduation ceremony, Günther and Magda sat together in the front row, seemingly in harmony.

For the past five and a half years, home for Harald had been with his mother and stepfather, a domicile complicated by the ever-growing number of half siblings and parental infidelities. Since his affair with Lida Baarová had ended, Goebbels was mostly living by himself during the week, in a palatial residence in central Berlin, lavishly financed by his ministry, which was located nearby. But overall, the fractious Goebbels household remained centered at the family villa on swanky Schwanenwerder Island and at the minister's country estate north of Berlin. And Harald, like millions of other young men, would soon have a new home — the ravaging battlefields of World War II, spread across the European continent.

Harald had already witnessed the atrocities of war and occupation in his work as a courier on the Polish front and in the areas now brutally ruled by the Nazis. He spoke extensively to Magda and Goebbels about what he had seen there — seemingly the start of German war crimes. On October 28, 1939, Goebbels wrote in his diary that Harald "had experienced all sorts of things in Poland. The children have now already become men." The next day, Goebbels celebrated his forty-second birthday, and Harald again spoke of his experiences in Poland to his stepfather. After their conversation, Goebbels wrote in his diary that his stepson "is already a real man and a soldier" who "has mightily improved." To Goebbels, what Harald had witnessed seemed to result in some positive character building. But the teenager was deeply affected by what he saw. On November 2, 1939, one day after Harald's eighteenth birthday, Goebbels wrote: "Talked to Magda about Harald in the evening. He worries us a bit."

In the intervening days, Goebbels had surveyed the situation in the Nazi-occupied parts of Poland with his own eyes. He flew to Lodz on October 31, 1939, where he was welcomed by *Gauleiter* Hans Frank, who was a banking client of Merck Finck, and his deputy, Arthur Seyss-Inquart, Austria's former chancellor. Goebbels then rode through the Jewish ghetto in Lodz. (Some 230,000 people — one-third of Lodz's population — were Jewish.) He got out of the car to inspect everything in detail himself.

Goebbels didn't like what he saw. In the diary entry — which he concluded by confiding his concern for Harald — Goebbels described what he witnessed in the ghetto: "It's indescribable. They are no longer human beings, they are animals. This is therefore not a humanitarian task, but a surgical one. One must make incisions here, and quite radical ones at that. Otherwise Europe will perish from the Jewish disease." The ghetto held about 160,000 Jews when the Nazis closed its gates six months later, imprisoning the residents. All in all, some 210,000 Jews passed through the Lodz ghetto, which served as a collection point for extermination camps across occupied Poland but mainly nearby, at Chelmno.

The next morning, Goebbels traveled on to Warsaw by car. He arrived in the Polish capital after a journey "across battlefields and past completely shot-up villages and towns. A picture of devastation. Warsaw is hell. A demolished city. Our bombs and shells have done their job. Not a single house is intact. The population is shocked and shadowy. People creep through the streets like insects. It's repulsive," Goebbels wrote. He flew back to Berlin at 2 p.m., glad to be leaving "this place of horror," and landed at dusk on Tempelhof, just in time for Harald's birthday celebrations. The next day, Goebbels reported to Hitler about his quick trip to Poland. "Especially my presentation of the Jewish problem meets his full approval. Jewry is a waste product," Goebbels wrote in his diary. "More a clinical than a social matter."

On November 1, 1939, while Goebbels surveyed the rubble of Warsaw,

Harald's real father closed a major deal in nearby Poznan. That day, Günther Quandt's DWM received trusteeship over the expropriated Cegielski weapons complex, Poznan's largest factory works. The Cegielski plants were famous for their production of locomotives, artillery, and machine guns; the Nazi arms authorities had classified them as the city's most important weapons manufacturers. Luckily for Günther, the Reich minister of economic affairs, Walther Funk, had favored his old pal over the other suitors eager to get their hands on the Cegielski complex.

The Cegielski factories would also be Harald's next destination. After returning to Poland, he started an internship at the foundry of DWM's locomotive construction department. In mid-January 1940, Magda visited her son in Poznan. She reported back to Goebbels that Harald was "behaving fabulously there. He has become a real man with a pronounced social sensibility. Now he only has to join the Wehrmacht to stand his ground there." Harald's next destination was indeed the battlefield, but in a far more daring role than his mother and stepfather had ever envisioned.

2.

Harald Quandt had been living with his mother, his stepfather, and his half siblings ever since he was twelve and a half years old, when the couple decided not to return to him to Günther after the 1934 Easter holiday. Despite the bitter custody battle that ensued, Magda and Goebbels allowed Harald to visit Günther once every other weekend. Even though Harald was growing up in arguably the Third Reich's most radical family, he was no Nazi. In fact, Harald couldn't have cared less about Nazism. He could afford not to. As Goebbels's stepson, Harald could do what he wanted. And as a teenager, he had more important things on his mind than embracing a fascist ideology: girls, motorcycles, and cars, most prominently.

As a result, Harald's record in Nazi youth organizations was a disaster. At fourteen, he flunked out of a trial membership at the navy's Hitlerjugend, an auxiliary force of the Nazi youth movement, where he received pre-military training. The pubescent Harald didn't like the drills, and he got into fights with his platoon leader. He shirked his duties and convinced Magda to write him excuses for his absences "because of school difficulties." His attendance record was so spotty that he was told not to return in autumn 1936. When it came time for Harald to register as a member of the NSDAP in 1938, he didn't fill out the forms and actually never joined the Nazi Party.

Harald later said that Goebbels's goal was to remove him "as far as possible from my father's ideas. I was to become a naval officer, not a businessman or an engineer." But Harald didn't join the navy. He entered the Luftwaffe. In June 1940, during his internship in Poznan, Harald volunteered for its elite paratrooper division after his best friend at school, serving as a tank commander during the German invasion of France, was killed. "Nothing is keeping me here anymore. I'm no different from everybody else," Harald wrote from Poznan to another school friend. Goebbels was happy that his stepson was about to join the military, to be "properly honed"; Magda had started complaining about her eldest son's lack of discipline. "He's in his teens and behaving scandalously," Goebbels wrote in his diary in late July 1940. During his internship at his father's factory, Harald got himself a girlfriend, a stage actress at Poznan's Metropolitan Theater. Magda despised her. During her next visit to Poznan, Magda stormed into the artistic director's office and demanded that he fire the actress. The director refused. He was soon arrested and forced to work at Günther's plant in Poznan.

Luckily for his mother, Harald's paratrooper training with the First Parachute Division began just a few weeks later. He was stationed in Dessau, a two-hour drive southwest of Berlin. When Harald came home for a two-day break in mid-October 1940, Goebbels wrote approvingly of him: "The military has straightened him out."

In early November 1940, a few days after his nineteenth birthday, Harald returned to Berlin for a weeklong holiday. He brought Ursula and Silvia Quandt with him. Ursula had just divorced Herbert, Harald's older half brother. Silvia was Ursula's three-year-old daughter from that broken marriage. After Harald returned to Dessau, Ursula and Silvia stayed with the Goebbelses in Berlin — for almost three months, as it happened. In a bizarre turn of events, the women with whom Goebbels spent Christmas Day,

1940 — Ursula, Magda, and her best friend, Ello — had all once been married to a member of the Quandt dynasty that Goebbels so deeply despised.

Christmas Day was spent at Goebbels's estate at Bogensee, just north of Berlin. Goebbels had transformed the cozy timber cottage, where he had spent so many nights with Lida Baarová, into a massive country house with about thirty rooms, a service building with some forty rooms, and a garage complex. In the afternoon, Goebbels and the women went on a two-hour ride on the family's new horses through the snow-covered landscape of Brandenburg. In the evening, the group read, listened to music, and told one another stories, likely gossiping about Günther, Herbert, and the other Quandts. Goebbels's opinion of Herbert hadn't improved since first meeting him years earlier, when he deemed the Quandt heir "slightly retarded." Goebbels wrote in his diary that Ursula "now looks quite lovely" since divorcing "her horrible husband." Herbert was indeed in the midst of "a particularly dark chapter" in late 1940, and one that Goebbels approved of.

3.

In October 1940, Günther Quandt, his right-hand-man Horst Pavel, and Herbert explored Nazi-occupied France for almost ten days. Günther had drawn up a "wish list," noting a dozen takeover targets in France, including Jewish-owned firms, for his AFA battery business. And 1940 was a big year for Herbert. He turned thirty; he joined AFA's executive board in charge of staffing, advertising, and the AFA subsidiary Pertrix; he divorced Ursula; and, befitting his new status as an executive, he became a member of the Nazi Party. The start of World War II had reconciled Herbert and his competitor Pavel. Herbert later recalled how their rivalry ended: "When the war came, the work became harder . . . I had to solve some tasks together with my colleague Dr. Pavel . . . In short, the war brought us . . . closer." These tasks included buying up Aryanized firms formerly owned by French Jews. Or, as Herbert later cryptically put it, "Industrial firms or factories there had been offered or suggested to individual firms for acquisition."

Now that war had arrived, Günther was determined to do what he did in any circumstance: profit from it. In August 1940, two months before the scouting trip, Günther sent one of his most trusted employees, Corbin Hackinger, to France. For the sake of appearance, Hackinger quit his job at AFA in Berlin before moving to Paris, where the mustachioed man in his early fifties set up shop on the fourth floor of 44 rue La Boétie, near the Élysée Palace. "Bureau Hackinger," a barely camouflaged branch of AFA, covered Nazi-occupied and Vichy France. Hackinger's many tasks there included identifying Jewish-owned companies and aiding in their Aryanization. Hackinger helped appropriate such firms for AFA via the use of front companies, trustees, straw men, and straw women, including his own mistress.

Günther, Herbert, and their cronies regarded French battery firms as easy marks for takeover. But they were wrong. Whereas the French authorities did eagerly collaborate with the Nazis, they didn't want their companies falling into the hands of German industry, and they obstructed most Aryanizations that the foreigners tried to carry out. The French authorities preferred expropriating the Jewish citizens themselves. Hackinger lamented at the control exercised by French bureaucrats, but he dared do little more than complain.

Out of AFA's seven known attempts at Aryanization, five failed. The two Aryanized French factories that Günther did succeed in buying came into his hands thanks to his elder son's eager efforts. On behalf of Pertrix, Herbert and Pavel negotiated the takeover of the Aryanized Hirschfeld sheet-metal factory in Strasbourg, the capital of Nazi-occupied Alsace. It was much easier for German firms to operate in that region because Nazi authorities ruled it. Still desperate to prove himself to his father, Herbert would sometimes negotiate over the weekend in Strasbourg, so that he could be back in Berlin at the start of the week. This earned him praise from his fellow executives.

After his success with Hirschfeld, Herbert helped AFA acquire a majority stake in Dreyfus, another Aryanized sheet-metal business, this one located in the suburbs of Paris. Hackinger called it the "best . . . object" he had come across. The sheet metal factories could be used to produce flashlights, a staple product of Pertrix. Herbert had carved out his own territory at Pertrix, where he had started his career and was now a leading executive. But it wasn't until he took on these new wartime responsibilities at AFA that Herbert finally earned the respect of his father. "Since that time . . . I have rarely made a decision, or considered a possibility of some significance without consulting him," Günther later wrote of his elder son. It didn't matter to father and son that they took over the seized livelihood and life's work of Jews. To them the only thing that mattered was the expansion of the Quandt empire. And expand it they would. Belgian, Polish, Croatian, and Greek firms soon fell prey to the Quandts' gang of corporate raiders.

4.

Harald Quandt loved being a paratrooper. He felt at home among his comrades on the base in Dessau. Besides learning how to parachute, he was trained to shoot rifles and pistols, likely the ones made by his father's arms company, and learned the paratroopers' battle song: "Green is our parachute, strong the young heart, steel our weapons, made of German ore." Everyone was young and adventurous within the German band of brothers. There were parties and pranks, which almost got Harald kicked out of the Luftwaffe before he ever saw combat. "Harald has messed up his military career for the time being because of a very stupid thing," Goebbels wrote in his diary on February 12, 1941. "A real childish prank with a more serious background. Now he has to pay for it. Hopefully he won't pull any more pranks, or it will be over for good." It's impossible to know for sure, but Harald had probably pulled some stunt following a night of heavy drinking. That Harald had gone "really out of line" kept Goebbels preoccupied for days. He was determined to get his stepson out of trouble. He even sent an aide down to Dessau to check on Harald, who was, of course, not your average soldier. As Goebbels's stepson, he enjoyed protection unlike anyone else in the Wehrmacht. After the aide returned to Berlin, Goebbels noted curtly: "The issue is solved."

Early in the morning of May 20, 1941, Harald finally went to war. His first mission was the spectacular invasion of Crete. Allied forces wanted to build a bomber base on their remaining bastion in Greece, and the Germans wanted to prevent this at all costs. Dubbed Operation Mercury, it was the first largely airborne operation in military history. In his war memoir, the British prime minister Winston Churchill wrote, "Never was a more reckless, ruthless attack launched by the Germans."

Harald and his comrades took off from their base on the Greek mainland before sunrise, "with a fiery heart in proud confidence of our wartime good fortune." Flying over the mainland coast, German fighter planes appeared on all sides to escort the paratroopers to their jump site over the island. British anti-aircraft guns started firing on the plane carrying Harald as soon as it flew over Crete's coastline. Then Harald got the command: "Ready to jump," followed by the green light. The nineteen-year-old leapt from the plane and free-fell into battle.

The jump was magnificent. Harald had clear weather and perfect altitude, and the German paratroopers were dropped over their designated jump sites with "pinpoint accuracy." They came under heavy British machine-gun fire, but Harald and most of his comrades managed to land on Crete without injury. More than forty shells had punctured Harald's parachute, causing him to drop much faster and hit the ground at great speed. After unbuckling his harness, he retrieved his weapon container, which had landed fifty-five yards away.

The fighting began immediately. Harald and his comrades particularly feared the many snipers hidden in trees and hedges. They were also wary of the heat. On their first day of combat, it was 125 degrees Fahrenheit in the shade, and that was by no means the hottest day they experienced. After a long and difficult battle, German troops finally conquered the island on June 1, 1941. But the carnage wasn't over. Local civilians put up widespread resistance; this was the first time during the war that the Germans met with such opposition. Led by the Luftwaffe general Kurt Student, the Nazi forces executed thousands of Cretans in reprisal. German troops burned several villages to the ground to quell the resistance. Student's deputy made good on an order he had issued during battle: ten Cretans were to be shot for every German soldier killed or wounded.

The invasion was ultimately a success for the paratroopers, though al-

*Harald Quandt, in uniform, with Magda and Joseph Goebbels
and his six half siblings, 1942.*

most six thousand German men had been killed or wounded in action. Even Winston Churchill was impressed. "The German Air Corps represented the flame of the Hitler Youth Movement and was an ardent embodiment of the Teutonic spirit of revenge for the defeat of 1918," he wrote. "The flower of German manhood was expressed in these valiant, highly trained, and completely devoted Nazi parachute troops. To lay down their lives on the altar of German glory and world-power was their passionate resolve."

Harald thrived in his first deployment. He was awarded the Iron Cross First Class. Magda had been worried about her son. She had heard of mutilations suffered by German prisoners of war in Greece. Goebbels, who wasn't told in advance about the mission or Harald's deployment, was immensely proud of his stepson, as was Hitler. In mid-June 1941, Goebbels told the führer about "Harald's bravery, which makes him exceptionally happy. He's still very attached to the boy."

Harald returned to Germany six weeks later, just in time for his father's sixtieth-birthday party in Berlin. He was soon promoted to under officer and penned an article for AFA's company magazine, detailing his experiences in Greece. "Operation Crete has shown us once again that there is no such thing as 'impossible' for German paratroopers," Harald wrote defiantly. "We all have only the desire to deal the death blow to the Englishman, preferably on his own island." His father echoed that sentiment. During the Blitz and the Battle of Britain, Günther wrote to AFA employees that the Luftwaffe had "already made a lethal and decisive strike against our first and last enemy," the British. At home too "everyone does their duty and utmost to contribute to the victorious end of the German struggle for existence." But the invasion of Britain was called off. Instead, the eastern front awaited Harald.

5.

On June 26, 1941, Operation Barbarossa, the fateful Nazi invasion of the Soviet Union, was four days underway when, in Berlin's Bellevuestrasse, Friedrich Flick had his auditor write an important letter to the Reich Ministry of Finance. Flick had big plans for his succession. He intended to make his two youngest sons, twenty-one-year-old Rudolf and fourteen-year-old Friedrich Karl, shareholders of the holding company that controlled his massive steel, coal, and weapons conglomerate. Almost exactly four years earlier, Flick had done the same for his eldest son, Otto-Ernst, just one day after he turned twenty-one. This move coincided with Flick's legal conversion of his group of industrial businesses into a namesake, family-owned conglomerate. But Flick was no longer so sure about designating his "crown prince" Otto-Ernst as his successor.

Being the firstborn son of the imperious magnate was a special burden, and Otto-Ernst felt the pressure. He had to prove himself in the shadow of his cold, cerebral father. The two couldn't have been more different. Growing up in the family villa in Berlin's leafy Grunewald neighborhood, surrounded by household staff, Otto-Ernst enjoyed jogging, music, cinema,

Friedrich Flick and his sons, Otto-Ernst (in the back), Rudolf (in the front, at right), and Friedrich Karl (left), at their family villa in Berlin Grunewald, early 1930s.

and theater. Flick preferred that his sons compete in rowing matches. "A boy from a normal bourgeois milieu could have never survived such an upbringing," Otto-Ernst once remarked. Ambitious and intelligent, he was also socially inept and overreacted in stressful situations. His lack of ease was compounded by his large frame. At six feet four, he was gangly and towered awkwardly over the rest of his family.

It seemed apparent that Otto-Ernst wasn't cut out to one day succeed his father, but it wasn't for lack of trying. In early 1939, after Otto-Ernst had spent one semester studying business administration in Berlin, his father forced him to drop out. Flick ordered his son to take over the management of a new grenade-pressing plant at the family's steel complex in Thuringia. But Otto-Ernst's first executive job didn't go well. Determined to make his mark, he got into a fierce dispute with one of the factory managers.

Flick's middle son, Rudolf, had the steely steadfastness that his older brother lacked. The Flick family "daredevil" enlisted in 1939 and became a lieutenant in the Luftwaffe's elite General Göring Division, which often supplied the *Reichsmarschall*'s bodyguards. On June 28, 1941, tragedy struck the family. Six days into Operation Barbarossa, Rudolf was advancing with his regiment through the Ukrainian town of Dubno when he was struck by an artillery shell and killed.

Flick was hit hard by Rudolf's death. He developed a terrible skin rash. Flick asked Hermann Göring to have his son's body repatriated, but the request was denied. Instead, the *Reichsmarschall* arranged for Flick to be flown to Rudolf's grave, near Lviv. The middle son's stake in the business was divided between Otto-Ernst and the teenage Friedrich Karl, whom his father called "the little lad." Flick had no idea how much trouble his remaining sons would give him, and the rest of Germany, for that matter.

In mid-September 1941, Flick sent Otto-Ernst to Lorraine for his next assignment: working at the expropriated Rombach steelworks. After a blitz of lobbying on the part of Flick, Göring had delivered the French factory into Flick's care. Twenty-five-year-old Otto-Ernst would work there under his future father-in-law, who directed the complex. Now that Rudolf was dead, Otto-Ernst felt even greater pressure to prove himself to his father — much to the detriment of the people forced to work at Rombach.

6.

On a muggy day in August 1941, Ferry Porsche arrived in East Prussia's Masurian forest to demonstrate a prototype to Hitler and Himmler at the Wolf's Lair, the führer's military headquarters for the eastern front. Ferry's father had been busy converting the Volkswagen for military purposes. In collaboration with the Wehrmacht, Ferdinand Porsche had designed the Kübelwagen (the bucket car): a light, all-terrain vehicle that was being used by General Rommel's troops in the North African campaign. Thirty-one-year-old Ferry had been summoned to the Wolf's Lair to present his father's latest design, the Schwimmwagen (the swimming car), an amphibious off-road vehicle that he was developing in collaboration with the Waffen-SS, the military branch of Himmler's terror machine. Ferry's father didn't come along for the trip; he had already moved on to the next project.

Ferry Porsche (in suit) standing by as Hitler inspects
the swimming car, with Himmler behind him, 1941.

The success of the bucket car had landed the sixty-five-year-old Porsche
yet another Nazi design job. The day before Operation Barbarossa began,
Hitler appointed Porsche as head of the tank commission, to design new
armored fighting vehicles for the eastern front. While Ferry continued to
oversee the design firm in Stuttgart, Porsche had his son-in-law, Anton
Piëch, take over as director of the Volkswagen factory in Fallersleben.

Production of weapons and military vehicles had taken off there since
spring 1940, when the massive complex was finally completed. Bucket
cars, the V-1 flying bomb, anti-tank mines, bazookas, parts for tanks, the
twin-engine bomber Ju 88, and the world's first jet fighter, the Me 262, were
all being made at the plant to build up the Nazi war machine. Increasingly,
forced labor was making it happen. Since June 1940, hundreds of Polish
women and jailed German soldiers (most of them insubordinates or de-
serters) were put to work at the Volkswagen complex, though there weren't
enough of them to meet production demands. They received little pay, endured terrible living conditions, and had no freedom to leave the factory
complex or spend their paltry wages outside it. These workers were kept

in a part of the factory camp surrounded by barbed wire, and the guards heavily abused them. Now, if all went as planned and Hitler approved the prototype, their calloused hands would soon be assembling parts for the Third Reich's swimming car.

Following Ferry's demonstration, Hitler himself inspected the amphibious car for a long time. He asked detailed questions of Ferry, who deemed the führer "more sympatico [sic] if you knew him personally." Hitler was concerned for the soldiers who would have to drive the vehicle. In addition to fighting the Russians, they were fending off swarms of mosquitoes on the eastern front. "Couldn't you devise some kind of mosquito net for this car that would give them protection while in transit?" the führer asked Ferry. At that very moment, a general standing next to Hitler was bitten on the cheek by a mosquito. With lightning speed, the führer slapped at the general, killing the insect. Blood immediately began running down the man's face. "Look!" Hitler cackled. "The first German general to shed blood during this war!"

Ferry later claimed that Himmler invited him for a stroll through the forest that evening and made him an honorary SS officer on the spot. But in fact, Ferry had voluntarily applied to the SS in December 1938 and had already been admitted as an officer on August 1, 1941, before his demonstration to Hitler and Himmler.

Thousands of swimming cars soon went into production at the Volkswagen complex in Fallersleben. In early October 1941, weeks after Ferry's demonstration, the factory became one of the first in the Third Reich to take in Soviet prisoners of war as slave labor — 650 men in total. They arrived severely underfed and could barely walk. Many collapsed at the machines. Within weeks twenty-seven of them died. Millions of their comrades were about to follow them into enslavement, torture, and death.

7.

On November 19, 1941, Friedrich Flick, three of his closest aides, and a few other steel tycoons received "some interesting reports" from occupied

Ukraine. Flick was about to go into business again with his rival, Paul Plei-ger. The Reichswerke CEO's empire had continued to expand since the war began. Göring first had Pleiger oversee Nazi Germany's coal industry. Now the *Reichsmarschall* was about to put him in charge of pillaging certain industries in the Nazi-occupied parts of the Soviet Union. As the region's new "economic dictator," Pleiger soon proposed a joint venture between one of Flick's steel firms and the Reichswerke. Its goal was to exploit expro-priated steel factories on the Dnieper River, which ran from north to south through the industrial heart of Ukraine. Flick readily accepted.

It wasn't your average steel-industry report that was read at Flick's head-quarters in Berlin's Bellevuestrasse that cold day. The eyewitness report, written by an industry expert, Ulrich Faulhaber, stonily detailed the hor-rors of the eastern front. Outside Kyiv, Faulhaber passed endless columns of Soviet prisoners of war guarded by German troops. When prisoners stumbled and couldn't walk any farther, they were executed. During the night, Faulhaber witnessed cannibalism among the starving Soviet sol-diers; they "fried and ate their own comrades" in a German transit camp for prisoners. German patrols shot the cannibal soldiers "because of their lack of discipline."

Faulhaber also wrote about the mass murder of Ukrainian Jews in his report. The so-called Einsatzgruppen ("deployment groups") were roving across Eastern Europe, massacring some 1.3 million Jews. Under orders from Himmler and supervised by his deputy, Reinhard Heydrich, these death squads were culled from the ranks of the Waffen-SS, the Gestapo, the police, and other Nazi security forces. As the Germans advanced across Eastern Europe, the Einsatzgruppen roamed behind the front lines, mur-dering along the way. Some of Ukraine's biggest cities, including Kyiv and Dnipro, were now "free of Jews . . . Those who did not escape were 'liqui-dated,'" wrote Faulhaber. He described Kyiv's inner city as being "in ruins," though he couldn't help but muse that the view toward the eastern plains from the west bank of the Dnieper was "unforgettably beautiful." At least there was that.

Death was everywhere. On Christmas Eve, 1941, Rudolf-August Oetker arrived in Varėna, a town of fewer than two thousand people in southern

Rudolf-August Oetker (center rear) in his Wehrmacht uniform, behind his mother, Ida, and Westphalia's Gauleiter Alfred Meyer, 1941.

Lithuania, near the Belorussian border. Because his father had been killed at the Battle of Verdun in World War I, members of Rudolf-August's family didn't want their only male heir out on the front lines again, and they used family connections to get him a different assignment. When Rudolf-August was drafted, he joined the Wehrmacht's catering service in Berlin. In Varėna, the twenty-five-year-old pudding prince from Bielefeld would supply food to German soldiers passing through on their way to the eastern front. He was billeted in town with a Polish seamstress who spoke German. Rudolf-August drank vodka to keep himself warm during the freezing nights and to keep the town's ghosts at bay.

Varėna was indeed haunted. Three and a half months before Rudolf-August arrived, one-third of the town's inhabitants had been murdered. On September 9, 1941, 831 Jews were rounded up in the town's synagogue by Einsatzkommando 3, led by the SS colonel Karl Jäger. The next day, they were taken to a grove of trees alongside the main road one mile outside of town. There, two large pits had been dug, eighty feet apart: one for men and boys, the other for women and girls. Colonel Jäger recorded the shooting of 541 men, 141 women, and 149 children in the pits that day. Then the

Einsatzkommando was off to the next town. And the next. And the next. On December 1, Jäger took a tally of the number massacred by his group since early July 1941: 137,346 people.

Rudolf-August later feigned surprise that "he was still alive at all" because Varėna had been located "in the middle of a partisan area." But the actual Baltic partisans were fighting the Soviets, not the Germans. The Nazis used the term "partisan" as a euphemism for the extermination of Jews and the brutal crackdown on locals in occupied territories on the eastern front. The atrocities in Varėna certainly didn't make Rudolf-August reconsider joining the SS. Already on July 1, 1941, he had been accepted as a volunteer for the Waffen-SS, whose members made up about one-third of the roaming Einsatzgruppen.

A prominent new friend in Berlin named Rudolf von Ribbentrop had given Rudolf-August Oetker a glimpse of what life in the Waffen-SS was like. Rudolf was the eldest son of Joachim von Ribbentrop, Nazi Germany's sycophantic foreign minister and führer-worshipper; no one liked him. Goebbels joked that the social-climbing von Ribbentrop had "married his money and bought his name." Von Ribbentrop was married to an heiress of Henkell, one of Germany's largest producers of sparkling wine. He also got himself adopted by a very distant relative so that he could include the particle "von," used by the nobility, with his surname, despite the fact that his non-aristocratic biological father was still very much alive.

In late 1940, Rudolf-August Oetker met von Ribbentrop's nineteen-year-old son in Berlin. They became fast friends. Wounded while serving as a Waffen-SS company commander, Rudolf was recuperating near the capital. His war tales clearly impressed Oetker; by January 1941 the pudding prince had started his application to the Waffen-SS. Back in Bielefeld, the secretary of his stepfather, Richard Kaselowsky, was busy wrangling the documents to prove Oetker's "Aryan descent" up to his great-grandparents, one of the many requirements for admission to the "racially pure" Waffen-SS. In Varėna, Oetker waited to be discharged from the Wehrmacht so he could leave the Lithuanian bloodlands and report for training to become a Waffen-SS officer.

8.

In late December 1941, Harald Quandt returned to the paratrooper base in Dessau after his first stint on the eastern front. He wasn't happy. Near Leningrad's front line, Harald's battalion had been deployed as ground infantry rather than dropping in behind enemy lines as usual. The carnage he witnessed on the battlefield had left him rattled and disillusioned. He spent New Year's Eve with the Goebbelses and their movie star guests at the minister's country estate north of Berlin. As everyone sat around the large dining table, they reflected on the events of the past year. Goebbels talked to his guests about the prospect of imminent victory. Harald suddenly interrupted his stepfather: "That's all nonsense. The war . . . will last at least two more years." Goebbels shot to his feet and began shouting at Harald. The twenty-year-old paratrooper stood his ground. The clash escalated, so much so that Magda had to summon all her strength to hold Goebbels back from her son. People had been executed for far less insubordination.

Not Harald, of course. Over the next year, he was continually deployed across war-torn Europe. He contracted jaundice in occupied France, where he was sent on mine-laying missions. In late July 1942, he returned home to Berlin on convalescent leave. He told his stepfather "interesting things" about the Wehrmacht's preparations in anticipation of a possible British attempt to establish a second front. Harald and his comrades were still eager to fight the British. "They have a special rage against them, because the constant waiting prevents them from having any vacation or leisure time. It would be desirable that the English, if they want to come at all, come as soon as possible. Our soldiers are ready to give them a warm and cordial welcome," Goebbels wrote in his diary.

But the British didn't come, not yet. In mid-October 1942, Harald returned to the eastern front. He was much looking forward to his next deployment and had "vigorously" resisted being assigned to the reserves. Magda and Goebbels worried about his return to combat. They prayed that he would "get through the coming difficult mission safe and sound." He was posted near Rzhev this time, west of Moscow, in the midst of a fourteen-month battle around the city, which had already taken the lives of millions of German and Soviet soldiers. The body count was so high, the front had become known as the "Rzhev meat grinder." And Harald was "living more dangerously than anyone else," according to a war comrade. Harald would go out alone at night on reconnaissance missions to scout enemy positions, and he ran into "trouble with Soviet partisans" at Rzhev, Goebbels told Hitler.

On February 23, 1943, Goebbels received a letter from Harald, thanking his stepfather for a package he had sent to the Rzhev front, which was stuffed with propaganda. Harald flattered Goebbels by praising his latest speeches. Goebbels had given his most fateful address to date just five days earlier. On February 2, the Wehrmacht and its allies had surrendered at Stalingrad, and the Red Army seized the moment to advance farther west. Their long approach to Berlin began. "Total war" was declared, now that battle had turned against Hitler and his troops. On the evening of February 18, Goebbels took the stage at Berlin's Sportpalast in front of thousands, as he had done so many times before. High above him hung a massive red-and-white banner bearing the regime's new propaganda motto in full caps: TOTAL WAR — SHORTEST WAR. For the tens of millions of Germans listening, Goebbels conjured a phantasmagoric scenario: hordes of Soviet soldiers approaching, followed by "Jewish liquidation commandos," all of them reducing Germany to mass starvation, terror, and anarchy. At the end of his speech, the minister asked his audience: "Do you want total war? If necessary, do you want it to be more total and more radical than we can even imagine today?" The crowd went wild. It was pure, raw hatred, stoked into flame.

In the middle of the speech, when speaking of the Jews, Goebbels let slip the word "eradication"; he quickly replaced it with "suppression." He didn't want to draw attention to what was already taking place: the systematic murder of millions of Jews in extermination camps that had been secretly built across Nazi-occupied Poland. One year earlier, during a conference led by Reinhard Heydrich in a villa on Berlin's Wannsee Lake, "the Final Solution to the Jewish Question" had been discussed to ensure that all responsible regime departments cooperated in its implementation. "A fairly

*Joseph Goebbels giving his "Total War" speech at Berlin's
Sportpalast, February 18, 1943.*

barbaric procedure, not to be described in any detail, is being used here,
and not much is left of the Jews themselves," Goebbels confided to his diary.

9.

While his younger son, Harald, was fighting across Europe, from France
to the eastern front, Günther Quandt was in Berlin, busily occupied with
labor shortages and bargaining with banks. Over the course of 1942, Günther had been caught up in tough negotiations with Germany's big three
banks: Deutsche Bank, Commerzbank, and Dresdner Bank. He wanted to
finance a further expansion of his weapons firm DWM. The arms company
had sales of 182 million reichsmarks that year, which would double to 370
million reichsmarks in 1943. At the same time, DWM was also in severe
debt. Growth doesn't come cheap, particularly not in wartime. The banks
had already provided DWM almost eighty million reichsmarks in loans,

an inordinate amount of credit, and they were hesitant to supply more. It seemed "no longer justifiable" in their eyes. Even so, Günther wanted more, and he wanted it at any cost.

In his October 1942 negotiations with Deutsche Bank's executive board, Günther didn't hesitate to cite DWM's "use of unskilled workers (prisoners of war, conscripted foreigners etc.)" as a reason why the bank should grant him a lower interest rate on his next loan. Unskilled laborers (especially those who were enslaved, imprisoned, starved, and abused) cost money. The banks had caved over the summer and issued a new bond of fifty million reichsmarks for DWM. The company desperately needed the windfall that the bond provided. Demand was so high, the banks' order book for DWM's new bond was several times oversubscribed, and it closed within days. The capital markets had bested human capital once again. But after the bond was issued, the big banks cut Günther off. The Nazi war machine was stalling in its tracks, and their money was now at risk.

Because millions of German men were being drafted or had volunteered for the Wehrmacht, manpower quickly became incredibly scarce across Germany. The labor shortage became especially pressing with the unrelenting bloodshed on the eastern front, which was costing the Wehrmacht some sixty thousand soldiers every month, from June 1941 onward. To address the shortage, Hitler enabled "one of the largest coercive labor programs the world has ever seen" in early 1942. The Nazi functionaries tasked with expanding the use of forced labor were the Thuringian *Gauleiter* Fritz Sauckel, whom Hitler had appointed general plenipotentiary for labor deployment in March 1942, and the architect Albert Speer, whom the führer had made the Reich's new minister of armaments that same month.

Over the course of 1942, Sauckel rapidly increased the number of people being forcibly recruited or simply deported for work in German factories. Millions of people were brought in from all over Europe, but the vast majority, dubbed *Ostarbeiter* by the Nazis, were from the Soviet Union and Poland. Meanwhile, at a multiday conference in late September 1942, Hitler took up Speer's suggestion that prisoners in concentration camps be used in war production outside those camps. Hitler's decision massively increased German firms' use of concentration camp captives, spawning a rapid growth of sub–concentration camps, or subcamps, built on or near factory grounds across the country. At least twelve million foreigners were forced to work in Germany during the war: men and women, boys and girls. Two and a half million of them died there, many after being subjected to horrific work and living conditions.

IG Farben, Siemens, Daimler-Benz, BMW, Krupp, and various companies controlled by Günther Quandt and Friedrich Flick were some of the largest private-industry users of forced and slave labor. Any German business could request coerced workers and prisoners of war at the local labor office. From early 1942 onward, concentration camp captives could also be supplied to a business by the SS Economic and Administrative Organization (SS-WHVA), led by the SS general Oswald Pohl, a member of Himmler's Circle of Friends. A company would make the request, and the SS-WHVA then would review the business. After a company was cleared, a subcamp was built near the firm's factory and supplied with captives. The company would pay for this subcamp while "leasing" each enslaved prisoner from the SS for a daily fee of four or six reichsmarks, depending on the person's capabilities. Slave labor collaborations between SS-run concentration camps and German companies included Auschwitz with IG Farben, Dachau with BMW, Sachsenhausen with Daimler-Benz, Ravensbrück with Siemens, and Neuengamme with Günther's AFA, Porsche's Volkswagen, and Dr. Oetker.

10.

Before the war started, Günther Quandt had been adamant about building a new state-of-the-art factory complex somewhere in Germany for AFA, his battery business. As luck would have it, the city of Hannover was selling a big plot of land on its industrial outskirts, about a third of a mile in size, and it offered the land to AFA. Günther proudly wrote that he "worked long and intensively on the plans" for the new factory, with remarkable results. After the war, British inspectors dubbed AFA's new factory possibly the "largest single battery manufacturing plant in the world," a title that would make Tesla's Elon Musk seethe with jealousy nowadays. In fall 1940, AFA's Hannover plant began to produce batteries for the German navy's infamous U-boat submarines and for the G7e electric torpedoes they used to sink ships.

By early 1943, forced labor made up more than half of the total work-force (thirty-four hundred people) at AFA's Hannover factory, but so far no prisoners from a concentration camp had been brought in. The managers of Günther's plant had been negotiating unsuccessfully with the SS about using prisoners from Neuengamme concentration camp, near Hamburg. But AFA couldn't guarantee the separation of captives and free workers on the factory floor, a condition that the SS insisted on.

In March 1943 the SS decided to compromise on this condition and came to an agreement with AFA. A subcamp was built on the Hannover factory grounds, one of Neuengamme's eighty-five satellite camps in the area. The cost of its construction and supplies, from buildings to beds to barbed wire, and initially, food, fell to AFA. The SS was responsible for the camp command and the guards; the prisoners and their clothing, food, and "medical care" (if you could call it that); and transport from and to Neuengamme. AFA would pay the SS the customary six reichsmarks per working day for a skilled captive and four reichsmarks for an unskilled one.

That price point didn't mean that the enslaved captives at AFA were to be paid; in fact, they were regarded as "less than slaves." The SS and AFA cynically agreed to "provide the detainees with incentives to motivate them to improve their output for the good of the production plant." Instead of money, the prisoners would receive vouchers that could be used at the camp canteen, but only if they reached certain weekly targets through the bonus system developed by the SS. Of course, this system was rife with abuse, and it favored captives who were in strong health. So-called *Ka-pos* — prisoners to whom camp command had assigned supervisory tasks — would beat fellow captives to "motivate" them to reach their targets but then steal the bonuses to keep for themselves. One *Kapo* at the AFA sub-camp was a mentally ill criminal; he supervised captives in the kitchen who were too weak to work in the factory. He would beat them with the end of a cable and hose them with water during winter; once, wearing iron boots, he kicked a French prisoner so hard in the abdomen that the man died a few hours later.

In the AFA factory's lead department, captives weren't allowed to wear special masks or clothing to protect them from poisonous fumes. Those who contracted lead poisoning, with symptoms such as severe colic, were forced to keep working, despite searing pain. Prisoners had accidents with boiling-hot lead. Their limbs, marred by third-degree burns, had to be amputated. The hands and arms of captives often got stuck in Günther's machinery, where "while fully conscious — the flesh was largely pulled off their bones up to their upper arms," an eyewitness later said.

The construction of AFA's subcamp started in mid-July 1943. About fifty German, Polish, and Serbian prisoners from Neuengamme began building the barracks, which were only four hundred feet from the factory. About twenty SS men were supplied to guard the construction site, and they wasted no time in getting started with abusing the captives. The first leader of this subcamp was SS staff sergeant Johannes Pump, who supervised the construction. He "beat the prisoners with his wooden club, who weren't working fast enough for him," an eyewitness later testified. "When the women who worked at the battery plant watched, he beat the prisoners particularly brutally, to show off."

About fifteen hundred captives from Neuengamme were soon brought into the subcamp to do work at Günther's factory. They met with similar abuse, and much worse. In front of the barracks, the prisoners had to build a roll-call area equipped with a gallows, which could be seen from outside the subcamp. Captives who escaped and were rearrested were hanged before the other prisoners as an example. Other escapees were executed with a pistol shot to the neck. At least 403 people lost their lives at Günther's prized AFA complex. He, however, had other things on his mind.

On the evening of July 27, 1943, the night before his sixty-second birthday, Günther was at home in Berlin, discussing political developments with his sons, Herbert and Harald. Things were looking grim for Germany.

Hitler's ally Mussolini had been deposed in Rome just two days earlier, putting an end to twenty-one years of fascist rule in Italy. Allied forces had invaded Sicily. The Wehrmacht had lost North Africa and the Mediterranean.

Harald had returned home to Berlin two weeks earlier, on leave. The twenty-one-year-old paratrooper had survived the grueling eastern front, where he had "performed excellently" in combat and had been promoted to officer. His next destination was Italy, which was about to leave the Axis alliance and switch sides. Günther defended Italy's defection as he spoke to his sons. It was "the only sensible thing for a nation to do the moment it sees that the war is lost," he said. In fact, Günther argued, Germany should follow the Italians' example and seek peace at any cost.

Harald was furious. How could his father take such a defeatist stance? In fact, the newly minted Luftwaffe officer was so upset at his father that he told his mother the next day about her ex-husband's remarks. However, he begged her not to tell Goebbels what Günther had said. Magda kept her promise — but only until her son was well on his way to the southern front.

A few weeks later, Günther received a phone call at his villa. He had been summoned to Goebbels's private residence on Hermann-Göring-Strasse in central Berlin. Goebbels sent a car to pick him up, but when Günther arrived at the majestic residence overlooking the Tiergarten, the propagandist had already left for his ministry. Instead, Günther found his ex-wife waiting for him. Magda had a warning from her husband. Günther knew well what the cost was for making defeatist comments: the person's head. One more remark in that direction, Magda said, and Günther would be "finished."

11.

On July 10, 1943, Friedrich Flick turned sixty. Unlike Günther Quandt, who had celebrated turning the same age in grand fashion just two years earlier, Flick spent the day away from the limelight of the German capital. There would be no decadent dinner at a luxury hotel with prominent guests from the regime, the military, and business circles, although Flick did receive "a heartfelt personal telegram from the Führer himself." Instead of arranging a posh party, the press-averse mogul's closest aides mounted a tightly controlled PR campaign in German newspapers, with the help of Göring's press chief, to celebrate their boss "in the right light." Ironically, the articles mainly lauded Flick's ability to operate in silence. His conglomerate even put out a rare statement celebrating Flick's "peasant forebears" and criticizing those who had called him a mere "collector of industrial participations. That is about as justified as if one looked upon a builder as nothing but a collector of building materials," the statement said. That the public knew so little about him was "due to his tactful modesty," it added. "He avoids people."

Stealth had brought Flick very far in life. While the Nazi empire was beginning to fray in the summer of 1943, Flick's conglomerate was at its apex. Due to its decade-long expansion, it was now one of Nazi Germany's largest producers of steel, coal, and arms. Flick had even surpassed his rival Krupp; Flick's conglomerate had become the country's second-largest producer of steel. The asset value for Flick's seven largest firms — three of which he didn't own outright — stood at about 950 million reichsmarks by early 1943. That year's tax assessment estimated that Flick's stake in his conglomerate was worth almost 600 million reichsmarks. With the industrial empire he owned, Flick was one of Nazi Germany's wealthiest men, if not *the* wealthiest. Ranging from coal mines to steel mills to weapons factories, and stretching from occupied Ukraine to France to Nazi Germany, Flick's empire was massive in size and scope. When the Third Reich wanted more arms, Flick had it covered. When it needed more natural resources, he was there to help. Black and brown coal, iron and steel, cannons and shells — he had all the fuel the Nazi war machine required. However, Flick lacked one key resource, which was in short supply across German businesses: skilled workers. By 1943, those performing forced labor at Flick's coal mines increasingly consisted of women and children deemed fit for work in the open-pit mines. Many were Russian teenagers from thirteen to fifteen years of age. By the time Flick's sixty-first birthday came around, his conglomerate had 120,000 to 140,000 workers. About half of them were forced or enslaved.

Flick had started using concentration camp prisoners in September 1940, making his conglomerate one of the first private companies in Nazi Germany to do so. The director of Flick's Hennigsdorf steel factory near Berlin had struck a deal with the SS months earlier and began using some fifty prisoners from Sachsenhausen concentration camp. But unlike Günther, Flick hadn't yet managed to get a subcamp built at one of his many factories and mines. It wasn't for lack of trying. Plans for one subcamp at the Döhlen steel plant—a joint venture half-owned by Flick, half-owned by the state of Saxony—had failed. In late summer 1942, the suggested subcamp for "foreign Jews" never materialized, because by then, the führer had actually decided in favor of the immediate murder of Jews as opposed to capitalizing on their value as unpaid laborers.

Alongside the importing of slave labor, Flick was busy reining in his elder son, Otto-Ernst, in France over the summer of 1943. The twenty-six-year-old heir was wreaking havoc at the Rombach steelworks, which his father had received in the form of a trusteeship from Göring after the complex was expropriated in Nazi-controlled Lorraine. In February 1943, Flick had promoted his designated successor to director of the massive complex, which already produced more than 20 percent of Flick's crude steel. Otto-Ernst succeeded his father-in-law as Rombach's director, having worked zealously to obtain the position. Still desperate to prove himself to his father, Otto-Ernst embarked on an ambitious but expensive arms-production strategy at Rombach, which he euphemistically dubbed a "quality program."

The month of Otto-Ernst's promotion, Germany's Army Weapons Agency (HWA) made Rombach the general contractor for fifteen ammunition factories in Nazi-occupied France. Rombach was to provide the plants with high-grade steel while also producing grenades and projectiles for the Wehrmacht. Otto-Ernst's decision to prioritize supplying the Nazi weapons program with quality steel demanded an immense infrastructural overhaul at Rombach. It came at an enormous cost in both money and human lives.

Otto-Ernst's move to focus on expensive arms production immediately alarmed his father. Already by early March 1943, Flick senior had gotten involved with managing Rombach and pointing out the dangerous cost increases. They were proof enough to him "that the business couldn't be in order." But still, by June nothing had changed. In a letter to Otto-Ernst and his fellow managers, Flick reiterated that, at Rombach, "we must make the greatest possible contribution to armaments, and it's also imperative that we maintain our reputation and standing . . . We mustn't disgrace ourselves."

When, in August 1943, Rombach's financial losses were compounded by a sharp drop in production, Flick's patience with Otto-Ernst broke. He threatened to send one of his closest aides from Berlin to Rombach to reclaim control of the company from his son if earnings and production didn't improve. Otto-Ernst, not exactly known for his interpersonal skills, tried to play down his own role in the debacle by discrediting a fellow manager, a tactic that did not succeed with his father. It was clear to Flick that his son had let business get out of hand. Otto-Ernst had once again shown that he wasn't fit to lead the family empire.

Meanwhile, working conditions at Rombach were disastrous, "among the worst in Flick's factories," a historian later concluded. As labor shortages rapidly worsened over the course of 1942, Otto-Ernst's father-in-law had already started to rely heavily on coerced workers and Soviet prisoners of war. Hundreds of Russians were shuffled like human cattle among the expropriated steelworks in Lorraine.

When Otto-Ernst took over Rombach, the amount of forced labor assigned to the steelworks was growing. This enabled him to offset part of the cost for his expensive weapons program. By summer 1943, more than half of the sixty-five hundred workers at Rombach were coerced, held at four camps at the site. About a quarter of them were women, a stunningly high figure for a steel factory. And most of the women were *Ostarbeiter,* forced workers from Eastern Europe. The women performed hard labor in twelve-hour shifts, repairing railway tracks, loading and unloading coal and wagons, and even working in the steel-smelting furnaces. Pregnant women had to keep working up to the point when they gave birth. These workers were given half a liter of soup for lunch, "a mixture normally given to pigs," one woman later said. As many as thirty women had to sleep in a single tiny room, while rain poured through the roof of the drafty barracks. Those in forced labor received measly pay. The bomb shelter on the site was reserved for Germans only.

Rombach's factory foremen and heads of security, a succession of sadistic SS and Gestapo men, were aided by various henchmen. Most intimidated and abused the laborers simply because they could. One young *Ostarbeiter* was beaten to death. An interpreter threw herself in front of a train after being threatened with beatings and a transfer to a concentration camp because she had illegally bought a pair of shoes. Russian interpreters who stabbed two guards were hanged on the factory grounds. A historian who later detailed forced and slave labor in the Flick conglomerate wrote that these SS men "committed the crimes right in front of Otto-Ernst Flick, who could have reined them in at any time . . . Flick's son protected the regime of terror of the factory foreman, and his willingness to do so increased as his entrepreneurial activities in Rombach became a disaster."

12.

On May 27, 1943, a man named Josef Herrmann wrote a sobering letter to Ferdinand Porsche in Stuttgart. The German Jew had worked with the car designer at Austro-Daimler and needed help from his former colleague. Herrmann had fled to Amsterdam with his sister, who had already been deported and, unbeknownst to him, murdered in Auschwitz. Now he too was in danger. He asked if Porsche could send a letter to the Bavarian official in charge of SS security forces in the Netherlands, touting Herrmann's contributions to the "Austrian national economy and industry." Jews were occasionally put on an exemption list, sparing them from direct deportations to the extermination camps because of "peacetime merits." The requested letter was typed up but never sent. In mid-June 1943, Porsche's secretary wrote to Herrmann. Without clarifying the reasons for this decision, the letter said that Porsche "didn't feel able to send a confirmation of your past civilian services to the commander of the security police" after all. Herrmann was soon deported from Amsterdam. He died in Bergen-Belsen on March 30, 1945, one week after his seventieth birthday and two weeks before the concentration camp was liberated. When push came to shove, the well-connected and supposedly independent-minded Porsche didn't dare help a former colleague facing death.

During the summer of 1943, Porsche was mainly busy saving himself. He'd been a flop in his new job as head of the tank commission. The prototypes Porsche designed, including an unwieldy supertank named Mouse, weren't fit to take part in Operation Citadel, the last major German offensive in the Soviet Union. The armaments minister and rival designer Albert Speer was about to fire Porsche, now almost seventy, as head of the commission. His decade-long stint as Hitler's favorite engineer was coming to an unceremonious end.

Meanwhile, Porsche's son-in-law, Anton Piëch, was enacting a regime of terror at the Volkswagen factory in Fallersleben. The first sub–concentration camp on the complex was cynically named "Work Village." Following an agreement between Porsche and Himmler, the prisoners were tasked with finishing construction of a light-metal foundry. In return, Porsche provided the Waffen-SS with four thousand bucket cars. The captives were brought in from Neuengamme, followed by captives from Sachsenhausen

Ferdinand Porsche on top of a tank he designed, 1943.

and Buchenwald. Prisoners from Auschwitz and Bergen-Belsen were soon deported to the plant too, for different projects.

In mid-July 1943, the Gestapo and factory guards, armed with rubber truncheons and firearms, broke up a "spontaneous musical procession" involving Dutch and French laborers singing and playing guitars and flutes. Forty were sent to a brutal penal camp nearby; those who returned alive three weeks later had become "different human beings." That same summer, Piëch "bluntly declared . . . that he had to use cheap *Ostarbeiter* in order to fulfill the Führer's wish that the Volkswagen be produced for 990 reichsmarks." The number of *Ostarbeiter* quickly grew to more than forty-eight hundred, including teenagers. All were held in an overcrowded part of the factory camp fenced off by barbed wire. A sadistic canteen cook "laced kitchen leftovers with glass shards so undernourished inmates injured themselves while rummaging for food," a historian later discovered.

About half of all the *Ostarbeiter* at the Volkswagen complex were women. Some of the Polish and Russian women either arrived pregnant or soon became so at the camps. The mothers were forced to give up their babies immediately after birth, and the newborns were moved to the "Nursery for Foreign Children" in Rühen, a village nearby. The conditions in the nursery "defied belief," a British prosecutor later explained. "At night the bugs came out of the walls of those barracks and literally covered the children's faces and bodies . . . Some children had as many as thirty to forty boils or carbuncles on their bodies." At least 365 Polish and Russian babies died at the nursery in Rühen from neglect, infections, and insufficient care.

13.

At around 9 a.m. on December 12, 1943, a train belonging to the SS leader Heinrich Himmler pulled into Hochwald station in East Prussia's Masurian forest. Aboard were Richard Kaselowsky, Friedrich Flick, and thirty-six other members of Himmler's Circle of Friends. The group had left Berlin the night before. After a thirteen-hour journey in the sleeper train, the men had finally arrived at their destination. Himmler had invited them to visit his command post, code-named Black Lair, fifteen miles east of Hitler's Wolf's Lair. From the train station, the men took a bus to Himmler's war headquarters, where, after a breakfast of white sausages, the guests took a guided tour of the bunker. Himmler joined them for one hour at noon and gave a short speech. After lunch, there was a film screening and a concert presented by an SS choir. The visit ended with a light supper: over a cup of tea, Himmler once again joined his "friends" for an hour. Afterward, the participants returned to Berlin by train.

Some members later called the visit an "immense disappointment" and "dull . . . despite the white sausages which tasted good." As it turned out, Himmler hadn't divulged any inside information about how Hitler was going to turn the tide of the war. Flick wondered whether he had visited Himmler's headquarters or an insane asylum. But for the CEO of Dr. Oetker, Richard Kaselowsky, the tour had served its purpose. He drew inner strength from Himmler's speech. "According to the *Reichsführer SS* we still have a time of hard battles and trials ahead of us, in which we must all keep our chin up. But the *Reichsführer* has the firm belief that at the end of the struggle there will also be a German victory, which will secure our future. We want to plant this faith in our hearts and not let it be destroyed by the many difficulties of daily life," Kaselowsky wrote to a relative after the visit.

The pudding boss from Bielefeld had reason to be optimistic. Business at Dr. Oetker was booming because of the war.

More than half a billion packages of the firm's famous baking powder and pudding mixes were being sold in Nazi Germany by 1942, more than twice the amount before the start of the war. Dr. Oetker had an official baking-powder monopoly in the German Reich and was one of Hitler's frontline suppliers. The company's baking products were being shipped to German soldiers fighting across Europe. Dr. Oetker also participated in a nutritional joint venture with the Wehrmacht to send nourishing dried fruits and vegetables to German troops.

Kaselowsky's membership in Himmler's Circle of Friends provided him with even more business opportunities. Through the group, Kaselowsky had become acquainted with the SS general Oswald Pohl, head of the SS Main Economic and Administrative Office (SS-WVHA). Pohl oversaw all

*Poster showing boxes of Dr. Oetker Pudding Powder
for the Wehrmacht.*

concentration and labor camps run by the SS, the organization's myriad business endeavors, and the supplying of slave labor to German firms.

Kaselowsky's connection with Pohl came in handy in early March 1943. In a joint venture between Dr. Oetker and Phrix, a chemical fiber firm, factories for the production of yeast were being built. The two companies needed more slave labor for the bitterly difficult construction work. Management was dissatisfied with the work performed by weakened prisoners. After a visit to the building site in Wittenberge, Pohl promptly sent hundreds more captives from Neuengamme to a subcamp there. Kaselowsky found it "quite gratifying" that Pohl had lobbied Himmler to guarantee that the yeast factory would be completed. Ironically, Phrix yeast would later be sent to Neuengamme's main camp near Hamburg. It made its way to the sick bay there, where some of the starved prisoners who had built the yeast factories convalesced, if they were lucky.

Of course, no favor from the SS came without a catch. There was always a quid pro quo. In exchange for more slaves to build the factories, Kaselowsky agreed to Pohl's request that the SS be dealt into Dr. Oetker and Phrix's next yeast venture. In April 1943, Kaselowsky's stepson, Rudolf-August Oetker, joined the advisory board of this new endeavor. A few months earlier, Rudolf-August had started training as a Waffen-SS officer with an administrative leadership course at the SS-Führerschule in Dachau concentration camp, near Munich. He later falsely claimed that the school had been "shielded" from the neighboring prisoner camp, as if they were separate entities, and that he had "noticed nothing . . . of the ordeals" at Dachau. In truth, the school was an integral part of the larger complex. During his training at Dachau, the prisoners would clean the students' quarters, Rudolf-August later wrote. The twenty-six-year-old spoke to the captives who were forced to attend to his room and noted that they seemed "not badly fed." He concluded: "I suspect that it was done intentionally, so that the people who came into contact with them would say that the concentration camps weren't that bad."

In addition to combat and military training, Rudolf-August received ideological instruction at SS schools, which included courses with titles such as "Race Studies," "Tasks of Racial Policy," and "Population Politics." At his grandmother's wish, Rudolf-August was supposed to join Dr. Oetker's management board when he turned twenty-seven, the age of his biological father when he was killed at Verdun. But by the time of Rudolf-August's birthday in September 1943, he was still busy with his Waffen-SS officer training. A year later, however, a twist of fate would force him to abandon his paramilitary ambitions and take over as head of the family firm.

14.

In mid-January 1944, Harald Quandt returned home to Berlin from the southern front. As a staff adjutant with the First Parachute Division, Harald had been fighting across southern Italy against the Allied forces since late summer, trying to hold the Puglia and Abruzzo regions. The twenty-two-year-old officer was in weak health and had "only words of contempt left" for the Italians, who had switched sides and joined the Allies. Goebbels, however, was pleased with how the war had built up his stepson's character. "The experience at the front has had the best effect on him," the propaganda minister wrote in his diary on January 17, 1944. "You can see that the war not only destroys, but also builds up, especially in young people, for whom it has been the great teacher."

Goebbels was wrong. Harald was fed up with the war. In early February 1944, the officer was admitted to a military hospital in Munich with a severe cold. When Goebbels visited the city days later, he went to see his stepson. Goebbels urged Harald to get well as soon as possible and return to his unit. But Harald wouldn't be rejoining the battle anytime soon. "Harald causes us some worry. He . . . still can't leave for the front," Goebbels wrote on February 13, 1944. "This is all the more embarrassing to me because his division is currently engaged in the heaviest fighting on the southern front . . . Magda will visit him in Munich on Monday and chew him out."

The propaganda minister was afraid of losing face because of his stepson's illness. Harald mattered to Goebbels only so long as his heroics fueled his stepfather's propaganda campaigns. When Magda visited her son in the hospital, they got into a huge argument. Harald had grown weary of the war, and of his radical Nazi mother and stepfather. A rift opened between them. Harald "behaved anything but decently," Goebbels wrote after Magda lamented to him over the phone. The situation nagged at Goebbels for weeks, even after Harald had recovered and returned to the Italian front by mid-March 1944. Magda was still "very unhappy" with her son, so Goebbels wrote "a very energetic letter" to Harald at the front. "I believe that this is the only way to bring him back to his senses," Goebbels stated in his diary on March 16, 1944. "We mustn't pay any attention to the fact that he's standing in front of the enemy. It's better for him to know what we think of him than for him to be pushed further down the slippery slope by our indulgence."

A month later, Goebbels received a response to his "very stern letter."
Harald had written from the front at the relentless Battle of Monte Cassino,
south of Rome. His former misgivings seemingly had disappeared. Harald
promised Goebbels that "he would finally eliminate the black mark in his
life" that his stepfather had criticized; he wrote that "he had come to his
senses." Goebbels was delighted with the apparent success of the letter he
had sent, a sentiment he recorded in his diary on April 19, 1944, a day
before Hitler's fifty-fifth birthday. At about the same time Harald wrote a
letter from Italy to a school friend on the eastern front. "Keep your chin
up, old boy, it's about us," he told his friend. Harald knew that Germany
was losing. But though Harald was done with the war, the war was far from
done with him.

15.

In spring 1944, Günther Quandt traveled from Berlin to attend a roll call
in his honor at the Cegielski weapons complex in Poznan. He had bought
the expropriated arms works for DWM after first receiving it in trusteeship. Günther expanded the original plants and built a new factory there,
making it one of the largest arms and ammo complexes in the Third Reich.
His upgraded plants made flamethrowers, air torpedoes, artillery cannons,
machine guns, and on-board weapons for the Ju 88 bombers, which were
among the Luftwaffe's most important combat aircraft. There was almost
no limit to DWM's immense manufacturing prowess in the Polish city.
Even as late in the war as April 1944, the factory was manufacturing some
400 million infantry bullets.

For this, Günther relied on as many as twenty-four thousand people in
Poznan to perform forced labor, a historian later estimated. Tuberculosis
was a common affliction among these workers at the plant. Those who
worked in the foundry had to endure smoke, fire, and temperatures of up
to 180 degrees Fahrenheit. True medical care was available only to Germans. Polish workers received some basic treatment but were refused care

if it was deemed too expensive. Children as young as twelve had to work night shifts and perform grueling manual labor; the plant security guards and their commanding SS officer often beat up these youths. Some seventy-five people performing forced labor were executed at the plant.

Speaking before Cegielski's largely enslaved workforce, *Gauleiter* Arthur Greiser showered Günther and his firm with praise, comparing them to another legendary weapons producer. "The Wartheland [a Nazi-named region of occupied Poland] is proud of DWM's presence! Where would we be without Krupp, without DWM? Yes, with all its branches here in the east and west . . . and in the whole of the Greater German Reich, the DWM today represents the same power as Krupp, and the name 'Quandt' therefore has just a good a sound as the name 'Krupp' and is rightly feared by all our enemies around the world." Günther followed with a speech of his own, and quipped: "While people thought we were making cooking pots, we were already preparing for the Führer's war in 1934."

One German forced into labor at the plant who witnessed this scene was Reinhardt Nebuschka. He had worked as the artistic director of a theater in Poznan, but back in the summer of 1940, he had crossed the wrong person. While visiting Harald in Poznan, Magda had stormed into Nebuschka's office to demand that he fire the stage actress her son was seeing. Nebuschka refused and was arrested by the Gestapo a few months later. He was forced to work, of all places, at Günther's DWM plant in Poznan. Nebuschka later claimed that Goebbels had given the order "to finish me off." And yet, after witnessing Günther's speech at the plant, Nebuschka wrote letters addressed to Goebbels and Göring, accusing Günther and his factory executives in Poznan of shifting food rations, intended for Polish laborers and Russian prisoners of war, to Berlin. After sending the letters, Nebuschka was once again arrested by the Gestapo and moved to Fort VII, a prison in Poznan that also was the first concentration camp established by the Nazis in occupied Poland. He survived prison, returned to Germany, and soon wrote another letter detailing what he had witnessed at Günther's factory in Poznan. That letter, however, was addressed to someone else: America's chief prosecutor at Nuremberg.

16.

On May 9, 1944, Ferdinand Porsche, his daughter, Louise, and his son, Ferry, fled to safety in Austria with their families and most of Porsche's employees. They left Stuttgart because the city was beset by Allied air raids; the Porsche firm was among the targets. Next to the Porsche family villa, high up on a hill overlooking Stuttgart, an anti-aircraft command post had been established at the former home of the Porsches' Jewish neighbors. The post only increased the vulnerability of the car designer and his family. One morning, the Porsches stepped out of their bomb shelter into the open air as "a red glow of fire shone up from the basin. Stuttgart was burning," Ferry later recalled. It was time to leave.

The Porsche-Piëch clan waited out the rest of the war in Austria, moving between the Schüttgut estate that Ferdinand Porsche had bought in Zell am See and the bucolic mountain town of Gmünd, where Ferry began to develop the first Porsche sports car. Up until their departure, Ferry had been busy leading the design firm in Stuttgart, which exploited hundreds of coerced workers. In the summer of 1942, a forced labor camp was built near Porsche's new car factory, one part of it exclusively used by the family firm to hold *Ostarbeiter*. The family's exploitation of labor extended to the private sphere. In March 1943, Ferry and his wife, Dodo, started using a "lovely" sixteen-year-old Ukrainian girl as household staff at the family's Austrian estate. "If she is as hardworking as she is beautiful, then Ferry can be satisfied," a Porsche relative wrote to Louise Piëch, introducing the teenage girl.

With his wife, Louise, and their children safely in Austria, Anton Piëch continued his reign of terror at the Volkswagen complex in Fallersleben. In mid-May 1944, a Volkswagen engineer traveled to Auschwitz, where he selected three hundred Hungarian Jewish metalworkers. They were briefly used at the Volkswagen factory to help produce the V-1 flying bomb, one of the Nazis' "miracle weapons." But the men were quickly deported to help convert an iron ore mine into an underground arms factory in Nazi-controlled Lorraine. At the mine, the captives joined another group of five hundred Jewish prisoners, also selected from Auschwitz by Volkswagen. On May 31, about eight hundred prisoners from Neuengamme concentration camp were brought in to finish building a camp southwest of the Volkswagen complex meant to house those performing forced labor. The SS sergeant Johannes Pump was the first to take charge of the so-called Laagberg camp. Earlier that May, the sadistic SS man had been sent about sixty miles east, from the Neuengamme subcamp at Günther Quandt's AFA plant in Hannover to the one at the Volkswagen factory where Piëch was in charge. At both places, the rule of violence and brutality continued.

17.

In mid-September 1944, Sachsenhausen concentration camp moved one of its thirty subcamps in Berlin to Niederschöneweide, an industrial neighborhood in the eastern part of the capital. The subcamp was down the road from the Quandts' Pertrix battery factory. Günther's elder son, Herbert, was responsible for staffing at the Pertrix plant. The new subcamp was different from most: it held only female prisoners. Guarded by the SS on the southern bank of Berlin's Spree River, the women lived in a decommissioned boat shed on the grounds of Loreley, a former nightclub.

As many as five hundred women from the subcamp were forced to work as slaves at the Pertrix plant over the next months. Many had already spent years in police prisons or concentration camps. The Polish and Belgian women had been shuttled about a number times — to the boat shed from a previous subcamp and, prior to that, from Ravensbrück, the women-only concentration camp sixty miles north of Berlin. The Polish women had arrived at Ravensbrück from Auschwitz.

At Pertrix, all the women were forced to toil in twelve-hour shifts; though they had no protective equipment, they worked with battery acids that could badly bite into the skin. They had to wear work clothes with bold black-and-white stripes, as if to emphasize their status as prisoners, along with a cross on their back and wooden clogs on their feet. The SS guards, who kept a watch on them en route to the factory and while they labored there, frequently subjected the women to physical abuse. There was no infirmary for the sick, no soap in the subcamp for basic washing, and little proper food; there was, however, plenty of vermin. To sleep, two women had to share a single wooden platform in the boat shed.

Herbert Quandt wasn't responsible for just the female concentration-camp slaves at Pertrix. The thirty-four-year-old was trying to build his own subcamp, close to one of his homes. Some two decades after his father bought the property at Severin to secure a professional future for his ailing son, Herbert bought his own estate, Niewerle. Günther's designated successor had soured on Severin. The Goebbelses' wedding had defiled it, as did the betrayal of the family caretaker, who turned the beloved family countryside home into a Nazi stronghold.

Herbert stopped going to Severin. But he remained an avid outdoorsman with a penchant for breeding Trakehner horses. Despite his visual impairment, he also loved motorboats, fast cars, and sailboats. In the fall of 1942, Herbert bought the six-hundred-acre Niewerle estate in the Lower Lusatian countryside, some ninety-five miles southeast of Berlin. Over the next two years, whenever he could spare the time, he took the train from Berlin to the village closest to Niewerle. From the station, Herbert rode a horse-drawn carriage to his estate, some five miles away. He spent his weekends there "with really only very few exceptions." By December 1944, Herbert was using a dozen foreigners — including four Poles, four Ukrainians, and two prisoners of war — at his estate to labor in the garden, kitchen, and household.

Niewerle was conveniently located for Herbert. Because of the constant bombing raids on Berlin, AFA's and Pertrix's aircraft battery manufacturing was to be relocated to the remote eastern reaches of Nazi Germany — two towns in Lower Silesia — in order to protect production. In Sagan, one of those towns, Herbert became personally involved with planning and building a sub–concentration camp. He aimed to use camp prisoners to continue the production that was to be moved from Berlin. Sagan was only some twenty-five miles to the east of Niewerle. On October 27, 1944, an AFA engineer presented and discussed sketches for the camp barracks with Herbert and his fellow Pertrix directors. One week later, the engineer submitted an application to Organization Todt — the Nazi engineering entity that built concentration camps, among other murderous structures — to construct the barracks that would house the prisoners.

One month later, on December 2, 1944, the engineer had an introductory meeting with an SS officer from the nearby Gross-Rosen concentration camp, which had some hundred subcamps spread out across the Third Reich. Two days after the meeting, Günther's right-hand man, Horst Pavel, and Herbert were personally informed about the building progress in Sagan. Two of the barracks were almost completed, and it's likely that some twenty-five concentration camp prisoners were already working on the construction there. By mid-January 1945, forty train cars carrying machinery and equipment had been sent to Sagan. The Nazi authorities estimated that it would take three months to finish the subcamp. Only upon its completion could prisoners from Gross-Rosen be requested for slave labor projects. But that never happened; the Red Army was approaching. In late January, Herbert personally managed the evacuation of the incomplete subcamp just weeks before Soviet troops conquered Sagan and Niewerle.

18.

Saturday, September 30, 1944, was a sunny fall day. In East Westphalia the American bombers seemed to come out of nowhere. They started raining bombs on Bielefeld around 2 p.m., leveling large sections of the historic center. When the sirens sounded, Richard Kaselowsky, his wife, and their two daughters took refuge in the cellar of their villa on the Johannisberg, where they'd had an air-raid shelter installed. A direct hit on the house likely killed the family of four instantaneously, though in the end, the coal supply in the cellar may have suffocated them. Their obituary began with a refrain that had become very common: "Taken from us by a terrorist attack."

Rudolf-August Oetker was just weeks away from becoming a Waffen-SS officer when he received word that his mother, two young sisters, and stepfather had been killed. The loss wasn't just a personal tragedy for the twenty-eight-year-old aspiring officer; it was also a blow to one of Hitler's frontline suppliers, Dr. Oetker. Rudolf-August was granted leave from his duties to take control of the family's food company. A month later, having successfully completed his training, he was promoted to *SS-Untersturm-führer*, the lowest rank of commissioned officer in the terror organization.

Before the bombs fell on his childhood home, Rudolf-August had been assigned to work at the headquarters of the SS Main Economic and Administrative Office in Berlin. Oswald Pohl, the SS general and his stepfather's powerful acquaintance from Himmler's Circle of Friends, led the organization. But because of Kaselowsky's death, Rudolf-August would never start the position with the SS. As his paramilitary career abruptly ended, another one began. Rudolf-August was ready and able to follow in his stepfather's footsteps. "I couldn't imagine a better father than Richard Kaselowsky," Rudolf-August said in an interview with a German newspaper more than half a century later, "nor a better teacher for me."

In late October 1944, Rudolf-August visited his fellow SS officer Fritz Kranefuss, the driving force behind Himmler's Circle of Friends, in Berlin. Following that visit, Kranefuss advised the leader of the SS to send a letter of condolence to Rudolf-August instead of his older sister. "He's the real heir to the Oetker businesses and will now succeed his stepfather as director," Kranefuss wrote. He had already communicated Kaselowsky's death to the SS: "As is well known, Dr. Kaselowsky belonged to the Circle of Friends and, even if he wasn't one of our old friends from the time before the seizure of power, he proved himself extraordinarily well there. In both personal and professional respects, he has been a role model, as can be said of very few business leaders."

For Kaselowsky it hadn't been the business contacts and advantages that made Himmler's Circle of Friends so special. They were just a nice accessory. The circle and its gatherings were close to the Westphalian arriviste's heart because they helped him feel that he had truly made it. In mid-May 1944, months before his death, he mused in a letter about a group meeting in bombed-out Berlin: "The beautiful evening that we spent in the Reichsbank's casino garden, as if in an oasis of peace in the middle of a ruined world, will be a lasting memory for me."

19.

Disaster struck Harald Quandt in late summer 1944, as German troops were retreating in Italy. On September 9, Goebbels was personally informed by the Luftwaffe general Kurt Student that his stepson had been wounded in battle on Italy's Adriatic coast, near Bologna. Harald was missing and had likely been taken by the Allies as a prisoner of war. Goebbels decided not to tell Magda "for the time being, as to not worry her unnecessarily." He hoped that Harald was still alive, and he tasked the Red Cross with finding information about his stepson's fate through its international contacts.

Goebbels waited almost two weeks to tell Magda that her eldest son was missing and had likely been taken captive by the Allies. She took the news in stride. But the couple decided not to tell their six young children. Harald's twenty-third birthday came and went on November 1, 1944, but there was still no sign of him. Magda and Goebbels were becoming increasingly anxious that they would never see him again. One week later, a captain from Harald's battalion told Goebbels that his stepson had been shot in the lung before he went missing. It still wasn't clear whether he had survived the bullet or where he was. Goebbels cast a wider net, roping in the German embassies in neutral Switzerland and Sweden to aid in the search for Harald. Nazi Germany's foreign service, via its embassy in Stockholm, even contacted the Allied embassies to help determine the fate of Goebbels's stepson.

On November 16, 1944, more than two months after Harald was reported missing, Goebbels received a telegram from the Red Cross with good news: Harald had been located in a British prisoner of war camp in North Africa. Magda burst into tears after her husband broke the news to her over the phone. She felt as if her first child had been reborn. The next evening, the couple received a letter from Harald. He wrote that he had been badly wounded and had received two blood transfusions but that

German doctors were taking good care of him and patching him up in the prison camp. Hitler, who had been "very worried" about Harald, was also "very satisfied" that the young man had been located after all, Goebbels wrote in his diary.

Some two months later, on January 22, 1945, at Hitler's residence in the Reich Chancellery, Hermann Göring handed Goebbels and Magda a personal letter honoring Harald, along with the German Cross in Gold — with a pontifical swastika at its center. The medal was awarded in absentia to Harald for his combat achievements. Goebbels was moved by Göring's gesture; the two men had always had a testy relationship. However, Goebbels couldn't help but snipe afterward at his fellow cabinet member in charge of the Luftwaffe. "One always feels deeply touched by his human personality, but unfortunately, he doesn't achieve what should be achieved in his field, and the Reich and the German people have to pay very dearly for his failure," Goebbels lamented in his diary.

Harald's premonitions about the war had been right after all. Soviet and Allied troops were advancing on Berlin, and Nazi Germany's end was near. As it happened, Harald would never see his mother, stepfather, or his six half siblings again. The couple's parting words to their beloved Harald would reach him by letter well after they had met their fate.

PART IV

"YOU WILL LIVE ON"

1.

Days before the surrender of Nazi Germany on May 8, 1945, Harald Quandt was sitting in officers' quarters at the British prisoner-of-war camp 305, in the Libyan port city of Benghazi, where he was being held as prisoner #191901. He was having a glass of rum with his fellow prisoners when a BBC radio news report came on. It announced that the bodies of Harald's six half siblings had been found inside the Führerbunker, an air raid shelter in the garden of the Reich Chancellery in central Berlin. The bodies of his mother and stepfather, Magda and Joseph Goebbels, were discovered outside, in the Reich Chancellery Garden. Harald was devastated. The twenty-three-year-old former Luftwaffe paratrooper lieutenant had been close to his half siblings. He was shattered to hear that all six little ones were dead. A war comrade of Harald's was with him when he heard the news. He later said that Harald, "a man of strict self-discipline and cool reserve," had been distraught for hours.

Later on in his captivity, Harald received two farewell letters, seemingly from beyond the grave. The first was from his mother, Magda:

> My beloved son!
>
> By now we have been in the Führerbunker for six days already—papa, your six little siblings, and I—to give our national socialistic lives the only possible, honorable end. I don't know whether you will receive this letter. Perhaps a kind soul will make it possible to send you my final goodbye after all. You should know that I have stayed with papa against his will, and that last Sunday the Führer wanted to help me escape. You know your mother—we share the same blood, I didn't even consider it. Our glorious idea is perishing—and with it everything beautiful, admirable, noble and good that I have known in my life.

The world that will come after the Führer and National Socialism will not be worth living in, which is why I brought the children here as well. They are too good for the life that will come
after us, and a merciful God will understand me when I give
them deliverance myself. You will live on, and I have only one
request for you: Never forget that you are a German, never act
dishonorably, and make sure that through your life, our deaths
will not have been in vain.

The children are wonderful. Without any aid, they take
care of themselves in these worse than primitive conditions.
Whether they have to sleep on the floor, go without a wash,
have little to eat and so on — never a word of complaint or tears.
The impact [of the bombs] makes the bunker shake. The bigger
children protect the smaller ones, and their presence here is a
blessing, if only because they bring a smile to the Führer's face
every now and then.

Yesterday evening the Führer removed his golden Party
badge and pinned it onto me. I am proud and happy. May God
grant me the strength to do the last and hardest thing. We only
have one goal left: to remain loyal to the Führer until death.
That we should end our lives together with him is a blessing
from fate that we would never have dared to count on.

Harald, my dear boy — for your journey I pass on to you the
best thing that life has taught me: be true! True to yourself, true
to others and true to your country! In each and every way!

It's hard to start a new page. Who knows whether I will be
able to fill it. But there is still so much love that I would like to
give you, so much strength, and I want to take all your sorrow
away over our loss. Be proud of us and try to keep us in proud,
happy remembrance. Everyone dies one day, and isn't it better
to live a brief but honorable and courageous life than a long one
in disgrace?

The letter must go out now ... Hanna Reitsch will take it.

She is setting off again! I embrace you with the most intimate, heartfelt, motherly love!

My beloved son
Live for Germany!
Your Mother

The second letter was from Harald's stepfather, Joseph Goebbels:

My dear Harald,

We are sitting locked in the Führerbunker in the Reich Chancellery and are fighting for our lives and honor. God only knows how this battle will end. What I do know is that, alive or dead, we will emerge from it with only honor and glory. I don't believe we will see each other again. That is why these are probably the last words you will receive from me. If you survive this war, I expect you to bring nothing but honor to your mother and me. It is not at all necessary for us to be alive to affect the future of our people. You may be the only one to carry on our family legacy. Always do so in a way that wouldn't give us reason to be ashamed. Germany will survive this terrible war, but only if our people have examples to lift themselves up by again, and we want to be such an example.

You can be proud to have a mother like yours. Last night, the Führer gave her the golden Party insignia that he has worn on his coat for years, and she deserved it too. Going forward, you have only one task: to prove yourself worthy of the greatest sacrifice, which we are willing and determined to make. I know you will. Do not let the noise of the world that is about to begin confuse you. One day, the lies will collapse and the truth will prevail once more. It will be the hour when we stand above all, pure and immaculate, as our faith and pursuit have always been.

Farewell, my dear Harald! Whether we will ever meet again is up to God. If not, then always be proud to belong to a family

that, even in misfortune, has remained loyal to the Führer and
his pure, holy cause, until the last moment.

All the best and my heartfelt greetings,

Your Papa

Harald didn't yet know the gruesome details of their deaths; those
wouldn't come to light for some time. On the evening of April 28, 1945,
Magda and Joseph Goebbels each wrote a letter to their beloved Harald.
Magda gave the letters to Hanna Reitsch, Nazi Germany's famous test pi-
lot, who was visiting the Führerbunker as Soviet troops were nearing the
center of Berlin. Hitler gave Reitsch two cyanide capsules as a farewell gift.
Reitsch flew out of the German capital that night from an improvised air-
strip near the Brandenburg Gate. It was the last flight to leave Berlin before
the Red Army captured the city. The Soviets tried to shoot down the plane,
fearing that Hitler was escaping in it, but Reitsch took off successfully. She
was arrested by American soldiers after she landed in Austria, the letters
for Harald still in her possession. Although the US Army Air Force captain
who interrogated Reitsch kept the original letters, the American authorities later sent copies of them to Harald in Benghazi.

On April 30, 1945, two days after Magda and Joseph wrote to Harald,
Adolf Hitler swallowed a cyanide capsule, as did his wife, Eva Braun, who
was sitting beside him; he then shot himself in the head with his Walther
pistol. The two had married the night before, officially ending Hitler's vow
of celibacy, which had been his expression of dedication to the German
people. The couple didn't enjoy their marriage for long. The führer knew
that the Red Army had penetrated the city limits of Berlin and was just a
few blocks away, closing in on his reinforced concrete bunker. The couple's bodies were cremated in the Chancellery Garden, based on Hitler's
instructions.

In accordance with the führer's will, Harald's stepfather, Joseph Goebbels, was named the new chancellor of Germany. He held the position no
more than a day. Hitler's will stated that his successor was to escape Berlin
with his wife and children, but Goebbels refused. The man who had been

subservient to his führer for more than twenty years did not obey Hitler's last order.

The day after Hitler's suicide, Magda dressed her six children in white nightgowns and brushed their hair. The SS dentist Helmut Kunz gave each kid a morphine injection. When they were in a drugged stupor, Magda inserted a cyanide capsule into each child's mouth and made sure they bit down on the glass, assisted by one of Hitler's personal physicians, Dr. Ludwig Stumpfegger. Magda performed the deed in the family's private quarters to avoid worrying the staff. Rochus Misch, one of Hitler's bodyguards, afterward saw Magda playing solitaire, looking very pale, with bloodshot eyes and a "frozen" face.

A few hours after Magda murdered her children, she and Joseph went, arm in arm, up the steps toward the Chancellery Garden. Not long after, Goebbels's adjutant Günther Schwägermann found the couple's lifeless bodies there. They had taken cyanide as well. The führer's golden Nazi Party insignia was still pinned to Magda's dress. An SS soldier, on prior instructions from Goebbels, fired a few shots into the bodies for good measure, poured gasoline over them, and set them ablaze. The following day, Soviet troops found the charred corpses in the leveled garden, lying between concrete mixers.

Among the last people to see Magda alive in the Führerbunker was Albert Speer, Hitler's architect turned armaments minister. "She was pale and spoke only trivialities in a low voice, although I could sense that she was in deep agony over the irrevocably approaching hour when her children must die . . . Only as I was on the point of leaving did she hint at what she was really feeling: 'How happy I am that at least Harald . . . is alive,'" Speer later reported in his memoir.

2.

In early March 1945, Magda had visited her best friend, Ello, Harald's godmother, at a sanatorium on the hills overlooking Dresden, two weeks after the Allies' bombs had leveled the city. Magda didn't arrive in her custom limousine, but rather in the delivery van of a cigarette company; she was sitting up front with the driver. She had come to say farewell to her best friend of twenty-five years. Their first meeting, in rural Pritzwalk, was a lifetime ago. They had been Quandt wives, then Quandt divorcées. But Ello had never remarried. She later said that Günther had offered to help Magda save her children. According to Ello, Günther had arranged a safe house for them in Switzerland; he offered to provide for them and their education. But Magda refused. Her children would die with her. Ello later recalled Magda's soliloquy, how she had rationalized doing the unthinkable to her children in a final attempt to reckon with her complicity in the mass atrocities of the Third Reich:

> We have demanded monstrous things from the German people, treated other nations with pitiless cruelty. For this the victors will exact their full revenge . . . Everybody else has the right to live. We haven't got this right — we have forfeited it . . . I make myself responsible. I belonged. I believed in Hitler and for long enough in Joseph Goebbels . . . In the days to come Joseph will be regarded as one of the greatest criminals that Germany has ever produced. His children would hear that said daily, people would torment them, despise and humiliate them. They would have to bear the burden of his sins; vengeance would be wreaked on them . . . You know how I told you at the time quite frankly what the Führer said in the Café Anast in Munich when he saw the little Jewish boy, you remember? That he would like to squash him flat like a bug on the wall . . . I could not believe it and thought it was just provocative talk. But he really did it later. It was all so unspeakably gruesome, perpetrated by a system to which I belonged. It has amassed such lust for revenge all over the world — I have no choice, I must take the children with me, I must! Only my Harald will survive me. He's not Goebbels's son . . .

Magda spent the night with Ello at the sanatorium. The next morning, Ello walked her to the delivery van, where her driver was waiting. Magda sped off through the remains of Dresden, back toward the ruins of Berlin, en route to the Führerbunker, her final destination. She knelt on the front seat and waved at Ello through the side window until she could no longer see her friend.

3.

On April 25, 1945, one week before his ex-wife killed six of her children and then herself, Günther Quandt fled Berlin and the approaching Soviet troops. He first tried to get away to Switzerland, purportedly for "business meetings," according to his request for an entry permit; but since he was registered at Swiss immigration as a financial supporter of Hitler, he was denied. The tycoon then split to Bavaria. News had leaked that the southern German state would become part of an American occupation zone. Not unreasonably, tycoons like Günther, Friedrich Flick, and August von Finck expected "business-friendly" policies from the capitalist Americans.

Günther began renting a "modest room" in a castle in Leutstetten, a pastoral village near Lake Starnberg, twelve miles south of Munich. American and British soldiers soon occupied the castle. But instead of being arrested by the Allies, Günther was taken in by the town's mayor, who was living in a house in the mountains. For the time being, the mogul believed that "the only right thing to do" was "to stay in the background as much as possible." Günther had every reason to keep a low profile. In addition to his mass production of arms and all the firms he had Aryanized, the magnate had subjected as many as 57,500 people to forced or slave labor across his factories, according to a historian's later estimations.

On April 18, 1945, one week before Günther fled Berlin, the Office of Strategic Services (OSS), the CIA's predecessor organization, had published a four-page memo on the tycoon. The spy agency had been keeping tabs on the bald businessman since the summer of 1941, when he so lavishly celebrated his sixtieth birthday. The OSS described Günther as "one of Germany's leading industrialists whose holdings, considerable before 1933, have greatly expanded since Hitler's rise to power." He "shares in the responsibility for formulating and executing Nazi economic policies and for the economic exploitation of German dominated territories." Günther's business methods had ensured success "without great noise of battle." Investigators from the US Treasury Department soon added Günther to a list of forty-three German business leaders to be indicted for war crimes at a military tribunal in Nuremberg. When Günther learned he was on the list, he wrote an irate rebuttal and asked that it be forwarded to the US Senate.

Before considering an escape to Switzerland or Bavaria, Günther had planned to flee from Berlin to Bissendorf, a town twelve miles north of AFA's Hannover factory, which was about to come under British occupation. He wanted to be present to lead his battery firm but then thought better of it; there was too much heat on the mogul. Since February 1945, a group of Günther's managers had been shuttling back and forth between Berlin and Bissendorf to set up alternative headquarters near AFA's state-of-the-art factory. The group included Günther's elder son, Herbert, who, after personally evacuating AFA's unfinished Gross-Rosen subcamp in Lower Silesia in late January, would now move closer to his father's prized new factory, where more horror was unfolding.

With Allied forces approaching, Günther's plant in Hannover shut down in late March 1945. Factory management burned all files, except for a list of prisoners' names. Around the same time, hundreds of additional ill and weak captives arrived at the AFA factory subcamp from Neuengamme's main concentration camp. One week later, on April 5, about a thousand of AFA's subcamp prisoners, those deemed "fit" enough, were forced to walk to Bergen-Belsen concentration camp, thirty-three miles to the north, in a death march. They were in disastrous health, and they lacked sufficient food, clothing, and shoes. On the first day alone, an SS paramedic likely shot as many as fifty captives who couldn't walk any farther. More of the prisoners were executed in the days that followed. On April 8, the remaining group arrived at Bergen-Belsen. Those who were still alive a week later were liberated by British troops.

Those left behind at the AFA subcamp in Hannover awaited a horrific fate. As many as six hundred captives had been too ill or weak to join the march. But now they had to be moved. On April 6, the day after the death march to Bergen-Belsen began, an SS commander ordered the AFA camp to evacuate. Two days later a freight train arrived, apparently at AFA's request, to remove the captives. But the train stalled in a rural area in Saxony-Anhalt; the bombed-out remains of another train was blocking the rails, and prisoner transports from concentration camps across Germany were stranded there. The people on these trains were cleared out. Already, sixty-five captives from Hannover had died during the ride. Now, most of the prisoners were forced to continue on foot; a few farm wagons transported the weakest. They ended up at the town of Gardelegen, where US troops were closing in. After discussing the situation with SS and Wehrmacht officials, the local Nazi leader decided to lock the captives in a barn on the edge of town and set it on fire. SS forces threw hand grenades onto the burning structure and gunned down prisoners who tried to flee. On April 15, 1945, American soldiers discovered the charred bodies of 1,016 people. Many had been burned alive.

Ten days later, US Army colonel George Lynch addressed Gardelegen's residents: "Some will say that the Nazis were responsible for this crime. Others will point to the Gestapo. The responsibility rests with neither — it is the responsibility of the German people . . . Your so-called Master Race has demonstrated that it is master only of crime, cruelty and sadism. You have lost the respect of the civilized world."

4.

In the night that stretched from April 7 to 8, 1945, one day after the SS evacuated the AFA factory subcamp in Hannover, Herbert Quandt and Günther's right-hand man, Horst Pavel, fled Berlin and relocated to Bissendorf with twenty employees. Provisional company headquarters were set up at Bissendorf's spa resort, and the group of colleagues moved to barracks in a pine forest just outside the village. The living arrangements there were primitive. There was little food, the grounds frequently flooded, and the men used shards from an anti-aircraft searchlight as shaving mirrors.

British soldiers occupied AFA's Hannover factory on April 20, 1945. It was practically undamaged, and they quickly restarted operations there. The plant, where just weeks earlier slave laborers had toiled under the most horrible circumstances to make batteries for U-boats and torpedoes, began producing dry batteries for the British army. Herbert was placed under surveillance; he was suspected of being a "tool of his father." The British barred him from entering the plant and working for AFA. Instead, Horst Pavel was appointed as the factory's trustee.

It was up to Pavel to save AFA's Hannover plant from being fully dismantled. Günther, in Bavaria, couldn't stand the fact that he had been forced to give up all control. He became paranoid, believing that his trusted lieutenant was plotting against him. Even Herbert didn't escape his father's suspicion. The heir wrote to Günther that he had to put his distrust aside if they intended to overcome the present challenges.

Weeks before fleeing Berlin, Herbert had had the opportunity to buy an Aryanized firm for himself; Max Franck, a leading underwear producer in Chemnitz, was offered to him for sale. He seriously considered buying the formerly Jewish-owned firm just so he could for once make a decision beyond "the shadow of his great father." In the end, however, Herbert decided against it.

Despite the enormous suffering that the two Quandt men had caused, Herbert was grateful for all that he had learned from Günther during the war. "I believe that it was especially in these most difficult years, from an industrial point of view, that I was able to learn more from my father in this way than would otherwise have been possible for me under . . . normal circumstances," he later recalled. What was left of their business empire hung precariously in the balance by summer 1945. But their troubles paled in comparison to those of Friedrich Flick; the scrutiny now trained on him and the chaos that gripped some of his firms under the leadership of the ever-disappointing Otto-Ernst.

5.

Friedrich Flick fled from Berlin to Bavaria in February 1945. He absconded to his Sauersberg estate, just an hour south from where Günther was hiding out. Flick had acquired the Sauersberg property from the persecuted Jewish beer brewer Ignatz Nacher years earlier. (The estate is still owned by one of Flick's granddaughters.)

Just before Allied forces liberated the Rombach steel complex in France, in late summer 1944, Otto-Ernst Flick fled back to Germany, where his father tasked him with yet another job. This time, it was leading the Gröditz weapons plant in Saxony. More than a thousand underfed concentration-camp prisoners were making artillery cannons and shells there. The captives were brought in from Flossenbürg and Dachau in Bavaria, Mauthausen and Gusen in Austria, and finally, Auschwitz. They were held and abused by the SS in the plant's attic. In October 1944, Flick inspected the Gröditz factory hall when he came to install the twenty-eight-year-old Otto-Ernst as its director. Afterward Flick went for dinner at the factory's casino to celebrate his son's new job. As at Rombach, this appointment backfired. Within weeks of his arrival, the rash Otto-Ernst tried to oust two of his father's trusted longtime executives.

Otto-Ernst had failed in each of his management positions since the war started. His father gave him another major promotion anyway. On February 1, 1945, Flick appointed Otto-Ernst as the CEO of Maxhütte, a major steel company with mills and ore mines across Bavaria and Thuringia. As at Rombach, Otto-Ernst succeeded his father-in-law, who was pushed into early retirement. The Flick heir started his new job on March 7, 1945, as the entire world seemed to be collapsing.

At Maxhütte, factory managers had been working the *Ostarbeiter* and prisoners of war for almost a hundred hours a week. The workers became far too weak to press on. Still, the managers cut their already minimal food rations as punishment for "faking" being incapacitated. "The Russian eats a lot, and they didn't get that much," an employee later concisely concluded.

Accidents and deaths were frequent; women who performed forced labor worked barefoot in the steel mills — "a bad thing in bad weather," one of the firm's executives dryly remarked.

In mid-March 1945, an epidemic of spotted fever spread through Gröditz, killing some 150 prisoners in a matter of days. Weeks later, with the Red Army and US troops fast approaching the plant, the SS sent the remaining Gröditz captives on a ten-day death march toward Prague. But not before shooting about 185 prisoners who were deemed too weak to walk and burying them in a gravel pit near Flick's factory.

While prisoners were being starved and massacred at his firms, Flick — safe and sound at his Sauersberg estate, on a hill west of Bad Tölz — initiated the so-called Tölzer program. He had already split his headquarters between Berlin, Düsseldorf, and Bavaria. Now, to provide himself with a postwar nest egg, Flick tried to transfer assets from his conglomerate to his personal ownership. But the maneuver failed.

In June 1945 the US Counter Intelligence Corps (CIC), the military security agency tasked with detaining and questioning many of Nazi Germany's most notorious suspects, put Flick under house arrest. By that time the industrialist had been able to transfer only one of his businesses. As it happened, the Fella firm hadn't made weapons during the war — it was Flick's sole machinery company that hadn't done so. Flick's steel and coal conglomerate was now at risk of being seized entirely. More than half of his factories and mines lay in the Soviet zone and would soon be expropriated. The rest of Flick's plants were placed under the Allies' control, for now. His continental empire of weapons, slaves, and plunder had finally fallen.

Flick's arrest had been months in the making. In a memo of May 1945, the OSS called him "the most powerful individual business leader sharing the formulation and execution of Nazi economic policies," who "has shared in the spoils of Nazi conquest in Europe." After weeks spent under house arrest, Flick was officially detained and moved to Kransberg Castle (code name Dustbin), an Allied detention center north of Frankfurt. Other high-profile suspects such as Albert Speer, Hjalmar Schacht, and Wernher von Braun were being interrogated there. Robert H. Jackson, a Supreme

Court justice and the recently appointed chief US prosecutor at Nuremberg, received a memo written by an aide, which outlined a possible trial of industrialists, listing Flick, "Germany's most powerful industrialist," as a potential defendant.

In early August 1945, Flick was transferred from Kransberg to Frankfurt and handed over to the US Office of Military Government for Germany (OMGUS), which had occupied IG Farben's former headquarters in the city's Westend district. Days before Flick was moved, the last Allied Conference concluded in Potsdam. There, the American president, Harry Truman; the Soviet dictator, Joseph Stalin; and the new British prime minister, Clement Attlee, came to an agreement on their goals for the occupation of Germany: "democratization, denazification, demilitarization, and decartelization."

Truman had long sanctioned the first official American occupation policy for Germany, which would keep certain parts of industry, instead of destroying all of it, and hold proper judicial proceedings against Nazi war criminals, rather than summarily executing them. Days after the Potsdam Conference concluded, the Allied powers, including France, signed the charter to establish the International Military Tribunal (IMT) in Nuremberg. The IMT would indict and try twenty-four of Nazi Germany's most important political and military leaders on war crimes, crimes against peace, and crimes against humanity. The IMT was to be just the first of many Nuremberg cases, however, including a possible second trial held by the Allies to be focused exclusively on German industrialists, financiers, and CEOs. Given how deeply intertwined with the Nazi war machine these industrial conglomerates and cartels had been — take Flick and Krupp's steel and coal conglomerates and IG Farben's enormous chemicals interests, for example — the Allies opted for a divide-and-conquer approach. They planned to break up these industrial behemoths and prosecute their owners and executives.

After his father's arrest, Otto-Ernst seized the chance to fill the power vacuum and embarked on a rash reorganization. He started firing longtime Maxhütte managers whom he didn't trust and replaced them with those he perceived as loyalists, including two former members of the SS and the SA. The American authorities in Bavaria didn't take kindly to that move. They promptly arrested Otto-Ernst and held him for a few days; they canceled the changes to personnel he had made at Maxhütte. But after his release, the Flick heir picked up right where he'd left off. On July 30, 1945, Otto-Ernst reinstated himself and the Nazi managers. The US authorities had seen enough and barred the twenty-eight-year-old from entering Maxhütte. Otto-Ernst was soon rearrested and brought to the Frankfurt prison where his father was confined. With both of them jailed and all their mines and factories occupied, the future of the Flick conglomerate was looking grim indeed.

6.

Baron August von Finck had a much quieter war than Günther Quandt and Friedrich Flick did. The two teenage sons of the forty-six-year-old aristocrat were still too young to be trained as his successors. He had completed the Aryanizations of Berlin's Dreyfus bank and Vienna's Rothschild bank well before the war started. As a result, the financier could just sit back and oversee the growth of his private bank, Merck Finck, and supervise his family investments in Allianz and Munich Re; he did not have to worry about weapons production, slave labor, and all the other wartime headaches that his peers were grappling with. (One unexpected wartime headache for von Finck: he got divorced.) He raised another eight million reichsmarks for Munich's Haus der Deutschen Kunst after Hitler "expressed a desire" for a separate building for exhibitions related to architecture. Because of the war, the structure was never built. Von Finck also continued to exercise his knack for looting. Even a dead friend of Günther wasn't safe from the baron's greed. In 1941, Merck Finck and IG Farben expropriated an Austrian magnesite mining firm after its American owner, Emil Winter, died. Winter was a gentile German immigrant who had become a steel industrialist in Pittsburgh. Günther deeply admired Winter and his firm. He and Magda had visited him at his stately mansion in Pittsburgh during their trip to the United States. Alas, it was a dog-eat-dog world.

But the Wehrmacht's surrender on May 8, 1945, abruptly disturbed von Finck's peace and quiet. The anti-Semitic Aryanizer was promptly put under house arrest by American soldiers at his Möschenfeld estate, just east of Munich. The famously frugal financier had been awaiting their arrival in the freezing cold, wrapped in an ancient, completely moth-eaten fur, even though he had plenty of wood at his disposal for a fire. Von Finck quickly removed from his piano a photo of Hitler with a handwritten dedication from the führer. The aristocrat's files were confiscated and sent to Munich; there, the US authorities put Merck Finck under property control, which was an Allied policy of taking custody of German assets. As the bank's trustee they appointed a concentration camp survivor. Von Finck was also removed as supervisory board chairman of Europe's two largest insurers, Allianz and Munich Re. But he remained the main shareholder of the two companies, for now.

Von Finck's private bank had already been singled out in 1944, in a US Treasury memo on the removal of German bank officials: "Scrutinize especially the . . . private firms enriched by Aryanization (for instance, Merck, Finck and Co.)." The Allies were particularly keen on breaking up Germany's commercial and private banks, which had financed countless arms factories, Aryanizations, concentration camps, and extermination camps across the Third Reich. Günther Quandt's and Friedrich Flick's respective supervisory board memberships at Deutsche Bank and Dresdner Bank therefore made them even more suspect in the Allies' view.

Despite Hitler's downfall, von Finck's fealty to the führer remained unwavering until the very end. Kurt Schmitt, the former CEO of Allianz and the Reich minister of economic affairs who had so often accompanied von Finck on his visits to Hitler, told an American interrogator: "Even during the latter years of the war when leading personalities freely stated to me that Hitler . . . had led Germany to the edge of the abyss, v. Finck . . . never expressed to me any doubts or criticisms of the Führer's leadership." Hans Schmidt-Polex, another Allianz executive and an old friend of von Finck, declared to his American questioner that the baron banker had told him in the first months of 1945 that "he remained a convinced Nazi" who "would die for his belief if necessary."

Von Finck's close ties to Hitler landed his private bank smack in the crosshairs of the Americans and the Soviets. In May 1945, a report from the US Justice Department's Economic Warfare Section stated that von Finck's bank was "the holder and trustee of Hitler's private fortune." This claim has yet to be proven. Hitler's name wasn't on a list, submitted by the bank, of prominent Nazis who had opened private accounts at Merck Finck. Soviet propaganda alleged that during the führer's rule, von Finck made him a Merck Finck shareholder, but the bank denied this.

The American authorities' impression of von Finck worsened as they kept him under house arrest. A report by the US Treasury Department described the financier as "a pro-Nazi in every respect, tall, snobbish, reserved, pedantic and a bureaucrat. It is said that he is entirely cool in disposition, unsentimental to the degree of cruelty, and extremely over-ambitious." In late May 1945, American officers moved von Finck to an internment camp and interrogated him there. They found the financier to be "a somewhat tricky customer, who has for years tried to make the best out of two worlds—profiting vastly from the [re]organization of Jewish banking houses [Rothschild, Dreyfus etc.] under the guise of protecting them." But now that they had this crafty character in custody, what did the Americans plan to do with him? Very little, as it turned out.

7.

The Americans released Baron August von Finck from the internment camp in October 1945, after he'd spent five months in detention. An uncertain future awaited him. The aristocrat was barred from his bank and corporate boards, and the matter of his Aryanizations still had to be addressed. What remained of Vienna's S.M. von Rothschild bank had been liquidated. Some assets were eventually returned to Baron Louis von Rothschild, who had immigrated to the United States.

Willy Dreyfus, the former owner of his family bank, hadn't ventured that far. He had immigrated to Basel, Switzerland, after Merck Finck Aryanized the Berlin branch of his bank in 1938. When the war ended, Dreyfus started looking into whether he and the heirs of his deceased partner could hold von Finck financially responsible for the Aryanization. As Dreyfus had no interest in reopening the bank nor the option to do so, he wanted restitution. Despite an "understandable reluctance to set foot on German soil again," Dreyfus crossed the border to explore his options for recourse. There, at a meeting in Munich on September 29, 1946, he ran into von Finck by coincidence. When Dreyfus refused to greet him, von Finck was deeply insulted.

Von Finck told Dreyfus that "if the roles had been reversed, he would have come up and used this opportunity to thank him for the decent takeover of his business in 1937/38." When Dreyfus's legal adviser told von Finck the reason for the visit to Munich — to begin restitution proceedings against him — the baron looked "surprised" and "quite concerned." Von Finck agreed to settle the matter as quickly as possible. But Dreyfus was hesitant. He said that he would immediately break off discussions if the aristocratic banker "further trivialized the circumstances of the Aryanization."

Negotiations between the two men took place in a "very frosty" mood but wrapped up in a mere three days. On October 2, 1946, Dreyfus and von Finck signed an agreement. Dreyfus would receive about two million reichsmarks, mainly in Allianz and Munich Re shares, in restitution for the approximately 1.65 million reichsmarks Merck Finck had underpaid for Dreyfus's Berlin branch in March 1938, with a little goodwill thrown in. The heirs of Dreyfus's former partner, Paul Wallich, who had committed suicide soon after the Aryanization, were to receive about 400,000 reichsmarks, also in shares.

However, the deal between Dreyfus and von Finck stalled. Merck Finck was under American property control, so the baron wasn't even allowed to access the assets of his private bank; he certainly could not transfer shares to Switzerland, where Dreyfus lived and had become a citizen. Also, since a US restitution law for occupied Germany had not yet been put in place, the settlement had to be put on hold. Meanwhile, von Finck remained a key focus of American investigators. Though their findings were still a well-kept secret, it was all but assured that the baron would be brought to trial.

8.

Work stopped at the Volkswagen factory in early April 1945. There was barely any food left at the massive complex in Fallersleben. The Nazis began using it as a transit point for deportations from other sub–concentration camps. On April 7, the SS ordered the evacuation of the remaining Volkswagen factory subcamps. A hundred male prisoners from one of them died after being deported hours north to Wöbbelin, yet another Neuengamme subcamp. Six hundred and fifty female Jewish prisoners held in a Volkswagen factory hall were deported one hour northeast in freight cars to Salzwedel, a women-only concentration camp. One week later, American forces freed them.

US troops liberated the remaining laborers, both forced and enslaved, at the Volkswagen plant on April 11, 1945. One day before the American soldiers arrived, the sadistic factory director, Anton Piëch, fled the complex, but not before stealing more than ten million reichsmarks in cash from the Volkswagen coffers and sending about 250 factory militia troops to fight on the front line. He made off with the millions to his native Austria, where the Porsche-Piëch clan awaited him at the family estate in Zell am See. Over the prior eight years, the Porsche firm had already billed the Volkswagen plant about 20.5 million reichsmarks for design and development services. "This sum likely laid the financial foundation for the successful post-war development of the house of Porsche," two historians concluded decades later.

In mid-May 1945, an Allied investigation team in Austria raided the thousand-acre estate in Zell am See and the provisional Porsche company headquarters in Gmünd. They began questioning Ferdinand Porsche and his engineers about their development of tanks and military cars. As the interrogators came down harder on them, Porsche and his staff cracked, and they handed over the company's technical drawings. At the time of the raid, the OSS published a memo on the arms and car designer: through Hitler, "Porsche was entrusted with the execution of one of the favorite Nazi schemes": the Volkswagen. Porsche also "played an important part in equipping the Nazi war machine."

The CIC arrested fifty-year-old Anton Piëch and Porsche's son, Ferry, on July 29, 1945, and brought them to an internment camp near Salzburg. Ferdinand Porsche was detained five days later, but he was moved to Kransberg Castle in Germany. The sixty-nine-year-old star designer complained to his interrogators that he had already been exhaustively questioned in Austria. "Hitler's support was simply necessary in order to successfully implement my ideas," Porsche told them.

It wasn't just Ferdinand Porsche's arms production for the Nazis that had put him at the mercy of the investigators. If anything, the Allies wanted his trade secrets. And as for Porsche and Piëch's brutal management of the Volkswagen factory, where they had used about twenty thousand people as forced or slave labor, including some five thousand concentration camp captives, the Allies didn't care much about the moguls' deplorable labor practices. The investigators mainly focused on their money and accused the men of stealing Volkswagen's assets for their personal profit. And they weren't wrong. Piëch, after raiding the Volkswagen coffers, had continued sending invoices from Austria to the British military, the plant's new overseer, billing them more than 1.25 million reichsmarks for services rendered by the company, even after the British occupied the plant. Piëch, not yet officially removed as the factory director, felt justified in doing so.

Ferdinand Porsche denied that he had done any looting: it was, after all, his son-in-law who had done the stealing at Volkswagen. Porsche was released after five weeks, and he returned to Austria. Anton Piëch and Ferry Porsche were soon let out of the internment camp too; Ferdinand Porsche had spent weeks lobbying the Allied authorities for their release. But as the American and British investigators moved on, the trio had to face another of the Allies: the French.

9.

Rudolf-August Oetker's hometown, Bielefeld, was captured by US soldiers on April 4, 1945. Within days, he had three American army officers billeted in his house. Rudolf-August entertained them with bottles of Steinhäger schnapps, the local Westphalian gin, telling the officers he wanted to march with them against the Soviets. They clearly had no idea that they were being hosted and feted by a Waffen-SS officer.

Rudolf-August's fun ended when Nazi Germany capitulated on May 8. Bielefeld lay in the British occupation zone. As a Waffen-SS officer, the twenty-eight-year-old Rudolf-August was to be immediately arrested and removed from all professional positions. He had been leading his family's food company, Dr. Oetker, ever since his mother, stepfather, and half sisters were killed in an American air raid. On May 18, he reported to the British authorities in Bielefeld for questioning and was directly detained. Rudolf-August was told that he would be transported the next day to Staumühle, a massive British-led internment camp twenty miles south of Bielefeld. He and his fellow detainees were held overnight in a disused factory just outside town. The heir later recalled: "Suddenly some guys appeared, who started beating the hell out of us. I later heard they were Poles, but nobody really knew for sure. I didn't notice much either, because I was immediately hit on the head and passed out."

When Rudolf-August woke up in Staumühle, he was paralyzed. The heir was quickly transferred to a British military hospital set in a castle a few miles east of the Dutch border. During his recovery in detention, Rudolf-August read Thomas Mann's debut novel, *Buddenbrooks*. It chronicles the decline of a wealthy northern German merchant family over four generations; when Mann won the Nobel Prize in Literature, it was largely on the merits of this book. Reading it made Rudolf-August "very depressed." No wonder. He, the designated heir of a northern German business dynasty, was now immobile, imprisoned in his war-torn homeland, which was occupied by foreigners. At least he still had his wife, Susi. She came to visit him in captivity and smuggled in tobacco, board games, and, of course, chocolate-pudding powder. In mid-January 1946, Rudolf-August was released after eight months in detention. Over time he slowly began to walk again, though doctors said that he would need a cane for the rest of his life.

Rudolf-August thought the British authorities had held him for being "guilty by association" as the successor to his Nazi stepfather, Richard Kaselowsky. During Kaselowsky's reign at Dr. Oetker, the family had benefited from Aryanizations, arms production, the use of forced and slave labor, and close collaboration with the SS and the Wehrmacht to provide soldiers with better nutrition. Kaselowsky had also been a paying member of Himmler's Circle of Friends. But in fact, with Kaselowsky's death, these matters had receded from view. The British cared only about Rudolf-August's role as an officer in the Waffen-SS.

While Rudolf-August was detained, Dr. Oetker and its subsidiaries were put under British property control, and a trustee was appointed. Upon his arrest, Rudolf-August had been banned from rebuilding his family business. Now his assets were frozen too. He was out of a company, forbidden to work, likely to be tried as an SS officer, and still suffering from his injury. After his release, Rudolf-August moved with his wife and children to the guesthouse at his family estate near Bielefeld. Eager to get back to business, he found the work ban "frustrating." But he could do very little, apart from reading and learning to walk again. He took long strolls with his son, in landscapes dotted with sheep and goats. But Rudolf-August hadn't resigned himself to a life of leisurely obscurity just yet. The pudding prince was biding his time.

10.

Günther Quandt too thought it best to lie low after the war was lost. While his fellow moguls were being arrested in scores, in rural Bavaria he had miraculously evaded the Allies. He was considering a move to Hannover, where his elder son, Herbert, was based near the once-prized AFA battery factory, which the British now occupied. But while he was awaiting the

Americans' decision as to whether to indict him at Nuremberg, Günther also came under investigation by two German courts: one in Hannover and one in Starnberg, near the town to which he had fled. He nixed his moving plans in late 1945. It seemed more prudent to stay put in Bavaria.

By January 1946, Günther thought the upcoming midterm elections in the United States would herald a positive change for him in the American occupation zone. "The Republicans won't share the view that money is theft. One can already feel a breath of fresh air," Günther wrote to a friend. However, by the time the Republicans beat the Democrats by a landslide and retook Congress that fall, Günther had long since been arrested and placed in an internment camp.

In mid-March 1946, CIC investigators interrogated Günther for two hours in Starnberg. In his eyes, the CIC was nothing more than "the American version" of the Gestapo. When submitting his OMGUS questionnaire, Günther added a section titled the "Political Persecution of Dr. Günther Quandt," detailing his supposed mistreatment at Goebbels's hands. This didn't impress the American investigators. In mid-June 1946, they placed Günther under house arrest at the mayor's house on Leutstetten's Tierkopf mountain. "Quite a few gentlemen" were taking an interest in him now. The Americans confiscated all his files and sent them to Nuremberg. Then, on July 18, 1946, ten days before his sixty-fifth birthday, the CIC detained Günther. There would be no lavish celebrations this year.

Günther was first taken to prison in Starnberg. In late August 1946, he was moved to an internment camp in Moosburg, northeast of Munich, where he was registered as "wanted" for Nuremberg's industrialist trials, which were still under consideration. The Hannover inquiry into Günther had just finished. Investigators there considered him a "reactionary capitalist, early stormtrooper, and military activist. His influence against Nazi-ideology and War-economy had to have been more active in his position in economic life, in order to make his assertion to be a Nazi-opponent trustworthy . . . His private personal antagonism to Dr. Goebbels . . . can by no means be regarded as a political [exoneration]." The investigators also received "the urgent request" from AFA's labor representatives to remove Günther and his son Herbert from any involvement with the battery company "once and for all." Günther was deemed "NOT capable for any position" in Germany's economy going forward.

Günther started working on his defense. In August 1946, he retained an inexperienced local lawyer from Starnberg. It was hard finding any legal representation at all — millions of Germans were seeking it — let alone securing an ace attorney. He then ordered his family, employees, and lawyer to start compiling exculpatory statements and documents.

One of the lawyer's first stops was a visit to Magda's best friend and former Quandt, Ello, in Berlin. Ello had left the Nazi Party in 1935 but continued to be a beloved guest chez Goebbels. As part of his defense, Günther was claiming that he had been an opponent of the Nazis and a victim of Goebbels, who had blackmailed Günther into joining the NSDAP. Ello happily helped confirm his lie. "Goebbels took every opportunity to belittle and make fun of the 'hated Quandt,'" she declared in an affidavit of late August 1946. She spun a familiar tale about the two men's relationship: Günther was forced to submit to Goebbels's demands to join the Nazi Party out of fear that the propaganda master would seize guardianship of young Harald, "eliminate the influence of his father," and indoctrinate the boy with Nazi ideas. Yet even after Goebbels had successfully claimed Günther's son, Ello declared that Harald never succumbed to Nazi ideology and that "the love and affection for his father" persisted against all odds.

Such a declaration became known as a *Persilschein,* a Persil ticket, named after a famous German laundry detergent. It was a tongue-in-cheek term for any statement meant to wash clean the stain of Nazi collaboration and sympathies. Suspected Nazis could be exonerated by affidavits from family, friends, or colleagues who refuted their alleged crimes before the courts. Often, a *Persilschein* was enough to grant a German defendant accused of Nazism a certificate of good standing, which allowed the person to return to a job or, in the case of a tycoon, to regain control over a business empire and board positions. Of course, Günther needed far more than one *Persilschein.* Whereas his lawyer clearly had a hand in drafting Ello's affidavit, Günther personally instructed his younger brother Werner, who was

Ello's ex-husband, that "no promises or mention of any money matters" were to be made in obtaining further exculpatory statements from her and others in order to keep up an appearance of integrity.

In late October 1946, Harald sent a statement from the British prisoner-of-war camp in Benghazi, confirming the "facts" in Ello's affidavit: "I was never a member or candidate of the NSDAP. This rejection of the party and its organizations is due <u>solely</u> to my father's influence. I could afford it, because as 'Dr. Goebbels's stepson,' I wasn't often asked about such things." Harald longed for a fresh start. He considered traveling, or even immigrating to Australia, New Zealand, or Egypt once he was set free. But he soon changed his mind. By early 1947, the twenty-five-year-old was ready to return to Germany. Harald witnessed the release of dozens of his war comrades, but his turn had not yet come. "It's just not fun anymore. One wants to go home, to be a human being among humans again, and not a prisoner of war among a masterful people, who are very friendly, but never for a moment forget that one was 'a member of the defeated former Wehrmacht,'" Harald wrote to his father.

The most valuable kind of *Persilschein* was written by someone with a Jewish background or connection; such persons came to be known by the crass colloquialism "alibi Jews." Some provided a statement of support with genuine feeling. In October 1946, Georg Sachs, a former arms executive who had worked for Günther, wrote a letter from the United States to a DWM board member. Günther had supported Sachs financially so the man could flee Nazi Germany in 1936. Sachs now responded with empathy to Günther's imprisonment: "I feel for Quandt, because he always behaved quite decently. If he wishes, I can issue him an affidavit . . . if he expects difficulties. Has his son escaped the Goebbelses' mass suicide? . . . You can't reasonably expect me to judge the situation in Germany particularly mildly. Of course, I feel sorry for the many people who, through no direct fault of their own, are now experiencing such awful difficulties. But, on the other hand, any educated or uneducated person should have soon realized what swine were in power." Günther very much wanted Sachs's affidavit. And Sachs, now a professor of physical metallurgy in Cleveland, Ohio, gave it. He testified that Günther had arranged for a "generous financial arrangement," which helped him move his family and their belongings. Sachs now wished "sincerely that Dr. Quandt will not be considered as a war criminal."

While he was being held in Moosburg's internment camp, Günther started writing a memoir. He wrote about his childhood, his start as an entrepreneur, his foreign travels, and his conquest of various companies during the Weimar Republic. He devoted almost thirty pages to life with Magda, taking the opportunity in the end to paint himself as a victim of the Nazis because, in contrast to his ex-wife and Goebbels's fanaticism, he did not support Hitler and his ideas. He wrote almost nothing about his business activities during the Third Reich. He did mention, three times, his arms business, Deutsche Waffen- und Munitionsfabriken, though he referred to it solely by the acronym DWM, which sounded rather bland, with no military overtones. Furthermore, he insinuated that the firm made only locomotives, industrial parts, and machines. Günther couldn't help but gloat that DWM's overall number of "employees" had grown to 150,000 during the war, yet he failed to mention the tens of thousands pressed into forced and slave labor at his plants. He did allude to the extra hard work that the war expansion had required of him and his "employees," but proudly wrote in conclusion: "It sufficed."

The memoir was Günther's unsubtle attempt to whitewash himself, conceal his role in the Third Reich, and get on the good side of the Americans as the Nuremberg trials approached. He apportioned an entire chapter to his travels across the United States and his admiration for the country, concluding on a schmaltzy note: "America! How often I think: the rise of this continent is one of the most wonderful chapters in the history of mankind." Elsewhere Günther admitted that, given his vast wealth and connections, he could have left Nazi Germany whenever he wanted to, but even though he had never served in a war, he fashioned himself a loyal soldier: "A businessman like me could have broken away. I had friends abroad, in North and South America, who would have taken me in at any time. But I would have considered that desertion. I remained at my post. I was in close contact with my closest colleagues, took care of the large number of my workers and staff and tried to keep the factories and companies entrusted to me intact."

Even Günther's sole reflection on his "guilt" cast him in a positive light. He wrote about reading Hitler's *Mein Kampf* early on, whereas his fellow Germans did not: "In it was written what we would face if this man joined the government. It spoke not only of work and bread, but also of war and oppression of other peoples. Unfortunately, most Germans didn't read this book in time. Had they done so, we might have been spared the most terrible chapter in German history. I reproach myself for not having taken Hitler seriously. If me and some other people had printed an excerpt from *Mein Kampf* and handed it out by the millions, on the condition that they would read it, we would have gotten off cheaper!"

The mass arms producer wrote that he had welcomed the rebuilding of the German armed forces in the 1930s "because I believed that it was the only way to curb the arbitrary rule of the party. That it would one day be used for a new world war, I held as impossible for a long time. Hitler's repeated assertions that he wanted peace deceived me."

Germany's defeat had cost Günther materially. For starters, some of the businesses he had Aryanized were returned to their rightful owners or the surviving heirs. Günther also mourned the loss of his Berlin townhouse, his Severin estate, and his "machinery," battery, and textile factories. Many were destroyed, seized, or lay in Soviet-occupied territory. "I admit that these losses do not weigh much in view of the general catastrophe that has befallen the German people. Nevertheless, it hurts me deeply," Günther wrote, in a faint attempt to dispel his self-pity. "In every lost factory, in every machine, considerations, plans and hopes were invested." He wrote to a friend that the number of people dead was "bad" but also questioned "who even had the slightest idea how many victims the Nazis had on their conscience?"

Life in the Moosburg camp, which held more than ten thousand German prisoners, was tough on the aging mogul. Günther shared a barrack with about a hundred men. He got up at 5:30 a.m. to have the washroom, which had only two water taps, to himself. The industrialist ate from a tin can and wore ill-fitting camp clothes and shoes that were too big; he made them fit by using eight cardboard inlays. His back was getting crooked from sitting on benches and stools without backrests for weeks on end.

To avoid "pondering his fate," he attended evening lectures offered by the camp's school: "Tibet 3x, East Africa 2x, China 1x, 6x agriculture, music theory 2x, pedagogy 2x, European-American educational circle 6x, India 2x, Christian religions over time 3x, and at least 20x medicine from 7–8."

By mid-September 1946, US and German investigations into Günther's empire were continuing unabated, and no indictment against him had yet been filed. Instead, he was transferred from camp to camp, including one located on the grounds of the former Dachau concentration camp. Circumstances there had much improved since the Nazis left. "Central heating, large washrooms, which you have to yourself, if you get up at 6 o'clock sharp, not difficult since 21–6 night, 13–15 midday rest. Running cold water, hot water three times a week," Günther wrote to a friend. When the mogul was brought to the Dachau Military Hospital because of heart problems, he described feeling like a "guest of the U.S. government in the best sanatorium in Germany. It wasn't bad, the beautifully warmed rooms, the running water, the baths and the good and plentiful food. Plus, there is the outstanding medical care."

11.

Father and son Flick were giving their American questioners quite the headache. The interrogations of the two in Frankfurt were proving to be "not very satisfactory, inasmuch as the Flicks were most elusive and contradictory in their responses," according to a memo by US investigators. Flick senior was portraying himself as an opponent and victim of the Nazis, who had been coerced into working with them. He spun the truth of his Aryanizations into a favorable tale: they were deals cut to help Jewish business owners escape the Nazis. Flick also emphasized the supposedly decentralized nature of his conglomerate, pretending that all decision-making responsibility lay with the individual managers. He therefore claimed to have had no hand in the production of arms or the requests for workers to perform forced or slave labor. Flick's lieutenants, most of them arrested by early 1946, stuck to similar lines of defense.

During questioning, Otto-Ernst shifted all responsibility for the working and living conditions of these laborers at the Rombach steel complex to
the Nazi authorities and his fellow managers. The *Ostarbeiter* were housed
in rooms that were "almost too beautiful," the Flick heir declared during
one interrogation. Otto-Ernst said that he had wanted to have as little involvement as possible with their working conditions, but he claimed to
have noticed that "the *Ostarbeiter* could walk around freely" and "how well
fed the people looked. The food was excellent. Barbed wire fencing? I don't
know." Otto-Ernst denied that any difference in pay existed between regular workers and those who did forced labor: "In principle, the Reich had
the policy of equal work, equal performance, it was completely irrelevant
who did the work."

In response to Otto-Ernst's bizarre answers, Josif Marcu, an American
investigator assigned to the Flicks, threatened him with forced labor or
ten years in prison if he continued to lie. It had no effect. Instead, the Flick
heir complained about being imprisoned along the same hallway as the
notorious SS slaughterers Oswald Pohl and Otto Ohlendorf. Ironically,
those same men had been, with Otto-Ernst's father, members of Himmler's
Circle of Friends. Flick senior had even attended a presentation by Ohlendorf at Goebbels's Ministry of Propaganda in 1943, where, supported by
film shot on the eastern front, Ohlendorf spoke about his service as commander of Einsatzgruppe D, responsible for the massacre of more than
ninety thousand people, mostly Jews, in the Soviet Union.

In March 1946, the chief prosecutor, Robert H. Jackson, appointed
Telford Taylor as his deputy for the first and main Nuremberg trial. Taylor would also preside over the Subsequent Proceedings Division, which
formed the basis for the Office of Chief of Council for War Crimes, an
American prosecuting authority in Germany partly tasked with investigating big business. That month, Josif Marcu informed the press of Flick's
official arrest, calling him the "greatest single power behind the Nazi war
machine." He strongly endorsed the idea of trying the tycoon, along with
other industrialists.

When he finally submitted his findings to the affable, Harvard Law
School–educated Taylor, Marcu made it clear that Flick was a strong can-

didate for Nuremberg. Marcu called Flick "the modern self-made German Robber Baron," who "was characterized by a perverse desire for absolute power. His industrial rise was based on unscrupulous and ruthless operations; he supported individuals and acts now condemned by an indignant world; he deprived honest workers of the fruits of their labor; he participated in aryanization programs of tremendous scales; in spoliation of goods and properties in countries brutally attached and subjugated; he used tens of thousands of male and female slave laborers dragged forcibly away from their homes and countries. He was the largest individual producer of armaments for the Nazi war of conquest." Concluding his memo to Taylor, Marcu stated that Flick, "who employed Ukrainian slave labor at his spoliated properties in France and French slave labor on his spoliated plants in the Ukraine, the man who tore down the national frontiers of Europe to further his own personal desire for power," belonged in the dock at Nuremberg.

In November 1946, father and son Flick were transferred from OMGUS's decartelization branch in Frankfurt to Nuremberg's war crimes section. This move occurred a month after the final verdicts in the first Nuremberg trial had been handed down. Flick's old comrade Hermann Göring was sentenced to death, but he committed suicide the night before his execution was to occur. In his place, the former Nazi minister of foreign affairs Joachim von Ribbentrop became the first of the Nuremberg convicts to be executed by hanging. Von Ribbentrop's social climbing ended at the gallows. The slave driver Fritz Sauckel was hanged one hour later. Robert Ley, who had funded Ferdinand Porsche's Volkswagen factory, also committed suicide before the trial began. Günther Quandt's old friend Walther Funk was sentenced to twenty years in prison, as was Porsche's wartime rival Albert Speer. The former Chancellor Franz von Papen, whose desire for revenge had brought Hitler to power, was acquitted, as was Flick's friend Hjalmar Schacht, the former Reichsbank president.

Flick had already hired Schacht's trial lawyer to mount his own defense. But there was still no indictment. It wasn't even clear if there would be a trial at all. Nevertheless, Flick was preparing to put up a fight.

As the main trial at Nuremberg ended, it became clear that a second one, led by the Allies and focused on German businessmen, wasn't going to happen. The acquittal of Hjalmar Schacht had set a bad precedent, for one thing. Furthermore, the Allies worried about "a Soviet-dominated, anti-capitalist show trial" and a lack of public appetite for another lengthy set of cases, which might "detract from the real achievements of the first" Nuremberg trial. The war-weary British were also concerned about additional financial costs. Instead, the Americans would go it alone. Telford Taylor, who succeeded Robert H. Jackson as chief prosecutor, agreed to oversee twelve subsequent trials at Nuremberg—solely under the purview of the United States—including three against German industrialists and executives. An important question remained: which of them would Taylor pick?

12.

In early November 1945, a French army lieutenant paid a visit to the Porsche-Piëch estate in Austria's Zell am See. The American and British authorities had recently released Ferdinand Porsche, his son, Ferry, and his son-in-law, Anton Piëch, pending further investigation. Now the French officer approached the trio with an invitation. A French commission, headed by the Communist minister of industry, wanted to work with Ferdinand Porsche on developing a French version of the Volkswagen, aided by the state-owned Renault company, which had been nationalized after its collaboration with the Nazis.

Eager to again work with a government, Porsche promptly provided reams of drawings and technical data to the French. He then started negotiating with the commission in Baden-Baden, the base of the French occupation authorities and close to Germany's border with France. In mid-December 1945, Porsche, Piëch, and Ferry traveled to Baden-Baden for the second round of negotiations. There, plainclothes French army officers suddenly arrested them on suspicion of war crimes.

As it turned out, Porsche's competitor Peugeot, after catching wind of the negotiations, had complained to the government. According to Peugeot, it was unpatriotic for the French to reach out to Ferdinand Porsche, given his prior relationship with Hitler and the Volkswagen's association with the Nazis. (What Peugeot actually feared was increased competition from Renault.) More damning, though, was Peugeot's accusation that Porsche and Piëch had committed war crimes. Seven managers at a French Peugeot plant looted by Volkswagen had been deported to concentration camps; three of them were killed. And all this while Porsche and Piëch were in charge of the Volkswagen complex, where thousands of French civilians and soldiers were pressed into forced and slave labor. But, as was typical of the Allied authorities, the tycoons' brutal labor practices weren't even a point of interest for the French government.

Instead, it was the deportation of Peugeot's staff and the accusation of murder that prompted French forces to arrest the trio and detain them in Baden-Baden. Ferry was released from jail in March 1946 but was kept under house arrest in a rural village in the Black Forest until July, when he was finally allowed to return to Austria. Meanwhile, Porsche and Piëch were moved to the outskirts of Paris, where they were held in the servants' quarters of a villa formerly owned by the Renault family. Instead of spending his pretrial detention in jail, Porsche was asked to give advice on the development of the Renault 4CV. Although Porsche contributed to crucial aspects of the minicar's design, Renault's CEO told the government that Porsche had done a miserable job. The company's director, a hero of the French Resistance, couldn't bear seeing the German star designer, accused of committing war crimes against French compatriots, receive a sliver of credit for helping design the French car. In mid-February 1947, Porsche and Piëch were moved from the Paris suburbs to a harsh military prison in Dijon to await trial.

With the two men in prison, Porsche's children, Louise Piëch and Ferry, had to save the family business on their own. It was facing serious challenges. The Porsche plant in Stuttgart — abandoned since the clan and its employees fled to Austria — was being used as a car repair shop for the US Army after it, along with Ferdinand Porsche's private assets, fell under American property control. Given the family's flight to Austria, the

Americans were seriously considering liquidation of the Porsche firm in Germany. Meanwhile, Ferdinand Porsche's application to become an Austrian citizen was rejected because he was in custody. Citizenship would have allowed him to transfer his firm and assets out of US property control to Austria, but alas. He would need to find another way to slip past the Americans.

Desperate times called for desperate measures. In early 1947, the Porsche siblings decided to formally split the family business. Louise had retained Austrian citizenship through her marriage with Anton Piëch. She incorporated a new firm in Salzburg, under the Porsche name, to which the family's Austrian assets were transferred. Ferry held on to his German citizenship to save the Porsche company in Stuttgart. But because of the Americans' property control, Ferry had to undertake this from the safety of the company's Austrian base in the Alps, where he was busy fulfilling his father's dream of designing the first sports car bearing the family name: the Porsche 356.

From prison, Anton Piëch wrote to his Porsche cofounder, Adolf Rosenberger, asking for a thousand dollars to help him and Ferdinand Porsche make bail. This, after the two had Aryanized Rosenberger's stake in Porsche more than a decade earlier. Now Piëch offered Rosenberger the Porsche patent license in the United States, though Piëch had coldly rejected Rosenberger's request for it in 1938. Rosenberger had immigrated to America in 1940 and was living under the name Alan Robert in Los Angeles. After the war, Rosenberger had sent a telegram to Louise Piëch. In her response, Louise expressed the hope that business relations with him might resume after the property control was lifted. They were soon writing to each other regularly. Rosenberger also corresponded with Ferry and even sent care packages to their family estate. Rosenberger clearly hoped to be part of the company once again.

With Ferdinand Porsche and Anton Piëch facing trial in France, and the next generation fighting for the survival of the Porsche company, it seemed that the Jewish Rosenberger might actually return to the car design firm he had cofounded.

13.

After having spent a year in the limbo of internment camps, Günther Quandt was told in mid-September 1947 that he wasn't going to be among the tycoons indicted in Nuremberg's trials of industrialists. Instead, the sixty-six-year-old was transferred to German jurisdiction by Telford Taylor's war crimes office, along with all evidence compiled against him. "Among the first 30 turned over to the Germans . . . was Guenther Quandt, German armaments manufacturer and former husband of Mrs. Paul Joseph Goebbels," the Associated Press wrote on October 27, 1947, covering the handover at Dachau. A prosecutor in Starnberg had filed an indictment against Günther. He stood accused of being a major offender during the Nazi regime, but only on the charge of having profited from producing arms and ammunition.

As the Cold War commenced in early 1947, the Truman administration's priorities began to shift from punishing Germany to enabling its economic recovery. In short, the United States wanted a bulwark against Communist expansion in Europe, and the western part of Germany, which had the potential to become Europe's largest economy, might serve as the key to containing the Soviet Union and reviving the rest of the continent. Secretary of State George C. Marshall soon announced his namesake aid plan, which gave Germany and other Western European countries the sum of $15 billion. OMGUS's military governor, Lucius D. Clay, replaced America's punitive occupation policy with one aimed at German self-governance. The US and UK occupation zones in western Germany had already merged to coordinate this shift in policy.

Momentous changes ensued. Allied authorities accelerated a handover of suspected war criminals and Nazi sympathizers to so-called German denazification courts, which were regional judicial panels with a setup similar to a criminal trial. Defendants hired their own lawyers if they could afford one. But given the overwhelming number of the accused, the judges and prosecutors were largely, and crucially, laymen, except in the most serious cases. An indicted individual would be charged as a major offender, an offender, a lesser offender, or a follower. If a defendant was convicted, the punishment would be prison, labor camp, a fine, or some combination of these. Those acquitted were categorized as "person exonerated."

Naturally, most Germans were none too keen on judging their own compatriots, who were being tried for crimes and political convictions that many of those sitting in judgment had participated in themselves. Nor did the millions of defendants feel particularly inclined to tell the truth about their Nazi sympathies or their transgressions during the war. Countless crimes and secrets remained buried.

Even after the handover, Günther was kept in Dachau. He was considered a flight risk and was moved to a part of the camp where other German war-crime suspects were awaiting denazification trials. From there, Günther went on the offensive. In late October 1947, he wrote a letter to his lawyer, claiming that he had abandoned weapons production at DWM after he bought the firm in 1928 and returned to arms manufacturing only when the Nazi authorities had ordered him to, in 1943. Günther's lawyer conveyed this brazen lie, along with several affidavits supporting it, to the Starnberg court. The ploy worked. In early December 1947, the prosecutor in Starnberg lessened the charge against Günther from major offender to offender, though on unclear legal grounds. Günther was also moved from Dachau to a more comfortable internment camp in Garmisch-Partenkirchen, a mountain town on the border with Austria.

But that wasn't enough for Günther. On January 10, 1948, he wrote another letter to the Starnberg court, complaining that he had been "imprisoned for over 1 1/2 years without any real reason." He asked to be released immediately and tried as a lesser offender, shamelessly maintaining in the letter that his "party membership came about under extortionate circumstances" and that he had been "persecuted by the national-socialist government for years in the most serious manner."

Günther was released ten days later, pending further proceedings. The Starnberg court let him go without bail. They inexplicably no longer considered him a flight risk. That same month, Julius Herf was appointed as the new prosecutor in the case. Günther had a mighty opponent in Herf, a prominent public plaintiff. The "stone-cold logician" had prosecuted members of the SA in Berlin before 1933 and was now in charge of Bavaria's most high-profile denazification cases. With his "biting wit, sharp formulations and cutting prosecutorial tone," and his natty suits (he kept a small perfumed cloth in his jacket pocket), Herf was feared across Germany.

On February 8, 1948, Herf filed a revised indictment against Günther in Starnberg's court. Offering far more substance than the initial charge had, Herf began by stating that even if Günther's NSDAP membership was the result of Goebbels's extortion, the mogul "didn't suffer any disadvantages from the alleged enmity of the party. No obstacle was put in the way of the consolidation and expansion of his commercial or industrial interests." In fact, Günther "received the full support of the competent Reich authorities in his business interests," Herf argued. To underline this, the prosecutor listed twenty-nine executive positions that Günther held in Nazi Germany at the firms he controlled, such as AFA and DWM, as well as his supervisory board posts at Deutsche Bank, Daimler-Benz, and AEG.

In addition to citing the mogul's arms and ammo production, Herf centered the case against Günther on the mogul's failed expropriation of a majority stake in Tudor, a Brussels-based battery business. Herf did this despite having much documentary evidence of other successful and attempted Aryanizations and expropriations across Nazi-occupied Europe undertaken by Günther, his son Herbert, and their AFA aides. All because, unlike these other cases, for this one Herf had a key witness, Léon Laval, Tudor's largest shareholder. Günther and his associates had pressured Laval to sell his stake while he was in the custody of the Gestapo and while his son was being held captive in a concentration camp.

In late February 1948, Günther replaced one inexperienced lawyer with another; this one had only just been admitted to the bar. It was a bad sign; the trial loomed close. Günther's new lawyer obtained a one-month trial postponement to familiarize himself with the case and to buy time. The defense strategy was aggressive. In response to Herf's indictment, Günther wrote a 164-page biography and rebuttal, demanding to be exonerated. Günther contended that Herf's claims were based on circumstantial evidence and "pseudo-arguments." He added about thirty *Persilscheine* to his file, including affidavits from Herbert and other close business associates, who attested to Günther's moral fiber and to their own. The gang of men who had been so foundational to the Quandt empire's mass arms production, Aryanization strategy, and use of slave labor were now rallying to scrub the record clean.

14.

Günther's denazification trial in Starnberg opened on April 13, 1948. One week before it started, he moved from Bavaria to a small prefab house in Stuttgart, in Ferdinand Porsche's neighborhood. Günther would commute to Starnberg on trial days; eight were planned, from mid-April to late July. Harald and Herbert were set to testify in person. Harald had been released from the British POW camp in Benghazi in April 1947. The twenty-six-year-old had spent half of his life so far living in the Goebbels household, on the front lines, and in prison camp. Now he was laboring as a welder, bricklayer, and foundry worker, but he would soon start studying mechanical engineering in Hannover. Since Harald had never joined the Nazi Party, he didn't have to go through denazification.

Harald's half brother, Herbert, had been "denazified" in late 1946, in Hannover. Herbert — who had voluntarily became a Nazi Party member, was involved with Aryanizations in France, helped plan and build a sub-concentration camp in Lower Silesia, and was responsible for staffing at a Berlin battery factory in which hundreds of female concentration-camp prisoners were abused — was exonerated by a denazification panel unaware of these offenses. The judges ruled that the heir had "never actively supported the party, but, on the contrary, openly criticized the party's policies." Herbert was free to go.

Günther's sons were among the first to testify as defense witnesses. Harald spoke about how Goebbels had disparaged his father for not being a Nazi, while Herbert described fights between Günther and Magda related to her anti-Semitism. Soon after the siblings had done their part for their father, Léon Laval came to the stand. Herf hadn't done himself any favors by building his case around Laval. The Tudor situation was complex, and Laval was no perfect witness. He had a well-connected Nazi contact during the attempted Tudor takeover in Herbert Göring, the *Reichsmarschall*'s corrupt half brother, a fact that did not improve the optics for the prosecution. Even less helpful was Laval's dislike of Günther. He held the mogul responsible for his arrests by the Gestapo. Laval had no proof of this, but his indignation colored the trial; testimonies devolved into shouting matches. Laval's own lawyer admonished him for his emotional behavior and for calling several associates to the witness stand who then proceeded to undermine the case.

Günther witnessed all of this with glee. He believed his "complete rehabilitation" was almost a given. In his closing arguments, Herf argued that Günther had tried to force Laval to sell his shares when he was at his most defenseless. The prosecutor also invoked Günther's efforts at Aryanization and expropriation across Nazi-occupied Europe to show that the mogul's "quest for power" covered the continent; it went beyond Laval and Tudor. Herf recommended that Günther, as a supporter of the Nazis and a profiteer, be ruled an offender, fined 500,000 deutsch marks, and sentenced to a labor camp for one and a half years, with credit given for time served.

The Starnberg court didn't agree. In its ruling on July 28, 1948, Günther's sixty-seventh birthday, he was classified as a mere follower of the Nazis. His only punishment: paying for the trial costs. The court deemed Günther an "apolitical human" who had wholly rejected Nazism. While his quarrels with Magda and Goebbels couldn't be viewed as "active resistance," the judges believed that the propaganda minister had forced Günther to become a member of the Nazi Party. The lay court also didn't consider the industrialist to have been a beneficiary of Hitler's regime. The judges ruled that Günther "refused to harness the factories he directed to the service of the tyrants' armament policy" — though he in fact had been one of the largest producers of weapons in the entire Third Reich. According to the court, his Aryanization efforts across Europe couldn't be seen as "an unacceptable expansion policy"; but the judges took a negative view of Léon Laval, declaring that he had turned a business quarrel into a political issue.

The many affidavits given in Günther's support, particularly those provided by people with a Jewish background or connection, also impressed
the judges. Those testimonies spoke to Günther's "human disposition," the
court thought. To top it all off, the judges concluded that "foreigners were
properly taken care of" in Günther's firms. Only one victim of forced labor
had come forward as a witness to testify otherwise, and he hadn't accused
Günther of any personal wrongdoing, the court (falsely) concluded.

Herf appealed the ruling. The related hearings took place in Munich
in late April 1949, and Günther himself wasn't present, for health reasons.
In his closing arguments, Herf invoked Max Weber's book *The Protestant
Ethic and the Spirit of Capitalism* to explain Günther's personality: "It's the
intoxication of the pursuit of power, the intoxication of building a huge
corporation, the obsession with self-affirmation that is at the root of all
this, and it's the belief in the value of one's own work, not only because
work is something moral, but because building the corporation is the ultimate good, and because anything that resists building it out is bad," the
prosecutor contended.

Herf repeated his recommendation for the sentencing of Günther. But
the Bavarian appellate chamber upheld the lower court's verdict. There
was no "clear proof" that Günther had procured "excessive advantages" for
himself, the court ruled. However, the judges conceded that the assessment
was difficult "in the case of a man who has proven throughout his life that
he knows how to build up a great fortune and a great economic power."

On May 23, 1949, four weeks after the verdict of the Munich appeals
court, the country officially split in two: the Federal Republic of Germany,
informally called West Germany, came to merge three occupation zones
— American, British, and French — into a new self-governing state, with
its capital in Bonn and with Chancellor Konrad Adenauer as its leader. The
previous summer, the deutsch mark had replaced the reichsmark as the
country's official currency, to help halt rampant inflation. The Soviet-occupied zone was soon established as the German Democratic Republic,
better known as East Germany, with East Berlin as the capital of this Communist state.

Herf appealed the verdict on Günther one last time. In December 1949,

Bavaria's court of cassation upheld the decision of the appeals chamber, concluding that in Günther's case there was no "conclusive proof of guilt." Though the mogul was initially upset that he wasn't fully exonerated, he soon praised the ruling as a "most brilliant judgment."

But Günther wasn't in the clear just yet. That same December, he came under investigation in Berlin for the mistreatment of laborers at his Pertrix factory, where, among many others, some five hundred female concentration-camp prisoners were used and held in a nearby subcamp during the final stages of the war. Günther claimed he had visited the battery plant only twice during the war and denied having any knowledge of "a so-called *Judenlager*" (Jew camp) at Pertrix. He protected his son Herbert too; a similar investigation in Berlin, concerning Herbert's actions at Pertrix, had led nowhere. In a letter to his lawyer, Günther lied some more and wrote that Herbert, as the firm's commercial director during the war, hadn't been responsible for staffing. In truth, Herbert would have had "precise knowledge" of the use of forced and slave labor at the factory, a historian later concluded.

On February 24, 1950, a Berlin denazification court ruled to rehabilitate Günther, after the city's remaining Jewish community gave no objection. The mogul charged the 29,500 deutsch marks in lawyer fees to AFA and went back to work. Günther was a free man. A new decade had started, and with that a new era for Germany, one of massive prosperity and grave silence.

15.

Though Julius Herf had been forced to accept Günther Quandt's quasi acquittal, the dogged attorney wasn't finished with the profiteers of the Third Reich. He had another chance at justice in his prosecution of one Baron August von Finck. Despite heavy scrutiny from American investigators, Bavaria's richest man wasn't, in the end, a serious contender for a trial at Nuremberg. In early November 1948, Herf indicted von Finck as an offender: a committed Nazi who had raised twenty million reichsmarks for Hitler's art museum. The regime had lavishly rewarded von Finck for his efforts, Herf showed. His Aryanizations of two banks, Berlin's Dreyfus and Vienna's Rothschild, quadrupled the balance sheet of his private bank, Merck Finck: from 22.5 million reichsmarks in 1933 to 99.2 million reichsmarks in 1944.

The denazification trial against von Finck took place in Munich in late December 1948. The main witness against the banker was Willy Dreyfus. Although Dreyfus and von Finck had come to a swift private settlement in October 1946, they hadn't been allowed to execute it; they had to settle in formal restitution proceedings under American occupation law. After the restitution law was put in place in November 1947, the two men reopened negotiations. In August 1948, after exhaustive talks, they came to an agreement that exactly mirrored the one they had concluded two years earlier.

Dreyfus was to receive shares to restore what Merck Finck had underpaid for the Berlin branch of his bank, as were the surviving relatives of Dreyfus's former partner, Paul Wallich. Dreyfus held that Wallich, who committed suicide after the Aryanization, "suffered indignities at the hands of the management of Merck, Finck & Co., which . . . contributed lagerly [*sic*] to breaking his spirit." But then Dreyfus moved to change one final passage in the settlement, which would have forced him and Wallich's relatives to return all restitution shares if a future German law nullified the settlement. Seeing a chance to regain shares that were slipping away, von Finck backtracked. All of a sudden, he claimed that the American restitution law wasn't applicable to their settlement and any insinuation that his bank was responsible for Wallich's suicide was offensive. The agreement was off.

On December 22, 1948, at the trial's start, the usually relentless Herf, for reasons that weren't clear, changed the category of von Finck's indictment from offender to lesser offender. That same day in court, von Finck denied all charges. According to the financier, the Dreyfus transaction had been concluded in good faith in 1938, and his bank's acquisition of Rothschild was meant to protect the owners' assets from the Nazis. He argued that his fundraising efforts as the chairman of the museum's board of trustees, to which he was appointed on Hitler's explicit instruction, hadn't been an expression of Nazi sympathies. Rather, it was just a good way to promote his business interests, von Finck contended. He claimed that networking also accounted for his bank's growth during the Nazi era.

About forty *Persilscheine* had been submitted to the court, each attesting to von Finck's apolitical, even anti-Nazi stance; they included several affidavits from former colleagues and clients who were Jewish. This defensive move had become all too common in denazification proceedings. But then von Finck's trial took a series of strange turns. It was unusual enough that Herf had reduced the seriousness of the indictment against the banker. Then, allegedly incriminating correspondence, confiscated from the baron's estate by US investigators, disappeared from the court dossier; the judges suddenly ordered the part of the trial that dealt with the Rothschild Aryanization to be handled behind closed doors, "for reasons of state security"; prosecution witnesses who had been summoned to testify against von Finck failed to appear in court or suddenly reversed the substance of their testimony before the judges.

A former confidant of von Finck later told *Der Spiegel* magazine that one potential prosecution witness, "who knew a lot and hated Finck," was paid the staggering sum of 500,000 deutsch marks (about $120,000 at the time) not to appear in court. The bribe was said to have been paid without the knowledge of the frugal financier.

The subterfuge didn't stop there. Julius Herf was gay — this was already an open secret. In the early 1930s, the nickname of the criminal prosecutor in Berlin's underworld had been Schwule Jule, or "Gay Jules." Just before von Finck's trial commenced, someone showed up at Herf's office and openly alluded to the lawyer's sexual orientation; he also "betrayed knowledge of certain details of a very delicate nature, the disclosure of which would have been devastating for the prosecutor," the erstwhile confidant of von Finck told *Der Spiegel*. "His conduct before the court must be considered in this light." Homosexual acts were a criminal offense in Germany (and remained so until 1994), and much gossiped about. Rumors circulated about Herf's and other prosecutors' involvement with younger men, and no doubt von Finck's henchmen were eager to exploit them.

In addition to lessening the charges against von Finck, Herf also announced, near the end of the trial, that he would no longer consider the

Rothschild Aryanization in his closing arguments, claiming to believe the banker's defense that he seized the company to protect its assets. Whereas Willy Dreyfus's testimony was considered credible, another key prosecution witness, a half-Jewish Dreyfus director initially retained by Merck Finck after the Aryanization, was dismissed as an unreliable drunk by former colleagues.

On January 14, 1949, Munich's denazification court ruled that von Finck was just a follower of the Nazis and ordered him to pay two thousand deutsch marks to a general restitution fund. The judges sided with the banker, accepting the claim that his role at the museum hadn't been an expression of Nazi sympathies; it was solely for promotion of his own business interests. The court agreed that Dreyfus had suffered serious economic disadvantages as a result of the Nazi regime's discriminatory laws but also held that von Finck wasn't personally responsible for those laws, nor did he take advantage of the situation. The judges determined that in the Rothschild case, von Finck "behaved in such an exemplary manner that every word about it to the contrary is too much." According to the court, the fifty-year-old financier had conducted himself as a "royal merchant" who actually put himself in considerable danger vis-à-vis the Nazi authorities in the transaction. The judges went so far as to call his "efforts" in the Rothschild matter "active resistance."

Herf soon regretted giving in to blackmail. One month after the ruling, the prosecutor filed an appeal against von Finck. But again, the same visitor showed up at his office with the same veiled threats. A week after Herf filed the appeal, he withdrew it without explanation, in a terse one-sentence note to the Munich court.

As for von Finck, he wasn't completely satisfied with the trial's outcome and appealed his sentence. He applied for amnesty based on a World War I knee injury, to avoid paying any restitution. The amnesty was granted. Von Finck was "denazified" and returned to work.

Herf and Dreyfus weren't so lucky. Soon after the trial, Herf was suspended as a public prosecutor on charges of homosexual "offenses," after flirty letters he had written to younger men were leaked to the public. In 1951, according to Dreyfus, his own lawyer went behind his back and settled with von Finck for a fraction of the initial agreement. The baron had stalled the deal long enough for the balance of power to shift in his favor. Dreyfus then pursued a case against von Finck in American courts. His litigation proceeded all the way up to the Supreme Court, but in 1976 the Court refused to hear the case. Willy Dreyfus died the next year, at the age of ninety-one.

16.

The denazification of Rudolf-August Oetker never even went to trial. He was "denazified" by an internal subcommittee at his own company after he appealed his dismissal as CEO of Dr. Oetker; British authorities had stripped him of his position because he had been a Waffen-SS officer. On April 9, 1947, his case came before Dr. Oetker's denazification panel in Bielefeld, which was made up entirely of company employees. The thirty-year-old's bogus defense went like this: He had been ordered to leave the Wehrmacht's catering service to join the Waffen-SS. He then applied to regain the rank of officer, which he had lost after being "forcibly" moved to the Waffen-SS. He did this because he had been told that the rank of officer was a prerequisite to becoming a company director.

Many *Persilscheine* had already been submitted on Rudolf-August's behalf. Now several employees of Dr. Oetker testified in his favor before the panel. There were no witnesses for the prosecution because "no one noticed any political activity" from the company heir. The five-member denazification committee accepted Rudolf-August's explanation and exonerated him, noting that in addition to being compelled to join the Waffen-SS, he had also been declared unfit for military service.

A few months later, British authorities confirmed his exoneration. In August 1947, Rudolf-August was reinstated as Dr. Oetker's CEO, after an absence of more than two years. His majority stake in the company was released from British property control the next month. Days later, Rudolf-August cleared the final hurdle. On September 20, 1947, Rudolf-August's thirty-first birthday, the British-appointed trustee was officially dismissed from his oversight of Dr. Oetker. Rudolf-August was back in control of his family's baking goods firm. The pudding prince would rise again.

17.

Seven weeks earlier, on July 31, 1947, Ferdinand Porsche and Anton Piëch were released from Dijon's military prison after Louise Piëch put up one million French francs in bail. The men had been in near-constant detention for two years now. They returned to Austria, where they were allowed to wait out a trial in France on war crime charges. The two had been indicted for the looting of a Peugeot factory, which had been expropriated by Volkswagen, and for the deportation of seven Peugeot plant managers to concentration camps — three of them were killed.

On May 5, 1948, a military tribunal in Dijon acquitted Porsche and Piëch. The case, already considered weak, collapsed after French witnesses testified in the tycoons' favor. The court found that neither man had played a role in the looting of the Peugeot factory nor in the deportation of its managers. It was said that both had actually lobbied for the release of prisoners. Not even mentioned in the trial: Porsche and Piëch's use of thousands of French civilians and soldiers as forced and slave labor at the Volkswagen complex.

During the two men's detention, the siblings Ferry and Louise were busy saving their family business by formally splitting it in two: Louise Piëch incorporated a new firm under the Porsche name in Salzburg, while Ferry revived the original Porsche company in Stuttgart. One question, however, remained: what to do with Volkswagen? The factory complex in Fallersleben had come under control of the British military, who renamed the town built around the plant, calling it Wolfsburg, and began mass-producing the original Volkswagen. Hitler's "people's car" was becoming the much-beloved Beetle. Still, Ferdinand Porsche had designed it, and during the war he had negotiated an initial remuneration contract with Volkswagen in the event that the car ever went into mass production.

That moment had at long last arrived. In mid-September 1948, a few months after Ferdinand Porsche and Anton Piëch were acquitted in France, the families entered into negotiations with the new Volkswagen CEO, Heinrich Nordhoff. The British-appointed executive also had a rather tainted recent history. Like Ferdinand Porsche, Günther Quandt, and Friedrich Flick, Nordhoff had been appointed *Wehrwirtschaftsführer* by the Nazi regime while serving as a car executive at Opel, where he had used some two thousand people as forced labor. But after Nordhoff's denazification, the British authorities disregarded his past sins.

The negotiations took place in the Bavarian spa town of Bad Reichenhall, bordering Austria and just ten miles north of Hitler's former mountain retreat on the Obersalzberg, where, twelve years earlier, Porsche had presented the test Volkswagens to the führer and convinced him to put the car into production. Now a different agreement was negotiated: how to remunerate Porsche in the years to come for the Volkswagen Beetle he designed.

Enormously, that's how. The car would become a massive success. The Porsche family ended up negotiating a 1 percent licensing fee on every Beetle sold — that would be about 21.5 million models worldwide by the time production stopped, in 2003. What's more, Louise and Anton Piëch's newly incorporated Porsche company in Salzburg received exclusive rights to import Volkswagens. Their company became Austria's largest car dealership and was sold back to Volkswagen for $4.6 billion in 2011. Another formal agreement enhanced the dynasty: Heinrich Nordhoff's daughter soon married a son of Louise and Anton Piëch.

Unlike the other German business dynasties, the Porsche-Piëch clan had entered the Nazi era, in January 1933, on the verge of bankruptcy. Now, in the wake of the war, the Bad Reichenhall deal secured its place alongside the other dynasties and would make the Porsche-Piëchs one of the wealthiest families in both Germany *and* Austria. And all this in mid-September 1948, before the first Porsche sports car was put into production and while the original Porsche factory in Stuttgart — the one that would one day produce millions of the world's most desired cars — was still under property control of the US Army.

From Austria, Ferdinand Porsche wrote: "I mourn my Stuttgart factory . . . every day." Although the American control of Porsche's firm and private assets in Stuttgart was lifted in early March 1949, the release proved to be short-lived. Adolf Rosenberger and the Porsche company had been engaged in a heated legal battle since summer 1948. Rosenberger hadn't returned to the company. The Jewish émigré now wanted restitution — to be reinstated as a shareholder in the firm he had cofounded, with the same stake Ferdinand Porsche and Anton Piëch had acquired from him in their 1935 Aryanization. After the Porsche company consistently refused any settlement, Rosenberger requested another asset freeze on the Stuttgart firm. It was granted in October 1949.

As the case went to court in late September 1950, a lawyer for Porsche and Piëch proposed a settlement to Rosenberger's attorney: fifty thousand deutsch marks plus a car. Rosenberger was offered a choice: a luxury version of the Volkswagen Beetle or a Porsche 356, the first sports car under the family name, designed by Porsche's son, Ferry. Rosenberger hadn't yet returned to Stuttgart. He was still in Los Angeles, caring for his wife, who was ill. So, Rosenberger's lawyer accepted the settlement without consulting him. Instead, he informed Rosenberger by letter after the matter was concluded. The Porsche firm was released from American property control; Rosenberger ended up picking the Volkswagen Beetle.

Ferry had already returned to Stuttgart from Austria with his sports car design. Now his father could at last follow. While the legal battle with Rosenberger raged in June 1949, Ferdinand Porsche had initiated his denazification proceedings. At his estate in Austria, where the denazification measures were generous and lax, he had waited for the zeal back home to wane. His lawyers' line of defense was essentially the same one that so many other Germans had used: "Professor Porsche has always been only a technician, a designer . . . political issues of the day were and still are completely outside his sphere of thought." On August 30, 1949, a denazification court near Stuttgart exonerated the car designer, whom Hitler had once considered his favorite engineer.

Ferdinand Porsche was particularly happy with this because it meant that he didn't have to pay for the court proceedings, which amounted to some thirty-nine thousand deutsch marks. With his firm intermittently under an asset freeze, he had been living off his two children and the rental income from his Stuttgart villa: "I was *entbräunt* free of charge. That 'free of charge' was very important to me," he wrote to a friend some months after the verdict. Because SA uniforms were brown, to be "*entbräunt*," or to have lost one's tan, meant to be "denazified." Ferry, who had been a voluntary SS officer and was also exonerated in a denazification court, was less preoccupied by the colors of his new associates' former Nazi uniforms (SS black and field gray, to be precise). To market the first Porsche sports car, Ferry teamed up with Albert Prinzing, an early member of the NSDAP who had served as an officer in Heydrich's SS security service and had cultivated ties to Mussolini's fascist party in Italy. A true believer, in short. Prinzing had spent three years in Allied custody, until he was judged a lesser offender by a denazification court in May 1948. He was then hired by his childhood friend Ferry as Porsche's commercial director, and along the way he helped Ferdinand Porsche successfully navigate his denazification proceedings.

Prinzing was put in charge of assembling *Persilscheine* for Ferdinand Porsche. The car designer was most grateful to his new employee. In mid-January 1950, Porsche wrote to Prinzing that he was thankful and aware "how hard you worked for us and how much you have contributed to everything that has been achieved." While the frail Porsche was no longer playing a significant role at the car design company that bore his name, the two former SS officers, Ferry and Prinzing, were only just getting started. In November 1949, production of the Porsche 356 began in Stuttgart. Within eighteen months, the factory had churned out five hundred. Prinzing then introduced the Porsche 356 to the United States, the world's largest market for automobiles. It was an enormous success. Wealthy Americans quickly became Porsche's most important clientele outside Germany. In the end, it wasn't the firm's persecuted Jewish cofounder and German émigré Adolf Rosenberger who brought the prized name of Porsche to America. It was Prinzing, a former *SS-Hauptsturmführer*.

18.

While most of the Third Reich's tycoons were walking away with little more than a slap on the wrist, one industrialist notably did not. On March 15, 1947, Friedrich Flick was led into the cramped dock at Nuremberg's Palace of Justice, alongside five of his associates. Telford Taylor, the US chief prosecutor for the trial, read out the indictments against them. Flick and the other defendants were charged with war crimes and crimes against humanity for the mass use of forced and slave labor. Flick and four of the other accused were indicted for the looting of expropriated companies in Nazi-occupied France and parts of the Soviet Union. Flick, his former right-hand man, Otto Steinbrinck, and Flick's cousin Konrad Kaletsch were indicted for several major Aryanizations in Nazi Germany before the war. Flick and Steinbrinck were also indicted for financially supporting the SS and its crimes as members of Himmler's Circle of Friends. The six defendants all pleaded not guilty.

The Flick case was the fifth out of twelve American-led trials at Nuremberg's Military Tribunal, and the first of three trials involving industrialists. The cases against Alfried Krupp, his directors, and the executives of the chemicals conglomerate IG Farben rounded out the business triumvirate. (Nazi economic functionaries Wilhelm Keppler and Paul Pleiger were each sentenced to a decade in prison in the so-called ministries trial.) Flick had been one of the Third Reich's largest arms producers, Aryanizers, and exploiters of forced and slave labor through his steel, coal, and machinery conglomerate. During the war, the number of people coerced into making cannons and shells in Flick's steel factories, or digging coal in his mines, may have been as high as 100,000.

No other tycoon had benefited from Nazi Germany as Flick had. Only Alfried Krupp, the other steel giant, whose trial would commence later that year, and his father, Gustav, who was too senile to stand trial, could compete in magnitude of weapons production and appetite for forced and slave labor. But Flick had built his own industrial empire from the ground up

*Friedrich Flick standing between court marshals
at his Nuremberg trial, 1947.*

in only thirty years, rather than inheriting it over a century, as the Krupps had. Hitler had often publicly invoked the Krupps as a model for German industry — even creating an inheritance law just for them, to regulate succession — but Flick had done it all under the radar, in stealth and silence, since 1933. The press-hating mogul would now, for the first time, be exposed to the entire world.

On April 19, 1947, Flick's trial began in earnest. In his opening statement, Telford Taylor emphasized the broad co-responsibility of German industrialists for Nazi crimes and for keeping Hitler afloat. "A dictatorship is successful, not because everybody opposes it, but because powerful groups support it," he contended. "The Third Reich dictatorship was based on this unholy trinity of Nazism, militarism, and economic imperialism." Taylor then quoted from the speech Hitler had given during the now-infamous February 1933 meeting in Berlin with the group of tycoons that had included Flick, Günther Quandt, and August von Finck, in which the führer had said: "Private enterprise cannot be maintained in the age of democracy." The titans of industry and finance had agreed with the Nazi leader, the attorney declared. As their moral values became corrupt, so did their business practices, Taylor argued.

The prosecutor concluded his opening statement on a stern note:

The story of this case is . . . a story of betrayal. The defendants were men of wealth; many mines and factories were their private property. They will certainly tell you that they believed in the sanctity of private property, and perhaps they will say that they supported Hitler because German communism threatened that concept. But the factories of Rombach and Riga belonged to someone else. The defendants will tell you that they were not anti-Semitic, and even protected individual Jews against the Nazis. Yet it was not beneath them to appear in public with, and pay a king's ransom to Himmler, who all but rendered the Jews extinct in Europe. They fattened on the misfortunes of wealthy Jews. Their mines and factories were worked by human labor and they, of all men, should have understood the true dignity of toil. Yet they turned back the clock and revived slavery in Europe. These men shamelessly betrayed whatever ideals they might have been expected to possess and, in the end, they betrayed Germany. In this lies their true guilt.

Over the next five weeks, Taylor and his deputies presented the prosecution's case against Flick and the five other defendants. There was overwhelming evidence for the use of forced and slave labor in the Flick conglomerate, as well as the firm's Aryanization and expropriation of companies. But it wasn't easy for the prosecutors to pin down Flick and the others who stood accused when it came to individual knowledge of and responsibility for these mass transgressions. The three judges from American state courts didn't help. They struggled at times with the complexity of the case and the reams of corporate documents translated from German.

On July 2, 1947, Flick's lawyer, Rudolf Dix, opened the case for the defense. Flick had beat Günther Quandt to Dix and retained him just after the lawyer had successfully defended Hjalmar Schacht in the main Nuremberg trial. In his opening statement, Dix spoke about the powerlessness of German industry and the accused businessmen in the face of the all-powerful Nazi state. He argued that the regime, not Flick, was responsible for slave labor and Aryanizations. The mogul hadn't plundered the expropriated companies abroad—he had invested in them, Dix contended. And just being a member of a group like Himmler's Circle of Friends could hardly be considered criminal, he said. Overall, Dix argued, the Americans had indicted Flick only to serve as a symbol, a representative of all of German industry.

Three days later, Flick was the first of the accused to take the witness stand. Over the next eleven days, and for up to six hours a day, the aging industrialist defended himself in cross-examination, standing upright the entire time. Flick painted a picture of himself as someone who in 1933 had entered the Nazi era with a target on his back. He said that he was nationally despised after secretly selling his majority stake in the country's largest industrial conglomerate, the VSt, to a weakened German state at the height of the Depression, and at a major premium, no less. He also contended that his large donations to political parties and candidates other than the NSDAP, just before Hitler seized power, made him a mark. Flick denied that the Nazi regime had helped him build his fortune: "I was glad if I was left alone and if I had my security. I did not ask for more because I wanted to live in peace and quiet and continue with the work of my life. Of course, I needed some protection for that, because after all, I had a political record."

Flick fashioned himself a victim of the Nazis, a man with ties to the Resistance, and a defender of the dispossessed and oppressed. He said that he had been "an advocate" of the Jewish Petschek families, whose massive brown coal assets he actually had looted, and stated that he had been "representing their interests in this desperate economic situation." Flick dismissed any anti-Semitic actions or statements attributed to him as "howling with the wolves." He claimed that his membership in Himmler's Circle of Friends was part personal insurance, part networking, and part support of the SS leader's hobbies and cultural interests. Flick also said that he had invested in seized factories such as Rombach and had made improvements to the nutrition provided for those in forced and slave labor there.

Faced with the prosecution's enormous documentary evidence, the defense chose to deploy an array of strategies. One was to shift all responsibility to coercion from the state. Another was to emphasize the decentralized nature of the Flick conglomerate, making it seem as if all decision-making authority lay with individual managers, not with Flick himself. The defense flooded the judges with *Persilscheine,* submitting 445 affidavits for the defendants, many attesting to their apolitical or anti-Nazi virtues. The defense also took to discrediting the prosecution's witnesses, most notably those who had survived forced and slave labor in Flick's factories. This led to several bizarre confrontations. One defense lawyer lectured a woman, a former *Ostarbeiter,* stating that the average German currently had less to eat than she had in a Rombach forced-labor camp. Dix trivialized a description of the use of French forced labor in one of Flick's factory kitchens by saying that the French were, after all, the "best cooks in the world." The presiding judge epitomized just how painfully uninformed the American magistrates were when, in all seriousness, he asked a former concentration camp prisoner at Flick's Gröditz factory whether there hadn't been red wine for dinner there.

Flick's feckless elder son, Otto-Ernst, played along with the charade. He had somehow escaped indictment for his leading roles at the Rombach and Gröditz steel plants; still, he was called up as a defense witness. The thirty-one-year-old heir testified about "strolling" around the Rombach complex in the French Lorraine, observing what he considered to be the more or less comfortable living conditions of the coerced workers. He also declared that he had provided underused female laborers with the opportunity to work in his garden on Sundays, so that they "would get something particularly good to eat."

The defense took three months to present its cases for the six accused men. Then, in late November 1947, the prosecution began closing arguments. Telford Taylor urged the American judges not to give in to the defense's argument that this trial was "a mere anachronism" in a rapidly changing Germany. Instead, Taylor argued that "the reconstruction which the world needs is not merely material but also moral reconstruction." The prosecutor stated that while the accused gave "every indication of devotion to the profit system . . . they are less ardently attached to certain other fundamental principles upon which the business community of any civi-lized nation must depend." Their "devotion to the capitalist system" wasn't above the law, he said. "Free enterprise does not depend upon slave labor, and honest business does not expand by plunder." The attorney concluded, "Surely . . . businessmen must be held to the same standard of steadfast-ness, and of unwillingness to commit crimes, whether in the face of temp-tation or threat, that the law requires of all individuals."

Dix summarized his closing arguments in defense of Flick with words from his opening statement: "The defendants lived in the Third Reich un-der a government which forced those they governed to do impious and iniquitous acts. It was their tragedy, but not their guilt, not even their tragic guilt." The lawyer for Bernhard Weiss, Flick's nephew, wasn't as subtle and questioned the "large scope" of the prosecution in the proceedings: "This first trial of industrialists is not an attack on Dr. Flick and his assistants, but an attack on the entire German economy, on German capitalism and its industrialists."

Flick agreed. He had the final word before the judges, making a state-ment on behalf of all six defendants. He had worn a scowl, black-rimmed reading glasses, and a fading gray double-breasted suit almost every day over the past eight months. "I am here as an exponent of German industry," thundered the white-haired mogul. "By having sentence passed on me, the prosecution is endeavoring to lend truth to their contention that it was German industry which lifted Hitler into the saddle, which encouraged him to wage aggressive wars, and instigated the ruthless exploitation of the human and economic potential of the occupied territories . . . I protest against the fact that in my person German industrialists are being stigma-tized in the eyes of the world as slave owners and spoliators . . . Nobody . . . who know [sic] my fellow defendants and myself, will be willing to believe that we committed crimes against humanity, and nothing will convince us that we are war criminals."

The presiding judge then ordered a recess. The magistrates would re-turn to the court in four weeks to rule on the Flick case — just in time for Christmas.

19.

On December 22, 1947, more than nine months after Telford Taylor read the indictment against Flick and his five accomplices, the American judges returned to give their ruling. Over six full months had been spent in session, almost fifteen hundred pieces of evidence had been introduced, and almost sixty witnesses, including the six defendants, had been heard. The English transcript of the proceedings ran to over eleven thousand pages. It had been a monster of a trial.

The judgment was bound to disappoint, on all sides. Friedrich Flick was sentenced to seven years in prison, credited against time served since he was arrested in mid-June 1945. Otto Steinbrinck was sentenced to five years in prison. Lastly, Flick's nephew Bernhard Weiss was sentenced to two and a half years in prison. The remaining three men, including Flick's cousin Konrad Kaletsch, were acquitted.

Of the six men, only Flick and Weiss were found guilty of using forced and slave labor, and at only one of their factories. Flick alone was found culpable of looting, but only at the expropriated Rombach steel complex in France. The charges of Aryanization were dismissed entirely — the transactions had been concluded before the war started, and the court said that its jurisdiction pertained only to crimes committed during the war or related to it. Flick and Steinbrinck were found guilty of having financially supported the SS and its crimes via Himmler's Circle of Friends. Steinbrinck was sentenced on an additional charge: as an SS officer, he had been part of a criminal organization.

In his final report on Nuremberg's subsequent proceedings, Taylor came to call the Flick ruling "exceedingly (if not excessively) moderate and conciliatory." Especially considering what would happen to Alfried Krupp: he would be sentenced to twelve years and his assets would be confiscated. In Flick's case, the judges followed the defense's line of argument on its most important point: that the program of forced and slave labor was created by the Nazi regime and operated beyond the control of the six accused, and German industry as a whole. Only in one factory did the prosecution prove, beyond any doubt, that Flick and Weiss had gone above and beyond to procure Russian prisoners of war to increase productivity, according to the American judges.

The judges also held that the steel firms expropriated in the Soviet Union had previously been state, not private, property, so in the context of war, Flick's seizure of them had been permissible. The mogul was deemed guilty on that count only for withholding the Rombach steel complex from its French owners. At the same time, the court somehow also concluded that Flick had left the place better than it had been when he seized it. The judges dismissed the charges of Aryanization because of a lack of jurisdiction, but they also failed to see how these transactions were criminal in character. It was best left to a civil court, the judges contended: "A sale compelled by pressure or duress may be questioned in a court of equity, but . . . such use of pressure, even on racial or religious grounds, has never been thought to be a crime against humanity."

However, the three judges didn't buy Flick and Steinbrinck's claim that their membership fees to Himmler's Circle of Friends merely supported the SS leader's esoteric hobbies and cultural interests. Though the court considered it a mitigating point that membership may have constituted some sort of personal insurance for the two men, it must have also been clear to them at some point that their substantial annual financial contributions went, at least in part, to maintaining a criminal organization that was undertaking the mass extermination of Jews and other people. Flick and Steinbrinck gave Himmler "a blank check" and it was "immaterial whether it was spent on salaries or for lethal gas," the American judges said.

Flick's next destination was Landsberg Prison, where more than two decades earlier Hitler had dictated *Mein Kampf* to two aides while they were jailed after the failed Beer Hall Putsch in nearby Munich. Flick too would rise again. Long before the ruling came down, he hired a lawyer in America. Flick was the one Nuremberg convict to appeal his sentence in the American court system, and it went all the way up to the Supreme

Court. But in 1949 the Court refused to hear his case. His conviction stood.

20.

From prison, Flick had to delegate tasks in order to rescue what remained of his industrial empire. Whereas about half of his conglomerate had been expropriated by the Soviet authorities in their occupation zone, the other half stood under American and British property control. That latter half had to be safely guided as the Allies planned a restructuring of West Germany's steel and coal conglomerates. The Americans and the British wanted to deconcentrate the German economy and eliminate the risk of rearmament. After his trial ended in December 1947, Flick dispatched two acquitted associates to the American and British occupation zones, one to each. The two would negotiate with Allied and German authorities about what that restructuring would look like.

These complex negotiations were still going on when Flick was released from Landsberg Prison. After the establishment of West Germany, President Truman appointed John J. McCloy, a Republican lawyer who had been an architect of American occupation policy and the Nuremberg tribunal, as the first US high commissioner for occupied Germany. Over 1950 and 1951, McCloy oversaw a series of controversial acts of clemency affecting more than a hundred Nuremberg convicts. He not only pardoned industrialists such as Alfried Krupp, even returning his assets, but he also commuted death sentences and reduced prison time for many high-ranking SS officers, all of them responsible for massacring hundreds of thousands of people, mostly Jews, across Nazi-occupied Europe. McCloy's decision was political. It was intended to placate an important new ally: the West German government and citizens. Many were pushing for these reduced sentences.

Telford Taylor was furious. In early 1951, the former Nuremberg prosecutor condemned McCloy's decision in *The Nation* as the "embodiment of political expediency, distorted by a thoroughly unsound approach to the law and the facts, to say nothing of the realities of contemporary world politics." But those politics now favored the convicted German war criminals. The Truman administration was getting bogged down in the Cold War and the Korean War, and it needed a good relationship with West Germany. Certain sacrifices had to be made.

Flick was released on August 25, 1950, after McCloy reduced his sentence by two years for good behavior. The sixty-seven-year-old tycoon had spent five years behind bars, partly working as registrar at Landsberg Prison's library. Flick had neglected this job so much that his successor had to work off a four-month backlog of returned books. Now it was time for Flick to get back to the real work. As the prison gates opened, reporters and photographers were awaiting the mogul and the other Nuremberg convicts released alongside him. Flick, who still abhorred press attention, hid behind an umbrella and made a beeline to a waiting limousine, where he joined his wife, Marie, in the back. The limo then sped off into the Bavarian countryside. Friedrich Flick was a free man.

When speaking to friends and colleagues, Flick was dismissive about his conviction at the Nuremberg trial: "My court was clearly an American court. Everyone, secretaries, auxiliary staff and judges, were Americans. Besides, they prayed for the USA twice a day. The rejection of my appeal was only in accordance with the national interest of the USA." Flick had undergone denazification proceedings in prison and was classified as exonerated in the British occupation zone. Because he had moved the seat of his conglomerate to Düsseldorf, which lay in that zone, Flick was allowed to return to work directly after his release and take over the delicate negotiations for the restructuring of his business.

And he did that quite successfully. In late 1951, Flick sold a quarter stake in his massive Maxhütte steel firm to the Bavarian state. One year later, the Allied High Commission signed off on Flick's restructuring plan. By May 1954, Flick had sold the majority stakes in his two remaining coal companies. All these sales netted Flick about a quarter billion deutsch marks. He reinvested part of the proceeds in a French and a Belgian steel firm, which made Flick a most undesirable trailblazer of the nascent economic integration of Western Europe. And he still had some 150 million deutsch marks left to invest. What to do with all that money? Flick soon found a place for it in one of the world's largest car companies: Daimler-Benz. By the end of the decade, the convicted Nazi war criminal was once again on top. He was Germany's wealthiest man.

PART V

"NINE ZEROS"

1.

On December 27, 1954, Günther Quandt traveled to Egypt for a holiday. Since his denazification trials concluded he was working harder than ever, laboring away in a nondescript office in Frankfurt to restructure what remained of his business empire. But his health was frail. He had rapidly recovered from a minor stroke in 1950, but he still had to check in at a hospital every three to six months for a few weeks to address various other health issues. Günther always arrived at the hospital with a suitcase full of work documents. Now he wanted to flee Germany's brutal winter and spend a couple of weeks down in Africa. For this post-Christmas holiday, the traveler had assembled an itinerary that included a sightseeing trip to the pyramids at Giza, on the outskirts of Cairo. He stayed at the capital's famed luxury hotel, Mena House. But he never made it to the pyramids. On the morning of December 30, 1954, Günther died in his hotel suite, with its views of the Sphinx. Whether he died alone remains a mystery. It was long rumored that the mogul succumbed following "a little death." Günther was seventy-three years old.

The mood in West Germany had changed earlier that year. German pride was back. After the country beat Hungary in the 1954 World Cup soccer final, the Nazi era chant "Deutschland, Deutschland über alles" ("Germany, Germany above all") rang through the stadium in Bern. Germany was back, but Günther was gone.

The 1950s were more than just a new decade. They were the dawn of a new German era, all of it thanks to the US government. The outbreak of the Korean War in June 1950 was the spark that ignited West Germany's economic resurgence. As the Truman administration began spending billions on rearmament, it turned many American factories over to the manufacture of weapons. As a result, production of many other goods bottlenecked, and scarcities spiked. West Germany stepped in to pick up the slack. A key Western industrialized nation, it was able to fill that manufacturing vacuum and likewise could handle the massive global demand in consumer goods by means of its export prowess. By 1953, West Germany's economy had quadrupled. Any lingering aversion to buying German products clearly and quickly vanished from other countries.

In the new federal republic of West Germany, led by Chancellor Konrad Adenauer, the *Wirtschaftswunder*, or economic miracle, heralded an age of unprecedented economic growth and massive prosperity for most Germans. In particular, those "denazified" tycoons and their heirs in the West entered an epoch of unfathomable global wealth, which persists to this day. But this newfound windfall entirely bypassed the millions living in the Soviet-led Communist state of East Germany. And as that inequity festered, a culture of silence also permeated the divided Germany. It buried the horrors of the Third Reich and the diabolical roles that many Germans had played in it. As West Germany's moguls turned their tens or hundreds of millions of reichsmarks into billions of deutsch marks and dollars, and (re)gained control of swaths of the German and global economy, they rarely, if ever, looked back. These tycoons left their heirs with firms and fortunes worth billions — but also with a bloodstained history waiting to be uncovered.

2.

On January 8, 1955, a memorial service was held for Günther Quandt in the assembly hall of Frankfurt's Goethe University. Hermann Josef Abs — one of the Third Reich's most influential bankers, who was now rapidly becoming West Germany's most powerful financier as the chairman of Deutsche Bank — had this to say of Günther in his eulogy: "He never submitted servilely to the overbearing state." It was the exact opposite of what Abs had said about Günther during the mogul's lavish sixtieth-birthday bash in Berlin, in 1941. Back then, speaking to the Nazi elite, the banker had lauded Günther's servility: "But your most outstanding characteristic is your faith in Germany and the Führer."

Horst Pavel, Günther's closest aide and a key architect of AFA's Aryanization strategy, also delivered a eulogy, which barely mentioned the Nazi era, except to say how extremely hard his boss and mentor had worked during the war. Instead, Pavel spoke admiringly about Günther's "brilliant" ability to capitalize on Germany's many financial and political disasters: "He . . . prepared his actions carefully and then operated as skillfully as he did tenaciously until the set goal was ultimately achieved."

Although the Soviet authorities had expropriated Günther's firms, factories, houses, and estate in East Germany, he still retained many assets in West Germany: the AFA battery factory in Hannover, several DWM weapons plants plus its subsidiaries Mauser and Dürener, and what remained of Byk Gulden, a massive chemicals and pharmaceuticals firm that had already been Aryanized when Günther bought it during the war, to name just a few. He also had an almost one-third stake in the oil and potash giant Wintershall left and a 4 percent interest in Daimler-Benz; until 1945, he had served as a supervisory board member of the Stuttgart-based car giant. It was a prescient move. Mass motorization was growing around the world, and West Germany's economic future lay with the auto industry. In the years before his death, Günther restructured AFA, positioning it as key supplier of accumulators and starter batteries for cars.

Restructuring in West Germany meant reckoning with some ugly truths. DWM's full name — Deutsche Waffen- und Munitionsfabriken — was changed to something that sounded more innocuous: IWK (for Industriewerke Karlsruhe). Plus, the firm was barred from making weapons and ammo, for now anyway. Günther's Byk Gulden had grown into one of Germany's largest pharmaceuticals businesses by the end of the war, but it partly consisted of Aryanized subsidiaries. After the war, heirs of the original Jewish owners initiated restitution proceedings. These negotiations were discreetly concluded, and land, buildings, and machinery were turned over to the heirs. Günther's attorney approached these matters pragmatically: "There wasn't a single German company that did not conduct Aryanizations during the war, so there were restitution proceedings here and there, and lawyers were needed for this," he later recalled.

Günther had fought these proceedings tooth and nail where he could. In 1947, Fritz Eisner, a German Jewish chemist who had fled to London, filed a restitution claim against AFA in the British occupation zone. Günther had Aryanized Eisner's electrochemical companies outside Berlin in 1937, and now Eisner wanted to be compensated to make up for Günther's pittance of a payment to him. But the firms now lay in the Soviet occupation zone and had been expropriated. Instead of apologizing to Eisner for extorting and underpaying him, Günther had AFA's lawyers fight the claim on jurisdictional grounds. Eisner's restitution claim was rejected in 1955, not long after Günther died.

3.

What was Günther Quandt's business legacy, exactly? Kurt Pritzkoleit, a business journalist who documented German industrialists, gave this title to a book chapter on Quandt in 1953: "The power of the great unknown." Pritzkoleit was the first reporter to expose the sheer size of Günther's industrial empire and his penchant for secrecy:

> Quandt developed the talent of shielding his work from the view of the outsider into a skill that is rarely found . . . hardly anyone has been able to fully grasp the scope and universality of his activities, apart from those close to him. His mimicry, the ability, so rare among us weak and vain people, to take on the protective color of the surroundings, is developed to perfection: Among textile manufacturers he appears as a textile manufacturer, among metalworkers as a metalworker, among weapons specialists as a weapons specialist, among electrical engineers as an electrical engineer, among insurance experts as an insurance expert, among potash miners as a potash miner, and in every manifestation he appears so genuine and convincing that

the observer who encounters him in an area of his multifaceted
activity believes the protective color to be the original and only
one, innate and unchangeable.

Dynastic and entrepreneurial continuity had been crucial to Günther. The mogul had seen other business families fall prey to infighting related to succession. He wanted to avoid that at all costs, so he meticulously laid out plans for after his death. His sons, Herbert and Harald, were each to take over a specific part of his industrial empire. Harald was the more technically gifted of the two. He had graduated as a mechanical engineer in 1953 and as a student had already served on numerous supervisory boards at his father's firms. Therefore it made sense for him to oversee the weapons and machinery firms IWK, Mauser, Busch-Jaeger Dürener, and Kuka. Harald's decade-older half brother, Herbert, would supervise AFA plus the Wintershall and Daimler-Benz stakes.

Günther left behind a fortune of 55.5 million deutsch marks (about $135 million today), mostly consisting of company shares. He left them to Herbert and Harald in almost equal parts through two holding companies. But since Günther had already transferred many assets to his two sons over the previous decade — a strategy to avoid inheritance tax, which many of the world's wealthiest still exploit today — the actual size of his estate was impossible to calculate. Suffice it to say, it was larger than 55.5 million deutsch marks. The Quandts' constructions of ownership and debt through various holding companies were so complex that even the most experienced auditors gave up. "To what extent the securities were acquired with personal funds or with bank loans cannot be specified in detail . . . These transactions . . . are so interwoven that it is impossible to establish a connection between purchases of securities and individual borrowings," read a German government-ordered review from 1962.

Nonetheless, the business transitioned smoothly to the next generation of Quandts. Günther's son Herbert later quipped: "With all due reverence for my father: If his death hadn't been in the newspaper, no one would have noticed it businesswise." Work at the Quandt factories was suspended in tribute during Günther's memorial service. But in no time at all, it was back to business. Herbert and Harald lived three hundred feet apart from each other in Bad Homburg, a spa town north of Frankfurt. They were keen on expanding the Quandt business empire and leaving their own legacy. Directly after their father's death, the half brothers began to increase a share package they had inherited in Daimler-Benz, the manufacturer of Mercedes. But unbeknownst to them, another German mogul, with even more money at his disposal, had investment plans of his own and spare millions to execute them. That mogul was Friedrich Flick. He too had his sights set on Germany's largest car firm. "The battle for Daimler" was about to erupt.

4.

In mid-July 1955, at Daimler-Benz's annual meeting in Stuttgart, two new major shareholders registered and were elected to the carmaker's supervisory board: Herbert Quandt and Friedrich Flick. Herbert registered a sizable 3.85 percent stake in Daimler, which he and Harald had inherited from Günther. But Flick took everyone by surprise by filing a 25 percent interest, a blocking minority. The mogul, fresh out of prison, had secretly started buying shares in Daimler. The Quandt siblings and Flick now wanted more. Herbert and Harald desired a 25 percent interest. Flick was eyeing majority control. As two of Germany's wealthiest business dynasties went head to head to increase their stakes, Daimler's share price rose feverishly. In January 1956, a third investor emerged: a speculating timber merchant from Bremen who had amassed an 8 percent stake. He wanted to sell his share package to one of the two parties at a massive premium: double the stock price.

United by the presence of a common enemy, the Quandts and Flick now called a truce. They made a secret deal to squeeze out the new investor. Flick rejected the speculator's offer, which forced the latter to sell the stake to Herbert and Harald at a much lower price. The Quandt siblings and Flick then split the share package and continued to increase their stakes. At Daimler's next annual general meeting in June 1956, Harald Quandt and

Flick's elder son Otto-Ernst joined the supervisory board of the Stuttgart carmaker.

By late 1959, Flick was Daimler-Benz's largest shareholder, with about a 40 percent stake. The Quandts held some 15 percent. Between them stood Deutsche Bank, with a 28.5 percent interest. The triumvirate of Hermann Josef Abs — Deutsche Bank's chairman *and* Daimler-Benz's supervisory board chairman — the Flicks, and the Quandts would rule over Europe's largest carmaker for the next decades. And it was hardly a contentious reign. Flick placed part of his Daimler stake in a holding firm owned by Herbert Quandt, which allowed Herbert to qualify for a tax break. The dynasties were now officially in cahoots.

But whereas Herbert and Flick wound up closely collaborating at Daimler, in an attempt to rescue BMW they found themselves on opposing sides. The Munich carmaker was on the brink of bankruptcy in the late 1950s, due to a lack of variety in car models and bad management. Herbert asked Harald's permission to buy BMW shares on his own account, separate from the Quandt group. It was a risky investment, but Herbert, who loved fast cars, wanted a shot at restructuring the firm.

Herbert began buying BMW shares and convertible bonds. The press first suspected that Flick was behind the rising share price, but he denied it. However, at BMW's annual meeting in December 1959, a Flick-backed restructuring plan was proposed. It included issuing new shares exclusively to Daimler-Benz, which then would have held a majority stake in its competitor. Flick, as Daimler's largest shareholder, saw it as a cheap way of bringing BMW under his control. But the restructuring plan that Flick supported ultimately was not accepted at the shareholders' meeting in Munich, which was quite heated. Following Flick's attempted corporate coup, Herbert firmly took the reins and began to reorganize BMW himself, after becoming its largest shareholder.

Herbert's decade-long restructuring of BMW proved successful. He installed new management, expanded the range of car models, and continued buying shares. In 1968, BMW hit one billion deutsch marks in revenue, and Herbert held 40 percent of its stock. That summer, he sold the family's longtime stake in the oil and gas giant Wintershall to the chemicals behemoth BASF for about 125 million deutsch marks. He used part of the proceeds to become BMW's controlling shareholder. To this day, two of his children still retain that level of control over the carmaker, making them Germany's wealthiest siblings.

5.

For the Quandts and many other German business dynasties, the ghosts of the Third Reich were never far off. This was mainly because the moguls themselves kept inviting them back. Harald Quandt hired a couple to join his household staff in Bad Homburg; each had worked for the Goebbelses during the Nazi era. "The same man who had chauffeured his mother in the 1930s now drove his daughters to school by car," a biographer of the Quandt dynasty later revealed. Such hires weren't limited to Harald's private life, though. In the early 1950s, Harald brought two of Joseph Goebbels's closest aides from the Ministry of Propaganda into the Quandt group, assigning them to high-ranking positions. The most prominent was Werner Naumann, Goebbels's appointed successor in Hitler's political testament. Naumann had been yet another lover of Harald's mother, Magda. When Harald hired him as a member of the board of directors at Busch-Jaeger Dürener, Naumann had just recently been released by the British authorities in Germany; in 1953 Naumann and a group of neo-Nazis had attempted to infiltrate a German political party, but the British had thwarted the plot. Apparently this didn't bother the Quandt heir. Speaking to a friend, Harald defended his decision to hire Naumann, deeming him "a clever fellow and not a Nazi." But Naumann had joined the NSDAP in 1928 and was appointed SS brigadier general in 1933. He was a committed Nazi by any measure.

And Harald wasn't alone in maintaining ties to Germany's dark past as he amassed dynastic wealth. The two former SS officers Ferry Porsche and Albert Prinzing were busy making the Porsche 356 an enormous global success during the 1950s. Ferry surrounded himself with yet more former

SS officers at the Porsche company in Stuttgart. In 1952, he put Baron Fritz Huschke von Hanstein in charge of Porsche's global public relations and made him the director of its auto-racing team. Von Hanstein had been a wartime racing icon, driving Himmler's favorite BMW while wearing overalls embellished with the initials ss—which he dryly explained stood for "Super-Sport." Von Hanstein's career in the SS wasn't limited to racing. As an SS captain, he assisted with the "resettlement" of Jews and Poles in Nazi-occupied Poland. But von Hanstein fell out of favor with Himmler after he was reprimanded by an SS court for attempted rape.

In January 1957, Porsche hired Joachim Peiper, who had been released from Landsberg Prison just four weeks earlier, when a US-German clemency committee commuted his death sentence. Peiper, a former adjutant to Himmler, had been sentenced by a US military court in Germany after the war for having commanded the SS tank unit responsible for the Malmedy massacre in 1944, in which eighty-four American prisoners of war were murdered. At Albert Prinzing's prompting, Porsche hired the Nazi war criminal as its head of sales promotion. Peiper was all too pleased with his new position. "You see . . . I silently swim in the big slimy floods of the Federal Republic's economic wonder. Not at the top, but also not at the bottom. In the middle, without making any waves," Peiper wrote to his lawyer. But in the end, Peiper's employment at the car company rocked the boat a little too much, even for a firm so well stocked with former SS officers (Hitler's former chauffeur Erich Kempka and the SS general Franz Six were other recent hires). In 1960, Porsche concluded that his ongoing employment could potentially harm the firm's reputation in the country most important to its export business: the United States. Peiper was fired.

In the same period, yet another former SS officer, Rudolf-August Oetker, was massively profiting from West Germany's economic miracle. His family firm, Dr. Oetker, hit a new sales record in 1950, selling about 1.25 billion packages of baking powder and pudding mixes. With those profits, Rudolf-August turned his Bielefeld-based baking goods business into a worldwide conglomerate. He increased his family's stake in the shipping firm Hamburg Süd and invested in more beer breweries. Rudolf-August also entered new industries: he bought the private bank Lampe and ap-

pointed the Nazi banker Hugo Ratzmann as its general partner. During
the Third Reich, Ratzmann had helped Günther Quandt, Friedrich Flick,
August von Finck, and many other tycoons conduct Aryanizations and expropriations in Germany and Nazi-occupied Poland.

Four years after Ratzmann died, in a 1960 car accident, Rudolf-August
appointed Rudolf von Ribbentrop as a managing director at Lampe. He
was the eldest son of Nazi Germany's social-climber foreign minister, the
first man to be hanged at Nuremberg's gallows. Rudolf-August and Rudolf
von Ribbentrop had been friends since 1940, but von Ribbentrop's career
in the SS had been far more successful than that of the pudding prince. Von
Ribbentrop served as a highly decorated tank commander in the elite First
Panzer Division Leibstandarte SS Adolf Hitler. His mother was an heiress
to Henkell, one of Germany's largest producers of sparkling wine. She had
nominated her son as managing partner of Henkell after he was released as
a prisoner of war, but her relatives and Henkell's chairman, Hermann Josef
Abs, blocked the appointment. They thought that the Ribbentrop name
would be bad for business. But Rudolf-August had no such qualms. He
"convinced me to stay away from the family clique and go to work for him,"
von Ribbentrop later wrote in his memoir. "The business opportunity he
made available to me constituted a greater challenge for me than I could
have imagined. I shall ever be grateful to him."

Rudolf-August first gave von Ribbentrop a job at a hand puppet factory he had invested in. Meanwhile, von Ribbentrop reinforced ties to his
Waffen-SS network. In January 1957, he asked Rudolf-August to provide financial aid for veterans of his SS tank division who had been sentenced for
the Malmedy massacre and had recently been released from prison. This
group of Nazi war criminals included the SS unit's former commanding
officer and recent Porsche hire, Joachim Peiper. It was a small world after
all. Rudolf-August was happy to financially support these old SS comrades,
but the miserly magnate wanted to avoid direct payments; those weren't tax
deductible. Instead, Rudolf-August suggested using the Dr. Oetker conglomerate, as had been done before, he intimated, to channel money to
Stille Hilfe (Silent Help), the secretive relief organization for convicted and
fugitive members of the SS; it still exists today.

Rudolf-August soon promoted von Ribbentrop to general partner of Lampe bank. But the former SS comrades' ties truly came full circle when Rudolf-August bought the Henkell family's sparkling wine business for 130 million deutsch marks in 1986.

6.

One of the tycoons did face actual business repercussions because of his actions during the Third Reich, and he responded radically. In November 1954, Baron August von Finck was at the foot of the Alps, planning his revenge. The chief hunter he employed, a man named Bock, had put snow chains on the old jeep sitting in Bavaria's Mittenwald village, on the border with Austria. Accompanied by his servant, his cook, and his hunting dog, Dingo, von Finck drove the breakneck roads up to the Vereinsalm, his rustic mountain cabin, which was decorated with antlers. He wanted to catch his breath in the snowy solitude below the Karwendel mountain range. He had just weathered the first exchange of blows in his power struggle with two of the world's largest insurers.

Already back at the helm of his private bank, Merck Finck, for some time now, the fifty-six-year-old aristocratic financier was staging a hostile takeover of Allianz *and* Munich Re, the insurance giants cofounded by his father. The reason behind von Finck's attempt at such a drastic coup: a recent demotion. In 1945, the American occupation authorities had removed the baron from his role as supervisory board chairman at both insurers; he had, however, been allowed to return as a supervisory board member, but not chairman, at Munich Re soon after his denazification trial ended. This wasn't enough for von Finck. He wanted *both* his old positions back. Given von Finck's recent history as a staunch supporter of Hitler and a major profiteer of private bank Aryanizations, it was inconceivable that the two renowned global insurers would let him return as chairman. So he angrily quit the board of Munich Re. "The year 1945 threw so much tradition overboard, and the new men at Allianz wanted their own circle. At that time, after all, the American tanks were rattling through the country, and heads had to roll," von Finck, ensconced in his cabin, complained to a reporter from *Der Spiegel*.

Through his father's inheritance and private bank, von Finck was still the largest shareholder at both insurers, whose share capital was closely intertwined. So, in response to the snub, the financier began secretly buying up Allianz shares via straw men over the course of 1954. He aimed to increase his 8 percent stake to at least a 25 percent blocking minority in order to gain control of both companies. Von Finck received no support for his hostile bid from Germany's commercial banks, which had close ties to the insurers. But Bavaria's wealthiest man had plenty of money to spend on his own. In an exceptionally uncharacteristic move, the frugal financier went so far as to buy 16.5 percent of all Allianz stock. However, the insurer blocked the registration of his new shares, so he couldn't leverage his full voting rights. Meanwhile, the aloof baron, never one for the common man, failed to convince enough smaller shareholders to join his side and form a blocking minority.

A solution had to be found. After dogged negotiations, von Finck and the insurers reached an agreement in late January 1955. In exchange for getting his new shares registered, von Finck withdrew his plan to put proposals related to restructuring to a vote at an extraordinary shareholders' meeting he had called. But the financier still remained a major shareholder of the two insurers; he could still be a massive headache for them down the line. More negotiations followed, and the insurers struck a different deal with their former chairman. In exchange for a large part of his Allianz and Munich Re shares, von Finck would receive a considerable minority stake in a major steel firm, Südwestfalen.

To von Finck's great dismay, he soon had to contend with a new majority shareholder at Südwestfalen. It was none other than the baron's longtime acquaintance Friedrich Flick. The mogul was wheeling and dealing everywhere in the 1950s, making up for lost time and business after his stint in prison. The Düsseldorf-based Flick conglomerate had almost entirely said farewell to coal, was ramping up its investments in steel, and venturing into the automobile and chemical industries. At the same time, another trade that was all too familiar to the mogul was having a renaissance in West Germany: weapons manufacturing. Flick wanted in, and he wasn't the only one. There were lucrative defense contracts to be won, and plenty of tycoons eyeing them. Germany's arms race was on again.

7.

Harald Quandt, the former paratrooper lieutenant in the Luftwaffe, was in charge of the arms and ammunition branch of the family's sprawling business empire. He was the head of IWK — formerly known as DWM — which was making a quick comeback as one of West Germany's largest weapons manufacturers. The country owed its rearmament to America's involvement in the Korean War and the Cold War. After the Korean War ended, the Eisenhower administration demanded that its Western allies take up a more equal share of the military burden related to the Cold War. Chancellor Adenauer seized on this as an opportunity to argue for the re-armament of West Germany. In May 1955, the country joined NATO and was allowed to have an army again. Six months later, West Germany established its new military, the Bundeswehr. Soon after, the Quandts' IWK and its rifle-making subsidiary, Mauser, were permitted to manufacture weapons again.

The decision to rearm was grist to the mill for a technology geek like Harald. He had a fully automatic shooting range installed in his basement; a radiation-proof bunker was built beneath a Quandt family villa in Bad Homburg. In 1957, the engineering graduate even got the opportunity to develop the prototype for a tank. The French and West German armies had agreed on producing one together and issued a design competition. A consortium led by Harald's IWK won. But the Franco-German tank project eventually fell through. West Germany withdrew from it because the government wanted the country to build its own tank: the Leopard.

West Germany ordered a massive number of the new battle tank. The West German army wanted between a thousand and fifteen hundred Leopard tanks, built at a unit price of 1.2 million deutsch marks; this first order could go as high as 1.8 billion deutsch marks. Harald felt confident that he would win this contract, but he faced stiff competition from two tycoons with far more experience in building and designing tanks: Friedrich Flick and Ferry Porsche. Although Flick's right-hand man declared to the press in 1956 that the convicted weapons producer "has a deep aversion to any kind of armament," he reentered the business that same year. One of Flick's steel subsidiaries started building aircraft parts for the new Luftwaffe's Noratlas military transport plane, the Fiat G91 jet fighter, and the Lockheed F-104 fighter-bomber.

This was just the beginning of Flick's weapon-production plans. When the orders for locomotives dried up at Krauss-Maffei, which Flick controlled, he had the company enter arms production through the Leopard tank tender, teaming up with Daimler-Benz for the engine and with Porsche for the design. But the Stuttgart auto firm was missing two of its cofounders. Ferdinand Porsche had died at seventy-five in 1951, followed the next year by Anton Piëch, who died unexpectedly at fifty-seven from a heart attack. The two men had never fully recovered from their detention in a French military prison.

Ferry Porsche and his sister, Louise Piëch, stepped in to fortify their respective Porsche companies. After having constructed the first car bearing the family name, Ferry now once again succeeded where his father had failed: sending off the prototype of a Porsche tank for wide production. In 1951, during a skiing holiday in Davos, Switzerland, Ferry met with a member of the Tata family, industrialists from India. They wanted to build trucks and tanks in India with Daimler-Benz, having had good experiences working with Krauss-Maffei in locomotives production. Of course, West German firms weren't allowed to build tanks at the time. So Ferry came up with a loophole: they would start a Swiss-based joint venture with Daimler for the tank design, thus circumventing the requirement that Germany not produce arms. The result: a Tata-Daimler factory in India that churned out tanks based on Ferry's design.

A decade later, Krauss-Maffei and Daimler-Benz, now both under Flick's control, returned the favor by bringing the Porsche company aboard the Leopard tank tender, to create the design. Harald Quandt thought he had the better plan, but he underestimated Flick's political connections. Whereas Harald wanted to bring production to left-wing Hamburg, Flick proposed having the Leopard made in Bavaria, the conservative home of Franz Josef Strauss, Germany's former defense minister and the mighty chairman of Bavaria's ruling political party, the Christian Social Union (CSU). With Strauss's backing, Flick and Ferry beat Harald; they were awarded the contract in 1963.

The Leopard tank was an enormous success. Flick's Krauss-Maffei estimated its stake in the first contract at 408 million deutsch marks alone. Not long after, the armies of several of West Germany's NATO allies were putting in their orders as well. About thirty-five hundred Leopard tanks had been built by 1966, and a new and improved model was soon ordered. Ferry Porsche had no qualms about the fact that his automobile firm had returned to arms development. "We never know in which direction politics will develop. According to the concept by which it's structured, our army is based on the principle of defense. For this task we must equip it with the best weapons available," Ferry wrote in one of his autobiographies.

Despite losing out on the Leopard, Harald continued undaunted with arms development and production. He led another consortium, this time to design the prototype for a German American tank. The expensive project failed to take off as well. Harald and Ferry were also busy designing their own amphibious cars. Ferry's military prototype — none too different from his father's bucket car — wasn't picked up by the Bundeswehr. And Harald's civilian "amphicar" was a flop worldwide. His IWK had more success making land mines, and the company supplied more than a million anti-personnel and anti-tank mines to West Germany's military and many of its allies. Some of IWK's anti-personnel mines were directly exported to or resold in African war zones. IWK's unexploded mines have been discovered in Ethiopia, Eritrea, and Angola, among other countries. Intended to maim or kill soldiers, they may have ended up killing even more children and other civilians. Many of those land mines likely lie dormant beneath African soil to this day, long after the death of Harald Quandt.

8.

At 10:30 p.m. on September 22, 1967, Harald Quandt's Beechcraft King airplane took off from Frankfurt Airport. Its destination was Nice, specifically Harald's villa on the Côte d'Azur, which he planned on selling. Also aboard were his mistress and two other guests. The weather over Frankfurt was stormy that evening, and the pilots soon lost radio contact with air traffic control. The next day, a shepherd in the last foothills of the Alps found the remains of the private jet. It had flown into the mountains of the Piemonte region, not far from Turin. Harald, all his passengers, and the pilots were killed.

Harald was only forty-five years old when he died. He left behind his wife, Inge, their five young daughters who ranged from two months to sixteen years of age, plus twenty-two executive and supervisory board positions. These numbers were, however, surpassed by his half brother, Herbert, who had six children from three marriages and held more board positions than any other West German industrialist. When Harald died, the only German richer than the Quandts was Friedrich Flick.

Flick, as well as high-ranking officers of the West German and American military, attended Harald's memorial service in Frankfurt. They paid tribute to an enterprising, charming industrialist who had loved people and parties. Harald's closest associates were "filled with horror" at his early death but weren't particularly surprised by it. They had long feared this day would come. Harald always prized living dangerously. After all he had witnessed and endured, he still had a childlike zest for life. This attitude stood in stark contrast to that of his conservative older half brother, Herbert, the visually impaired savior of BMW who didn't like strangers. But in truth, Harald was the burdened one. One of Harald's daughters once asked him whether she had so many siblings because he once had six of them himself. He didn't respond kindly to that question. While these tragic matters weren't totally taboo, they were largely left undiscussed. But Harald carried this macabre past with him wherever he went.

A German journalist once described running into Harald at a party in Frankfurt that was hosted by a famous Jewish architect: "Among the excited, cheerful faces, one, pale as the moon, gazed, still and silent with bright watery eyes . . . looking nowhere. The pale face, smiling politely but laboriously, remained motionless. It seemed to me as if a distant storm was raging behind those waxy eyes, a memory of an incurable misfortune. Harald Quandt, rich heir, son of Magda Goebbels . . . Everyone who looked at him remembered the terrible sacrifice of Baal that his mother had made in the Führerbunker when everything came to an end." Harald never forgave his mother and stepfather for murdering their own children, his beloved siblings, nor did he ever get over their murder-suicide. When a lawyer representing Goebbels's estate contacted Harald about his stepfather's inheritance, he had wanted nothing to do with it. Harald told the lawyer that he preferred to cherish the memories of the house on Berlin's Schwanenwerder Island — with his six siblings and mother alive in it.

Harald's death tore the Quandt clan apart. At the same time, the Flick family was coming undone as well. One business dynasty would survive the inner turmoil. The other would fall apart.

9.

Baron August von Finck wore a blue suit of simple make and brown shoes with worn heels on the chilly day in early spring 1970 when a reporter from *Der Spiegel* magazine met him at his Möschenfeld estate, east of Munich. The journalist was there to profile the seventy-one-year-old for a piece on land reform. The collar and cuffs of the banker's shirt looked threadbare, and his necktie hung askew. "It isn't difficult for the old man to disprove the saying that clothes make the man. Beyond the billion-mark, the rules of peasantry apply once again," the reporter wrote at the start of his twelve-page profile, titled "Nine Zeros." The aristocrat "drinks little and smokes moderately — at most cheap straw Virginias, which disproves the proverbial saying that money doesn't stink." By 1970, Friedrich Flick, August von Finck, Herbert Quandt, and Rudolf-August Oetker made up West Germany's top four wealthiest businessmen, in descending order of fortune.

August von Finck in the 1970s.

All four were former members of the Nazi Party; one of them had been a voluntary Waffen-SS officer; they had all become billionaires.

The aristocratic financier's private bank, Merck Finck, was valued at one billion deutsch marks, but the vast portion of his fortune lay in land. Von Finck's main estate extended almost unbroken for twelve miles outside Munich. The five thousand acres of land on the outskirts of Germany's wealthiest city — that's two hundred million square feet of potential building land, worth about two billion deutsch marks at the time — was one-third meadows and farmland, two-thirds forest. On Sundays, the baron would drive his beat-up Volkswagen to the Bavarian countryside and trudge for miles through his forests, wearing a worn loden-green coat. In Bavaria, August von Finck was omnipresent. "It's like the fairy tale of the hare and the hedgehog," a union builder complained to the journalist from *Der Spiegel.* "Wherever we go — [von] Finck is already there."

Bavaria's richest man remained its stingiest as well. Von Finck didn't carry small change. If he needed money, he drilled his unkempt fingers into his vest and mumbled, "Oh, don't I have anything in my pocket?" He would accept coins with an open hand from anyone who stood nearby, and he hitched rides to the hairdresser in a nearby village because it was fifteen pennies cheaper than a haircut in Munich. He "doesn't understand the world of necessary social change and doesn't even want to understand it," the reporter wrote. "As if in a museum, he continues to live in the era in which he grew up." And von Finck wasn't the only tycoon holding on to a darker era.

The former Waffen-SS officer Rudolf-August Oetker was still cozying up to Nazis. He hadn't stopped at employing his old SS comrade von Ribbentrop or donating to Stille Hilfe. In the early 1950s, Rudolf-August's second wife, Susi, left him to marry a prince who soon became a prominent politician for the NPD, West Germany's neo-Nazi party. In 1967, at the pinnacle of the party's fringe popularity, *Der Spiegel* reported that Rudolf-August privately met with some of the neo-Nazi politicians. He met the NPD's founder through his ex-wife's new husband while hosting another NPD leader at his mansion in Hamburg. In May 1968, the German newspaper *Die Zeit* included the Dr. Oetker and Flick conglomerates on a list of the NPD's corporate backers. Both companies denied that they supported the party.

In late September 1968, despite massive protests, a public museum opened in Bielefeld bearing the name of Richard Kaselowsky, Rudolf-August's beloved Nazi stepfather and member of Himmler's Circle of Friends. To design the museum, Rudolf-August had commissioned the American star architect Philip Johnson, who had been a supporter of the Nazis as well. When the naming controversy flared up again decades later, the city council removed Kaselowsky's name from the museum. In response, Rudolf-August pulled his funding from the museum, along with the artworks he had loaned to it.

10.

In December 1967, Adolf Rosenberger died as Alan Robert in Los Angeles from a heart attack. The persecuted cofounder of Porsche and émigré was only sixty-seven. After his settlement with the firm and the deaths of Ferdinand Porsche and Anton Piëch in the early 1950s, Rosenberger had traveled back to Stuttgart and met with Ferry. Rosenberger offered him patents and hoped to represent Porsche in California. After everything that had transpired, Rosenberger still wanted to be a part of the company he had helped establish. Ferry responded in a noncommittal way, and nothing came of it.

Almost a decade after Rosenberger's death, Ferry published his first autobiography: *We at Porsche.* In it, the sports car designer not only twisted the truth of Rosenberger's Aryanization and escape from Nazi Germany but also did the same with the stories of other German Jews who were forced to sell their firms and flee Hitler's regime. Ferry even accused Rosenberger of extortion after the war. What's more, the former SS officer used blatant anti-Semitic stereotypes and prejudice in his warped account: "After the war, it seemed as though those people who had been persecuted by the Nazis considered it their right to make an additional profit, even in cases where they had already been compensated. Rosenberger was by no means an isolated example."

Ferry, now in his midsixties, supplied an example of a Jewish family who had voluntarily sold their factory after leaving Nazi Germany for Mussolini's Italy, only to return after the war and claim "payment a second time," at least according to his interpretation of events. Ferry continued: "It would be hard to blame Rosenberger for thinking in a like manner. He no doubt felt that since he was Jewish and had been forced out of Germany by the Nazis who had done so much harm, he was entitled to an extra profit."

Ferry then falsely claimed that his family had saved Rosenberger from imprisonment by the Nazis. But it hadn't been Ferry, his father, or his brother-in-law, Anton Piëch, who got Rosenberger released from a concentration camp in late September 1935, just weeks after the car moguls Aryanized his stake in Porsche. In fact, Rosenberger's successor at Porsche, Baron Hans von Veyder-Malberg, had negotiated with the Gestapo for Rosenberger's release and later helped Rosenberger's parents escape Germany. But Ferry stole credit for these morally sound actions from the dead baron on behalf of the Porsche family: "We had such good connections that we were able to help him, and he was set free. Unfortunately, all this was forgotten when Mr. Rosenberger saw what he thought was an opportunity to make more money. However, not only Jewish people, but most emigrants who had left Germany felt the same way."

11.

When their father died, Herbert and Harald "vowed to each other that there would be no fratricidal war in the Quandt house." But after Harald died in the 1967 plane crash, the relationship between his widow, Inge, and his half brother, Herbert, deteriorated. Inge started dating her late husband's best friend, who began criticizing Herbert's business decisions. The two branches of the Quandt family initiated a separation of assets. After long, difficult negotiations, Inge and her five daughters received four-fifths of the dynasty's 15 percent stake in Daimler-Benz from Herbert. Other assets were soon divided between the two families as well.

Inge was ill-suited to the life of a Quandt heiress. She became addicted to prescription pills and smoked about a hundred cigarettes a day. On the morning of Christmas Eve, 1978, Inge was found dead in her bed. She had perished from heart failure at fifty. She must have died with a cigarette in her hand, as two of her fingers were found to be scorched. Her daughters were orphaned, but yet another drama awaited them. The next evening, on the night of Christmas Day, Inge's new husband lay down next to his dead wife, whose body had been laid out at home in Bad Homburg. He put a gun in his mouth and pulled the trigger. One of his stepdaughters discovered his body the next day.

Despite another tragedy for Harald's daughters, at least they were well provided for. The Quandts had started shopping their Daimler-Benz stake around in 1973. The Flick family wasn't interested. They were dealing with problems of their own. The Quandts quickly found another buyer. In November 1974, the families sold the stake. The buyer, initially kept a secret, was soon revealed: the Kuwaiti Investment Authority, the world's oldest sovereign wealth fund. The sale was controversial in West Germany, coming hot on the heels of the 1973 oil crisis, but it netted the Quandt families almost a billion deutsch marks, the largest share transaction in German history. Harald's daughters were set for life. As it happened, within six weeks their sale of shares was eclipsed by an even larger one: a Daimler stake, double the size, was sold for two billion deutsch marks by a Flick heir. The Flick conglomerate and the family who owned it were collapsing too.

12.

In the early 1960s, a heated legal battle had erupted between Friedrich Flick and his elder son, Otto-Ernst. Succession was at stake, as was the future of the Flick conglomerate, West Germany's largest privately owned group of companies. As it had for Günther Quandt, dynastic and entrepreneurial continuity meant everything to Flick. But, unlike Günther, Flick never put in place the structures that would allow for smooth corporate succession as a way to pass the torch to his sons. To make matters worse, Otto-Ernst's desire to separate himself from his controlling father turned him into an authoritarian and brusque leader in the Flick boardroom, alienating those he worked with.

Otto-Ernst was the opposite of his cool, cerebral, and calculating father. During one tense family meeting in Düsseldorf, which had been called to discuss Otto-Ernst's professional future, he accused his father of being a coward. Flick responded that he "was the most good-natured person on the face of the earth, but not a coward," adding that his son would soon find that out for himself in court. The verdict that Flick's wife, Marie, delivered concerning her son was particularly brutal: "You were a person who justified great hopes. However, your few bad qualities have become so strong in the course of your life that . . . you lack the character requirements and the professional suitability to succeed your father."

After more years of tense disputes, Flick finally concluded in late 1961 that Marie was right: his elder son just wasn't cut from the right cloth. Flick amended his conglomerate's shareholder agreement in favor of his younger

*The Flick family in 1960. Otto-Ernst at the far left, Marie and Friedrich
in the center, and Friedrich Karl at the far right.*

son, Friedrich Karl, who was promoted over his eleven-year-older brother.
In response, Otto-Ernst sued his father and brother for breach of contract,
and he requested in court that the Flick conglomerate be dissolved and
divided up.

The court proceedings in Düsseldorf dragged on for years. Otto-Ernst
lost two trials. An out-of-court settlement was reached in fall 1965. Otto-
Ernst was bought out of the family conglomerate for about eighty million
deutsch marks, and his 30 percent stake was transferred to his three children. His younger brother, Friedrich Karl, now controlled the firm's majority of shares. Flick didn't particularly approve of this son either, but he
was running out of time and options for succession. He now set his hopes
on his two grandsons — both sons of Otto-Ernst — who went by the names
Muck and Mick.

Months after the conclusion of the settlement that tore her family apart,

Marie died. Flick's wife of more than fifty years had viewed both her surviving sons as incapable successors to her husband. Otto-Ernst "has always
been talented, capable, and industrious, but he doesn't get along." Friedrich
Karl "wasn't talented, capable, or industrious, but he gets along." That was
her merciless assessment.

After his wife's death, Flick, who suffered from a bronchial disease after
a lifetime of smoking cheap cigars, moved from Düsseldorf to southern
Germany for the fresh alpine air. He ended up taking permanent residency
in a hotel on Lake Constance, just minutes from Switzerland. Flick died at
the hotel, in his suite, on July 20, 1972, ten days after his eighty-ninth birthday.

13.

At the time of his death, Friedrich Flick was West Germany's wealthiest
man and among the world's five richest people. He controlled the nation's
largest privately owned conglomerate, with 103 majority and 227 significant minority stakes, annual revenue of almost $6 billion, and more than
216,000 employees, including those who worked for Daimler-Benz.

And yet Flick had refused to ever pay a cent in compensation to those
who performed forced or slave labor at factories and mines he controlled.
In the early 1960s, the Jewish Claims Conference submitted a claim against
Dynamit Nobel, an explosives turned plastics producer controlled by Flick.
During the war, it had used about twenty-six hundred Jewish women from
Hungary, Czechoslovakia, and Poland as slaves to make ammunition in
underground factories. The women were picked from the Auschwitz and
Gross-Rosen concentration camps and deported to Buchenwald sub-
camps, where they were put to work for the explosives firm. About half of
the women survived this ordeal. As it happened, Flick didn't own Dynamit
Nobel during the war. He became its majority shareholder only in 1959.
Cruelly, he didn't just reject the women's compensation claims outright.
Instead, he strung the negotiators along for years before pulling out of the

talks entirely. Even John J. McCloy, the former US high commissioner for occupied Germany who had ordered Flick's early prison release, got involved. He appealed to Flick's moral obligation, but of course he got nowhere.

In the fifteen years before the claim concerning Dynamit Nobel landed on his desk, Flick had gained a lot of experience with negotiations for restitution. During that period, the mogul settled three highly complex Aryanization cases. Without admitting any guilt, Flick restored a mere fraction of the massive industrial firms he had forcibly bought or helped seize from the Hahn and Petschek families, who had all immigrated. Not only was he able to hold on to all remaining assets, but Flick even managed to turn a profit by negotiating government compensation for all the coal he had given up to the Nazi conglomerate Reichswerke Hermann Göring in the Ignaz Petschek Aryanization.

It wasn't a surprise, then, when Hermann Josef Abs, the ubiquitous chairman of Deutsche Bank, struck a far more sober note during his eulogy at Flick's memorial service in Düsseldorf than he had at Günther Quandt's in Frankfurt. After settling with the Ignaz Petschek heirs for his own dubious role in the Aryanization, Abs mediated with the German government and Flick on behalf of the heirs. Ever the go-between, Abs then did the same for Flick in his callous dealings with the Jewish Claims Conference. At Flick's funeral, Abs said that any assessment of the tycoon's life's work should be "left to more objective historiography than is currently customary in our so tormented and beaten country."

It wasn't just Flick's — or his own — unholy dealings during the Third Reich that led Abs to this uncharacteristically morose declaration in late July 1972. In the 1960s the student protest movement had marked a cultural shift in West Germany. A more progressive generation had come of age, one that was born after the war and critical of the country's power structures, the Third Reich's continued stranglehold over high-ranking positions in virtually all aspects of society, and the lack of any real reckoning over Germany's Nazi past. The old reactionary men who led Germany's big industries were perplexed. They grew up in an era when authority was unquestionable and painful matters were simply swept under the rug. On top of that, after almost twenty-five years of relentless growth, West Germany's boom economy was finally cooling off. Flick left behind a rapidly aging conglomerate and a disintegrating family tasked with keeping it all together.

Otto-Ernst didn't attend his father's memorial service in Düsseldorf. Almost eighteen months later, he succumbed to a heart attack—a broken man at only fifty-seven years of age. His younger brother, Friedrich Karl, wasted no time in making the Flick conglomerate his own, succeeding his late father as CEO. In mid-January 1975, he announced the sale of a 29 percent stake in Daimler-Benz to Deutsche Bank for two billion deutsch marks. There had been rumors floating around that Friedrich Karl was negotiating to sell the Flicks' entire Daimler stake to the shah of Persia — the West German government found this unacceptable, especially since it came only six weeks after the sale of the Quandts' Daimler stake to Kuwait. So, Deutsche Bank stepped in. Friedrich Karl needed the liquidity for urgent family matters. The next month, he bought out his nephews, Muck and Mick, and his niece, Dagmar, for 405 million deutsch marks. Thus Otto-Ernst's three children were cut out of the family business, and Friedrich Karl now ruled over the Flick empire alone.

Unlike his stern, workaholic father, who preferred an austere lifestyle, Friedrich Karl enjoyed the trappings of wealth. He jetted between his mansions in Bavaria and Düsseldorf, a hunting estate in Austria, a villa on the Côte d'Azur, a penthouse in New York, a castle near Paris, and a two-hundred-foot yacht named the *Diana II*. His Munich parties were legendarily debauched. The Flick heir was smart but lazy and not overly interested in running the family business. He left that largely to his childhood friend, Eberhard von Brauchitsch, a dashing lawyer whom Flick senior had promoted to management. The two best friends now sat atop a pile of cash.

They made a deal with the West German Ministry of Finance: the billions from the sale of Daimler-Benz would be largely tax exempt, so long as the money was reinvested within two years into the German economy or in eligible assets abroad. So in the following years, several Flick-owned firms in Germany were upgraded, and hundreds of millions were reinvested in

American businesses such as the chemicals company W. R. Grace. The tax exemptions for West Germany's largest privately owned conglomerate were granted just in time.

But it all came crashing down in early November 1981, when tax authorities raided the office of the Flick conglomerate's chief accountant in Düsseldorf; he was suspected of personally evading taxes. What investigators found was far more insidious: documents detailing that, for more than a decade, von Brauchitsch had paid almost twenty-six million deutsch marks in bribes to West Germany's three largest political parties in order to facilitate the tax exemptions. A Catholic mission had been used to launder Flick-donated money back to the Flick conglomerate for cash distribution to its largest recipient: the CDU/CSU, an alliance of two conservative political parties, the Christian Democratic Union and Bavaria's Christian Social Union. Von Brauchitsch euphemistically referred to the bribes as "cultivating the political landscape."

The Flick affair, Germany's largest political corruption scandal to date, shook the country to its core. *Der Spiegel* called it "the bought republic." In the inquiry that followed, hundreds of current and former parliament members were implicated, including the new chancellor, Helmut Kohl. He got to keep his job, but his minister of economic affairs, Count Otto von

Eberhard von Brauchitsch and Friedrich Karl Flick, 1982.

Lambsdorff, was indicted for accepting bribes from the Flick conglomerate. He resigned his post. Friedrich Karl denied any knowledge of the payoffs and blamed everything on his friend von Brauchitsch. In 1987, the fired director was convicted to a two-year suspended prison sentence and a fine for tax evasion. Von Brauchitsch moved to Zurich and Monaco. He and Friedrich Karl remained close friends but seemingly out of necessity. Von Brauchitsch's later memoir carried a telling title: *The Price of Silence.*

By then the Flick conglomerate had ceased to exist. In December 1985, as many of the investigations into the Flick affair still went on, Friedrich Karl sold his entire business to Deutsche Bank for 5.4 billion deutsch marks ($2.2 billion), setting a new record for the largest corporate transaction in West Germany. Almost sixty years old, Friedrich Karl had had enough of big business. He cashed in and soon immigrated to tax-friendly Austria. Almost seventy years after his father started his first secret takeover of a steel firm, the Flick conglomerate dissolved. The bribery affair turned out to be one scandal too many for the notorious family business. As a German historian later concluded, all that remained of Friedrich Flick's once mighty firm was "the enormous fortune of his heirs and the bad sound of a name."

Like his father, Friedrich Karl steadfastly refused to compensate those who had performed forced and slave labor for the Flick conglomerate. He left it to Deutsche Bank to satisfy the claims of the Jewish Claims Conference against Dynamit Nobel. The bank did so promptly in January 1986, paying five million deutsch marks ($2 million) to those Jewish women who were still alive. A change was at hand in Germany, one that would dredge up the suppressed Nazi past of its most eminent business patriarchs.

14.

While the Flick empire was crumbling, other German business dynasties were imploding. The Porsche-Piëch clan had been generating headlines in the 1970s and '80s, but not for exciting new sports car designs. It was rather their sordid, intrafamilial sex scandals and infighting over succession that made the news. Added to these somewhat typical dynastic squabbles was the threat of abduction. In 1976, one of Rudolf-August Oetker's sons was kidnapped at the campus parking lot of the Bavarian university he attended. The student was held for forty-seven hours in a wooden box, where he received electric shocks. After his father paid a ransom of twenty-one million deutsch marks ($14.5 million) the young man was freed, but the ordeal left him disabled.

Still, of all the tragedies that could befall a business dynasty, a patriarch's death remained the most dangerous. On a sunny day in late April 1980, Baron August von Finck collapsed behind his writing desk at his Möschenfeld estate and died. He was eighty-one. At the time of his death, the reactionary aristocrat was considered Europe's richest banker, with an estimated fortune of more than two billion deutsch marks ($1.2 billion). He left behind the Merck Finck private bank as well as thousands of acres around Munich, some of the world's priciest land. The baron had five children from two marriages. The "penny-pinching tyrant ... subjected his five children to a Teutonic version of 'daddy dearest,' tightfisted and demanding, cold and remote," according to a profile in *Fortune* magazine. Von Finck bought his only daughter out of his will for mere crumbs and disinherited his son Gerhard in 1978 for "leading a dishonorable lifestyle" after immigrating to Canada. (Gerhard now works as an upmarket real estate broker in Toronto, where he offers "a combination of German efficiency and Canadian courtesy" to his clients.)

This left von Finck's three remaining sons to split the estate. The two eldest sons, August Jr. and Wilhelm, dutifully followed in their father's footsteps and took over Merck Finck. Their younger half brother, Helmut, chose a different path. He joined the mystical sect of Bhagwan Shree Rajneesh in Oregon. His arch-conservative siblings didn't take a shine to this. In February 1985, the duo summoned Helmut to a Munich notary, where he was asked to sign over his inheritance in exchange for sixty-five million deutsch marks. He accepted, left the Rajneesh movement, and became a horse breeder in Germany. Five years later, his half brothers sold Merck Finck to Barclays for 600 million deutsch marks.

It took another two decades for Helmut to remember that he had been addicted to alcohol and drugs when he signed over his inheritance, and therefore, according to him, he had not been legally competent. His half brothers had also violated their father's will by selling the family bank and other assets, Helmut argued. He sued, claiming the two owed him hundreds of millions of euros. In 2019, a court ruled that Helmut had been legally competent when he signed the agreement. He lost. Meanwhile, August Jr. had followed in his father's footsteps in other ways. He took to financing far-right politics.

15.

While other business dynasties fought, faltered, and even faded, the Quandts somehow survived. In early June 1982, Herbert Quandt died unexpectedly from heart failure while visiting relatives in Kiel, weeks before his seventy-second birthday. Herbert left behind six children from three marriages. Like his father, he had transferred much of his fortune before his death. His eldest daughter, a painter, received shares and real estate. The next three children received a majority stake in Varta, the battery behemoth formerly known as AFA. He left the jewels of his fortune to his third wife, Johanna, and their two children, Susanne and Stefan. They inherited about half of BMW plus Altana, the pharmaceuticals and chemicals firm formerly known as Byk Gulden. When Friedrich Karl Flick immigrated to Austria, this last batch of Herbert Quandt's heirs became Germany's wealthiest family.

Even though Herbert surpassed his father's success by saving and buying BMW, the visually impaired Quandt heir was unable to ever truly leave Günther's shadow. At a memorial service in Frankfurt's former opera house, Herbert's closest aide remembered his boss as someone who "remained in his innermost being the son who found his pride in not having disappointed his father's expectations."

After his death, the two branches of the Quandt dynasty began to manage their fortunes in neighboring office buildings near Bad Homburg's city

Herbert Quandt on his seventieth
birthday, 1980.

limits. Herbert's and Harald's heirs are separated not only by a street and
billions in net worth but also by different styles of doing business and contrasting outlooks: while one looks to the past, the other looks to the future.
Whereas Susanne and Stefan Quandt's office is housed in a plain brutalist
building from the 1960s named after their grandfather Günther, Harald's
heirs make their investments in sleek bungalow-type offices adorned with
greenery and named after their father and mother. They commissioned
portraits of Harald and his wife, Inge, from Andy Warhol. Harald's portrait
hangs in the foyer of their family office. The other Quandts put a stern portrait of Günther above the reception desk and placed busts of the Quandt
patriarch and Herbert in the entrance hall. Susanne and Stefan inherited
immense economic responsibility through control over BMW and Altana.
Harald's daughters, on the other hand, invest their money freely, aided by
their family office. They once got an offer to buy New York City's Chrysler
Building, but their mother couldn't come to a decision. The two Quandt
branches differ just as much as Herbert and Harald did: the older conser-

vative, myopic sibling desperate to please his father; the younger one modern and forward-looking, in spite, or because, of everything.

In a stunning historical reckoning for the more modern Quandt branch,
one of Harald's five daughters converted to Judaism. When Colleen-Bettina
Quandt was orphaned in 1978, she was only sixteen. Earlier that year, she'd
first learned that her grandmother was Magda Goebbels, the First Lady
of the Third Reich. Her family didn't break the news to her — it had come
from her Jewish boyfriend. Just like Magda during her teenage years in
Berlin, Colleen-Bettina befriended a group of young Jews in Frankfurt. She
too felt alienated at home, was searching for a way to belong, and became
fascinated by Judaism. The news that a granddaughter of Magda Goebbels
had a Jewish boyfriend spread like wildfire through Frankfurt's tight-knit
religious community. "In the end, the whole Mishpacha knew," she later
told a biographer of the Quandt dynasty. Not everyone in the Jewish community welcomed her with open arms. Some of her friends' parents even
refused to talk to her.

Colleen-Bettina ended up moving to New York City to study jewelry
design at Parsons School of Design. As in Frankfurt, most of her friends
in New York were Jewish, and it was there that she decided to convert to
modern Orthodox Judaism. In 1987, at age twenty-five, Magda's granddaughter converted in front of three rabbis. Soon after this event, she met
Michael Rosenblat, a German Jew who had moved to New York to work in
the textile trade. Rosenblat grew up in an Orthodox Jewish household in
Hamburg. His father had survived a concentration camp. His family now
had to get used to the fact that he was dating not just a convert but also the
granddaughter of the Third Reich's most notorious matriarch.

But love prevailed. In 1989, the German couple married in a New York
synagogue. Colleen-Bettina was glad to lose her maiden name. "Quandt,
this name only annoyed and destroyed. Bodyguards, conflict, endless lone-
liness. Terribly envious people and hypocrites — I don't want to have anything to do with that anymore," she told a German journalist in 1998. She
and Rosenblat had divorced the year before, but she carries his surname to
this day.

PART VI

THE RECKONING

1.

In 2019, Stefan Quandt and Susanne Klatten, Herbert Quandt's youngest children and the two heirs to BMW, no longer could claim to be Germany's wealthiest family. Another dynasty, even more reclusive, overtook them that year: the Reimanns. No picture of a Reimannn heir had ever become public. No one even knew where the family lived. This clan of shareholders controlled JAB, a consumer goods investment firm that was based, for tax reasons, in Luxembourg. Since 2012, JAB has spent more than $50 billion to acquire all-American food and beverage brands such as Snapple, Dr Pepper, Krispy Kreme doughnuts, Peet's Coffee, Einstein Bros. Bagels, Stumptown Coffee Roasters, Keurig Green Mountain, Panera Bread, and Pret A Manger. In Europe, the firm bought Douwe Egberts. The Reimann family also controls the beauty label Coty and the fashion brand Bally. They once owned Jimmy Choo.

But the roots of the Reimann family fortune run far deeper than doughnuts, bagels, coffee, lipstick, and stiletto heels. They lie in the bleak industrial city of Ludwigshafen, a one-hour drive south of Frankfurt. For four generations, the Reimann dynasty owned and ran Joh. A. Benckiser (JAB), a specialty chemicals firm that operated out of Ludwigshafen. Under Albert Reimann's leadership in the 1960s, the family firm branched out into household consumer goods, forming the basis for an empire that is omnipresent in our lives as consumers. Albert was the father of the current Reimann heirs. He died in 1984. Like so many German tycoons of his generation, Albert had led a double life, hiding many dark secrets. His Nazi past was just one facet of a bizarre history that began to unfold, in real time, as four of his heirs emerged as Germany's wealthiest family.

News of the Reimanns' Nazi history first broke when the British tabloid *Mail on Sunday* revealed, in September 2018, that Albert had been a member of the NSDAP. The reporters had found his membership card in a German archive, which they had been digging through after JAB's $2 billion acquisition of Pret A Manger, the global sandwich chain founded by a Jewish Londoner. That founder, who had died in 2017, could not respond to the tabloid story, but his sister did: "I am horrified . . . My brother would have been mortified. We are a Jewish family." Spokespeople for JAB and the Reimann family told the tabloid that they were aware that Albert had been a member of the Nazi Party and confirmed that his company had made use of forced labor and prisoners of war. But that was it, for now. The article contained no other details.

After reading the story in fall 2018, I called up the Reimann family's longtime spokeswoman in Düsseldorf. I had reported for years on JAB's global spree of acquisitions while I was still at *Bloomberg News*. In fact, the first story I ever broke at *Bloomberg*, back in 2012, identified the four reclusive Reimann shareholders behind JAB. In addition to their names and ages, my colleague and I found out that most of them were trained chemists who ran a children's charity and had never actually worked in their father's consumer goods business. Their family office was based in Vienna. The Reimanns had traded in their German passports for Austrian ones, a tax-avoidance move that many wealthy German families took advantage of. (Among its various fiscal benefits, Austria has no inheritance tax.) We discovered little more than that at the time.

In fall 2018, the spokeswoman assured me over the phone that there was nothing more to the Reimann Nazi story that had just been published. Yes, Albert Reimann had belonged to the NSDAP, but that was it, she said. Suppressing my reporter's instinct, I accepted her explanation. For a year already, I had been working on this book about German business dynasties and their Third Reich histories. The last thing I wanted was to add yet another family to the story.

That soon changed. In late March 2019, the front page of *Bild am Sonntag*, Germany's largest Sunday tabloid, carried a major scoop: the Nazi history of the Reimann dynasty. A *Bild* reporter had discovered in archives that Albert Reimann, his sister Else, *and* their father were early believers in the Nazi cause and virulent anti-Semites. The father-and-son duo began donating to the SS in 1931 and became members of the NSDAP in 1932.

The two men even successively joined Ludwighafen's city council, representing the Nazi Party. In May 1933, Albert's father told his employees: "The Jew Karl Marx gathered only the worst people around him to carry out his idea, while Hitler has gathered the best." In July 1937, Albert wrote a letter to Heinrich Himmler, saying, "We are a purely Aryan family business that is over 100 years old. The owners are unconditional followers of the race theory." Albert Reimann was thirty-eight years old at the time, and the firm's chief executive. His sister Else married an SS man.

The *Bild* reporter also found that by 1943, 30 percent of the Reimanns' workforce at their chemicals plant, or some 175 people, consisted of forced labor or French prisoners of war. The firm's factory foreman brutally abused these workers and even tortured a Russian woman in the coal cellar of Albert's private villa. Albert encouraged this mistreatment. His foreman ordered female coerced laborers to stand naked outside their barracks in the middle of the night so he could grope them. During an Allied air raid in 1945, the foreman kicked dozens of workers out from the company's bomb shelters. One Russian was killed; others were injured.

After the war, Ludwigshafen fell within the French occupation zone. The Allies arrested Albert and held him in an internment camp. The family firm's assets were seized, and their shares were frozen. In February 1947, the French authorities dismissed father and son Reimann from their own firm and banned them from other positions in business. But the two men engaged in occupation zone arbitrage. They appealed their sentence in Heidelberg, which was in the American occupation zone; they owned a second home there. And like so many other Germans, the father and son then procured *Persilschein* statements, falsely attesting to their stance against the Nazis and their active involvement in the Resistance. The two were classified as Nazi followers in their denazification trials. They had to pay a small fine; then their company was returned to them. Over the next decades, Albert turned his family firm in Ludwigshafen into a major consumer goods business, producing Kukident denture adhesive cream and Calgonit dishwasher detergent.

None of the Reimanns commented on the revelations in *Bild am Sonntag*. But Peter Harf, JAB's chairman and the Reimanns' longtime family confidant, confirmed all of the reporting and added that father and son Reimann "should have gone to prison." Harf announced that the family would donate ten million euros ($11.3 million) to a suitable organization. He also revealed that the Reimanns had long before commissioned a prominent German history professor to research their family's Nazi history, creating an independent study that would be available to the public. Weeks before the *Bild* story broke, the historian had presented an interim report to five Reimanns and to Harf: "We were ashamed and went white as a sheet. There is nothing to gloss over. These crimes are disgusting," Harf said.

The fallout from the Reimann revelations was swift. Most of the brands the family controls are based in the United States and deeply embedded in American culture. Headlines like "Krispy Kreme Owners Admit to Family History of Nazi Ties" circled the globe. Calls for boycotts soon followed. The *Boston Globe*'s Jewish American food critic wrote a searing column called "I Found Out Nazi Money Is Behind My Favorite Coffee. Should I Keep Drinking It?" My personal favorite was a parody piece in *McSweeney's*, titled "This Is Embarrassing, but It Turns Out Our Fake Jewish Bagel Chain Was Funded by Nazis." The Reimanns desperately needed damage control, and fast, lest their reputation and their brands be marred beyond repair. The family had to issue a response. When they finally did, they made global headlines once again.

The Reimanns leaned on Peter Harf—arguably too much. The Cologne-born, Harvard Business School–trained economist is primarily responsible for creating the Reimanns' fortune, estimated at around thirty-two billion euros ($39 billion) in 2020. Harf's steering of their assets also made him a billionaire. Albert Reimann's heirs appointed Harf as CEO of the family business in 1988, seven years after he left Boston Consulting Group and joined the company in Ludwigshafen. Over the next decades, Harf and a Dutch protégé turned the family firm into Reckitt Benckiser, one of the world's largest consumer-goods companies. In 2012, Harf and two lieutenants used the money from Reckitt dividends and sales of shares to establish JAB as the Reimanns' own investment firm, with a strategy focused on coffee, carbs, beauty, and luxury goods. In 2019, JAB expanded into pet care.

Harf is bald, with an intense gaze and a ready smile. He has a penchant for jeans, colorful designer shirts worn untucked, and glasses with heavy black frames mostly seen on architects and artists, not staid German executives. But he's more cosmopolitan than your average global executive — living variously in London, Milan, and New York — and better connected too. Harf modeled JAB after his idol's firm, Berkshire Hathaway. Although Harf's returns haven't been as good as Warren Buffett's, everybody who's anybody seems keen to stake some of their money with JAB. From Buffett and his favorite banker, the former Goldman Sachs partner Byron Trott, to the Brazilian investment firm 3G, to France's Peugeot family, to Belgian and Colombian beer dynasties: all have invested in JAB and worked with Harf. During my prior reporting on the company, Harf's brief answers via email were always carefully crafted and rather generic, revealing little. Everything about JAB and the Reimanns was shrouded in mystery, a communications strategy orchestrated by Harf and executed by an expensive PR firm in New York for the business side and a spokeswoman in Düsseldorf for the family. *Bild*'s revelations were a blow to that meticulously controlled image. But they also presented an opportunity for change. "By assuming responsibility for the past, damage to the company in the present and in the future had to be averted," Harf later wrote to me. "If I had had to choose between the interests of the company and responsibility for the past, I think I would have chosen the latter."

2.

During the 1990s, external pressures forced German businesses to deal with a part of their Nazi past that they had avoided for decades: the brutal use of millions of people in forced and slave labor. The Berlin Wall and the Soviet Union fell. The Cold War ended, and Germany was finally reunified. More than a million surviving coerced laborers were freed after decades behind the Iron Curtain, and some turned their anger on the German firms that had exploited them under the Nazi regime. In the United States, survivors sued German businesses in class action lawsuits, while advertisements called for boycotts of German companies and their products. In a globalizing world, German firms began to feel the damage that their unresolved involvement with the Nazis could do to their share prices, sales, and standing. Some firms opened their archives to allow historians to research the company's role in the Third Reich; a few even commissioned the research themselves. Daimler-Benz, Volkswagen, Allianz, and Deutsche Bank were the most prominent among them.

By the time these studies were initiated, none of the global German companies that had commissioned them were controlled by a business dynasty. The Flicks and Quandts were long out of Daimler, as were the von Fincks from Allianz and Munich Re. The dynastic influence over Volkswagen was limited to Ferdinand Piëch, a mighty descendant of Anton Piëch and Ferdinand Porsche. He began leading the Volkswagen Group in 1993, years after a study was commissioned but not before disgruntled executives who had been passed over for the job leaked the story that Piëch was an inappropriate choice to head the company, given that his father and grandfather had used tens of thousands of people as forced and slave labor during their reign at Volkswagen. Piëch's enemies insinuated that his appointment would cause bad press in America, Volkswagen's most important growth market. Piëch survived the attack, and none of the other German business dynasties made any effort during the 1990s to shed light on their families' roles in the Third Reich.

A branch of the Flick dynasty — specifically the sons of Otto-Ernst Flick, Muck and Mick — was the first to experience public blowback, after attaching their surname to philanthropic giving in academia and art. The two had been bought out of the Flick conglomerate for hundreds of millions of deutsch marks by their uncle Friedrich Karl, back in 1975 — alongside their sister, Dagmar, who received much less money than her brothers, as she had been given half as many shares to begin with.

In 1992, Muck, who was based in London, was appointed to Oxford University's court of benefactors, following his initial donation of 350,000 pounds. This money was used to create a professorship under the Flick name at Balliol College. But in 1996, Muck withdrew his name and his money amid a wave of protests over the Flick family's past. Protesters were incensed that the Flicks had thus far refused to compensate any survivors of forced and slave labor. Although, in an open letter to the *Daily Telegraph*, the multimillionaire Muck expressed his "total abhorrence of what took place in Germany during the Third Reich" and his "profound personal shame for the involvement of my grandfather in these dreadful events," he told the *Jewish Chronicle* that compensation could leave him "destitute," adding, "How can you compensate for human tragedy with money?"

Although the uproar in Oxford died down after Muck withdrew his money, the Flick controversy concerning compensation was only just beginning. In August 2000, a foundation named Remembrance, Responsibility, and the Future (EVZ) was established in Berlin by the German state and German companies. The EVZ was founded following an agreement between the US and German governments. Compensation payments would be made to survivors of forced and slave labor on the condition that no more legal cases would be brought against German firms before American courts. As one historian put it: "In this way, the German government and German industry together developed a rhetoric of responsibility with, yet again, no explicit or individual admission of legal liability . . . the German government occupied the moral high ground, while significant perpetrators conveniently disappeared behind a veil of apparent responsibility without actual guilt." The negotiator for the German state was Count Otto von Lambsdorff, the only minister who had been forced to resign because of the Flick bribery scandal. The former politician was even convicted of tax evasion in the affair, but that was clearly no impediment to becoming the head of the negotiations for compensation.

Between 2001 and 2006, the EVZ paid out about 4.4 billion euros (around $5.85 billion by December 2006) to more than 1.66 million former coerced laborers. To the almost 300,000 surviving slave laborers used in concentration camps and ghettos, the highest compensation was 7,670 euros each (about $10,000). To the 1.35 million who had survived forced labor, it was 2,560 euros each (about $3,500). In all, the state of Germany and German businesses contributed equally to the 5.2 billion euros (almost $7 billion) that the foundation had at its disposal. But more than 60 percent of that money had been contributed by just 17 firms out of the 6,500 German companies paying into the EVZ fund. These 17 businesses included major global names such as Allianz, BMW, Daimler, Volkswagen, Siemens, and Krupp. About 1,560 German firms contributed only some 500 euros each ($665) to the foundation — a symbolic gesture at best.

All the money that was pledged by German companies was supposed to have been paid by the time the EVZ foundation was established in 2000. However, when the EVZ started its operations that year, it was still missing hundreds of millions in contributions that various German firms and their owners had pledged. Companies controlled by the Quandts and Reimanns had already paid in, as had those owned by the Porsche-Piëch clan and the Oetkers. Now, the Flicks were called upon by the foundation to do the same. But with no immediate effect.

In 2001, when Muck's younger brother, Mick, announced the building of a museum in Zurich, to be designed by Rem Koolhaas as a place to house Mick's contemporary art collection, the compensation controversy reignited. Major protests broke out against the proposed museum. Mick withdrew the plan and instead lent his collection to a museum in Berlin in 2004. Again, the story caught fire. At the height of the uproar, Mick's sister, Dagmar, wrote an open letter in *Die Zeit*, announcing that she had anonymously contributed millions to the EVZ in early 2001 and that she was commissioning a group of German historians to chronicle the Flick firm and family during the twentieth century. Dagmar's brothers soon followed her example. Mick mimicked his sister particularly closely: he first donated millions to the EVZ, and then funded the work of five historians who investigated the operations of the Flick conglomerate during the Third Reich.

3.

Despite the commotion they caused, those three siblings actually were the small fry of the Flick dynasty. They were merely worth millions. The family billions belonged to their uncle, Friedrich Karl. He immigrated to Austria a few years after selling the Flick conglomerate for $2.2 billion to Deutsche Bank, and he died there at the age of seventy-nine, in 2006.

But even in death, Friedrich Karl couldn't escape the Flick dynasty's no-toriety. In 2008, grave robbers removed the 660-pound coffin containing his body from a mausoleum in the Austrian lakeside town of Velden. They demanded a ransom of six million euros ($7.5 million) from his widow, Ingrid, a petite blonde constantly surrounded by bodyguards. Friedrich Karl's remains were later recovered in Hungary and reburied in Velden. "Finally, my husband is back home," Ingrid told a German tabloid. "The hoping and fearing have ended. The prayers were answered."

Like his father, Friedrich Karl refused to compensate survivors of forced and slave labor, and he never contributed to the EVZ. Friedrich Karl's four children, from two different wives, each inherited a quarter of his $6 billion fortune in 2006. His youngest children, a set of twins, were only seven years old when he died. At his death, those twins, a boy and a girl, became the world's youngest billionaires. Their money is invested by the Flick family office in central Vienna, near the State Opera. And their mother, Ingrid, a carpenter's daughter and former hotel receptionist, is tasked with steering their fortune and foundation.

Ingrid prides herself on her philanthropic giving. "I help wherever I consider it useful and necessary," she told a regional Austrian newspaper in 2019. Five years earlier, for example, Ingrid had donated "a very substantial

Ingrid Flick.

amount" to the Tel Aviv Museum of Art, which would be used in part "for a cross-cultural exchange of Jewish, Muslim and Christian children called 'The Art Road to Peace.'" However, helping victims of the Flick empire was apparently never a cause worth taking up for the billionaire branch of the Flick family after Friedrich Karl's death. Despite their largesse, Ingrid and Friedrich Karl's eldest daughters haven't contributed a dime to the EVZ.

Meanwhile, Ingrid chairs the Friedrich Flick Foundation in Düsseldorf. She directs money to educational, medical, and cultural causes, primarily in Germany and Austria, through a family foundation still named after a convicted Nazi war criminal in whose factories and mines tens of thousands of people worked and died in forced or slave labor, including thousands of Jews. But looking at the foundation's website, you would never know of the Flick fortune's tainted past, nor that of its founding patriarch. In fact, Ingrid's "main concern" as chair is to "continue the foundation's philanthropic activities in the spirit of the founder, Dr. Friedrich Flick" and her late husband — two men notorious for many things, but not charity.

Flick established his namesake foundation in 1963, evidently for purposes of whitewashing. Through his philanthropy, the Nuremberg convict hoped to restore and add luster to his name in order to be granted one of Germany's highest federal honors, the Order of Merit, for his eightieth birthday. It worked. Then, in 2006, Ingrid Flick took over as the foundation's chair and kept its name intact — but another institution took a different path. In 2008, Friedrich Flick's name was removed from a high school in the town of his birth, Kreuztal, after years of intense local debate, which received much national attention. A school shouldn't be named after a convicted Nazi war criminal, argued the side in favor of replacing his name. But another more prominent educational institution hasn't seemed as ardent about placing the facts of history above the desire for funding.

Since 2015, the Friedrich Flick Foundation has been cofunding several prominent academic initiatives at Frankfurt's renowned Goethe University, including a prestigious German student scholarship. In 2018, the Flick charity took over the cofinancing of a visiting professorship in financial history at the university from the Edmond de Rothschild Group, the Swiss

French branch of the Jewish banking dynasty. The Flick money has since helped bring in professors from Princeton, Berkeley, and Oxford. The spending hasn't gone unrewarded. The Friedrich Flick Foundation has earned a seat on the university's foundation board of trustees.

It's not the first time that Goethe University has accepted money from a foundation named after a Nazi profiteer and thereby honored him. In 2015, the university christened a campus lounge with the name Adolf Messer, following a decade-long series of donations by his namesake foundation. It was no secret that Messer had been an early member of the NSDAP who profited from arms production and the use of forced labor at his machinery firm. But students protested this travesty. "Adolf Messer is in no way a role model for students and teachers at Goethe University," they argued. Eventually the outcry had an effect. The lounge was renamed in 2019, after four years of protest and debate. The Messer family rechristened its foundation too.

But donations from the Friedrich Flick Foundation have continued to roll in, hidden in plain sight — until now.

Many more foundations in Germany have been named after businessmen who backed and benefited from the Nazi regime and were convicted for this after the war. Take the foundations named for Alfried Krupp and Fritz Thyssen, for example. At least they cannot be accused of completely hiding the past. Whereas the Friedrich Flick Foundation continues to bury its Third Reich legacy, the charitable institutions associated with Krupp and Thyssen are more transparent; each provides information on its website about the Nazi convictions or crimes of its eponymous tycoon. Anyone receiving a donation from one of these foundations can at least learn something about the person whose name it honors.

Ingrid Flick once said this about her twins: "The kids have to learn that they are nothing special, but that the name Flick obliges." But what exactly does it oblige, in the case of Ingrid? If the Flick matriarch's penance for her family's tainted wealth and vicious past is any indicator, it's not much.

And though Ingrid Flick may be complicit in burying the sins that cling to her inherited fortune, the Austrian heiress is far from the only one.

4.

On the evening of September 30, 2007, near midnight, a documentary screened, without advance notice, on Germany's primary public broadcast channel. It was titled *The Silence of the Quandts*. The ominous audio set a tense tone as the introduction posed a question: are the Quandts, Germany's wealthiest dynasty, deliberately hiding their family past? In the twenty-five years since Herbert's death, his wealthiest and most visible heirs — those who control BMW — had maintained a near-total silence in the media. While many brutal facts about their patriarchs' activities during Third Reich had emerged in a bestselling family biography in 2002, Herbert's BMW heirs did not comment in it on the dark part of the Quandts' history, which it laid bare. But the broadcast finally forced all the Quandts to speak out.

The documentary's visceral power lay in the testimony of two surviving slave laborers who had toiled in AFA's Hannover factory while held captive in its subcamp. One of them, a Danish man in his eighties, was interviewed at the former site of the Quandt-owned factory and the SS-led subcamp. There, he spoke about the sheer hellishness of the place. "Whenever I dream, I'm here in the camp," Carl-Adolf Soerensen said as he looked around in horror. "This will stay that way for as long as I live."

AFA's successor company, Varta, had declined the request for a grant from a group of surviving Danish slave laborers in 1972. "Since we recognize neither a legal nor a moral obligation that could be derived from culpable behavior on the part of our company, we ask for your understanding if we do not take your request into account," the Quandt-owned firm answered. In the documentary, Soerensen responded to this statement: "They reacted harshly and arrogantly. They humiliated us."

In the late 1980s, Varta eventually did grant money for a different but related purpose: to preserve the Neuengamme concentration camp as a memorial site. But even then, the chairman of the charity making the request had to work hard to convince those at Varta to do so. And after Varta finally sent the check in support of the memorial — only five thousand deutsch marks, an amount so low the chairman thought it was a mistake — the battery behemoth then asked that an expense receipt be sent along to the company, to make the grant tax deductible.

Whereas the wealthiest Quandts declined to be interviewed for the documentary, one of Herbert's other children did speak. Sven Quandt had inherited part of Varta and sat on its supervisory board. On screen, Sven smilingly rejected any moral responsibility for his inherited fortune and minimized his father's and grandfather's involvement in the crimes of the Third Reich. The Quandt heir also urged Germany to move on from its Nazi past: "We must try to forget about this. Similar things happened ... all over the world. Nobody talks about those anymore."

The broadcast drew millions of viewers. For the Quandts it was a public relations disaster. The compelling testimony of the surviving slave laborers and Sven's dismissive, tone-deaf comments created a dissonance that could not be ignored. Unfortunately, the documentary was also flawed. It introduced the false premise that the Quandts' wealth had started with Nazi era profits — a fortune built on the backs of laborers both forced and enslaved. This was given as the reason for their utter silence. But this conclusion was misleading. Günther Quandt was already one of Germany's wealthiest men when Hitler came to power.

On October 5, 2007, five days after the broadcast, Herbert's and Harald's heirs issued a terse joint statement. The documentary's accusations had "moved" the family, it said. The Quandts admitted that they had failed to own up to their Third Reich history. They now planned to commission a historian who would independently research the family's Nazi past, open their archives to facilitate the inquiry, and publish the findings. In conclusion they asked the media "to treat our history as a German business family with care and fairness." That was rich, coming from a dynasty that still denied basic respect to the survivors of forced and slave labor exploited by their firms. The family statement did not even include an apology to them.

Although Germany's richest family rarely gave interviews, Herbert's BMW heirs had been bestowing a journalism award since 1986 — the Herbert Quandt Media Prize, annually endowed with fifty thousand euros ($60,000) and named after a man once described as having "an almost pathological inclination for secrecy." Months after the documentary was broadcast, three editors in chief resigned from the board of the Quandt foundation that awards the prize. They no longer wanted to be involved with bestowing an award in Herbert's name while the research into the family's Nazi past was ongoing. But the BMW Quandts continued to confer the media prize that year, and have every year since.

During the June 2008 award ceremony, Stefan Quandt, Germany's wealthiest heir, was the first of the dynasty to publicly state his regret for the use of forced and slave labor at Quandt-owned firms during the Third Reich. While he stopped short of apologizing, Stefan expressed his grief for the many coerced workers who suffered and died in Quandt factories during the war. But although the family-commissioned study was three years away from completion, Herbert's youngest son was already defending his forebears and deflecting any criticism of them. During the Third Reich, Günther and Herbert had been forced to operate "in a climate of fear and insecurity," Stefan argued. A puzzling claim, considering that even Günther hadn't seen it that way. In his memoir, the Quandt family patriarch wrote that he could have left Nazi Germany whenever he wanted to, but he had stayed to keep his firms and factories running.

Five months after Stefan's statement, in November 2008, his older sister, Susanne Klatten, Germany's wealthiest woman, for the first time opened up to a journalist about her personal life. The reasons for the sudden transparency with the *Financial Times Deutschland* were many. For one, Susanne was emerging from a sordid affair. That previous fall, while the documentary on her family's Nazi era history rocked Germany, the married Quandt heiress was being blackmailed by her former lover, Helg Sgarbi. He was demanding millions from her. The swindler from Switzerland had had an accomplice secretly tape the couple while they were having sex in a hotel room. If she refused to pay, Sgarbi would send the sex tapes to her family, to the press, and to BMW's management — she served on the company's supervisory board. Eventually Susanne went to the police and Sgarbi was arrested. Now the extortion case was making headlines all over the world.

The interview, therefore, touched only briefly on her family's Nazi past.

Susanne didn't deflect the matter or jump to conclusions as her younger brother had. "A light has been cast on something dark," said the Quandt heiress. "That's always better than when it grows powerful in the dark . . . It's better to know what was there than to ignore it." The forty-six-year-old Susanne said, in conclusion, "I will never lose respect and love for my father. No one can judge what it was like to live back then."

It took another three years for the Quandt-commissioned history professor, Joachim Scholtyseck, and his researchers to complete their study. The 1,183-page book, published in September 2011, provided a wealth of evidence for the complicity of Günther and Herbert, their top executives, and Quandt-owned companies in the crimes of the Third Reich. Günther was a ruthless opportunist, not a committed Nazi, according to Scholtyseck. Regardless, his entrepreneurship was "inseparably" linked to Nazi crimes, the historian wrote. Günther's desire to increase his fortune was so strong that it "left no room for fundamental questions of law and morality." Scholtyseck concluded: "The family patriarch was part of the Nazi regime."

Günther had removed Jewish board members "lightheartedly and shamefully early," the professor wrote. He also discovered more Aryanizations carried out by father and son alike: "Quandt wasn't one of the 'friendly' buyers who fulfilled their obligations . . . Rather, he belonged to the large group of 'Aryanizers' who consciously and coolly exploited the plight of the Jewish owners in order to take over their available firms," Scholtyseck explained. "Doubts about the legitimacy of the 'Aryanizations' or moral reservations cannot be found . . . with Günther Quandt, his son Herbert, or their managers."

The historian judged Herbert's role in the Nazi era harshly: "There can be no doubt that Herbert . . . was aware of the extent of the Quandt Group's involvement in the regime's acts of injustice regarding the use of forced labor and concentration camp prisoners, but also with regard to the Aryanizations. To the best of present knowledge, he didn't express any reservations about his father's management, not at the time nor in hindsight. What's more, in the course of his ascent to the top of the firm, he himself bore direct responsibility for the injustices committed."

5.

In September 2011, Stefan Quandt and his cousin Gabriele, a daughter of Harald, sat down with two journalists from *Die Zeit*, Germany's highbrow weekly newspaper, for the family's first and only interview, to date, on the study's findings. One of the interviewers was Rüdiger Jungbluth, writer of the 2002 bestselling Quandt family biography and the first to bring the dynasty's Nazi past to a larger audience.

Gabriele expressed her horror and shame at the way forced and slave laborers were treated in Quandt-owned firms during the Third Reich. She concluded: "It hurts. Günther Quandt is our grandfather. But we would have liked to have had another one. Or rather: we would have liked to have had him differently." The documentary, though flawed, had put things in motion, Gabriele said. She "found the insinuation that our publicity shyness suggested that we had skeletons in the closet, and that our money came from dubious sources, painful and outrageous. But it woke us up."

Apparently not everyone woke up. Stefan again went on the defensive. The interview began with Germany's richest heir recounting the things that the study confirmed his grandfather Günther was *not:* ". . . not an anti-Semite. Not a convinced National Socialist. And not a warmonger." Günther's many Aryanizations were news to the forty-five-year-old Quandt heir. He described the revelations as "painful." But even so, Stefan didn't share Scholtyseck's conclusion that his grandfather was a part of the Nazi regime: "I would prefer 'part of the Nazi system.' I interpret 'regime' as political leadership, to which he didn't belong. He took advantage of the opportunities the system offered industrialists, but he didn't pursue its ideological goals."

And although Stefan acknowledged that coerced workers endured terrible circumstances in the family factories and found it "a sad truth that people didn't survive forced labor in Quandt companies," the BMW heir argued that Günther "didn't pursue the goal of killing people. This is something that is close to my heart as a grandson. That line wasn't crossed. The employment of forced labor was necessary in the system at that time to maintain production. The German men were at the front." Stefan ignored the fact that Günther had directly benefited from the frontline killing, simply by being one of Nazi Germany's largest producers of arms and ammo.

Whereas Stefan conceded that his father, Herbert, was also a part of that same Nazi system and participated in the use of forced and slave labor, he considered the Third Reich era too short a period to serve as a basis for understanding Herbert or inferring his "entire personality from his actions. He stood in his father's shadow." Stefan announced in the interview that, together with his mother, Johanna, and his sister, Susanne, the three BMW heirs would make a donation to Berlin's forced labor documentation center. The center is located in an intact camp that had imprisoned two hundred enslaved women at the Pertrix factory, for which Herbert was responsible during the war. His heirs would give more than five million euros (about $6 million) toward its renovation, as well as its educational programs and exhibitions, including one on Pertrix's use of forced and slave labor. Stefan had visited the center, and he was impressed by the remembrance work being done there.

When the interviewers asked Stefan about his half brother's statement that Germany should just forget about its Nazi past, he eventually admitted that Sven's answers were unfortunate: "I don't see any point in time in Germany when we can say: We shouldn't think about the Nazi era anymore, or no longer reflect on it. But it also can't be that this country defines itself only through the twelve years of National Socialism." But Stefan had at first stood up for Sven, stating that he "was not prepared for these questions." Stefan seemed to find it unfair that a reporter might ask him, or one of his relatives, a question without forewarning or a chance to vet it beforehand. This from the steward of an annual journalism prize.

Stefan described the family's distancing from his father and grandfather as necessary but a "massive and painful" inner conflict. And yet, despite these admissions, little seemed to change among the younger, more penitent Quandts. The BMW Quandts wouldn't remove Günther's name for their headquarters in Bad Homburg. "We cannot and do not want to erase Günther Quandt from our history, but we will remember him with his light and dark sides. Everything else is too easy," Stefan said in the interview.

Germany's wealthiest family also decided to retain Herbert's name for the media prize and one of their foundations. Stefan believed his father's "life's work" justified it. The Quandt heir didn't find it strange that they awarded a media prize in the name of a man who rarely spoke to the press, let alone one who bore "direct responsibility" in the crimes of the Third Reich. Like Herbert before him, Stefan was apparently unable or unwilling to escape his father's shadow.

Stefan said in the interview that the family's most important goals in commissioning the study of their history were "openness and transparency." But, for an entire decade following the interview, when you visited the website of the Herbert Quandt Media Prize and read the biography of its namesake, you would find no mention of his activities during the Nazi era except one: he joined the executive board of AFA in 1940. Nothing was written about his crimes, those of his father, or those of their firms. The website's description of Scholtyseck's study was bafflingly vague. The reason for the study and the weight of its findings were absent, nor was the Third Reich mentioned anywhere. From this one could have parsed the study's real impetus — public pressure, but not an honest desire to confront a challenging history. This euphemistic statement was as close as the website got to expressing the reason for the study: "As with other important firms and entrepreneurial families of the 20th century, there was a loud call for an overall presentation of the family business history."

Only in the last week of October 2021, more than a decade after the study was published but just days after the latest in a series of inquiries from me, was Herbert's whitewashed biography on the website suddenly replaced with an expanded one. This version included some of his activities during the Third Reich, part of Scholtyseck's findings and conclusions, and the reason the study came about: public pressure.

6.

At first, it seemed that things were going more smoothly for members of the Oetker dynasty as they reckoned with their father's sins. In mid-

October 2013, two years after the interview with the Quandt heirs, two journalists from *Die Zeit* again sat down with a press-averse business heir to discuss the findings of yet another family-commissioned study into its firm and the family's history during the Third Reich. Again, Rüdiger Jung-bluth was one of the journalists. He had followed up his 2002 biography of the Quandts with one focused on the Oetkers; it had been published in 2004. Though Jungbluth had been denied access to the Oetker archives, he still found plenty about their Nazi connections. And now that the pa-triarch had passed away some years earlier and the study was about to be published, one Oetker was finally ready to speak.

Rudolf-August Oetker had died in Hamburg at the age of ninety, in Jan-uary 2007 — the last of the Nazi billionaires. The former Waffen-SS officer, partly trained at Dachau, left behind a global conglomerate in Bielefeld with an annual revenue of $15 billion and interests in shipping, food, bev-erages, private banking, and luxury hotels. Dr. Oetker's frozen pizzas and pudding powder were known around the world. His eight children from three marriages had each inherited an equal stake in the family business, making them individual billionaires. At Rudolf-August's death, the heirs were also left with some questions.

Their father had rarely spoken with his children about the Nazi era and the war, but they knew that he had been to Dachau. The year before his death, Rudolf-August published a private memoir, *Spoiled by Luck*, which apparently revealed little about that period of his life. In 2008, a year after his death, Rudolf-August's children, on their own initiative, commissioned three historians to research the activities of their firm, their father, and his stepfather, Richard Kaselowsky, during the Third Reich. Their father had vetoed such a study while he was alive, but the documentary about the Quandts prompted the Oetkers to bring some clarity to the subject before the press did it for them.

That clarity finally came in fall 2013. The historians concluded in their study that "Kaselowsky, and with him the family and the Oetker company, bore responsibility for the political system in which they lived. They were pillars of Nazi society, they sought proximity to the regime, and profited from its policies." It was Oetker's eldest son, August, who spoke in October

2013 to Jungbluth and a *Zeit* colleague about the imminent publication of the study and his father's past. August was born in 1944, while his father was in training to be a Waffen-SS officer. He had succeeded his father as CEO of the family conglomerate and had no problem distancing himself from the patriarch. "My father was a National Socialist," August said in the interview. "Now the fog is being lifted." He also confirmed that his father still harbored far-right sympathies long after the war. What was left undiscussed: the Oetker heirs continued to maintain two foundations under the name of their father and their grandparents, all of whom were committed Nazis.

During the interview, a generational rift among the Oetkers became apparent. The five eldest siblings — born in the 1940s and early '50s — had insisted on commissioning the study, whereas the three youngest ones — born in the late 1960s and '70s — were initially hesitant to agree to that, according to August. He also said that his younger half siblings hadn't yet distanced themselves from their father the way he and his siblings had.

On the day the study was published, in late October 2013, Maja, Oetker's widow and the mother of his three youngest heirs, criticized the 624-page book and her stepson August in an interview with a regional Westphalian newspaper. The matriarch claimed that the historians were only out to prove that her late husband and his stepfather, Kaselowsky, had been committed Nazis. Maja also disputed her stepson's assertion that his father still held far-right sympathies after the war. "We have always agreed with conservative ideas. Left-wingers may consider conservative thinking as something negative. For us, conservative means holding on to Christian values and preserving good traditions that have stood the test of time," she said in the interview. Maja admitted having deliberately read only the parts of the study that dealt with her husband, but she claimed to have found several unproven insinuations. She failed to specify what those insinuations were.

Both interviews were a sign of things to come. Three months later, in late January 2014, a power struggle between the two camps of Oetker siblings burst into the German press and rocked the nation's sedate business world. The dispute revolved around sibling succession for the position of CEO at Dr. Oetker. The battle lines were again generational: the five eldest Oetkers versus their three younger half siblings. Years of strife followed.

Lawsuits were drawn up; mediation was initiated. For the first time, the company appointed a CEO who was not a member of the family. But this didn't end the bickering.

In late July 2021, Rudolf-August Oetker's worst nightmare came true: eight of his heirs announced that they were splitting the Dr. Oetker conglomerate into two independent groups. The family business he built was falling apart, a *Buddenbrooks* scenario of sorts. Although the billionaire heirs have carved up the Oetker business empire, it still caters to all sorts of cravings: for cake and pudding and pizza, for Radeberger beer, for Henkell Freixenet's sparkling wine, and for famed luxury hotels, such as London's Lanesborough, Paris's Le Bristol, and Cap-Eden-Roc in Antibes.

Following the split, the eldest Oetker heirs rechristened the foundation named after their Nazi grandparents, Richard and Ida Kaselowsky. However, Rudolf-August's three youngest children kept their foundation and art collection named after their Waffen-SS-officer father. But again, you wouldn't learn any of that history from reading their new conglomerate's website. It is yet another dark past that remains obscured.

7.

In March 2019, the Ferry Porsche Foundation announced that it would endow Germany's first-ever professorship of corporate history, at the University of Stuttgart. The Porsche firm had established the foundation a year earlier — seventy years after Ferry had designed the first Porsche sports car — with hopes of "reinforcing its commitment to social responsibility." In a statement, the charity's then chairman said: "Dealing with one's own history is a full-time commitment. It is precisely this critical reflection that the Ferry Porsche Foundation wants to encourage, because: to know where you're going, you have to know where you've come from." The chairman added that "the endowed professorship is . . . an invitation to family companies in particular to engage with their history even more intensively and candidly, and the results and possible consequences of it." A particularly bold statement, given Ferry's lies about his SS application, his blatant use of anti-Semitic stereotypes and prejudices in his first autobiography, and the enduring silence of the Porsche family in the face of it all.

In 1998, Ferry died in his sleep at eighty-eight years of age, in Austria's Zell am See. The sports car icon of global renown had published his second autobiography a decade earlier. But in this version, Ferry had changed his tune. The anti-Semitic statements were gone, and he reduced the Adolf Rosenberger affair to just two paragraphs. The billionaire continued to deny the Aryanization of Rosenberger's stake in Porsche undertaken by his father, Ferdinand, and his brother-in-law, Anton Piëch. Instead, Ferry played the pity card: "As bad as these events were for Rosenberger at the time, under the circumstances we always behaved fair and correct towards him. For us, too, the situation was anything but easy back then."

One constant in Ferry's later autobiography was his claim that he had not wanted to be an SS officer; Himmler had bestowed the rank on him, and it was merely honorary. He still explicitly denied having voluntarily applied to the SS. In his new autobiography Ferry claimed that having been given this "honorary position" offered no proof that he was an SS man: "if you are made an honorary citizen of Salzburg, are you then an Austrian national?" But Ferry's postwar fabrications were dispelled in 2017, when three German historians revealed, in a study of the Porsche firm's origins, that Ferry had indeed voluntarily applied to the SS in 1938. They had dug up the SS forms, filled out and signed by Ferry, thereby "exposing the denial of an actively pursued SS membership as one of the widespread excuses for obscuring one's own past," the historians wrote. Ferry's lifelong lie had been laid bare. Still, the Porsche family remained silent about it.

The study of Porsche's origins had been funded by the company itself. In 2012, the Stuttgart sports car firm became a full subsidiary of the now Porsche-Piëch-controlled Volkswagen Group. The Wolfsburg-based behemoth has some $250 billion in annual sales and more than 665,000 employees manufacturing and selling luxury cars such Audi, Bentley, and Lamborghini, as well as the "family" brands, Volkswagen and Porsche. The dynasty's fortune has grown to $21 billion.

In fact, the reason why the Ferry Porsche Foundation endowed the professorship at the University of Stuttgart was because members of the university's history department wrote the firm-funded study. The car company had been happy with its findings, though no one from the Porsche-Piëch clan publicly reacted to them. In response to its revelations, a plaque was mounted at the Porsche factory in Stuttgart to commemorate the laborers held captive and forced to work there during the war. However, the public soon raised a question: was the study truly based on independent, objective analysis of the historical record?

In June 2019, a documentary about Porsche's forgotten cofounder, Adolf Rosenberger, aired on German public television. The broadcast detailed how crucial a role Rosenberger had played in the founding of Porsche, how his cofounders, Ferdinand Porsche and Anton Piëch, had Aryanized his stake in 1935, how Rosenberger fought for recognition, and how he was eventually written out of Porsche's company history.

The documentary also confronted one Wolfram Pyta, a professor of modern history at the University of Stuttgart and the main author of the study that Porsche had commissioned; somehow none of Rosenberger's personal papers had been included in the research. Pyta said that a relative of Rosenberger in Los Angeles had denied him access to the papers she had inherited. But in the documentary, Rosenberger's cousin disputed this. She said that one of Pyta's researchers did contact her, but that Pyta never followed up in order to come and see the papers in her possession.

Equally dubious was another finding — or lack thereof — in the study. Rosenberger was bought out of Porsche in 1935 for the exact same amount he had paid for his founding 10 percent stake in the company back in 1930, even though Porsche's profits had hugely increased in the intervening period. Plain and simple, Rosenberger had been stiffed and did not receive the full value of his shares. Although Pyta wrote that "there was no hesitation about drawing an economic advantage from Rosenberger's precarious situation" and "one cannot shake off the impression that Rosenberger . . . was cheated" out of his Porsche shares, the professor refused to call the transaction what it plainly was: an Aryanization.

In the documentary, Pyta said that Ferdinand Porsche and Anton Piëch conducted the transaction to strengthen the firm's family character, not because Rosenberger was Jewish. But paying a Jewish shareholder in a German company far below the actual market value of his stake in Hitler's Germany of 1935 could mean just one thing: the transaction was an Aryanization. Eighty-two years later, a Porsche-funded historian intentionally chose not to acknowledge that fact.

8.

In late November 2018, *Der Spiegel* published a bombshell cover story titled "The Billionaire and the AfD." In the 2017 federal elections, the Alternative für Deutschland (Alternative for Germany) became the largest opposition party in the country's national parliament, and the first far-right party to hold seats there in almost sixty-five years. Since its founding in 2013, the AfD has risen rapidly.

But the octogenarian billionaire mentioned in the headline, Baron August von Finck Jr., still kept to the shadows. After selling his family's private bank, Merck Finck, to Barclays for about $370 million in 1990, the aristocrat rose to become one of the world's wealthiest and most reclusive investors. A few of his investments, at least the ones that are known, have included German and Swiss firms such as the construction business Hochtief, the hotel chain Mövenpick, the goods testing company SGS, and the insulation maker von Roll. Von Finck Jr.'s fortune, estimated at more than $9 billion, is managed at the family's corporate headquarters on Munich's tony Promenadeplatz. Though the von Finck assets are said to include about half of Munich's city center, and much of the land around it, he mostly lived abroad. In 1999, von Finck Jr. immigrated with his wife, Francine, and their four children to tax-friendly Switzerland. One of their bases there became a medieval castle bought by his father. It overlooks the town of Weinfelden, near the German border.

Von Finck Jr. was even more secretive than his father. The heir, nicknamed "Gustl," never gave an interview to the press. The few images of him showed a tall man with white hair and sharp green eyes, often dressed in a dark-gray suit, wearing a Hermès tie, and alternating between two facial expressions: a stern look and a smile. He inherited some of his father's odd-

August von Finck Jr. in the 2000s.

ball thriftiness. Although he liked to commute between his stately homes
by helicopter, he drove his cars until they rusted through and broke down.
He brought his own meat, cheese, and bread to parties, and he served his
wealthy guests a slice of meatloaf at family celebrations. Von Finck Jr. never
commissioned a study of history that reckoned with his father's adulation
of Hitler, his Aryanizations of private banks, and his dubious denazification. Among the traits inherited from his father, Gustl had a preference for
reactionary politics. Whereas his father raised twenty million reichsmarks
for Hitler's Haus der Deutschen Kunst, von Finck Jr. became well established as a donor to German right-wing and far-right political organizations.

The documented start of Gustl's political giving began soon after he sold
the family's private bank. In 1993, a banker friend of the aristocratic investor
quipped to *Der Spiegel:* "To the right of Gustl is only Genghis Khan." Flush
with cash after the sale to Barclays, von Finck Jr. started backing reactionary
causes. Between 1992 and 1998, he gave 8.5 million deutsch marks (about
$5 million) in cash to the founder of a fringe right-wing party in Germany,
which campaigned against the introduction of the euro. The politician was
later convicted for tax evasion related to the donated cash, which was often
hand-delivered by Ernst Knut Stahl, Gustl's right-hand man.

After this initial failure, von Finck Jr. moved on to support parties that were better established. To retain a certain anonymity, he only once donated under his own name. All other donations came from entities he controls. Between 1998 and 2008, some of his subsidiaries donated about 3.6 million euros (about $5 million) to Bavaria's Christian conservative CSU. In 2009, one of his entities gave 1.1 million euros (approximately $1.5 million), in three tranches, to the free-market FDP. Soon after receiving his donations, the coalition parties successfully pushed for lower tax rates on hotel stays; it happened that von Finck Jr. owned a part of the Mövenpick hotel chain at the time. The FDP was ridiculed as the "Mövenpick party." The media viewed the scandal as a small-scale version of the Flick affair, a German synonym for bought politics.

Von Finck Jr. donated to causes that could be categorized as free-market conservative, anti–European Union, and anti-euro; his political outlook was best described as libertarian. In 2003, he donated millions to a lobbying organization that advocated for a smaller German government. The now defunct group's longtime chair, Beatrix von Storch, is currently one of the AfD's deputy leaders. Germany's Ludwig von Mises Institute — named for the economist whose writings in favor of the gold standard are a longtime staple of libertarians, as are gold investments — is based at the von Finck headquarters in Munich. So, in 2010, with Europe in the grip of a financial crisis, Gustl entered the gold-trading business. His venture came with a lurid though not entirely unsurprising lack of historical sensitivity.

To brand his gold-trading firm, one of Gustl's entities paid two million euros ($3 million) for the trademark rights to Degussa, an acronym for German Gold and Silver Separation Institute. The infamous chemicals conglomerate Degussa had helped produce the cyanide-based pesticide Zyklon B and had smelted precious metals plundered by the Nazis. In a 2004 company-commissioned study, a Northwestern University history professor, Peter Hayes, detailed how a subsidiary of Degussa developed the pesticide and how the SS became one of its trusted customers. Between 1941 and 1945, the SS used Zyklon B to gas more than a million people, almost all of them Jews, in extermination camps. After murdering millions in the camps or the ghettos, the Nazis stripped the corpses of gold teeth and fillings. Many of those metals ended up in Degussa's smelting factories, generally in compressed form but sometimes in their original state. Degussa also refined and resold gold and silver worth millions; some of it had been stolen by the Nazis across Europe, some of it from Jews sent to concentration camps and death camps.

In a perverse twist of history, von Finck Jr., a right-wing billionaire whose Hitler-obsessed, anti-Semitic Nazi father grew his private bank by Aryanizing Jewish-owned assets in the Third Reich, ended up carrying the Degussa banner. Today Degussa gold and silver are marketed in high-end shopping locations across Europe. A Degussa shop sits next to the von Finck headquarters in Munich, and anyone can buy and sell precious metals there. But von Finck Jr. didn't stop at this. He also installed a far-right CEO at Degussa, who once described the monetary policy of the European Central Bank as the "engine room of autogenocide."

9.

August von Finck Jr.'s political funding was far less successful than his business investments. Then an opportunity arose that could benefit both areas of interest. In early 2013, the anti-euro AfD party was founded. Days after its first party convention, a think tank affiliated with chancellor Angela Merkel's ruling CDU speculated in a memo that von Finck Jr. would become a major donor to AfD. To this day, there is no direct proof that their prediction came true, but the signs are there.

There are no limits on donations to political parties in Germany. But anonymous individuals and companies can donate only up to ten thousand euros (about $12,000) at a time to a political party. Any amount above that, and the party has to disclose annually the identity of the donor. In cases when more than fifty thousand euros (about $60,000) are given in a single contribution, the donation must be published immediately by the national parliament's presidium, along with the donor's name. It is easy to deduce, for example, that the Quandt heirs in control of BMW have donated millions of euros, mostly to the CDU, since at least 2002. But von Finck Jr., on the other hand, used more secretive methods to finance political parties at a sizable scale — while still trying to maintain anonymity.

Even before its failed first bid in a national election, in September 2013, the AfD was next to broke. It had precious few paying members or donors. At the time, an AfD spokeswoman, who financed some of its events and expenses, was also managing Degussa's publicity. *Der Spiegel* followed the money trail and later reported that a portion of those bills seem to have been paid by von Finck Jr. via his trusted right-hand man: Ernst Knut Stahl. This, despite the fact that it would be illegal in Germany to act as a conduit to finance a political party. To raise more funds, the AfD also opened an online gold store while drumming up fears that the euro currency was collapsing. Still hot on von Finck Jr.'s trail, *Der Spiegel* discovered that Degussa was one of two producers of the store's gold products.

The AfD's online store sold two million euros' worth of gold products in both 2014 and 2015, boosting Degussa's sales. Meanwhile, the AfD reaped state subsidies; German political parties receive government financing if they manage to generate external funding from donations, membership fees, or other income. But in December 2015, an amendment to Germany's law concerning political parties meant that the AfD's online gold shop no longer sufficed to qualify for subsidies. German party law wasn't the only shakeup in the works. The AfD's own political platform was changing too. During Europe's 2015 migrant crisis, the AfD rebranded itself: no longer an anti-euro party, it became an anti-immigrant party, stoking and exploiting fears that Merkel's decision to accept more than a million refugees from predominantly Muslim countries would change Germany's cultural identity.

In February 2016, two months after the AfD's state subsidies were curtailed, the party started receiving a different kind of campaign help, seemingly out of nowhere. Thousands of billboards and posters began to pop up across two German states, Baden-Württemberg and Rhineland-Palatinate; each was in the middle of an election cycle. A free newspaper was delivered to some two million households. The message was always the same: vote AfD. But the campaign material hadn't come from the AfD itself. It was paid for by a mysterious organization, the Association for the Preservation of the Rule of Law and Citizen Freedoms, a nonprofit similar to an

American-style "dark money" interest group. The association could receive and spend unlimited amounts of money, and it wasn't required by law to disclose its donors, so long as it didn't directly collaborate with the political party or candidate it supported. If evidence ever emerged of any collaboration, the association's campaigns would count as illegal donations. The AfD would get hit with massive fines, and the association's donors would be outed. Over 2016 and 2017, this association staged election campaigns in support of the AfD across Germany. Meanwhile, the AfD denied any cooperation with the nonprofit.

The story got murkier. In September 2016, *Der Spiegel* revealed that the association's campaigns were being designed by Goal, a Swiss-based political PR firm. The association's letterbox company in Stuttgart had a forwarding address: it happened to be Goal's address. Goal's owner is Alexander Segert, a German campaign guru for the leading right-wing parties. He has designed election campaigns for Switzerland's governing SVP, Austria's FPÖ, and some of the AfD's most prominent candidates, and his campaigns are notorious for their anti-immigrant messages and imagery. Goal is based at Segert's modern villa, protected with heavy security, in the bucolic village of Andelfingen, near the German border. His home office happens to be a mere twenty-minute drive west of von Finck Jr.'s Swiss castle in Weinfelden.

The tangled web of coincidences ran deeper. Since September 2016, the association has been headed by David Bendels, who has been seen in public with Segert on occasion. In July 2017, Bendels also became editor in chief of *Deutschland-Kurier,* a newly founded newspaper that was initially published by the association and still serves as a mouthpiece for the AfD. Adding another layer to the conspiracy, *Der Spiegel* revealed that Ernst Knut Stahl, von Finck Jr.'s right-hand man, was involved with founding the *Kurier.* Stahl had tried to recruit a publisher during a May 2017 lunch in Munich. "There's danger ahead," von Finck Jr.'s lieutenant said in the meeting. "There's a street in New York with lots of investment bankers, lawyers and so forth. Coincidentally, they are all Jews, but that's not relevant here. They want to push Germany into ruin. They control everything."

In September 2017, the AfD emerged as the major winner in Germany's national elections. It went from controlling zero parliament seats to being Germany's third-largest party. In no time at all, the AfD gained representation in all of the country's sixteen state parliaments. The association's countrywide campaigns had raised the national profile of the increasingly far-right party; meanwhile its big-money donors remain shrouded. Bendels has claimed that the association relied on grassroots donors but has never provided proof of it. According to an estimate by Germany's LobbyControl, the association has so far spent more than ten million euros ($12 million) in electoral campaign support for the AfD.

Bendels and the AfD continued to deny any cooperation. But in 2018, the AfD became mired in multiple scandals related to donations. Two involved Segert's Goal, which acted as a straw man to finance election campaigns for two prominent AfD politicians. In April 2019, the AfD was fined more than 400,000 euros ($500,000) for the affair. Days later, the public prosecutor's office in Berlin announced it was investigating the AfD's national treasurer because of the association's Goal-designed election campaigns in support of the political party. If prosecutors can prove that the association and the AfD cooperated, it would be Germany's largest political-donation scandal since the Flick affair. At the time of writing, in December 2021, the investigation is still ongoing. The AfD has so far been fined almost a million euros (some $1.2 million) for its various donation scandals.

Meanwhile, the AfD is becoming ever more radical. The party's politicians are attacking the country's culture of remembrance and its reckoning with the Nazi past. As the AfD's then co-leader Alexander Gauland so delicately put it in a 2018 speech: "Hitler and the Nazis are just a speck of bird shit in over a thousand years of successful German history." And he represents the party's moderate faction.

The AfD's extremist wing publicly embraces anti-Semitism, Islamophobia, and historical revisionism, including the downplaying of Nazi crimes and denigration of the Holocaust. Meanwhile, threats and attacks against immigrants, Jews, and politicians are rising in Germany. Most prominently, the February 2020 shooting spree in Hanau, where a gunman murdered nine people, all of them immigrants or Germans from immigrant families, plus his mother. Before that was the October 2019 synagogue shooting in

Halle, where an attacker killed two bystanders. And in June 2019, a local politician in Hessen who supported immigration was assassinated at home by a gunman. These attacks were all carried out by far-right extremists; some had ties to neo-Nazi groups.

That same June, von Finck Jr. was spotted sitting next to Bavaria's prime minister, Markus Söder, at a festive dinner in Munich. There were ties between the men. Söder's former right-hand man had recently joined Gustl's family office. Now they were attending the seventieth-birthday party of a well-known lawyer and noted Euroskeptic politician. Gustl had paid the attorney more than eleven million euros (about $12.5 million) in legal "consulting fees" while the lawyer was serving in the German parliament. But though the former parliamentarian's career was winding down, Söder's was just now rising. In the spring of 2021, Söder bowed out of a leadership contest to succeed Angela Merkel as the Christian conservatives' national candidate for German chancellor. But Söder isn't going anywhere. In late November 2021, August von Finck Jr. died at age ninety-one in London.

10.

The headline that accompanied the *New York Times* article in mid-June 2019 could have been the subtitle of a trashy novel: "Nazis Killed Her Father. Then She Fell in Love with One." But the article itself had a far more serious tone. For the first time ever, two members of the Reimann dynasty, now Germany's wealthiest family, had spoken on the record to a reporter. The story they told was both tragic and bizarre. During or soon after the war, Albert Reimann — dynasty patriarch, anti-Semite, and local Nazi Party politician — began a decades-long relationship with Emily Landecker, an employee of the mogul and the daughter of a Jewish man. In 1941, Emily was hired at Reimann's firm in Ludwigshafen. In 1942, her father, Alfred, was arrested by Gestapo officers at his home in Mannheim, and murdered soon after. His last message came from a ghetto in Nazi-occupied Poland, which served as a transfer point to the extermination camps Sobibor and Belzec.

From 1951 on, Albert Reimann fathered three children with Emily; two are current shareholders in the family conglomerate, JAB. Now, some of the Reimanns were ready to share their family's legacy. They were descendants of an ardent Nazi and a Jewish man murdered by the Nazis. They were the product of perpetrator and victim, and their story involved both reckoning and grief. But it got more complex. Throughout his romance with his employee Emily, Albert was also married to another woman. Their union remained childless, though, and in 1965 Albert formally adopted his children with Emily and continued their liaison. Albert and Emily spoke little of the war with their children. The only things Albert told them was that French prisoners of war were "often given some red wine on Saturdays" and that "forced laborers had loved the company so much, they cried when the conflict ended and they had to leave."

Wolfgang Reimann, the son of Emily and Albert, told the *Times* that when they asked their mother about the family's Jewish roots, she spoke vaguely of being raised in a "Jewish milieu" and then chided her children to quit talking about "that old stuff." They didn't discover that their father had been a fervent Nazi until the family-commissioned historian presented his interim report to them in January 2019. Emily had loved Albert, despite everything. "I never understood why," Wolfgang told the *New York Times*. "He was not very lovable from my perspective."

In the article, JAB's chairman and the Reimanns' confidant, Peter Harf, born exactly one year and one day after the war ended, revealed that his own father had been a Nazi too. He was worried about the rise of nationalism in the West and said it was time to take a stand. The billionaire thought that too few corporate voices were speaking out against the resurgence of populism. "In history, businesses have enabled populists," Harf told the *Times* reporter. "We mustn't make the same mistake today."

In a major breakthrough in corporate Germany's reckoning with the Third Reich, the country's wealthiest business dynasty announced that they would rename their family foundation. It would no longer honor the Reimanns' Nazi father or grandfather, but rather their Jewish grandfather who had been murdered by the Nazis. Furthermore, the Alfred Landecker Foundation would focus on educating people about the Holocaust. The Reimanns signaled their commitment to this goal with a massive family-funded endowment: 250 million euros ($300 million), every ten years, in perpetuity. They stacked the foundation's board with globally prominent names from academia, business, and politics, and announced the funding of a new program and chair at Oxford University to research the persecution of minorities in Europe. The family didn't stop there. The foundation began tracking down survivors of forced labor at the family firm, and then compensated them. To put it bluntly, Germany's new wealthiest business dynasty was putting their money where their mouth was, all in the name of a man who had been demonized by the family's founding tycoons. What's more, the website of the Alfred Landecker Foundation is transparent about the Reimann family's Nazi patriarchs and their crimes.

This stood in stark contrast to the Quandts of BMW. On June 20, 2019, six days after the *New York Times* article about the Reimanns came out, *Manager Magazin,* a German publication similar to *Forbes,* published a cover story about two of the Quandts. It was the first time Susanne Klatten and Stefan Quandt, Herbert's youngest children, had sat down together to give an interview. The magazine estimated their fortune that year at about 26.5 billion euros ($30 billion), making them Germany's second-wealthiest family, behind the Reimanns. The two Quandt siblings control about 47 percent of BMW, among many other investments. BMW gave them a total dividend of almost 800 million euros ($1 billion) in 2019, even though its share price lagged. In the interview, the family's Nazi history was left undiscussed. Apparently, the magazine thought that the topic had long since been exhausted.

Instead, Stefan used the opportunity to question the rationale of an inheritance tax. Susanne said that wealth redistribution doesn't work and argued for a meritocracy, saying that a fair society should allow people to pursue opportunities according to their abilities. "Our potential stems from our roles as heirs and in developing that [inheritance]," she told the magazine. "We work hard on that every day. The role as guardians of wealth also has personal sides that aren't so nice." One of those unpleasant aspects, according to the multibillionaire siblings, is dealing with jealousy concerning their immense inheritance: "Some people believe that we are constantly sitting around on a yacht in the Mediterranean," Susanne said.

Her brother had made a similar comment almost eight years earlier when discussing the family's Nazi history with *Die Zeit*. "We don't spend all day at the beach," Stefan had said back then. "I don't have a big money bin like Scrooge McDuck." He too seemed to view his inheritance as an immense cross to bear. The headline for this new interview directly quoted a question Susanne put forth, echoing, without a trace of irony, another of her brother's earlier musings: "Who Would Want to Trade Places with Us?"

On June 22, 2019, two days after the interview was published, the annual Herbert Quandt Media Prize was awarded, as usual, on the occasion of the mogul's birthdate. That day, Stefan published a version of his award speech as a column in the conservative-leaning *Frankfurter Allgemeine Zeitung*, one of Germany's largest and most influential newspapers. The title of his column was "Protect Private Property!" In it, he railed against supposed threats to property rights, the menace of a higher inheritance tax, and the specter of expropriations in today's Germany. The fact that his grandfather and father had flouted the private property rights of their Nazi-era victims and massively benefited from state-supported expropriations was seemingly lost on the BMW heir. Ten days later, Stefan joined the newspaper's supervisory board.

Stefan Quandt at the Jewish Museum Berlin, 2018.

To this day, the two Quandt siblings oversee their corporate empire from the Günther Quandt House in Bad Homburg. Stefan annually awards the Herbert Quandt Media Prize to German journalists. In 2016, BMW's charitable arm was consolidated under the Herbert Quandt Foundation. The foundation's assets were increased to a hundred million euros ($120 million); another thirty million ($35 million) were provided by Stefan and Susanne themselves. Its mission is to promote and inspire "responsible leadership" in the name of a man who once helped Aryanize companies in France, who supervised a factory in Berlin filled with female slave laborers, and who oversaw the planning and building of a sub–concentration camp in Nazi-occupied Poland. But none of that matters to BMW, apparently. If the foundation is to be believed, Herbert's entire biography consists of only one act: he "secured the independence" of BMW. The triumphs and travesties of his life are reduced to that one terse sentence.

In May 2021, the *Süddeutsche Zeitung* reported that a street in Munich named after Herbert Quandt was on a shortlist of streets that might be renamed. When a district member of the AfD argued that Herbert's business merits following the war should be considered during the deliberation, the historian in charge of recommending the renamings countered that anyone who had "profited from the Nazi system" and thus "sinned" against humanity's core values "doesn't deserve a relativizing overall view of his life's work."

Thus far, the scale remains tipped in favor of money and power. Many German business dynasties continue to sidestep a complete reckoning with the dark history that stains their fortunes, and so the ghosts of the Third Reich still haunt them.

EPILOGUE: THE MUSEUM

In late 2019, I flew to Tel Aviv to visit my German girlfriend for a week. She was working as a reporter in Israel and in the Palestinian Territories for a month, subbing for a colleague on leave. One evening in early December, we visited the Tel Aviv Museum of Art, a labyrinthine building with a mix of brutalist and modernist architecture. At the recommendation of a friend back in New York, we went to see an exhibition by the American artist Raymond Pettibon. The weather was still warm. And yet, upon arriving at the exhibition, I felt a chill run down my spine. Just before we entered, I noticed a list of names written in German and Hebrew on the wall. Above the names was a sign: THE GALLERY OF THE GERMAN FRIENDS OF THE TEL AVIV MUSEUM OF ART.

Between surnames listed beneath the sign, such as Gottesdiener and Gleitman, a few especially notable ones jumped out at me. Near the top: Gabriele Quandt. Gabriele, the granddaughter of Magda Goebbels and the daughter of Harald Quandt, the heir who grew up in the Goebbels household but never became a Nazi Party member — who tried to look to the future but could never escape the tragedies of his past.

At the very bottom of the list: Ingrid Flick, third wife of Friedrich Karl Flick, the man responsible for Germany's largest postwar corruption scandal and the third and youngest son of Friedrich Flick: the mightiest and most ruthless of all German industrialists, who was convicted at Nuremberg and rose to become Germany's wealthiest man in three different eras. Friedrich Flick, who couldn't let go of his creation, causing his empire, and his family, to fall apart. Friedrich Karl, who like his father refused to ever pay compensation to any of the tens of thousands of people used as forced or slave labor at Flick factories and mines; thousands died there, many of them Jews brought in from concentration camps. Friedrich Karl took his billions and fled to Austria, leaving the family's ghosts for his niece and nephews to publicly reckon with. Meanwhile, Ingrid Flick continues her late husband's tainted work. Still, she maintains a foundation in the name of her late father-in-law, a convicted Nazi war criminal who stole the livelihoods of so many to expand his empire.

To see the names Quandt and Flick honored in an Israeli museum, their names spelled out in Hebrew, was, as the Germans might say, *unheimlich*, eerie. The reigning generation of heirs still has the chance to alter course before passing their empires along — to commit fully to historical transparency and moral responsibility, and to strive, unconditionally, to repay to society the enormous debts their fathers incurred. Those heirs' children, in turn, will have the chance to use their power and wealth to help create a better world, one in which their grandfathers would have no place.

Beneath Gabriele's and Ingrid's names were those of their children: Gabriele's sons, now in their early thirties, and the Flick twins, the world's youngest billionaires, now in their early twenties. They are the next generation — my generation. "We will do better," I said to no one in particular. My girlfriend smiled at me. We skipped the exhibition and walked out of the museum, into the warm December evening and a new decade.

APPENDIX: FAMILY TREES

These are not complete family trees, as they omit certain spouses and members of older and younger generations. They include only those family members who are relevant to this book.

The Quandt Dynasty

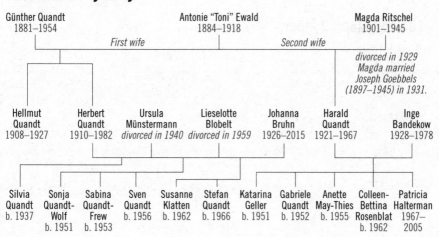

Günther Quandt
1881–1954

Antonie "Toni" Ewald
1884–1918

Magda Ritschel
1901–1945

First wife

Second wife

divorced in 1929
Magda married
Joseph Goebbels
(1897–1945) in 1931.

Hellmut
Quandt
1908–1927

Herbert
Quandt
1910–1982

Ursula
Münstermann
divorced in 1940

Lieselotte
Blobelt
divorced in 1959

Johanna
Bruhn
1926–2015

Harald
Quandt
1921–1967

Inge
Bandekow
1928–1978

Silvia
Quandt
b. 1937

Sonja
Quandt-
Wolf
b. 1951

Sabina
Quandt-
Frew
b. 1953

Sven
Quandt
b. 1956

Susanne
Klatten
b. 1962

Stefan
Quandt
b. 1966

Katarina
Geller
b. 1951

Gabriele
Quandt
b. 1952

Anette
May-Thies
b. 1955

Colleen-
Bettina
Rosenblat
b. 1962

Patricia
Halterman
1967–
2005

Note: All known years are given.

The Flick Dynasty

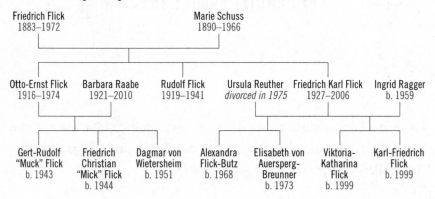

Friedrich Flick
1883–1972

Marie Schuss
1890–1966

Otto-Ernst Flick
1916–1974

Barbara Raabe
1921–2010

Rudolf Flick
1919–1941

Ursula Reuther
divorced in 1975

Friedrich Karl Flick
1927–2006

Ingrid Ragger
b. 1959

Gert-Rudolf
"Muck" Flick
b. 1943

Friedrich
Christian
"Mick" Flick
b. 1944

Dagmar von
Wietersheim
b. 1951

Alexandra
Flick-Butz
b. 1968

Elisabeth von
Auersperg-
Breunner
b. 1973

Viktoria-
Katharina
Flick
b. 1999

Karl-Friedrich
Flick
b. 1999

Note: All known years are given.

The von Finck Dynasty

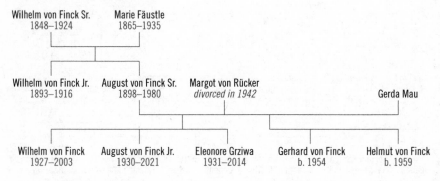

Wilhelm von Finck Sr.
1848–1924

Marie Fäustle
1865–1935

Wilhelm von Finck Jr.
1893–1916

August von Finck Sr.
1898–1980

Margot von Rücker
divorced in 1942

Gerda Mau

Wilhelm von Finck
1927–2003

August von Finck Jr.
1930–2021

Eleonore Grziwa
1931–2014

Gerhard von Finck
b. 1954

Helmut von Finck
b. 1959

Note: All known years are given.

The Porsche-Piëch Dynasty

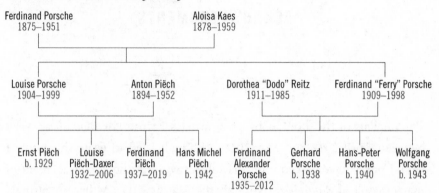

Ferdinand Porsche
1875–1951

Aloisa Kaes
1878–1959

Louise Porsche
1904–1999

Anton Piëch
1894–1952

Dorothea "Dodo" Reitz
1911–1985

Ferdinand "Ferry" Porsche
1909–1998

Ernst Piëch
b. 1929

Louise
Piëch-Daxer
1932–2006

Ferdinand
Piëch
1937–2019

Hans Michel
Piëch
b. 1942

Ferdinand
Alexander
Porsche
1935–2012

Gerhard
Porsche
b. 1938

Hans-Peter
Porsche
b. 1940

Wolfgang
Porsche
b. 1943

The Oetker Dynasty

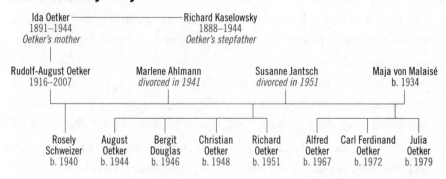

Ida Oetker ——————————— Richard Kaselowsky
1891–1944   1888–1944
Oetker's mother   *Oetker's stepfather*

Rudolf-August Oetker
1916–2007

Marlene Ahlmann
divorced in 1941

Susanne Jantsch
divorced in 1951

Maja von Malaisé
b. 1934

Rosely
Schweizer
b. 1940

August
Oetker
b. 1944

Bergit
Douglas
b. 1946

Christian
Oetker
b. 1948

Richard
Oetker
b. 1951

Alfred
Oetker
b. 1967

Carl Ferdinand
Oetker
b. 1972

Julia
Oetker
b. 1979

Note: All known years are given.

ACKNOWLEDGMENTS

The nucleus of this book consists of articles I wrote for *Bloomberg News* between April 2012 and May 2018. Although I left to write this book, I would never have delved into this subject without the encouragement of many people at *Bloomberg*. Not only did Matthew (G.) Miller unwittingly come up with the book title ("de Jong, do we have any more Nazi billionaire stories on the shelf?"), but he and Peter Newcomb (his suggestion, *Nazillionaires*, was a close second for the title) took a chance on me and then put me onto this beat. Thank you both. Matt, I think I took your assignment to "go and find the Nazi gold" a tad too seriously. Thanks also to Rob LaFranco and Pierre Paulden for their editorial guidance, and to Pamela Roux Castillo and Jack Witzig, two stalwarts of the Bloomberg Billionaires turned wealth team.

Thanks to Max Abelson for inadvertently leading me to the start and the end of this book: by introducing me at *Bloomberg* in fall 2011 and for telling me to see the Raymond Pettibon exhibition at the Tel Aviv Museum of Art in fall 2019. A big thanks to Donal Griffin, my favorite cantankerous Irishman, for taking the time to read early drafts. Thanks also to Caleb Melby, who, way back when, told me I should write a book about this subject; it firmly planted the idea in my mind. Thanks to my then editors Simone Meier, Elisa Martinuzzi, and Neil Callanan for encouraging me to take the plunge and write the book. Thanks also to Annette Weisbach and Matthew Boyle; I collaborated with them on some of my earliest reporting on the Reimanns and the Quandts.

I'm grateful to my agent, Howard Yoon, for believing in this project from the start and for his enormous help and encouragement, and to his associates at Ross Yoon, notably Dara Kaye. A massive thank-you to Alexander Littlefield, my discerning editor at Houghton Mifflin Harcourt/ HarperCollins, who remained unflappable and never lost sight of the big picture. Thanks also to Zach Phillips, Marleen Reimer, and Lisa Glover for helping out with so much, and to Susanna Brougham for her impeccable copyediting. Thanks to David Eber for the legal review and Mark Robinson and Chloe Foster for the cover and interior design. Thanks also to Glen Pawelski and the team at Mapping Specialists. I'm also very grateful to Arabella Pike and Jo Thompson at William Collins in London for their help with the book.

Many thanks to colleagues at Büro Hermann & Söhne, particularly Gerben van der Marel, Jan Zappner, and Peter Wollring, for the years of camaraderie in lieu of an actual newsroom. Pauline Peek, a true multi-talent, helped with research and fact-checked the book. A big thank-you to Martin Breitfeld and his colleagues at Kiepenheuer & Witsch in Cologne for all their help. Thanks also to Rüdiger Jungbluth, who once told me over lunch in Hamburg, "When it's not written in English it's not considered news"; it made me realize that these dark histories of money and power weren't known outside Germany. Thanks to all the German historians who were willing to speak to me at length about this subject — most notably Tim Schanetzky, Kim Christian Priemel, and Sven Keller.

Thanks, for various reasons, to Alex Cuadros, Alice Pearson, Ben and Jenny Homrighausen, Volker Berghahn, Yana Bergmann, Brittany and Sam Noble, Ruby Bilger, Daniel Sedlis, Nina Majoor, Eric Gade, Evan Pheiffer, Sven Becker, Janette Beckman, Daniel Steinmetz-Jenkins, Norman Ohler, Taunton and Nikki Paine, Sam Moyn, Majlie de Puy Kamp, Patrick Radden Keefe, Mary Vromen, Mathew Lawrence, Hayden Miller, Ryan Alexander Musto, Heather Jones, Joe Dolce, Lauren Streib, Henry Seltzer, Line Lillevik, and Max Raskin. Germany's dark history was never far away in Berlin, and sometimes it came bizarrely close. A big *danke* to the whole "clique" in the capital, most notably Elsa Wallenberg, Alexander Esser, Laura Stadler, Cäcilie von Trotha, Richard Meyer zu Eissen, Finn Weise, and all the other weirdos. A special thanks, also, to all my dear friends in Amsterdam.

Writing this book made me realize even more how fortunate I am to be surrounded by such wonderful families. An immense thanks to my parents, Helen and Philip, for their unconditional love and support, and also to my aunt Jacqueline, the de Zwarts, the Velaises, and the Tanns.

Finally, a big thank-you to Sophie, a true force of nature. Ever industrious; ever the explorer. Glad to be caught up in your whirlwind. Can't wait to find out where it will take us next.

A NOTE ON SOURCES

Members of almost all the German business dynasties detailed in this book declined to comment or be interviewed; others didn't respond to requests for interviews or questions sent to their spokesperson or family office representatives. But there was one notable exception.

Jörg Appelhans, the longtime spokesman for the two Quandt siblings who control BMW, declined my request for an interview with Stefan Quandt on the grounds that the academic study the family commissioned to examine their patriarchs' activities during the Third Reich was "ground-breaking and comprehensive. Hence, we didn't get further or new insights above the study's findings which are common knowledge since it was published in 2011." When I asked him where, and for whom, he considered the findings to be "common knowledge," Appelhans responded: "Common knowledge in the sense that they have been published and thus are accessible to everyone."

Accessible to everyone who can read German, that is. The Quandt study, and many similar ones commissioned by other dynasties, have never been translated into other languages, even though most of the victims of their patriarchs' activities during the Nazi era weren't German, and the dynasties' business interests, then and now, are global. Nonetheless, Appelhans wrote, "the Quandt Family is convinced that the goals of openness and transparency were achieved ... We don't believe that renaming streets, places or institutions is a responsible way to deal with historic figures because such 'damnatio memoriae' ... prevents a conscious exposure to their role in history and instead fosters its neglect." But so does commemorating historical figures with no mention whatsoever of their Nazi history.

In response to questions I sent to the BMW Group, including why the Munich carmaker is keeping its savior's name on its charitable foundation, which promotes "responsible leadership," even after his activities in the Third Reich were revealed, a representative of the BMW Foundation Herbert Quandt wrote, in a statement to me, that "[the foundation] draws on the entrepreneurial deeds of BMW and Herbert Quandt, which is why it made a conscious decision: The long-term and forward-looking actions with which Herbert Quandt acted from 1959 to his death in 1982 . . . should be represented in the name of the foundation."

I requested interviews with Gabriele Quandt and Colleen-Bettina Rosenblat, daughters of Harald Quandt, but they "decided against doing an interview," their family office spokesman, Ulrich von Rotenhan, wrote to me.

The documents detailing Günther Quandt's denazification trial and appeals, including many documents on the Aryanizations that Günther, Herbert, and their executives conducted in Nazi-occupied nations during World War II, can be found on microfiche copies of folders 1362 and 1363 at the Bavarian State Archives in Munich. The documents from the Quandt family archive that Joachim Scholtyseck cited in the commissioned study, and that the Quandts considered relevant enough to be made available to researchers, are accessible at the Hessian Business Archives in Darmstadt.

Antiquarian booksellers in Germany proved to be a gold mine of primary sources. They sold me Günther's bundled letters from 1938, his postwar memoir, Quandt company books from the 1930s, and much more. It felt particularly satisfying to buy Herbert's 1980 private biography that he commissioned, given the length that Herbert's handlers went to keep the book out of the hands of journalists, a scenario that is vividly described in archival correspondence. Joseph Goebbels's diaries, spanning 1923 through 1945 and edited by Elke Fröhlich, are available online at De Gruyter publishing company for an annual licensing fee.

Rüdiger Jungbluth's 2002 and 2015 biographies about the Quandt dynasty were equally indispensable sources, as was Joachim Scholtyseck's 2011 study.

. . .

Family office representatives for Ingrid Flick and her twins in Vienna declined to comment on a list of questions I sent about Ingrid's direct philanthropic giving and the philanthropy she conducts in the name of her father-
in-law, the convicted Nazi war criminal Friedrich Flick. After reaching out
to Frankfurt's Goethe University with questions about how it reconciles the
Flick foundation's annual financial contributions to the academic institution with its namesake's problematic place in history, a university spokesman sent me this statement: "Goethe University has been working with
the Friedrich Flick Foundation for six years and has come to know it as a
fair, reliable and generous partner. Thanks to the foundation's exemplary
commitment, it has been possible to finance projects in research and teach-
ing as well as scholarships for which no other funds would otherwise have
been available. The cooperation represents an important building block
in the context of the diverse commitment of sponsors to the university."
Friedrich Karl Flick's eldest daughters, Alexandra Flick-Butz and Elisabeth
von Auersperg-Breunner, did not respond to an interview request or to
questions sent to their respective family office representatives in Munich.

Out of all the German business dynasties detailed in this book, the only
family member to respond to my questions was Gert-Rudolf Flick, also
known as "Muck." He did so with candor. Friedrich Flick's eldest grandson,
and Otto-Ernst's eldest son, is almost eighty years old and has been living in London for decades, where he writes and teaches about Old Master
paintings. Muck was born in France in 1943, during his father's disastrous
reign at the expropriated Rombach steelworks in Nazi-occupied Lorraine.
He was close to his grandfather Friedrich up until the patriarch's death, in
1972, when Muck was almost thirty years old. Friedrich Flick had hoped
that Muck and his younger brother, Mick, both of them mentored by the
patriarch, would one day take the reins at the family conglomerate. But it
didn't turn out as planned.

I received permission from Muck to cite part of our email correspondence: "During his lifetime we did not discuss the war; my brother and
I obviously admired and venerated my grandfather who was a genius in
more ways than one," Muck wrote. "Now more ugly things have come out.
One could take a harsher view, but I remember him as a very gifted human

being, and I cannot change my feelings retroactively. I am deeply grateful to have known him and not only for the wealth he bestowed on us." Muck's siblings, Mick Flick and Dagmar von Wietersheim, did not respond to interview requests sent to Mick's foundations in Potsdam and Zurich and Dagmar's family office in Munich.

The 1947 Nuremberg trial proceedings against Friedrich Flick and his associates, including many documents, are available online. As secondary sources, I relied heavily on Kim Christian Priemel's PhD study from 2007, about the Flick conglomerate, and the studies that Dagmar and Mick, respectively, commissioned from two separate groups of German historians: the 2009 study about the Flick conglomerate in the twentieth century, conducted by Norbert Frei, Ralf Ahrens, Jörg Osterloh, and Tim Schanetzky; and the 2008 study about the Flick conglomerate during the Third Reich, conducted by Johannes Bähr, Alex Drecoll, Bernhard Gotto, Harald Wixforth, and again, Kim Christian Priemel. Günther Ogger's 1971 biography of Friedrich Flick has also withstood the test of time remarkably well. The Berlin-Brandenburg Business Archive has an entire Flick research archive, which contains original and copied documents used in the academic study that Dagmar commissioned. In a bizarre coincidence, the Flick archive is housed in what used to be a part of Günther Quandt's sprawling DWM arms complex in Berlin's Wittenau neighborhood. Unfortunately, due to the COVID-19 pandemic, I wasn't able to visit the archive.

In June 2021, Annemarie Thoene, the longtime secretary at August "Gustl" von Finck Jr.'s private office in Munich, informed me over the phone that their "communication policy" remained unchanged — von Finck Jr. still didn't give interviews, and there was no designated email address by which to request an interview. Previously, I have been referred to a fax number when seeking a comment from Gustl. But for this book, I was told to write a letter. Gustl did not respond to the interview request and other questions I sent by courier letter to his private office over summer and early fall 2021. Gustl died in London in late November 2021. His half brothers, Helmut and Gerhard, also did not respond to interview requests. Nor did the PR guru of Goal AG, Alexander Segert. David Bendels also did not respond to an interview request to discuss the alleged connections between the AfD and the mysterious Association for the Preservation of the Rule of Law and Citizen Freedoms. The AfD's spokesman, Peter Rohling, declined to make a member of the party's leadership available for an interview on the subject.

August von Finck Sr.'s original denazification trial documents are located in folder 409 at the Bavarian State Archives in Munich. Many of the documents detailing the Aryanization transactions of the Dreyfus and Rothschild banks by Merck Finck can be found at the National Archives and Record Administration in College Park, Maryland, or through its online partner, Fold3, which has digitized millions of records. Ingo Köhler's 2005 PhD study about the Aryanization of Jewish-owned private banks in Germany was a vital source, as was a 2001 study about Allianz during the Third Reich by Gerald Feldman. For the chapter about the connections between the AfD, the association, Goal, and August von Finck Jr.'s orbit, I relied on the groundbreaking reporting of the journalists Melanie Amann, Sven Becker, Ann-Katrin Müller, and Sven Röbel at *Der Spiegel;* Anna Jikhareva, Jan Jirat, and Kaspar Surber at *Wochenzeitung;* Friederike Haupt at the *Frankfurter Allgemeine Zeitung;* Christian Fuchs and Paul Middelhoff at *Die Zeit;* and Roman Deininger, Andreas Glas, and Klaus Ott at *Süddeutsche Zeitung.*

The Porsche company in Stuttgart declined to make Wolfgang Porsche, a son of Ferry Porsche and the speaker for the Porsche side of the Porsche-Piëch clan, available for an interview. In written responses to my questions, Sebastian Rudolph, the Porsche company's head of communications, characterized Ferry's anti-Semitic and discriminatory statements in his 1976 autobiography, *We at Porsche,* as testifying to "a lack of empathy on the part of Ferry Porsche towards the fate of Adolf Rosenberger and other Jewish families who had to leave Germany . . . Ferry Porsche believed that Adolf Rosenberger had at least been treated and compensated correctly by the company. This is the only way to interpret his annoyance at the renewed disputes after the Second World War."

A 1996 study about the Volkswagen factory complex during the Third Reich by Hans Mommsen and Manfred Grieger was an invaluable resource, as was Bernhard Rieger's 2013 study about the history of the Volkswagen Beetle. I also relied on various biographies about the Porsche-Piëch clan by the German and Austrian journalists Stefan Aust, Thomas Ammann, Georg Meck, Wolfgang Fürweger, and the documentaries about Porsche's Jewish cofounder Adolf Rosenberger by Eberhard Reuß.

The original German version of the 2017 study by Wolfram Pyta and his two colleagues about the Porsche firm's origins can be considered a credible source, despite its significant shortcomings. It's thoroughly researched, which makes Pyta's failure to inspect the private papers of Adolf Rosenberger even more confusing and troubling. While Pyta also failed to properly characterize the 1935 buyout of Adolf Rosenberger from the Porsche firm by Ferdinand Porsche and Anton Piëch as an Aryanization, the historian admitted to me in a Zoom interview that the transaction constituted an "Aryanization profit."

In the last days of fact-checking the book, the Porsche firm's spokesman suddenly sent me an access code to a digital-only English translation of Pyta's study. After four years of research, I was very surprised to learn that this version even existed. I had never come across it because there's almost no mention of it online. As it turns out, access to the English translation of Pyta's study is available only after one requests it from the Porsche firm or when the company chooses to provide it. That is one reason why the English translation of Pyta's study can't be considered a credible source. The second and more important reason is that words were added to at least one crucial paragraph in the English version, which give the impression that Ferry Porsche lied about his application to the SS only during the immediate postwar era. In truth, he lied about his voluntary membership in the SS for the rest of his life. Himmler, Ferry maintained, forced him to accept an honorary rank. The fabrication appears in both of Ferry's autobiographies and in a 1952 affidavit from Ferry to the United States consulate in Stuttgart, which the Porsche company provided to me.

Jörg Schillinger, the longtime spokesperson for the Dr. Oetker conglomerate in Bielefeld, declined to make any member of the Oetker family available to me for an interview. Christoph Walther, a spokesperson for the three youngest children of Rudolf-August Oetker, wrote to me, "They have no intention to go on record on this topic beyond what has already been published."

The 2013 study of the Dr. Oetker firm and the Oetker/Kaselowsky family during the Third Reich, by Jürgen Finger, Sven Keller, and Andreas Wirsching, was an indispensable source, as was Rüdiger Jungbluth's 2004 history of the Oetker dynasty and conglomerate. The Dr. Oetker archive in Bielefeld is generally open to researchers but has been closed since the start of the COVID-19 pandemic. For this reason, I wasn't able to visit it.

The longtime spokeswoman for the Reimann family declined to make a member of the Vienna-based clan available for an interview. She did set up an interview for me in Berlin with Peter Harf and two other executives from the Alfred Landecker Foundation. Unsurprisingly, Harf failed to show up. He did agree to answer most of my questions in writing, but my quest to one day interview the elusive billionaire in person continues. The Reimann-commissioned study about the family and its firm during the Third Reich is expected to be published in 2023. It will be paired with the publication of a biography of Alfred Landecker. The Bahlsen study is expected to be completed in the summer of 2023, according to a company spokesman, though he does not know yet when it will be published. In an interview with the *Süddeutsche Zeitung* in September 2021, Verena Bahlsen seemed to have come around. She told the newspaper: "We have failed for decades to create transparency about our Nazi history. I believe this will continue if we don't take advantage of this opportunity now. And I have to push my family to talk about it."

This book is a work of narrative nonfiction. It's comprehensively sourced with endnotes and has been independently fact-checked. In instances where the various sources cited provide differing accounts of the same event, I have chosen the most plausible version. Any errors that remain are my own.

NOTES

ABBREVIATIONS

ARD: Germany's main public broadcaster

HWA: Hessian Business Archives

NARA: National Archives and Records Administration, Washington

NDR: North German Broadcasting

NMT: Nuremberg Military Tribunals

NND: Designation for declassified documents

OMGUS: United States Office of Military Government for Germany

OSS: Office of Strategic Services

STAM: State Archives Munich

SWR: Germany's Southwest Broadcasting

TG: The Diaries of Joseph Goebbels (Die Tagebücher von Joseph Goebbels)

USACA: United States Allied Commission for Austria

USHMM: United States Holocaust Memorial Museum, Washington

Prologue: The Meeting

page

1 *"And there they stand"*: Éric Vuillard, *The Order of the Day* (London: Picador, 2018, trans.), 17.

about two dozen: For two (incomplete) attendance lists, see Dirk Stegmann, "Zum Verhältnis von Großindustrie und Nationalsozialismus, 1930–1933," *Archiv für Sozialgeschichte* 13 (1973), 478, 481; Henry Ashby Turner Jr., *German Big Business and the Rise of Hitler* (New York: Oxford University Press, 1985), 468 n81.

"explain his policies": NMT, Vol. VII, "The IG Farben Case" (Washington, DC: US Government Printing Office, 1953), 557, https://www.loc.gov/rr/frd/Military_Law/pdf/NT_war-criminals_Vol-VII.pdf.

2 *In tow was Walther*: Stegmann, "Verhältnis," 478.

settle the struggle: NMT, Vol. VII, 557–60.

"*Private enterprise*": NMT, Vol. VII, 558.

"*We must first gain*": NMT, Vol. VII,560.

3 "*the last election*": NMT, Vol. VII, 561.

"*for having given us*": NMT, Vol. VII, 562.

"*that with political pacification*": NMT, Vol. VII, 561–62.

4 *Göring's conclusion:* NMT, Vol. VII, 562.

election campaign fund: Stegmann, "Verhältnis," 480.

"*And now, gentlemen*": Cited in Louis Lochner, *Tycoons and Tyrant* (Chicago: Henry Regnery, 1954), 146–47.

twelve million reichsmarks: Günter Ogger, *Friedrich Flick der Grosse* (Bern: Scherz, 1971), 132.

5 *The largest donations:* NMT, Vol. VII, 567–68.

"*Göring brings the joyful*": Elke Fröhlich (ed.), *TG* (Munich: De Gruyter Saur, 1993–2008), Feb. 21, 1933.

Introduction

6 "*I am a capitalist*": Verena Bahlsen, "About the Future of Cookies," *Online Marketing Rockstars,* May 15, 2019, Youtube video, 18:53, https://www.youtube.com/watch?v=TauCu0aJ5Vs.

"*That was before my time*": "Zwangsarbeiter-Zoff um Keks-Erbin," *Bild,* May 12, 2019.

7 *seven hundred coerced workers:* "Bahlsen During National Socialism, 1933 to 1945," July 1, 2020, https://www.thebahlsenfamily.com/int/company/about-us/history/bahlsen-during-national-socialism-1933-to-1945/.

Spiegel *magazine dug in:* Felix Bohr, Jürgen Dahlkamp, and Jörg Schmitt, "Die Bahlsens und die SS," *Der Spiegel,* May 17, 2019; Nils Klawitter, "So wurden die NS-Zwangsarbeiter bei Bahlsen wirklich behandelt," *Der Spiegel,* July 5, 2019.

8 *attempted to flee:* Rob van den Dobbelsteen, "De Engelandvaarders die het niet haalden," *Provinciale Zeeuwse Courant,* Oct. 9, 1993.

separated during the war: Peter de Waard, *Schoonheid achter de Schermen* (Amsterdam: Querido, 2014), 105–19, 192–95.

9 *dynasty descended from:* David de Jong, "Nazi Goebbels' Step-Grandchildren Are Hidden Billionaires," *Bloomberg News,* Jan. 28, 2013.

10 *goal of "openness":* Rüdiger Jungbluth and Giovanni di Lorenzo, "NS-Vergangenheit der Quandts: Man fühlt sich grauenvoll und schämt sich," *Die Zeit,* Sept. 22, 2011.

12 *soon promoted her:* "Bahlsen Announces 'Next Generation' Leadership," March 11, 2020, https://www.thebahlsenfamily.com/int/press/2020/.

Part I: "Perfectly average"

15 *millions from the war:* Joachim Scholtyseck, *Der Aufstieg der Quandts* (Munich: C. H. Beck, 2011), 57.

16 "*happy years*": Herbert Quandt and Harald Quandt (eds.), *Günther Quandt Erzählt sein Leben* (Munich: Mensch & Arbeit, 1961), 27.

barred from marrying her: Scholtyseck, *Aufstieg,* 36; Quandt and Quandt, *Günther,* 41–42.

17 *"This is where I will":* Quandt and Quandt, *Günther,* 70–72.

"something irretrievable": Quandt and Quandt, *Günther,* 111.

18 *"Magda, this is where":* Quandt and Quandt, *Günther,* 112.

"I had invited in": Quandt and Quandt, *Günther,* 114.

On just their third date: Hans-Otto Meissner, *Magda Goebbels: The First Lady of the Third Reich* (New York: Dial Press, 1980, trans.), 28–30.

19 *Her Jewish ties:* Anja Klabunde, *Magda Goebbels* (London: Sphere, 2001, trans.), 37–38.

"Religion doesn't matter": Cited in Klabunde, *Magda,* 46.

20 *"unmissable conference":* Cited in Scholtyseck, *Aufstieg,* 197–98.

"fundamentally he was": Meissner, *First Lady,* 34.

21 *"tired and battered":* Citations in Scholtyseck, *Aufstieg,* 198.

22 *forty-five million:* Quandt and Quandt, *Günther,* 86.

23 *"I had nothing to say":* Quotes in Quandt and Quandt, *Günther,* 88.

straw men: Scholtyseck, *Aufstieg,* 118–19.

an anonymous ad: Quandt and Quandt, *Günther,* 97–99.

24 *raiders emerged victorious:* Scholtyseck, *Aufstieg,* 120–22.

"a little Krupp": Trial minutes, May 13–14, 1948, denazification court Starnberg, STAM, denazification court documents, Günther Quandt, carton 1362/4.

was in dire shape: Scholtyseck, *Aufstieg,* 142–46.

25 *He alleged that:* Quandt and Quandt, *Günther,* 185–88.

Now Flick paced: Thomas Ramge, *Die Flicks* (Frankfurt: Campus, 2004), 56.

stately office building: Norbert Frei, Ralf Ahrens, Jörg Osterloh, and Tim Schanetzky, *Flick: Der Konzern, die Familie, die Macht* (Munich: Pantheon, 2009), 51–52.

26 *enabled Flick to marry:* Frei et al., *Flick,* 18–19; Kim Christian Priemel, *Flick: Eine Konzerngeschichte vom Kaiserreich bis zur Bundesrepublik* (Göttingen: Wallstein, 2007), 49–52.

27 *financed a stealthy takeover:* Frei et al., *Flick,* 27–33.

transformed the firm: Priemel, *Konzerngeschichte,* 87 ff.; Frei et al., *Flick,* 36–85.

28 *"seized with the spirit":* Felix Pinner, *Deutsche Wirtschaftsführer* (Berlin: Weltbühne, 1924), 99.

began bribing journalists: See Ogger, *Grosse,* 25–27; Frei et al., *Flick,* 15.

control the entire VSt: Detailed account in Priemel, *Konzerngeschichte,* 121–48.

29 *"He belongs to those":* Cited in Scholtyseck, *Aufstieg,* 159.

Günther had been looking: Quandt and Quandt, *Günther,* 152–63.

"See, dear, how wrong": Cited in Meissner, *First Lady,* 47.

"I would have so gladly": Quandt and Quandt, *Günther,* 176.

"I lost my dear": Quandt and Quandt, *Günther,* 176.

30 *some suspected:* See Meissner, *First Lady,* 59–60; Klabunde, *Magda,* 73, 85–86.

"Everything he was destined": Quandt and Quandt, *Günther,* 178.

a visual disability: Quandt and Quandt, *Günther,* 73–74; Wilhelm Treue, *Herbert Quandt* (Bad Homburg: Varta/Altana, 1980), 29–31.

grand Severin estate: Quandt and Quandt, *Günther,* 92–94.

"always be kind": Quandt and Quandt, *Günther*, 175.

31 *giving her an allowance:* Scholtyseck, *Aufstieg*, 197.
    "Read and approved": Cited in Klabunde, *Magda*, 48–49.
    overtures from the Nazi Party: Kurt G. W. Ludecke, *I Knew Hitler* (New York: Charles Scribner, 1937), 316–17.
    "I lunched with him": Ludecke, *I Knew Hitler*, 317.

32 *and more money:* Meissner, *First Lady*, 61–66.
    marriage was dissolved: Certified copy of court decision, July 13/17, 1929, HWA, dept. 2017, folder 47; Meissner, *First Lady*, 67, 95.

33 *"In summer 1929"*: Quandt and Quandt, *Günther*, 230.
    "With all the stress": Quandt and Quandt, *Günther*, 180,
    "Even when our ways": Quandt and Quandt, *Günther*, 111.
    "in greatest harmony": Statement Herbert Quandt, Nov. 10, 1947, HWA, dept. 2017, folder 42; Meissner, *First Lady*, 67, 75–78.

34 *"With nothing to do"*: Ludecke, *I Knew Hitler*, 317.
    "after consuming considerable": Citations in Klabunde, *Magda*, 113.
    Joseph Goebbels: Peter Longerich, *Goebbels* (London: Vintage, 2015, trans.), 3–151.

35 *"Magda was inflamed"*: Cited in Rüdiger Jungbluth, *Die Quandts: Ihr leiser Aufstieg zur mächtigsten Wirtschaftsdynastie Deutschlands* (Frankfurt: Campus, 2002), 108.
    joined the Nazi Party: Meissner, *First Lady*, 79–81.
    "Who was that": Cited in Klabunde, *Magda*, 118.

36 *"A beautiful woman"*: Fröhlich, *TG*, November 7, 1930.
    "It was supposedly": Quotes in Quandt and Quandt, *Günther*, 230–31.
    "She became the most": Trial minutes, May 13/14, 1948, denazification court Starnberg, STAM, denazification court documents Günther Quandt, carton 1362/4.

37 *"admiration and gratitude"*: Statement, Herbert Quandt, Nov. 10, 1947, HWA, dept. 2017, folder 42.
    "A picture of misfortune": Quandt and Quandt, *Günther*, 68–69.
    Society for the Study: See Jungbluth, *Quandts* (2002), 122; Scholtyseck, *Aufstieg*, 263–64.

38 *At the club:* Scholtyseck, *Aufstieg*, 264.

39 *On Sunday morning:* Henry Ashby Turner Jr. (ed.), *Hitler — Memoirs of a Confidant* (New Haven: Yale University Press, 1985, trans.), 232–37.

40 *Wilhelm was a financier:* See Bernhard Hoffmann, *Wilhelm von Finck* (Munich: C. H. Beck, 1953); "Neun Nullen," *Der Spiegel*, May 18, 1970, https://www.spiegel.de/politik/neun-nullen-a-608eb41d-0002-0001-0000-000045152285?.

41 *"conjured up the specter"*: Turner, *Big Business*, 150.
    "absolutely convinced": Turner, *Confidant*, 237.
    "the kind of power": Turner, *Confidant*, 237.

42 *at twenty-five million:* Turner, *Confidant*, 238, 243.
    "I can't say that Hitler": Quandt and Quandt, *Günther*, 233.
    "The youngest Hitler Youth": Turner, *Confidant*, 239–40.

43 *"a Frau Quandt"*: Turner, *Confidant*, 240.
    "Even at first glance": Turner, *Confidant*, 241.
    "Magda Quandt comes": Fröhlich, *TG*, Feb. 15, 1931.

"*Magda . . . goes home late*": Fröhlich, *TG*, March 10, 1931.

"*Magda, the lovely*": Fröhlich, *TG*, March 15, 1931.

"*Magda . . . shoos*": Fröhlich, *TG*, March 22, 1931.

44 "*A lot of work*": Fröhlich, *TG*, March 26, 1931.

"*In the afternoon*": Fröhlich, *TG*, March 12, 1931.

"*a useful boy*": Fröhlich, *TG*, June 14, 1931.

loved Harald "idolatrously": Fröhlich, *TG*, Aug. 12, 1932.

"*Harald looks so sweet*": Fröhlich, *TG*, Oct. 19, 1931.

Magda spoiled Goebbels: Jungbluth, *Quandts* (2002), 115.

"*She stood by me*": Fröhlich, *TG*, April 9, 1931.

45 "*Small quarrel with Magda*": Fröhlich, *TG*, June 26, 1931.

the couple's favorite getaway: Meissner, *First Lady*, 95; Quandt and Quandt, *Günther*, 233.

"*Now we are clear*": Fröhlich, *TG*, May 31, 1931.

46 "*Magda . . . had a talk*": Fröhlich, *TG*, Sept. 14, 1931.

kept on flirting: Longerich, *Goebbels*, 157–58.

"*she could represent*": Turner, *Confidant*, 255–59; quote on 255.

"*the arrangement*": Longerich, *Goebbels*, 157–60.

"*Nausea: Mr. Günther Quandt*": Fröhlich, *TG*, Sept. 12, 1931.

47 *According to Günther's*: Quandt and Quandt, *Günther*, 233–35; quote on 235.

"*Our views were so*": Trial minutes, May 13/14, 1948, denazification court Starnberg, STAM, denazification court documents Günther Quandt, carton 1362/4.

"*instinctively felt*": Quandt and Quandt, *Günther*, 232.

48 "*a tactless lout*": Fröhlich, *TG*, Nov. 30, 1931.

"*Günther Quandt came*": Fröhlich, *TG*, Dec. 11, 1931.

"*from start to finish*": Meissner, *First Lady*, 95.

49 *Thus the wedding*: Meissner, *First Lady*, 95–96.

50 *Günther later wrote*: Quandt and Quandt, *Günther*, 232–33, 236.

"*furious like a lioness*": Fröhlich, *TG*, Dec. 29, 1931.

51 "*over the moon*": Fröhlich, *TG*, Feb. 19, 1932.

"*an idea of the public*": Quandt and Quandt, *Günther*, 235.

"*slightly retarded*": Fröhlich, *TG*, April 24, 1932.

"*a real prole*": Fröhlich, *TG*, Oct. 13, 1932.

"*the capitalist*" *Werner*: Fröhlich, *TG*, Aug. 6, 1934.

to be wiped out: For the most detailed account of the Gelsenberg affair, see Priemel, *Konzerngeschichte*, 220 ff.

52 *wanted financial backing*: For accounts of the meeting, see Turner, *Big Business*, 235–36; NMT, Vol. VI, "The Flick Case" (Washington, DC: US Government Printing Office, 1952), 349, https://www.loc.gov/rr/frd/Military_Law/pdf/NT_war-criminals _Vol-VI.pdf.

decorated navy veteran: See Frei et al., *Flick*, 39, 58, 150.

53 *he first met Hitler*: Frei et al., *Flick*, 717.

he managed to sell: Priemel, *Konzerngeschichte*, 236–46.

54 "*Giving money to Nazis*": Turner, *Big Business*, 254–57; quote on 257.

55 "*who will be at our*": NMT, Vol. VI, 285.

"*the wind was blowing*": NMT, Vol. VI, 349.

"*Goebbels . . . got it into*": Cited in Scholtyseck, *Aufstieg,* 245.

"*talked to G. Quandt*": Fröhlich, *TG,* Nov. 4, 1932.

Christmas break: Fröhlich, *TG,* Dec. 24, 25, 27, 30, 31, 1932.

56   "*Mr. Quandt came*": Fröhlich, *TG,* Feb. 5, 1933.

57   *forty thousand reichsmarks:* Stefan Aust and Thomas Ammann, *Die Porsche Saga* (Cologne: Bastei Lübbe, 2016), 73–74, 85–86.

terminated twice: See Hans Mommsen and Manfred Grieger, *Das Volkswagenwerk und seine Arbeiter im Dritten Reich* (Düsseldorf: Econ, 1996), 72–74; Wolfram Pyta, Nils Havemann, and Jutta Braun, *Porsche: Vom Konstruktionsbüro zur Weltmarke* (Munich: Siedler, 2017), 20–22, 28.

58   "*unemployable perfectionist*": Bernhard Rieger, *The People's Car* (Cambridge, MA: Harvard University Press, 2013), 61.

59   *turned down a job:* Ferry Porsche and John Bentley, *We at Porsche* (New York: Doubleday, 1976), 49–53.

"*whose genius creates*": Cited in Aust and Ammann, *Saga,* 84.

"*As the creator of many*": Cited in Aust and Ammann, *Saga,* 85.

"*We express the hope*": Cited in Pyta et al., *Porsche,* 59.

Porsche's first contact: Pyta et al., *Porsche,* 65.

60   *On May 10, 1933:* For accounts of this meeting, see Aust and Ammann, *Saga,* 116–17; Pyta et al., *Porsche,* 69–73.

"*at the first possible*": August von Finck interrogation, Sept. 22, 1947, NARA, OMGUS, RG 260, M1923, roll 7.

Flick donated royally: NMT, Vol. VI, 389.

61   *The smallest contribution:* NMT, Vol. VII, 567–68.

Günther Quandt joined the Nazi: Jungbluth, *Quandts* (2002), 125–26.

1.6 million Germans: Ian Kershaw, *Hitler* (London: Allen Lane, 2008), 291.

62   "*disapproving attitude*": Quandt and Quandt, *Günther,* 232.

"*never belonged to*": Günther Quandt response to public prosecutor's indictment, Feb. 8, 1948, HWA, dept. 2017, folder 38.

"*insane disadvantages*": Trial minutes, May 13/14, 1948, denazification court Starnberg, STAM, denazification court documents Günther Quandt, carton 1362/4.

"*Received Dr. Quandt*": Fröhlich, *TG,* April 29, 1933.

Günther was handcuffed: Unless otherwise noted, this account is based on Günther Quandt response to public prosecutor's indictment, Feb. 8, 1948, HWA, dept. 2017, folder 38; Trial minutes, May 13/14, 1948, denazification court Starnberg, STAM, denazification court documents Günther Quandt, carton 1362/4; Scholtyseck, *Aufstieg,* 253–60.

63   *allegedly "prevented"*: Scholtyseck, *Aufstieg,* 254.

"*in a courtly manner*": Günther Quandt response to public prosecutor's indictment, Feb. 8, 1948, HWA, dept. 2017, folder 38.

"*buy impunity from*": Cited in Scholtyseck, *Aufstieg,* 259.

64   "*the year 1933 formed*": Günther Quandt response to public prosecutor's indictment, Feb. 8, 1948, HWA, dept. 2017, folder 38.

"*lightheartedly and shamefully*": Scholtyseck, *Aufstieg,* 314.

"It became clear": Quandt and Quandt, *Günther,* 237.

"Günther Quandt arrested": Fröhlich, *TG,* May 5, 1933.

the *"G. Quandt case"*: Fröhlich, *TG,* May 7, 1933.

"Detention warrant": Fröhlich, *TG,* June 14, 1933.

65 *"Goebbels said he knew"*: Trial minutes, May 13/14, 1948, denazification court Starnberg, STAM, denazification court documents Günther Quandt, carton 1362/4.

The same couldn't be said: Klabunde, *Magda,* 193–99.

"downright torturous": Cited in Treue, *Herbert,* 37.

66 *"That danger wasn't small"*: Cited in Treue, *Herbert,* 63.

"a blank page": Cited in Treue, *Herbert,* 64.

Herbert then married: Treue, *Herbert,* 70–72.

did Herbert sign up: Scholtyseck, *Aufstieg,* 766–67.

"was anxious for": Gerald D. Feldman, *Allianz and the German Insurance Business, 1933–1945* (New York: Cambridge University Press, 2001), 73.

67 he quickly resigned: Feldman, *Allianz,* 102.

"outlook on the world": Kurt Schmitt interrogation, July 15, 1947, NARA, OMGUS, RG 260, M1923, roll 7.

"exercised on him": Hans Schmidt-Polex interrogation, Sept. 22, 1947, NARA, OMGUS, RG 260, M1923, roll 7.

"that he believed": Hans Hess interrogation, Sept. 17, 1947, NARA, OMGUS, RG 260, M1923, roll 7.

"felt that his contributions": Edgar Uexküll interrogation, June 9, 1947, NARA, OMGUS, RG 260, M1923, roll 7.

"You are my man": Cited in "Neun Nullen," *Der Spiegel,* May 18, 1970.

68 On October 15, 1933: Ines Schlenker, *Hitler's Salon* (Bern: Peter Lang, 2007), 50.

69 *"millions of decent"*: Cited in Rieger, *People's Car,* 57.

a twelve-page memo: Pyta et al., *Porsche,* 161–64.

taken inspiration from: See Paul Schilperoord, *The Extraordinary Life of Josef Ganz* (New York: RVP, 2012), 112–24.

Hitler summoned Porsche: Pyta et al., *Porsche,* 168–70.

70 Hitler had read somewhere: Aust and Ammann, *Saga,* 91.

Porsche's citizenship: Mommsen and Grieger, *Volkswagenwerk,* 91.

"I really don't see": Porsche and Bentley, *We at Porsche,* 76.

71 Goebbels complained: Fröhlich, *TG,* April 13, 1934.

"We'll now bring out": Fröhlich, *TG,* April 13, 1934.

"fight for Harald": Fröhlich, *TG,* April 18, 1934.

"They both support": Fröhlich, *TG,* April 20, 1934.

"I won't put up": Fröhlich, *TG,* May 5, 1934.

72 *"Now Günther Qu."*: Fröhlich, *TG,* May 9, 1934.

"Old fool!": Fröhlich, *TG,* June 5, 1938.

Part II: "The National Socialist haunt will soon pass"

75 his sixtieth birthday: Table setting for the sixtieth birthday of military economy leader Dr.-Ing. E. h. Günther Quandt, Hotel Esplanade, Berlin, July 28, 1941, Federal Archive

Berlin, 8119 F/P 1112; 60. Geburtstag Dr. Günther Quandt, July 28, 1941, Material Nr. 2240, Film archive Karl Höffkes Agency, 13:17, https://archiv-akh.de/filme/2240#1.

a "brilliant speech": Cited in Scholtyseck, *Aufstieg,* 279.

76 *"accomplished something":* Cited in AFA-Ring, Accumulatoren-Fabrik AG Berlin's workers community magazine, Year 8, Issue 5, September 1941, 9, STAM, denazification court documents Günther Quandt, carton 1363/6.

skyrocket by 300 percent: Jungbluth, *Quandts* (2002), 178.

more than half the country: Scholtyseck, *Aufstieg,* 77.

secretly buying up: Jungbluth, *Quandts* (2002), 179; Scholtyseck, *Aufstieg,* 591–95.

a 60 percent stake: Scholtyseck, *Aufstieg,* 411.

"Military cloth, accumulators": Cited in Jungbluth, *Quandts* (2002), 164–65.

"He almost certainly won't": Cited in Jungbluth, *Quandts* (2002), 183.

77 *nineteen-year-old Harald:* Scholtyseck, *Aufstieg,* 279–80.

he held a reception: Scholtyseck, *Aufstieg,* 191–93.

about ten paintings: Jonathan Petropoulous, *Göring's Man in Paris* (New Haven: Yale University Press, 2021), 139.

78 *As a birthday present:* Scholtyseck, *Aufstieg,* 297.

"the lynchpin of ": Cited in Petropoulous, *Göring's Man,* 138.

"You were able to make": Cited in AFA-Ring, factory magazine of AFA Berlin's workers community, Year 8, Issue 5, September 1941, 5, STAM, denazification court documents Günther Quandt, carton 1363/6.

financial stimulus package: Adam Tooze, *The Wages of Destruction* (London: Penguin, 2006), 53–56.

79 *pursuing a dual strategy:* Scholtyseck, *Aufstieg,* 365.

"It took no small effort": Vereines deutscher Ingenieure (ed.), *50 Jahre Deutsche Waffen- und Munitionsfabriken* (Berlin: VDI, 1939), I.

DWM's arms complex: Jungbluth, *Quandts* (2002), 133–35; Scholtyseck, *Aufstieg,* 366–68, 439, 447.

80 *"shackles of Versailles":* Cited in Scholtyseck, *Aufstieg,* 374.

"dream come true": Cited in Wolfgang Seel, *Mauser* (Zurich: Stocker-Schmid, 1986), 112.

Dürener was renowned: Scholtyseck, *Aufstieg,* 143, 440.

81 *new industrial empire:* Johannes Bähr, Alex Drecoll, Bernhard Gotto, Kim Christian Priemel, and Harald Wixforth, *Der Flick-Konzern im Dritten Reich* (Munich: Olden- bourg, 2008), 77–84.

82 *like a weapons catalog:* Frei et al., *Flick,* 190.

invited von Blomberg: Bähr et al., *Flick-Konzern,* 137.

"extraordinarily kind": NMT, Vol. VI, 236.

83 *"extremely agitated":* Cited in Frei et al., *Flick,* 191.

"should not hesitate": NMT, Vol. VI, 237.

expropriation of Donauwörth: See Priemel, *Konzerngeschichte,* 344–45; Bähr et al., *Flick-Konzern,* 142–43; Frei et al., *Flick,* 194–95.

classified a "state pest": Citations in Frei et al., *Flick,* 194.

so-called Montan scheme: See Priemel, *Konzerngeschichte,* 345–48; Bähr et al., *Flick-Konzern,* 143–47; Frei et al., *Flick,* 195; Scholtyseck, *Aufstieg,* 368.

84 *interested in buying Simson:* See Priemel, *Konzerngeschichte,* 349–52; Bähr et al., *Flick-Konzern,* 302–3; Frei et al., *Flick,* 196–97.

   "smooth cooperation": Cited in Priemel, *Konzerngeschichte,* 350.

   "if for general national-political": Cited in Bähr et al., *Flick-Konzern,* 302.

85 *"excess profits":* Priemel, *Konzerngeschichte,* 350.

   "We as a private group": Cited in Priemel, *Konzerngeschichte,* 351.

86 RESERVED FOR THE GUESTS: NMT, Vol. VI, 302.

   made no impact: Turner, *Big Business,* 244–45.

87 *many familiar faces:* For the guest list, see Reinhard Vogelsang, *Der Freundeskreis Himmler* (Göttingen: Muster-Schmidt, 1972), 149–50.

   nicknamed "SS-Bank": Cited in Tobias Bütow and Franka Bindernagel, *Ein KZ in der Nachbarschaft* (Cologne: Böhlau, 2004), 53.

   "physically impressive": Cited in Feldman, *Allianz,* 77.

   as a "mirror image": Cited in Vogelsang, *Freundeskreis,* 24.

88 *in zeal for Hitler:* Jürgen Finger, Sven Keller, and Andreas Wirsching, *Dr. Oetker und der Nationalsozialismus* (Munich: C. H. Beck, 2013), 123.

   work as peasant farmers: Heather Pringle, *The Master Plan* (London: HarperCollins, 2006), 40.

   hundreds of thousands: Finger et al., *Dr. Oetker,* 141–49.

89 *profitable regional newspaper:* Rüdiger Jungbluth, *Die Oetkers* (Frankfurt: Campus, 2004), 139–42; Finger et al., *Dr. Oetker,* 178–90.

   who invited him: Jungbluth, *Oetkers,* 142–43; Finger et al., *Dr. Oetker,* 191, 195.

   Every second Wednesday: Vogelsang, *Freundeskreis,* 78–81.

   Dachau concentration camp: Account of the visit in NMT, Vol. VI, 303–5.

   "very carefully prepared": NMT, Vol. VI, 305.

90 *"For the SS and my other":* Cited in NMT, Vol. VI, 326.

   "special account S": NMT, Vol. VI, 238.

   Millions soon flowed in: Vogelsang, *Freundeskreis,* 158.

   Kaselowsky was present: Finger et al., *Dr. Oetker,* 197.

91 *"If . . . you can't turn out":* Cited in Porsche and Bentley, *We at Porsche,* 76.

   1.75 million reichsmarks: Mommsen and Grieger, *Volkswagenwerk,* 83–84.

   "race defilement": Aust and Ammann, *Saga,* 87.

   neared 170,000 reichsmarks: Pyta et al., *Porsche,* 90.

92 *"It was held against me":* Adolf Rosenberger to Hermann Bienstock, Feb. 18, 1950. Cited in Eberhard Reuß, "Der Mann hinter Porsche—Adolf Rosenberger," ARD/SWR, June 24, 2019, Youtube video, 43:57. https://www.youtube.com/watch?v=VSQzYWHtl-0.

93 *"protective custody":* Aust and Ammann, *Saga,* 87.

   did nothing to secure: Reuß, "Rosenberger," ARD/SWR; Pyta et al., *Porsche,* 135; Aust and Ammann, *Saga,* 87.

   remained a foreign representative: Pyta et al., *Porsche,* 124–25.

   presented two test cars: Porsche and Bentley, *We at Porsche,* 91–92.

94 *"The way these Volkswagens":* Henry Picker, *Hitlers Tischgespräche im Führerhauptquartier* (Stuttgart: Seewald, 1977), 374.

   "pudding prince": "Der Puddingprinz," *Der Spiegel,* Dec. 17, 1957.

   "the most valuable thing": Cited in Finger et al., *Dr. Oetker,* 345.

She spoiled the boy: Finger et al., *Dr. Oetker,* 343–44.

95   *a Nazi family:* See Finger et al., *Dr. Oetker,* 120, 352, 354.

"a fun party": Cited in Finger et al., *Dr. Oetker,* 346.

96   *"It's out of the question":* Cited in Finger et al., *Dr. Oetker,* 224.

below their market value: Finger et al., *Dr. Oetker,* 225–26.

Lipmanns, a Jewish couple: Jungbluth, *Oetkers,* 169–71; Finger et al., *Dr. Oetker,* 226–29.

"desperate emigration efforts": Finger et al., *Dr. Oetker,* 227.

"After lengthy negotiations": Cited in Jungbluth, *Oetkers,* 170.

a few "friendly words": Cited in Finger et al., *Dr. Oetker,* 349.

"must have suffered": Cited in Finger et al., *Dr. Oetker,* 353.

"We thought nothing": Cited in Finger et al., *Dr. Oetker,* 353.

97   *a Jewish arms executive:* For the Sachs saga, see Scholtyseck, *Aufstieg,* 315–18.

"I'll decide who's a Jew!": Cited in Bryan Mark Rigg, *Hitler's Jewish Soldiers* (Lawrence: University Press of Kansas, 2002), 21.

at least 40 percent: Tooze, *Wages of Destruction,* 339.

despite his "dark spot": Cited in Scholtyseck, *Aufstieg,* 317.

"in the interest of": Cited in Scholtyseck, *Aufstieg,* 317.

98   *"old Quandt" proved:* Cited in Scholtyseck, *Aufstieg,* 318.

"foreign or Jewish capital": Leistungsbericht Kriegsjahr 1941/42, Dürener Metallwerke AG, HWA, dept. 2017, folder 54.

received the title: See Frei et al., *Flick,* 202; Wolfgang Fürweger, *Die PS-Dynastie* (Vienna: Ueberreuter, 2007), 73.

Günther later said: Scholtyseck, *Aufstieg,* 270–71.

decided not to attend: Scholtyseck, *Aufstieg,* 290.

"an unpleasant thing": Fröhlich, *TG,* August 1, 1936.

"I'm very depressed": Fröhlich, *TG,* August 2, 1936.

99   *were taking a stroll:* Fröhlich, *TG,* June 3, 1936; Longerich, *Goebbels,* 317–18.

100   *"national-socialistic model":* Jungbluth, *Oetkers,* 156–57.

to Aryanize assets: On these Oetker Aryanizations, see Finger et al., *Dr. Oetker,* 213–14, 231–35.

"extremely favorable": Cited in Finger et al., *Dr. Oetker,* 213.

stakes in three companies: Finger et al., *Dr. Oetker,* 235–46.

101   *Nacher's Bavarian estate:* Frei et al., *Flick,* 211, 711–12.

"white sausage temple": "Neun Nullen," *Der Spiegel,* May 18, 1970.

got their checkbooks out: Schlenker, *Salon,* 41–42.

"They have hung works": Fröhlich, *TG,* June 6, 1937.

102   *"display such muck":* Fröhlich, *TG,* June 7, 1937.

the chancellor was happier: Longerich, *Goebbels,* 349.

"The car has fabulous": Fröhlich, *TG,* Sept. 7, 1937.

103   *"Dr. Porsche delivers":* Fröhlich, *TG,* Dec. 9, 1937.

Quandt robbed another: On the Herny Pels Aryanization, see Scholtyseck, *Aufstieg,* 393–401, 951 n224; Hans-Dieter Nahme, *Ein Deutscher im zwanzigsten Jahrhundert* (Rostock: Hinstorff, 2007), 219–23.

"heroic death for": Cited in Scholtyseck, *Aufstieg,* 396.

104   *"the National Socialist haunt"*: Nahme, *Deutscher*, 220.
      Günther had discovered: Treue, *Herbert*, 74–76.
105   *"struggle for life"*: Quandt and Quandt, *Günther*, 73.
      "The principle of": Letter from Sept. 6, 1938, in Günther Quandt, Gedanken über Sü-
      damerika. Briefe in zwangloser Folge, Vol. I, Sept.–Dec. 1938.
      "for some time": Cited in Frei et al., *Flick*, 211.
      bought three estates: Frei et al., *Flick*, 211, 711–13.
      The Bavarian estate: Benjamin Engel, "Der Beraubte Bierbaron," *Süddeutsche Zeitung*,
      Oct. 11, 2020.
106   *the Austrian hunting grounds:* "Habe Rottenmann lieben gelernt," *Kleine Zeitung*, Aug.
      24, 2015.
      the Lübeck blast furnaces: On the Lübeck Aryanization, see Ogger, *Grosse*, 161–73;
      Priemel, *Konzerngeschichte*, 371–83; Bähr et al., *Flick-Konzern*, 307–21; Frei et al.,
      Flick, 213–23.
      "The discussion with this": Cited in Ogger, *Grosse*, 168.
107   *"seems to be a little"*: Cited in Bähr et al., *Flick-Konzern*, 320.
      "to accept a bill": Cited in Ogger, *Grosse*, 171.
      "You're lucky to get": Cited in Ogger, *Grosse*, 172.
108   *controlled about 65 percent:* Bähr et al., *Flick-Konzern*, 322.
      "matter of life": Citations in Bähr et al., *Flick-Konzern*, 326.
      "making trouble for": Cited in Priemel, *Konzerngeschichte*, 394.
109   *"created an outright parasitic"*: Quote and citation in Frei et al., *Flick*, 229.
      "Four Year Plan": See Tooze, *Wages of Destruction*, 219 ff.
      follow-up meeting: Bähr et al., *Flick-Konzern*, 327.
      with "angry silence": Bähr et al., *Flick-Konzern*, 328.
      complicated ownership structure: See Priemel, *Konzerngeschichte*, 392.
110   *the "Petschek problem"*: See NMT, Vol. VI, 442–60; Priemel, *Konzerngeschichte*, 396–
      98; Bähr et al., *Flick-Konzern*, 331–33; Frei et al., *Flick*, 230–31.
      "calming atmosphere": Cited in Frei et al., *Flick*, 231.
      "orders from top quarters": Cited in Priemel, *Konzerngeschichte*, 400.
      "German problem": Cited in Bähr et al., *Flick-Konzern*, 334.
      under constant surveillance: Frei et al., *Flick*, 232.
111   *"threatened . . . by the same"*: Cited in Priemel, *Konzerngeschichte*, 401.
      More political pressure: See NMT, Vol. VI, 469–71; Priemel, *Konzerngeschichte*, 404;
      Bähr et al., *Flick-Konzern*, 338; Frei et al., *Flick*, 233.
      "the spirit of all": Citations in Bähr et al., *Flick-Konzern*, 339–40.
      "the interests of his": Cited in Priemel, *Konzerngeschichte*, 405 n64.
112   *managed to sell:* See Bähr et al., *Flick-Konzern*, 384–85.
      almost $600,000: Priemel, *Konzerngeschichte*, 408.
      "rather good deal": Cited in Frei et al., *Flick*, 229.
      NSDAP and personal accounts: Ingo Köhler, *Die "Arisierung" der Privatbanken im
      Dritten Reich* (Munich: C. H. Beck, 2005), 307.
      He first attacked: Köhler, *Arisierung*, 366.
113   *"Today, the German"*: Cited in Köhler, *Arisierung*, 367.
      seized during Kristallnacht: Köhler, *Arisierung*, 371–73.

114 *responsible for the liquidation:* Harold James, *Verbandspolitik im Nationalsozialismus* (Munich: Piper, 2001), 181.

Von Finck's first Aryanization: For more on the Dreyfus Aryanization, see Köhler, *Arisierung,* 305–11; Christopher Kopper, *Zwischen Marktwirtschaft und Dirigismus* (Bonn: Bouvier, 1995), 257–59.

Julius Kaufmann estimated: Köhler, *Arisierung,* 503.

"friendly negotiations": Georg Siebert, *Hundert Jahre Merck Finck & Co.* (Munich: 1970), 45.

115 *"pure German blood":* Citations in Köhler, *Arisierung,* 310.

"bank of the Führer": Gerhard Lück interrogation, Oct. 17, 1947, NARA, OMGUS, RG 260, M1923, roll 7.

further "dejewification": Köhler, *Arisierung,* 311.

116 *the chance to Aryanize:* Peter Melichar, *Neuordnung im Bankwesen* (Vienna: Oldenbourg, 2004), 397–98.

Louis was arrested: Giles MacDonogh, *1938: Hitler's Gamble* (New York: Basic Books, 2009), 61, 69–71.

"undoubtedly goes back": Emil Puhl interrogation, Oct. 23, 1947, OMGUS, NARA, RG 260, M1923, roll 7.

"to discuss possible solutions": August von Finck interrogation, Sept. 23, 1947, OMGUS, NARA, RG 260, M1923, roll 7.

"up to tackling": Cited in Harold James, *The Deutsche Bank and the Nazi Economic War Against the Jews* (Cambridge, UK: Cambridge University Press, 2001), 137.

117 *private bank Anton Kohn:* Köhler, *Arisierung,* 414–15.

"Jewish clientele": Cited in Köhler, *Arisierung,* 415.

Aryanization of Simon Hirschland: See James, *Nazi Economic Wars,* 77–81; Köhler, *Arisierung,* 374–89.

Rothschild out of trusteeship: Melichar, *Neuordnung,* 399–402.

the bank's estimated value: See report on German External Assets in Austria: Private Bank E.V. Nicolai & Company S.M. V. Rothschild in Liquidation, March 19, 1947 ff., NARA, USACA, RG 260, M1928, roll 13.

After the sale: Erich Gritzbach interrogation, Oct. 24, 1947, NARA, OMGUS, RG 260, M1923, roll 7.

118 *closer to Göring:* See August von Finck interrogation, Sept. 23, 1947; Erich Gritzbach interrogation, Oct. 24, 1947, both in NARA, OMGUS, RG 260, M1923, roll 7; Ogger, *Grosse,* 131–32.

Von Finck later claimed: James, *Verbandspolitik,* 183.

paid some $21 million: "Baron Louis de Rothschild Dies; Freed by Nazis for $21 Million," *New York Times,* Jan. 16, 1955.

most of the capital: Melichar, *Neuordnung,* 401–2.

He was recommended: Egon von Ritter interrogation, Oct. 10, 1947, NARA, OMGUS, RG 260, M1923, roll 7.

"aggressive and elbowing": Hans Schmidt-Polex interrogation, Sept. 22, 1947, NARA, OMGUS, RG 260, M1923, roll 7.

assets quickly quadrupled: See indictment by public prosecutor J. Herf, Nov. 3, 1948, STAM, denazification court documents August von Finck, carton 409.

119 *"established itself as"*: James, *Verbandspolitik*, 183–84.

"I hate the word": Cited in Rieger, *People's Car*, 72.

two hundred million: See Mommsen and Grieger, *Volkswagenwerk*, 155–65.

morning of the ceremony: See Mommsen and Grieger, *Volkswagenwerk*, 182–86; Rieger, *People's Car*, 71–72.

120 *"In the cordoned-off"*: Rieger, *People's Car*, 71.

121 *"thousands and thousands"*: Cited in Rieger, *People's Car*, 72.

inundated with love letters: Porsche and Bentley, *We at Porsche*, 113.

in the midst of an expansion: Pyta et al., *Porsche*, 91, 215–17.

a Jewish family, the Wolfs: The Porsche firm later paid restitution to a Wolf heir. See Pyta et al., *Porsche*, 131–34.

122 *"on higher authority"*: Hans von Veyder Malberg to Adolf Rosenberger, June 2, 1938. Cited in Reuß, "Rosenberger," ARD/SWR, June 24, 2019.

suggesting two ways: Pyta et al., *Porsche*, 126.

shared their ideology: See Mommsen and Grieger, *Volkswagenwerk*, 915 n19; Pyta et al., *Porsche*, 308–9.

"Dr. Porsche has told": Cited in Pyta et al., *Porsche*, 126–27.

"My company does not": Cited in Pyta et al., *Porsche*, 126.

123 *a ménage à trois*: See Longerich, *Goebbels*, 391–92; Meissner, *First Lady*, 177–79.

"I've come to some very": Fröhlich, *TG*, Aug. 16, 1938.

124 *"Everything depends on"*: Fröhlich, *TG*, Oct. 11, 1938.

the "divorce mania": Fröhlich, *TG*, Feb. 3, 1937.

"terrible heart pains": Fröhlich, *TG*, Oct. 18, 1938.

"carry out my difficult task": Fröhlich, *TG*, Oct. 25, 1938.

no longer allowed to work: Longerich, *Goebbels*, 395.

"I'm not talking to": Fröhlich, *TG*, Oct. 22, 1938.

"It appears that he": Longerich, *Goebbels*, 394.

"Hanke has proven": Fröhlich, *TG*, July 23, 1939.

who brought her affair: Longerich, *Goebbels*, 420–21.

125 *quarter billion reichsmarks*: See Priemel, *Konzerngeschichte*, 410.

"These people want to": Cited in NMT, Vol. VI, 458.

across holding companies: See Priemel, *Konzerngeschichte*, 392.

"attitude is completely indifferent": NMT, Vol. VI, 485–86.

Dietrich also drafted: See NMT, Vol. VI, 480–84; Priemel, *Konzerngeschichte*, 411; Bähr et al., *Flick-Konzern*, 343–45; Frei et al., *Flick*, 236–37.

126 *670 million*: See Priemel, *Konzerngeschichte*, 412–14.

he was "very displeased": Cited in Priemel, *Konzerngeschichte*, 410.

a swap of brown coal: For more about the saga of the coal swap, see Priemel, *Konzerngeschichte*, 414–26; Bähr et al., *Flick-Konzern*, 345–70; Frei et al., *Flick*, 239–47.

127 *"Decree Concerning the Utilization"*: NMT, Vol. VI, 498–503.

128 *more than one-third*: Bähr et al., *Flick-Konzern*, 366–67.

129 *around 280 million*: Mommsen and Grieger, *Volkswagenwerk*, 198–200, 1032.

Porsche dared show him: Volkswagen, *Place of Remembrance of Forced Labor in the Volkswagen Factory* (Wolfsburg: Volkswagen, 1999), 18.

massive red-brick façade: Rieger, *People's Car*, 81–82.

dusty barracks camp: See Mommsen and Grieger, *Volkswagenwerk,* 283–311.

130 *relationship with Flick:* Priemel, *Konzerngeschichte,* 429–30.

"*The effort of a forced*": NMT, Vol. VI, 569–70.

an angry response: Frei et al., *Flick,* 176.

Flick's taxable income: See Bähr et al., *Flick-Konzern,* 162–63.

131 "*Most disturbing news*": Citations in Scholtyseck, *Aufstieg,* 366.

"*I didn't believe*": Quandt and Quandt, *Günther,* 11–12.

"*The German people*": Cited in Scholtyseck, *Aufstieg,* 274.

Günther projected that: Scholtyseck, *Aufstieg,* 419 for AFA, 421–22 for DWM.

"*If there's war, there's*": Cited in Treue, *Herbert,* 80.

"*sober corporate strategy*": Cited in Scholtyseck, *Aufstieg,* 417.

Part III: "*The children have now already become men*"

135 *sat together in:* Scholtyseck, *Aufstieg,* 248.

a palatial residence: Longerich, *Goebbels,* 404–5.

"*had experienced*": Fröhlich, *TG,* Oct. 28, Oct. 29, 1939.

136 "*Talked to Magda*": Fröhlich, *TG,* Nov. 2, 1939.

"*across battlefields*": Fröhlich, *TG,* Nov. 2, 1939.

"*Especially my presentation*": Fröhlich, *TG,* Nov. 3, 1939.

137 *DWM received trusteeship:* See Scholtyseck, *Aufstieg,* 573–76.

started an internship: Quandt and Quandt, *Günther,* 243.

"*behaving fabulously*": Fröhlich, *TG,* Jan. 14, 1940.

girls, motorcycles, and cars: Jungbluth, *Quandts* (2002), 147.

Harald's record in Nazi: See Jungbluth, *Quandts* (2002), 143–46; Scholtyseck, *Aufstieg,* 248.

138 "*because of school difficulties*": Cited in Jungbluth, *Quandts* (2002), 145.

"*as far as possible*": Trial minutes, May 13/14, 1948, denazification court Starnberg, STAM, denazification court documents Günther Quandt, carton 1362/4.

"*Nothing is not keeping me*": Cited in Jungbluth, *Quandts* (2002), 151.

to be "properly honed": Fröhlich, *TG,* July 21, 1940.

got himself a girlfriend: See Günther Reinhardt Nebuschka to Telford Taylor, Nov. 3, 1947, STAM, denazification court documents Günther Quandt, carton 1362/1.

Harald's paratrooper training: Jungbluth, *Quandts* (2002), 151.

"*The military has straightened*": Fröhlich, *TG,* Oct. 13, 1940.

Harald returned to Berlin: Fröhlich, *TG,* Nov. 5, 1940.

139 *Christmas Day:* Fröhlich, *TG,* Dec. 26, 1940.

massive country house: Longerich, *Goebbels,* 405–6.

"*her horrible husband*": Fröhlich, *TG,* Nov. 5, 1940.

"*particularly dark chapter*": Scholtyseck, *Aufstieg,* 518.

drawn up a "wish list": Scholtyseck, *Aufstieg,* 565.

member of the Nazi Party: Scholtyseck, *Aufstieg,* 766.

"*When the war came*": Cited in Treue, *Herbert,* 79.

"*Industrial firms or factories*": Cited in Scholtyseck, *Aufstieg,* 529.

140 "*Bureau Hackinger*": See Scholtyseck, *Aufstieg,* 493–96, 992 n394.

they were wrong: See Scholtyseck, *Aufstieg,* 519–21.

five failed: Scholtyseck, *Aufstieg,* 521–28.

the Aryanized Hirschfeld: See Scholtyseck, *Aufstieg,* 528–30.

majority stake in Dreyfus: See Scholtyseck, *Aufstieg,* 530–31.

the "best . . . object": Cited in Scholtyseck, *Aufstieg,* 530.

141 *"Since that time . . .":* Quandt and Quandt, *Günther,* 242.

expand it they would: See Scholtyseck, *Aufstieg,* 537 ff.

"Green is our parachute": Cited in Jungbluth, *Quandts* (2002), 153.

"Harald has messed up": Fröhlich, *TG,* Feb. 12, 1941.

probably pulled some stunt: Jungbluth, *Quandts* (2002), 153.

"really out of line": Fröhlich, *TG,* Feb. 13, 1941.

"The issue is solved": Fröhlich, *TG,* Feb. 20, 1941.

142 *"Never was a more":* Winston Churchill, *The Second World War* (London: Bloomsbury, 2013), 429.

"with a fiery heart": For Harald's report on the Crete invasion, see AFA-Ring, factory magazine of AFA Berlin's workers community, Year 8, Issue 5, Sept. 1941, STAM, denazification court documents Günther Quandt, carton 1363/6.

widespread resistance: See Jungbluth, *Quandts* (2002), 156.

143 *"The German Air Corps":* Churchill, *Second World War,* 429.

awarded the Iron Cross: Fröhlich, *TG,* June 14, 1941.

heard of mutilations: Fröhlich, *TG,* May 31, 1941.

"Harald's bravery": Fröhlich, *TG,* June 16, 1941.

144 *promoted to under officer:* Fröhlich, *TG,* Sept. 14, 1941.

"Operation Crete has shown": AFA-Ring, factory magazine of AFA Berlin's workers community, Year 8, Issue 5, Sept. 1941, STAM, denazification court documents Günther Quandt, carton 1363/6.

"already made a lethal": Cited in Scholtyseck, *Aufstieg,* 274.

write an important letter: Frei et al., *Flick,* 280–81.

four years earlier: NMT, Vol. VI, 192–94.

his "crown prince": Cited in Priemel, *Konzerngeschichte,* 735.

145 *"A boy from a normal":* Cited in Ramge, *Flicks,* 56.

forced him to drop out: Ogger, *Grosse,* 218.

got into a fierce dispute: Frei et al., *Flick,* 282.

Flick family "daredevil": Cited in Ramge, *Flicks,* 114.

146 *Rudolf was advancing:* Frei et al., *Flick,* 281.

hit hard by Rudolf's death: See Frei et al., *Flick,* 752; Bähr et al., *Flick-Konzern,* 257 n428.

"the little lad": Cited in Ramge, *Flicks,* 174.

sent Otto-Ernst to Lorraine: Bähr et al., *Flick-Konzern,* 452.

Ferry Porsche arrived: Porsche and Bentley, *We at Porsche,* 141; Ferry Porsche and Günther Molter, *Ferry Porsche* (Stuttgart: Motorbuch, 1989), 123.

Kübelwagen (the bucket car): See Mommsen and Grieger, *Volkswagenwerk,* 383–405.

147 *weapons and military vehicles:* See Mommsen and Grieger, *Volkswagenwerk,* 453 ff.

Increasingly, forced labor: Volkswagen, *Remembrance,* 23.

148 "more sympatico": Porsche and Bentley, We at Porsche, 141.

Ferry later claimed: Porsche and Bentley, We at Porsche, 162; Porsche and Molter, Ferry, 124–25.

applied to the SS: Pyta et al., Porsche, 307–8, 458 n16; Jens Westemeier, Himmlers Krieger (Paderborn: Ferdinand Schöningh, 2014), 540-541.

Soviet prisoners of war: Volkswagen, Remembrance, 35.

"some interesting reports": NMT, Vol. VI, 694.

149 "economic dictator": Cited in Bähr et al., Flick-Konzern, 419.

proposed a joint venture: See Priemel, Konzerngeschichte, 459–68; Bähr et al., Flick-Konzern, 420–30; Frei et al., Flick, 317–23.

It wasn't your average: NMT, Vol. VI, 695–98; quotes on 696, 698.

150 Wehrmacht's catering service: See Finger et al., Dr. Oetker, 355–58.

151 "still alive at all": Citations in Finger et al., Dr. Oetker, 357.

accepted as a volunteer: Finger et al., Dr. Oetker, 358.

"married his money": Cited in Michael Bloch, Ribbentrop (London: Abacus, 2003), 19.

They became fast friends: Finger et al., Dr. Oetker, 351.

started his application: Finger et al., Dr. Oetker, 358.

152 deployed as ground infantry: Scholtyseck, Aufstieg, 250.

"That's all nonsense": Cited in Veit Harlan, Im Schatten meiner Filme (Gütersloh: Mohn, 1966), 140.

"interesting things": Fröhlich, TG, July 23, 1942.

"vigorously" resisted: Fröhlich, TG, Oct. 18, 1942.

"get through the coming": Fröhlich, TG, Oct. 13, 1942.

153 "living more dangerously": Cited in Jungbluth, Quandts (2002), 200.

"trouble with Soviet partisans": Fröhlich, TG, March 9, 1943.

Goebbels received a letter: Fröhlich, TG, Feb. 24, 1943.

"Total war" was declared: See Jungbluth, Quandts (2002), 200–201; Longerich, Goebbels, 559–60.

154 "A fairly barbaric procedure": Fröhlich, TG, March 27, 1942.

He wanted to finance: See Scholtyseck, Aufstieg, 421 ff.

155 "no longer justifiable": Cited in Scholtyseck, Aufstieg, 423.

"use of unskilled workers": Cited in Scholtyseck, Aufstieg, 427.

issued a new bond: Scholtyseck, Aufstieg, 426.

The labor shortage: See Tooze, Wages of Destruction, 513–17.

"one of the largest": Tooze, Wages of Destruction, 517.

prisoners in concentration camps: See Marc Buggeln, Slave Labor in Nazi Concentration Camps (Oxford, UK: Oxford University Press, 2014, trans.), 20–21.

156 At least twelve million: See Mark Spoerer and Jochen Fleischhacker, "Forced Laborers in Nazi Germany: Categories, Numbers, and Survivors," Journal of Interdisciplinary History, vol. 33, no. 2 (Autumn 2002): 197, 201.

Slave labor collaborations: Tooze, Wages of Destruction, 531–32.

"worked long and intensively": Quandt and Quandt, Günther, 239.

"largest single battery": Cited in Scholtyseck, Aufstieg, 790.

157 began to produce: Scholtyseck, Aufstieg, 435–36.

from a concentration camp: On AFA's Hannover subcamp, see Hans Hermann Schröder et al. (eds.), *Konzentrationslager in Hannover* (Hildesheim: August Lax, 1985), 50 ff.; Jungbluth, *Quandts* (2002), 190–99; Marc Buggeln, *Arbeit & Gewalt* (Göttingen: Wallstein, 2009), 71–74, 188–92, 307–12; Scholtyseck, *Aufstieg*, 638–43, 664–70, 682–87.

"less than slaves": See Benjamin Ferencz, *Less Than Slaves* (Bloomington: Indiana University Press, 2002).

"provide the detainees": Cited in Buggeln, *Slave Labor*, 71.

Instead of money: Schröder, *Konzentrationslager*, 74–76, 80–104.

158 *"while fully conscious":* Cited in Schröder, *Konzentrationslager*, 83.

"beat the prisoners": Cited in Schröder, *Konzentrationslager*, 60–61.

discussing political developments: Unless otherwise noted, this account is based on trial minutes, May 13/14, 1948, denazification court Starnberg, STAM, denazification court documents Günther Quandt, carton 1362/4; Günther Quandt response to the indictment by public prosecutor, Feb. 8, 1948, HWA, dept. 2017, folder 38; Jungbluth, *Quandts* (2002), 202–4.

159 *"performed excellently":* Fröhlich, *TG*, June 20, 1943.

"the only sensible thing": Trial minutes, May 13/14, 1948, denazification court Starnberg, STAM, denazification court documents Günther Quandt, carton 1362/4.

would be "finished": Trial minutes, May 13/14, 1948, denazification court Starnberg, STAM, denazification court documents Günther Quandt, carton 1362/4.

160 *"a heartfelt personal telegram":* Cited in Priemel, *Konzerngeschichte*, 578.

"in the right light": Bähr et al., *Flick-Konzern*, 283.

"peasant forebears": Quotes in NMT, Vol. VI, 183–84.

The asset value: See Bähr et al., *Flick-Konzern*, 495–96.

That year's tax assessment: Frei et al., *Flick*, 396.

161 *forced or enslaved:* See Bähr et al., *Flick-Konzern*, 511; Frei et al., *Flick*, 328.

subcamp for "foreign Jews": Cited in Frei et al., *Flick*, 359.

in favor of the immediate murder: Priemel, *Konzerngeschichte*, 492.

at the Rombach steelworks: On Rombach, see Priemel, *Konzerngeschichte*, 447–52; Bähr et al., *Flick-Konzern*, 451–61; Frei et al., *Flick*, 299–306.

a "quality program": Cited in Bähr et al., *Flick-Konzern*, 459.

162 *"that the business couldn't":* Citations in Priemel, *Konzerngeschichte*, 449.

working conditions at Rombach: see Priemel, *Konzerngeschichte*, 495–97; Bähr et al., *Flick-Konzern*, 527–28, 546–48; Frei et al., *Flick*, 307–9.

"among the worst": Priemel, *Konzerngeschichte*, 497.

"a mixture normally": Cited Frei et al., *Flick*, 308.

163 *was beaten to death:* Frei et al., *Flick*, 308–9.

"committed the crimes": Bähr et al., *Flick-Konzern*, 548.

"Austrian national economy": Citations in Pyta et al., *Porsche*, 315.

164 *in his new job:* Mommsen and Grieger, *Volkswagenwerk*, 453–76.

named "Work Village": See Mommsen and Grieger, *Volkswagenwerk*, 496–515; Volkswagen, *Remembrance*, 81, 84; Buggeln, *Slave Labor*, 66–67.

165 *"spontaneous musical procession":* Quote and following citation in Volkswagen, *Remembrance*, 58.

Piëch "bluntly declared": Mommsen and Grieger, *Volkswagenwerk*, 756.

"laced kitchen leftovers": Rieger, *People's Car,* 83.

"Nursery for Foreign Children": See Mommsen and Grieger, *Volkswagenwerk,* 762–65; Volkswagen, *Remembrance,* 52.

"defied belief": Cited in Rieger, *People's Car,* 83–84.

Himmler had invited: For program and guest list, see NMT, Vol. VI, 273–75.

166 *"immense disappointment"*: NMT, Vol. VI, 366.

"dull . . . despite": Cited in "Treue im Chor," *Der Spiegel,* Oct. 12, 1965.

Flick wondered whether: NMT, Vol. VI, 336.

"According to the": Cited in Finger et al., *Dr. Oetker,* 201.

More than half a billion: Finger et al., *Dr. Oetker,* 286, 288 ff.

Kaselowsky had become: Finger et al., *Dr. Oetker,* 199–200.

167 *In a joint venture:* See Jungbluth, *Oetkers,* 186–88; Finger et al., *Dr. Oetker,* 311–24; Buggeln, *Slave Labor,* 67–68.

found it "quite gratifying": Cited in Finger et al., *Dr. Oetker,* 318.

168 *had been "shielded"*: Citations in Finger et al., *Dr. Oetker,* 365.

ideological instruction: Finger et al., *Dr. Oetker,* 358–64.

169 *"only words of contempt"*: Fröhlich, *TG,* Jan. 13, 1944.

"The experience at the front": Fröhlich, *TG,* Jan. 17, 1944.

fed up with the war: Jungbluth, *Quandts* (2002), 205.

"Harald causes us": Fröhlich, *TG,* Feb. 13, 1944.

"behaved anything but": Fröhlich, *TG,* March 15, 1944.

"very unhappy" with: Fröhlich, *TG,* March 16, 1944.

170 *"very stern letter"*: Fröhlich, *TG,* April 19, 1944.

"Keep your chin up": Cited in Jungbluth, *Quandts* (2002), 206.

Cegielski weapons complex: Scholtyseck, *Aufstieg,* 576–84.

twenty-four thousand people: Scholtyseck, *Aufstieg,* 680–81, 695–99, 709.

171 *"The Wartheland is proud"*: Reinhardt Nebuschka to Telford Taylor, Nov. 3, 1947, STAM, denazification court documents Günther Quandt, carton 1362/1; Scholtyseck, *Aufstieg,* 578.

"to finish me off": Reinhardt Nebuschka to Telford Taylor, Nov. 1, 1947, STAM, denazification court documents Günther Quandt, carton 1362/1.

172 *"a red glow of fire"*: Porsche and Molter, *Ferry,* 145.

hundreds of coerced workers: See Pyta et al., *Porsche,* 319–25.

"lovely" sixteen-year-old: Citations in Pyta et al., *Porsche,* 321.

his reign of terror: See Mommsen and Grieger, *Volkswagenwerk,* 766 ff.; Volkswagen, *Remembrance,* 88 ff.

173 *only female prisoners:* On the Pertrix subcamp, see Gabriele Layer-Jung and Cord Pagenstecher, "Vom vergessenen Lager zum Dokumentationszentrum? Das ehemalige NS-Zwangsarbeiterlager in Berlin-Schöneweide," *Gedenkstätten-Rundbrief* 111 (March 2003), 3; Gabriele Layer-Jung and Cord Pagenstecher, "Das Pertrix-Außenlager in Berlin-Niederschöneweide" (May 2004), 1–2; Scholtyseck, *Aufstieg,* 647–48, 673–74, 690.

174 *his own estate, Niewerle:* Treue, *Herbert,* 93.

"with really only very few": Cited in Scholtyseck, *Aufstieg,* 705.

a sub-concentration camp: Scholtyseck, *Aufstieg,* 648–49.

175 *"Taken from us by"*: Jungbluth, *Oetkers,* 196–98, citation on 198.

176 *Rudolf-August had been:* Finger et al., *Dr. Oetker,* 360.

"I couldn't imagine": "Einen besseren Vater könnte ich mir nicht vorstellen," *Welt am Sonntag,* Nov. 22, 1998.

"He's the real heir": Cited in Jungbluth, *Oetkers,* 199.

"As is well known": Cited in Jungbluth, *Oetkers,* 198.

"The beautiful evening": Cited in Finger et al., *Dr. Oetker,* 201.

177 *"for the time being"*: Fröhlich, *TG,* Sept. 10, 1944.

captain from Harald's battalion: Fröhlich, *TG,* Nov. 10, 1944.

Goebbels received a telegram: Fröhlich, *TG,* Nov. 17, 1944.

178 *"very worried" about Harald:* Fröhlich, *TG,* Dec. 2, 1944.

"One always feels deeply": Fröhlich, *TG,* Jan. 23, 1945.

Part IV: *"You will live on"*

181 *Harald Quandt was sitting:* Wolf Jobst Siedler, *Ein Leben wird besichtigt* (Berlin: Siedler, 2000), 317.

"strict self-discipline": Cited in Treue, *Herbert,* 103.

"My beloved son": Magda Goebbels to Harald Quandt, April 28, 1945, Robert E. Work collection, USHMM; letter reproduced in Rolf Hochhuth (ed.), *Joseph Goebbels: Tagebücher 1945* (Hamburg: Hoffmann und Campe, 1977), 549–50.

183 *"My dear Harald"*: Joseph Goebbels to Harald Quandt, April 28, 1945, USHMM; letter reproduced in Hochhuth, *Tagebücher 1945,* 547–48; Robert E. Work, last letters from Hitler's Air Raid Shelter, Nov. 1, 1945, USHMM. The sons of the air force captain donated the original letters to the museum in 2019.

184 *the evening of April 28:* On the events in the Führerbunker, see Hanna Reitsch, *Fliegen Mein Leben* (Munich: Ullstein, 1979), 324–29; Ian Kershaw, *Hitler* (London: Penguin, 2008), 938 ff.; Rochus Misch, *Hitler's Last Witness* (London: Frontline, 2017, trans.), 176–81; Longerich, *Goebbels,* x–xi, 686–87; Hochhuth, *Tagebücher,* 550–56.

kept the original letters: Steve Johnson, "How Goebbels' Final Letter Made Its Way from Hitler's Bunker to a Chicago Family — and at Last to the Holocaust Museum," *Chicago Tribune,* April 24, 2019, https://www.chicagotribune.com/entertainment/museums/ct-ent-goebbels-final-letters-chicago-family-0425-story.html.

185 *a "frozen" face:* Misch, *Witness,* 177.

"She was pale and spoke": Albert Speer, *Inside the Third Reich* (London: Phoenix, 1995, trans.), 643. Originally published in 1970.

visited her best friend: For the Dresden episode, see Meissner, *First Lady,* 239–43.

186 *"We have demanded"*: Meissner, *First Lady,* 239–42.

187 *"business meetings"*: Karl Bernd Esser, *Hitlers Gold* (Munich: 2004), 403.

"business-friendly" policies: Citations in Scholtyseck, *Aufstieg,* 730.

"the only right thing": Cited in Scholtyseck, *Aufstieg,* 731.

forced or slave labor: Scholtyseck, *Aufstieg,* 709.

188 *"one of Germany's leading"*: Quandt, *Günther,* April 18, 1945, Cornell Law Library, Donovan Nuremberg Trials Collection, vol. 17, sec. 53.051, https://lawcollections.library.cornell.edu/nuremberg/catalog/nur:01775.

"without great noise": Cited in Scholtyseck, *Aufstieg*, 731.

US Treasury Department: See Bernd Greiner, *Die Morgenthau-Legende* (Hamburg: Hamburger Edition, 1995), 238; Scholtyseck, *Aufstieg*, 732.

Günther had planned to flee: Treue, *Herbert*, 90; Scholtyseck, *Aufstieg*, 714, 730.

more horror was unfolding: On the AFA Hannover subcamp evacuation and Gardelegen massacre, see Herbert Obenaus et al. (eds.), *Konzentrationslager in Hannover* (Hildesheim: August Lax, 1985), 493 ff.; Jungbluth, *Quandts* (2002), 197–99; Buggeln, *Arbeit & Gewalt*, 638–40, 650–51; Scholtyseck, *Aufstieg*, 668–70.

189 *"Some will say that"*: Cited in Gardelegen, USHMM, https://encyclopedia.ushmm.org/content/en/article/gardelegen.

The living arrangements: Treue, *Herbert*, 90 ff.; Scholtyseck, *Aufstieg*, 714, 790–92, 822–23.

190 *"tool of his father"*: Cited in Scholtyseck, *Aufstieg*, 822.

couldn't stand the fact: Scholtyseck, *Aufstieg*, 823–24.

"the shadow of his great": Cited in Scholtyseck, *Aufstieg*, 765–66.

"I believe that it was": Cited in Treue, *Herbert*, 85.

191 *Friedrich Flick fled:* Frei et al., *Flick*, 464, 712–13.

still owned by: Engel, "Beraubte Bierbaron."

Just before Allied forces: Priemel, *Konzerngeschichte*, 452; Bähr et al., *Flick-Konzern*, 460.

the Gröditz weapons plant: On Gröditz slave labor, see NMT, Vol. VI, 770–88, 815–16, 828–29, 835–37; Priemel, *Konzerngeschichte*, 493–94; Bähr et al., *Flick-Konzern*, 530, 553–56; Frei et al., *Flick*, 359–60.

appointment backfired: Frei et al., *Flick*, 386.

another major promotion: Bähr et al., *Flick-Konzern*, 509–10.

"The Russian eats a lot": Cited in Frei et al., *Flick*, 358.

192 *"a bad thing"*: Cited in Priemel, *Konzerngeschichte*, 488.

about 185 prisoners: On the Gröditz massacre, see NMT, Vol. VI, 778–81; Priemel, *Konzerngeschichte*, 494; Bähr et al., *Flick-Konzern*, 530–31, 554–55; Frei et al., *Flick*, 360.

so-called Tölzer program: On Flick's asset transfers and seizures, see Priemel, *Konzerngeschichte*, 554–55, 591–615; Bähr et al., *Flick-Konzern*, 579–609; Frei et al., *Flick*, 388–89, 448–71.

"the most powerful": Bähr et al., *Flick-Konzern*, 878–79, 883.

moved to Kransberg: Priemel, *Konzerngeschichte*, 603.

193 *"Germany's most powerful"*: Bähr et al., *Flick-Konzern*, 883.

"democratization, denazification": Kim Christian Priemel and Alexa Stiller (eds.), *Reassessing the Nuremberg Military Tribunals* (New York: Berghahn, 2014), 5.

a possible second trial: For further reading, see Telford Taylor, *The Anatomy of the Nuremberg Trials* (New York: Knopf, 1992), 151–61; Donald Bloxham, *Genocide on Trial* (Oxford, UK: Oxford University Press, 2001), 24–25; Kim Christian Priemel, *The Betrayal* (Oxford, UK: Oxford University Press, 2016), 152–55; Priemel and Stiller, *Reassessing*, 166.

Otto-Ernst seized the chance: Priemel, *Konzerngeschichte*, 603–5; Frei et al., *Flick*, 467–68.

194 *"expressed a desire"*: August von Finck interrogation, Sept. 25, 1947, NARA, OMGUS, RG 260, M1923, roll 7.

his knack for looting: See preliminary report on Deutsche Heraklith AG; original exhibits Alpenländische Bergbau Gmbh, USACA Section 1945–1950, NARA, RG 260, M1928, rolls 22, 46, 47; Siebert, *Hundert Jahre*, 47–48.

Günther deeply admired: Quandt and Quandt, *Günther*, 135–36.

195 *awaiting their arrival*: "Neun Nullen," *Der Spiegel*, May 18, 1970.

"Scrutinize especially": Suggestion regarding removal of bank officials, Major Peery to Lt. Ladenburg, Denazification: Policy and Directives, NARA, OMGUS, RG 260, M1925, roll 3.

even more suspect: See Scholtyseck, *Aufstieg*, 1044 n46; Frei et al., *Flick*, 403.

"Even during the latter": Kurt Schmitt interrogation, July 15, 1947, NARA, OMGUS, RG 260, M1923, roll 7.

196 *"he remained a convinced"*: Hans Schmidt-Polex interrogation, Sept. 22, 1947, NARA, OMGUS, RG 260, M1923, roll 7.

"the holder and trustee": Guide for Investigation of Vereinigte Stahlwerke AG, Düsseldorf, Germany, May 31, 1945, Appendix B, 78, NARA, OSS, RG 226, M1934, roll 5.

Soviet propaganda alleged: Siebert, *Hundert Jahre*, 49.

"a pro-Nazi in every respect": Cited in James, *Verbandspolitik*, 300 n72.

"a somewhat tricky customer": Cited in James, *Verbandspolitik*, 301 n88.

had been liquidated: See German External Assets in Austria: Private Bank E. V. Nicolai & Company S. M. V. Rothschild in Liquidation, USACA, RG 260, M1928, roll 13; Melichar, *Neuordnung*, 404–8.

197 *"understandable reluctance"*: Cited in Köhler, *Arisierung*, 502.

"if the roles": Citations in Köhler, *Arisierung*, 502.

"very frosty" mood: Köhler, *Arisierung*, 503–6, citation on 505.

However, the deal: See affidavit Willy Dreyfus, Dec. 22, 1948, STAM, denazification court documents August von Finck, carton 409; Frank J. Miller to Albert F. Bender Jr., March 6, 1947, Deutscher Reichsanzeiger Re: J. Dreyfuss [*sic*] & Co. and Merck, Finck & Co., NARA, OMGUS, RG 260, M1923, roll 3.

198 *The Nazis began using*: Mommsen and Grieger, *Volkswagenwerk*, 798–99, 901–2; Volkswagen, *Remembrance*, 95, 100, 133.

not before stealing: Mommsen and Grieger, *Volkswagenwerk*, 926–27.

"This sum likely laid": Mommsen and Grieger, *Volkswagenwerk*, 643.

Allied investigation team: Porsche and Bentley, *We at Porsche*, 180–82; Pyta et al., *Porsche*, 341.

199 *"Porsche was entrusted"*: Porsche, Ferdinand, May 17, 1945, Cornell Law Library, Donovan Nuremberg Trials Collection, vol. 17, sec. 53.048, https://lawcollections.library.cornell.edu/nuremberg/catalog/nur:01772.

"Hitler's support was": Cited in Georg Meck, *Auto Macht Geld* (Berlin: Rowohlt, 2016), 79.

continued sending invoices: Mommsen and Grieger, *Volkswagenwerk*, 927–28, 940–41.

200 *Rudolf-August entertained*: Finger et al., *Dr. Oetker*, 374–77.

"Suddenly some guys": Cited in Finger et al., *Dr. Oetker*, 376.

"very depressed": Citations in Finger et al., *Dr. Oetker*, 377.

201 work ban "frustrating": Finger et al., Dr. Oetker, 385–87, citation on 385.
considering a move to Hannover: Scholtyseck, Aufstieg, 736–37.
202 "The Republicans won't": Cited in Scholtyseck, Aufstieg, 731.
"the American version": Cited in Scholtyseck, Aufstieg, 732.
"Political Persecution": Supplementary Sheet to Questionnaire Military Government of Germany, March 1, 1946, STAM, denazification files Günther Quandt, carton 1363/7.
"Quite a few gentlemen": Cited in Scholtyseck, Aufstieg, 733.
registered as "wanted": Cited in Scholtyseck, Aufstieg, 733.
"reactionary capitalist": Opinion Sheet, Denazification Panel District Hannover, Aug. 6, 1946, STAM, denazification court documents Günther Quandt, carton 1363/7.
203 working on his defense: Scholtyseck, Aufstieg, 737.
"Goebbels took every": Affidavit Eleonore Quandt, Aug. 27, 1946, STAM, denazification court documents Günther Quandt, carton 1362/1.
a hand in drafting: Jungbluth, Quandts (2002), 218.
204 "no promises or mention": Günther Quandt to Werner Quandt, Jan. 5, 1947, HWA, dept. 2017, folders 36/37.
"I was never a member": Certified statement Harald Quandt, Aug. 27, 1946, STAM, denazification court documents Günther Quandt, carton 1362/1.
He considered traveling: Günther Quandt to Lieselotte Dietermann, Oct. 11, 1946, HWA, dept. 2017, folders 36/37; Scholtyseck, Aufstieg, 253.
"It's just not fun": Cited in Liselotte Dietermann to Günther Quandt, Feb. 5, 1947, HWA, dept. 2017, folders 36/37.
"I feel for Quandt": Cited in Scholtyseck, Aufstieg, 320.
"generous financial arrangement": Affidavit Georg Sachs, Feb. 10, 1947, STAM, denazification court documents Günther Quandt, carton 1362/2.
205 "It sufficed": Quandt and Quandt, Günther, 111–26, 167–80, 191–92, 230–32, 240–44; quote on 241.
"America! How often": Quotes in Quandt and Quandt, Günther, 139, 184, 238–39, 245–46.
206 "I admit that these": Quandt and Quandt, Günther, 247–49.
was "bad" but also: Cited in Scholtyseck, Aufstieg, 731.
Life in the Moosburg camp: Quandt and Quandt, Günther, 252–53.
207 "pondering his fate": Cited in Scholtyseck, Aufstieg, 733.
"Tibet 3x, East Africa 2x": Quandt and Quandt, Günther, 252–53.
"Central heating, large": Cited in Scholtyseck, Aufstieg, 734.
"guest of the U.S.": Günther Quandt, Circular Christmas letter, Dec. 5, 1947, HWA, dept. 2017, folders 36/37.
"not very satisfactory": Cited in Priemel, Konzerngeschichte, 605.
Flick senior was portraying: See Priemel, Konzerngeschichte, 627–31; Bähr et al., Flick-Konzern, 582–85, 608–15; Frei et al., Flick, 410–11.
208 "almost too beautiful": Citations in Bähr et al., Flick-Konzern, 611–12.
threatened him with: Bähr et al., Flick-Konzern, 582, 610; NMT, Vol. VI, 261–62.
appointed Telford Taylor: Taylor, Anatomy, 274–92.
"greatest single power": Cited in Frei et al., Flick, 409.
209 "the modern self-made": Bähr et al., Flick-Konzern, 897.

after the final verdicts: Taylor, *Anatomy,* 587–624.

210 *wasn't going to happen:* See Bloxham, *Genocide,* 28–32; Priemel, *Betrayal,* 156–57; Telford Taylor, *Final Report to the Secretary of the Army on the Nuernberg War Crimes Trials Under Control Council Law No. 10* (Washington, DC: US Government Printing Office, 1949), 22–27, 73–85, 271–81, https://www.loc.gov/rr/frd/Military_Law/NT _final-report.html.

"a Soviet-dominated": Priemel and Stiller, *Reassessing,*167.

"detract from the real": Bloxham, *Genocide,* 30.

with a government: On the French episode, see Porsche and Bentley, *We at Porsche,* 189 ff.; Mommsen and Grieger, *Volkswagenwerk,* 942; Pyta et al., *Porsche,* 342 ff.

211 *save the family business:* Pyta et al., *Porsche,* 335–38, 362–63.

212 *split the family business:* Mommsen and Grieger, *Volkswagenwerk,* 937–38; Pyta et al., *Porsche,* 328–30, 364–67.

a thousand dollars: Reuß, "Rosenberger," ARD/SWR, June 24, 2019.

213 *Günther Quandt was told:* Scholtyseck, *Aufstieg,* 734.

"Among the first 30": "U.S. War Crimes Unit Seeks to End Task Early in '48," Associated Press, Oct. 27, 1947.

indictment against Günther: Indictment by the public prosecutor, denazification court Starnberg, Sept. 25, 1946, STAM, denazification court documents Günther Quandt, carton 1362/1.

priorities began to shift: For further reading, see James F. Tent, *Mission on the Rhine* (Chicago: University of Chicago Press, 1982), 254–318; S. Jonathan Wiesen, *West German Industry and the Challenge of the Nazi Past* (Chapel Hill: University of North Carolina Press, 2001), 43–44; Frank M. Buscher, *The US War Crimes Trial Program in Germany* (New York: Greenwood Press, 1989), 49–50; Jean Edward Smith, *Lucius D. Clay* (New York: Henry Holt, 1990), 378–87, 425–44; Frederick Taylor, *Exorcising Hitler* (New York: Bloomsbury Press, 2011), 277–331.

German denazification courts: For further reading, see Taylor, *Final Report,* 14–21, 54–56; Buscher, *War Crimes,* 30–31; Taylor, *Anatomy,* 278–87, Priemel and Stiller, *Reassessing,* 249–71; Office of Military Government for Germany, *Denazification (Cumulative Review): Report of the Military Governor (1 April 1947–30 April 1948),* no. 34; John H. Herz, "The Fiasco of Denazification in Germany," *Political Science Quarterly,* vol. 63, no. 4 (Dec. 1948), 569–94.

214 *kept in Dachau:* Arrest warrant Günther Quandt, denazification court Dachau, Oct. 24, 1947, STAM, denazification court documents Günther Quandt, carton 1362/1.

a letter to his lawyer: Günther Quandt to Herman Alletag, Oct. 11, 1947, STAM, denazification court documents Günther Quandt, carton 1362/1.

lessened the charge: Memo Dr. Carl Reiter, denazification court Starnberg, Dec. 13, 1947, STAM, denazification court documents Günther Quandt, carton 1362/1.

"imprisoned for over": Günther Quandt to denazification court chairman Starnberg, Jan. 10, 1948, STAM, denazification court documents Günther Quandt, carton 1362/1.

Günther was released: Scholtyseck, *Aufstieg,* 739.

215 *"stone-cold logician":* "Wie's den Ehemännern geht," *Der Spiegel,* June 21, 1950.

"biting wit, sharp": "Wie's den Ehemännern geht," *Der Spiegel,* June 21, 1950.

small perfumed cloth: Henriette von Schirach, *Der Preis der Herrlichkeit* (Munich: Herbig, 2016), 216.

filed a revised indictment: Indictment by the public prosecutor, Feb. 8, 1948, STAM, denazification court documents Günther Quandt, carton 1362/3.

pressured Laval to sell: On the Tudor and Laval case, see Scholtyseck, *Aufstieg,* 537–62; Jungbluth, *Quandts* (2002), 180–81.

one inexperienced lawyer: Scholtyseck, *Aufstieg,* 741.

216 *"pseudo-arguments":* Günther Quandt response to the indictment by public prosecutor, Feb. 8, 1948, HWA, dept. 2017, folder 38.

a small prefab house: Scholtyseck, *Aufstieg,* 742–43.

he was laboring: Treue, *Herbert,* 103.

"never actively supported": Scholtyseck, *Aufstieg,* 767–68, citation on 767.

first to testify: Trial minutes, denazification court Starnberg, May 13/14, STAM, denazification court documents Günther Quandt, carton 1362/4.

217 *no perfect witness:* Trial minutes, denazification court Starnberg, June 3, 4, 26, 1948; July 15, 1948, STAM, denazification court documents Günther Quandt, carton 1362/4.

Laval's dislike of Günther: See Jungbluth, *Quandts* (2002), 225; Scholtyseck, *Aufstieg,* 743–44.

"complete rehabilitation": Günther Quandt to Heidi von Doetinchem, June 29, 1948, HWA, dept. 2017, folder 35.

In his closing arguments: Public prosecutor plea, July 16, 1948, STAM, denazification court documents Günther Quandt, carton 1362/2.

In its ruling: Ruling denazification court Starnberg, July 28, 1948, STAM, denazification court documents Günther Quandt, carton 1362/1.

218 *"It's the intoxication":* Prosecutor statement, annex to the appeal minutes, Munich, April 29, 1949, STAM, denazification court documents Günther Quandt, carton 1362/5.

upheld the lower court's: Ruling appeals chamber Upper Bavaria, April 29, 1949, STAM, denazification court documents Günther Quandt, carton 1362/4.

219 *upheld the decision:* Bavaria's cassation court ruling, Dec. 2, 1949, STAM, denazification court documents Günther Quandt, carton 1362/5.

"most brilliant judgment": Günther Quandt to Heidi von Doetinchem, April 18, 1950, HWA, dept. 2017, folder 35.

came under investigation: Scholtyseck, *Aufstieg,* 748–49.

"a so-called Judenlager": Günther Quandt to Eckhard König, January 5, 1950, HWA, dept. 2017, folder 27.

"precise knowledge": Scholtyseck, *Aufstieg,* 705, 765.

ruled to rehabilitate: Scholtyseck, *Aufstieg,* 749.

220 *quadrupled the balance sheet:* Indictment by public prosecutor, Nov. 3, 1948, STAM, denazification court documents August von Finck, carton 409.

"suffered indignities": Cited in Köhler, *Arisierung,* 310–11 n375.

The agreement was off: See affidavit Willy Dreyfus, Dec. 22, 1948, and trial minutes, denazification court X Munich, Dec. 22, STAM, denazification court documents August von Finck, carton 409.

von Finck's indictment: Trial minutes, denazification court X Munich, Dec. 22, 1948,

STAM, denazification court documents August von Finck, carton 409; "Neun Nullen," *Der Spiegel*, May 18, 1970.

221　*series of strange turns:* Trial minutes, denazification court X Munich, Dec. 22, 23, 24, 27, 1948, denazification court documents August von Finck, carton 409; "Neun Nullen," *Der Spiegel*, May 18, 1970.

"for reasons of state": Otto von Dewitz to Julius Herf, Jan. 14, 1949, STAM, denazification court documents August von Finck, carton 409.

"who knew a lot": "Neun Nullen," *Der Spiegel*, May 18, 1970.

"Gay Jules": "Wie's den Ehemännern geht," *Der Spiegel*, June 21, 1950.

"betrayed knowledge of": "Neun Nullen," *Der Spiegel*, May 18, 1970.

Rumors circulated about: "Wie's den Ehemännern geht," *Der Spiegel*, June 21, 1950.

222　*claiming to believe:* Trial minutes, denazification court X Munich, Dec. 22, 27, 1948, STAM, denazification court documents August von Finck, carton 409.

denazification court ruled: Ruling denazification court X Munich, Jan. 14, 1949, STAM, denazification court documents August von Finck, carton 409.

same veiled threats: "Neun Nullen," *Der Spiegel*, May 18, 1970.

terse one-sentence note: Withdraw of appeal, Feb. 24, 1949, STAM, denazification court documents August von Finck, carton 409.

applied for amnesty: Fritz Berthold to Ludwig Hagenauer, April 19, 1949; Kurz to Ludwig Hagenauer, June 28, 1949, STAM, denazification documents August von Finck, carton 409.

Herf was suspended: "Wie's den Ehemännern geht," *Der Spiegel*, June 21, 1950; R. R. Bowie to Hans Weigert, Aug. 31, 1950; Sept. 27, 1950, NARA, RG 260, NND 775035.

after flirty letters: Julius Herf to Lorenz Willberger, April 29, 1950; Julius Herf to Günther Griminski, May 25, 1950, NARA, RG 260, NND 775035.

223　*refused to hear the case:* Eric Schnapper and William Schurtman, *Willy Dreyfus, Petitioner, v. August Von Finck et al.* (Washington, DC: Gale, 2011).

bogus defense: Finger et al., *Dr. Oetker*, 360–61, 378–80.

"no one noticed": Cited in Finger et al., *Dr. Oetker*, 379.

224　*back in control:* Finger et al., *Dr. Oetker*, 379–80, 386–87, 394.

wait out a trial: On French proceedings, see Mommsen and Grieger, *Volkswagenwerk*, 942–44; Pyta et al., *Porsche*, 357–58.

initial remuneration contract: Mommsen and Grieger, *Volkswagenwerk*, 939.

225　*Nordhoff had been appointed:* Mommsen and Grieger, *Volkswagenwerk*, 973; Rieger, *People's Car*, 109–10.

how to remunerate: On the Bad Reichenhall pact, see Porsche and Bentley, *We at Porsche*, 215–16; Mommsen and Grieger, *Volkswagenwerk*, 938; Meck, *Auto*, 110–13, 116.

226　*"I mourn my Stuttgart":* Cited in Pyta et al., *Porsche*, 376.

a heated legal battle: Pyta et al., *Porsche*, 377–78; Reuß, "Rosenberger," ARD/SWR, June 24, 2019.

proposed a settlement: Aust and Ammann, *Saga*, 234–35; Reuß, "Rosenberger," ARD/SWR, June 24, 2019; property control report of property transactions, Stuttgart, Oct. 26, 1950.

"Professor Porsche has": Cited in Pyta et al., *Porsche*, 311.

227   *"I was* entbräunt": Cited in Pyta et al., *Porsche,* 389.

    teamed up with Albert Prinzing: Porsche and Bentley, *We at Porsche,* 222–23; Pyta et al., *Porsche,* 379–82.

    "how hard you worked": Cited in Pyta et al., *Porsche,* 381.

228   *charged with war crimes:* NMT, Vol. VI, 9–25.

    as high as 100,000: Bähr et al., *Flick-Konzern,* 531.

    No other tycoon had: Harold James, *Krupp* (Princeton: Princeton University Press, 2012), 172–225; Taylor, *Final Report,* 22–27, 78–79, 184–201 ff.

229   *"A dictatorship is":* NMT, Vol. VI, 32–33.

230   *"The story of this":* NMT, Vol. VI, 114–15.

    But it wasn't easy: Priemel, *Konzerngeschichte,* 640–41; Bähr et al., *Flick-Konzern,* 627–30; Frei et al., *Flick,* 426.

    Dix spoke about: NMT, Vol. VI, 115–34.

231   *industrialist defended himself:* NMT, Vol. VI, 217–25, 382–83, 405 ff., 1015–16; Frei et al., *Flick,* 420.

    "I was glad if I": NMT, Vol. VI, 222–23,

    "an advocate" of: NMT, Vol. VI, 133.

    "howling with the wolves": Cited in NMT, Vol. VI, 997.

    an array of strategies: See Priemel, *Konzerngeschichte,* 635–41; Bähr et al., *Flick-Konzern,* 635–39; Frei et al., *Flick,* 421–23; NMT, Vol. VI, 4, 202 ff., 285 ff.

232   *"best cooks in the world":* Cited in Bähr et al., *Flick-Konzern,* 638.

    The presiding judge: Priemel, *Konzerngeschichte,* 640.

    testified about "strolling": Citations in Frei et al., *Flick,* 422.

    "a mere anachronism": NMT, Vol. VI, 974.

    "every indication of": NMT, Vol. VI, 1034–35.

233   *"The defendants lived":* NMT, Vol. VI, 115, 1172.

    the "large scope": NMT, Vol. VI, 1117–18.

    "I am here as": NMT, Vol. VI, 1186–87.

234   *monster of a trial:* NMT, Vol. VI, 3–4.

    The judgment was: For the ruling, see NMT, Vol. VI, 1187–228.

    "exceedingly (if not excessively)": Taylor, *Final Report,* 187.

235   *"A sale compelled":* NMT, Vol. VI, 1214.

    "a blank check": NMT, Vol. VI, 1221.

236   *His conviction stood:* NMT, Vol. VI, 1225–33.

    complex negotiations: See Priemel, *Konzerngeschichte,* 661–71; Frei et al., *Flick,* 476–86.

    McCloy's decision: Kai Bird, *The Chairman* (New York: Simon & Schuster, 1992), 359–75; Priemel, *Betrayal,* 352–68.

    "embodiment of political": Telford Taylor, "The Nazis Go Free," *The Nation,* Feb. 24, 1951, 171.

237   *Flick was released:* Ogger, *Grosse,* 254; Frei et al., *Flick,* 445–46.

    "My court was clearly": "Der Eisenmann," *Der Spiegel,* Sept. 16, 1958.

    undergone denazification: Frei et al., *Flick,* 436–37.

    quite successfully: Priemel, *Konzerngeschichte,* 671–702; Frei et al., *Flick,* 486–522.

Part V: "Nine Zeros"

241 harder than ever: Quandt and Quandt, Günther, 256–57; Treue, Herbert, 125.
"a little death": Jungbluth, Quandts (2002), 238.
"Deutschland, Deutschland": Cited in Liz Crolley and David Hand, Football and European Identity (London: Routledge, 2006), 70.

242 economy had quadrupled: Werner Abelshauser, Deutsche Wirtschaftsgeschichte (Munich: C. H. Beck, 2011), 152–81.
"He never submitted": Citations in Jungbluth, Quandts (2002), 238–39; see also Abs's and Pavel's full speeches in "In Memoriam Günther Quandt geb. 28.7.1881, + 30. Dec. 1954."

243 "prepared his actions": "In Memoriam Günther Quandt geb. 28.7.1881, + 30. Dec. 1954."
retained many assets: Quandt and Quandt, Günther, 253–56; Treue, Herbert, 92–94, 106–9, 131–33, 141; Scholtyseck, Aufstieg, 785–821.
restitution proceedings: Scholtyseck, Aufstieg, 801.
"There wasn't a single": Interview with Gerhard Wilcke, April 21, 1978, HWA, dept. 2017, folder 82.

244 filed a restitution claim: For more about the Eisner saga, see Scholtyseck, Aufstieg, 401–3, 953 n245.
"The power of the great": Kurt Pritzkoleit, Männer-Mächte-Monopole (Frankfurt: Karl Rauch, 1953), 70, 88.

245 Dynastic and entrepreneurial: Treue, Herbert, 103, 114, 120, 123, 130–33.
Günther left behind: Estate of Dr. Günther Quandt, HWA, dept. 2017, folder 44; Scholtyseck, Aufstieg, 159–70, 834–38.
larger than 55.5 million: Rüdiger Jungbluth, Die Quandts: Deutschlands erfolgreichste Unternehmerfamilie (Frankfurt: Campus, 2015), 199.
"To what extent the securities": Cited in Scholtyseck, Aufstieg, 160.
"With all due reverence": Cited in Scholtyseck, Aufstieg, 838.

246 "The battle for Daimler": Ogger, Grosse, 281.
went head to head: On their battle and deal for Daimler, see Ogger, Grosse, 281–96, 300–303; Treue, Herbert, 141–46; Jungbluth, Quandts (2002), 243–46; Frei et al., Flick, 524–26, 535–38.

247 found themselves on opposing: On their battle for BMW, see Ogger, Grosse, 296–300; Treue, Herbert, 146–56; Jungbluth, Quandts (2002), 246–56; Frei et al., Flick, 538–42.
decade-long restructuring: Treue, Herbert, 156–76; Jungbluth, Quandts (2015), 219–24.

248 kept inviting them: Jungbluth, Quandts (2002), 275–76; Scholtyseck, Aufstieg, 769–70.
"The same man who": Jungbluth, Quandts (2002), 275.
"a clever fellow and not": Jungbluth, Quandts (2002), 276.
Ferry surrounded himself: Jens Westemeier, Joachim Peiper: A Biography of Himmler's SS Commander (Surrey, UK: Schiffler Military History, 2007, trans.), 175–81.

249 stood for "Super-Sport": Cited in Westemeier, Peiper, 181.
"You see . . . I silently": Cited in Westemeier, Peiper, 180.
new sales record: Finger et al., Dr. Oetker, 404, 423.

worldwide conglomerate: Jungbluth, *Oetkers,* 212 ff.

250 *Hugo Ratzmann:* Finger et al., *Dr. Oetker,* 410; Jörg Osterloh and Harald Wixforth (eds.), *Unternehmer und NS-Verbrechen* (Frankfurt: Campus, 2014), 269–97.

"convinced me to stay": Rudolf von Ribbentrop, *My Father Joachim von Ribbentrop* (Barnsley: Pen & Sword, 2019, trans.), 428–30; quote on 430.

Rudolf-August first gave: Finger et al., *Dr. Oetker,* 410.

251 *Rudolf-August bought:* Jungbluth, *Oetkers,* 306.

responded radically: On the battle for Allianz, see "Kampf um Die Allianz," *Der Spiegel,* Dec. 14, 1954; Feldman, *Allianz,* 490, 496; Johannes Bähr and Christopher Köpper, *Munich Re* (Munich: C. H. Beck, 2016, trans.), 295–98.

"The year 1945": "Kampf," *Der Spiegel,* Dec. 14, 1954.

252 *wheeling and dealing:* Priemel, *Konzerngeschichte,* 724–29; Frei et al., *Flick,* 572–75.

253 *decision to rearm:* Wolf Perdelwitz and Hasko Fischer, *Waffenschmiede Deutschland* (Hamburg: Gruner + Jahr, 1984), 143–64; Jungbluth, *Quandts* (2002), 263–66, 272; Scholtyseck, *Aufstieg,* 805–17.

254 *"has a deep aversion":* Cited in Ogger, *Grosse,* 333.

Flick's weapon-production: Frei et al., *Flick,* 565–71, 647–48.

two of its cofounders: Porsche and Bentley, *We at Porsche,* 230–31, 245–46.

Ferry now once again: Porsche and Molter, *Ferry,* 203–4.

255 *an enormous success:* Frei et al., *Flick,* 648, 664–65; Porsche and Molter, *Ferry,* 207.

"We never know": Porsche and Molter, *Ferry,* 208.

led another consortium: Jungbluth, *Quandts* (2002), 266.

amphibious cars: Jungbluth, *Quandts* (2002), 272; Porsche and Molter, *Ferry,* 204–6.

success making land mines: Jungbluth, *Quandts* (2002), 267–70.

256 *Harald Quandt's Beechcraft King:* On Harald's death and memorial, see "In Memoriam Harald Quandt, Geb. 1. Nov. 1921 — Gest. 22. Sept. 1967," HWA, dept. 2017, folder 85; "Die Stille Gruppe," *Der Spiegel,* Oct. 1, 1967; Jungbluth, *Quandts* (2002), 284–85; Jungbluth, *Quandts* (2015), 241.

"filled with horror": "In Memoriam Harald Quandt, Geb. 1. Nov. 1921 — Gest. 22. Sept. 1967," HWA, dept. 2017, folder 85.

Harald always prized: On Harald's postwar life, see Jungbluth, *Quandts* (2002), 271–86.

257 *"Among the excited":* Helene Rahms, *Die Clique* (Bern: Scherz, 1999), 156.

When a lawyer representing: Willi Winkler, *Der Schattenmann* (Berlin: Rowohlt, 2011), 102.

"It isn't difficult": Neun Nullen," *Der Spiegel,* May 18, 1970.

four wealthiest businessmen: Michael Jungblut, *Die Reichen und die Superreichen in Deutschland* (Hamburg: Rowohlt, 1973), 65–97.

258 *"like the fairy tale":* "Neun Nullen," *Der Spiegel,* May 18, 1970.

259 *politician for the NPD:* Jungbluth, *Oetkers,* 215; Finger et al., *Dr. Oetker,* 409.

Rudolf-August privately met: "Trinkgeld für Ober," *Der Spiegel,* Feb. 12, 1967.

NPD's corporate backers: "Neonazis im Vormarsch," *Die Zeit,* May 3, 1968.

public museum opened: Jungbluth, *Oetkers,* 245–48, 337–45; Osterloh and Wixforth, *Unternehmer,* 331–61.

supporter of the Nazis: Marc Wortman, "Famed Architect Philip Johnson's Hidden Nazi Past," *Vanity Fair,* April 4, 2016, https://www.vanityfair.com/culture/2016/04/philip-johnson-nazi-architect-marc-wortman.

260 *met with Ferry:* Reuß, "Rosenberger," ARD/SWR, June 24, 2019.

"After the war, it seemed": Porsche and Bentley, *We at Porsche,* 227–29.

helped Rosenberger's parents: Pyta et al., *Porsche,* 306–7.

261 *"vowed to each other":* Treue, *Herbert,* 123.

a separation of assets: Treue, *Herbert,* 227–32, 279–80; Jungbluth, *Quandts* (2002), 296–305.

Inge was ill-suited: Jungbluth, *Quandts* (2002), 310–11.

sold the stake: Treue, *Herbert,* 232–34; Jungbluth, *Quandts* (2002), 301–2.

262 *"was the most good-natured":* Citations in Frei et al., *Flick,* 620–21.

263 *Otto-Ernst sued his father:* "Von Friedrichs Gnaden," *Der Spiegel,* June 4, 1963.

Otto-Ernst lost two trials: Frei et al., *Flick,* 632–41.

264 *"has always been talented":* Cited in Priemel, *Konzerngeschichte,* 737.

He controlled the nation's: Priemel, *Konzerngeschichte,* 727–28.

Jewish Claims Conference: Ferencz, *Less Than Slaves,* 158–69.

265 *negotiations for restitution:* For the proceedings, see Priemel, *Konzerngeschichte,* 703–15; Bähr et al., *Flick-Konzern,* 678–719; Frei et al., *Flick,* 588–604.

"left to more objective": Cited in Frei et al., *Flick,* 669.

266 *wasted no time:* Frei et al., *Flick,* 670–77; Ramge, *Flicks,* 188–206.

Friedrich Karl now ruled: Frei et al., *Flick,* 672–73; Ramge, *Flicks,* 207–12.

267 *The tax exemptions:* Frei et al., *Flick,* 678–86; Ramge, *Flicks,* 212–16.

almost twenty-six million: Frei et al., *Flick,* 687–88; Ramge, *Flicks,* 218–35.

"cultivating the political": "Die gepflegte Landschaft," *Der Spiegel,* Dec. 12, 1999.

"the bought republic": "Die gekaufte Republik," *Der Spiegel,* Nov. 29, 1983.

In the inquiry: Frei et al., *Flick,* 689–90, 697; Ramge, *Flicks,* 235–47.

268 The Price of Silence: Eberhard von Brauchitsch, *Der Preis des Schweigens* (Berlin: Propyläen, 1999).

ceased to exist: Frei et al., *Flick,* 692–93; Ramge, *Flicks,* 249–51.

"the enormous fortune": Priemel, *Konzerngeschichte,* 788.

The bank did so: James M. Markham, "Company Linked to Nazi Slave Labor Pays $2 Million," *New York Times,* Jan. 9, 1986.

Porsche-Piëch clan: Meck, *Auto,* 147–55, 162–63.

269 *threat of abduction:* Jungbluth, *Oetkers,* 262–75.

"penny-pinching tyrant": Louis S. Richman, "The Germans Survivors of Tumultuous Times," *Fortune,* Oct. 12, 1987.

"leading a dishonorable": Cited in Markus Schär, "Vermögen mit Verfalldatum," *Die Weltwoche,* Jan. 8, 2015.

"a combination of": See Gerhard von Finck, sales representative: http://gvfinck.com/about/.

split the estate: On the von Finck inheritance dispute, see Henryk Hielscher, "Schlammschlacht ums Milliardenerbe," *Wirtschaftswoche,* July 27, 2010; Sören Jensen, "Millionäre gegen Milliardäre," *Manager Magazin,* Oct. 20, 2011; Leo Müller, "Ein

Erbstreit sondergleichen," *Bilanz*, Dec. 8, 2015; "Urteil im Erbschaftsdrama," *Juve*, Sept. 13, 2019.

270 *much of his fortune:* Treue, Herbert, 286; Jungbluth, *Quandts* (2002), 312–17.

"remained in his innermost": "In Memoriam Herbert Quandt 22. Juni 1910–2. Juni 1982," HWA, dept. 2017, folder 85.

271 *contrasting outlooks:* See Astrid Becker, Johannes Jansen, Martina Padberg, and Sonja Pöppel, *Kunst im Harald Quandt Haus* (Bad Homburg: Harald Quandt Holding, 2008); Jungbluth, *Quandts* (2015), 252, 384.

272 *stunning historical reckoning:* For Colleen-Bettina Rosenblat's various accounts of her path to Judaism, see Jungbluth, *Quandts* (2002), 334–36; Bianca Lang, Andreas Möller, and Mariam Schaghaghi, "Heimat sind Rituale," *Der Spiegel*, Sept. 29, 2017; Yvonne Weiss, "Das Schwere Erbe der Colleen B. Rosenblat-Mo," *Hamburger Abendblatt*, Oct. 18, 2018.

"In the end, the whole": Jungbluth, *Quandts* (2002), 335.

"Quandt, this name": Dagmar von Taube, "Colleen B. Rosenblat; Klare Ansichten," *Welt am Sonntag*, Dec. 20, 1998.

Part VI: The Reckoning

275 *Germany's wealthiest family:* Christoph Neßhöver, "Die Reimanns sind die reichsten Deutschen," *Manager Magazin*, Oct. 1, 2019.

clan of shareholders: See JAB Holding Company, https://www.jabholco.com/.

276 *"I am horrified":* Adam Luck and Alan Hall, "Nazi Slavery Past of Family Buying Pret A Manger — Which Was Founded by Jewish Businessman — for £1.5 Billion," *Mail on Sunday*, Sept. 15, 2018.

reclusive Reimann shareholders: David de Jong and Annette Weisbach, "Billionaires Unmasked as Coty Persists in Pursuit of Avon," *Bloomberg News*, April 9, 2012; David de Jong and Matthew Boyle, "The Caffeine Fix," *Bloomberg Markets*, Feb. 11, 2015.

A Bild reporter had: Maximilian Kiewel, "Die Nazi-Vergangenheit von Deutschlands Zweitreichster Familie: Die SS-Liebe von Else Reimann," *Bild am Sonntag*, March 30, 2019.

277 *"The Jew Karl Marx":* Citations in Maximilian Kiewel, "Sie sind 33 Milliarden Euro Reich: Die Nazi-Vergangenheit der Calgon-Familie," *Bild am Sonntag*, March 24, 2019.

278 *"should have gone":* Maximilian Kiewel, "Reimann-Vertrauter Peter Harf zu den Enthüllungen: Es gibt nichts zu beschönigen," *Bild am Sonntag*, March 24, 2019.

"Krispy Kreme": Chris Isidore, "Krispy Kreme Owners Admit to Family History of Nazi Ties," *CNN Business*, March 25, 2019.

"I Found Out": Devra First, "I Found Out Nazi Money Is Behind My Favorite Coffee. Should I Keep Drinking It?" *Boston Globe*, June 4, 2019.

"This Is Embarrassing": Rebecca Saltzman, "This Is Embarrassing, but It Turns Out Our Fake Jewish Bagel Chain Was Funded by Nazis," *McSweeney's*, March 27, 2019.

the Reimanns' fortune: On Harf and JAB, see de Jong and Boyle, "Caffeine Fix"; Franziska Scheven, "Buying into Success," *Handelsblatt*, Aug. 4, 2018; "A Peek Inside JAB

Holding," *Economist*, June 20, 2020; Sven Clausen, "Clan ohne Klasse," *Manager Magazin*, April 23, 2021.

279 *"By assuming responsibility"*: Peter Harf to author, June 30, 2021.

forced German businesses: See Osterloh and Wixforth, *Unternehmer*, 365–79; Susanne-Sophia Spiliotis, *Verantwortung und Rechtsfrieden* (Frankfurt: Fischer, 2003), 25–67; Mary Fulbrook, *Reckonings* (Oxford, UK: Oxford University Press, 2018), 343–44.

280 *Piëch was an inappropriate*: Dietmar Hawranek, "Porsche and Volkswagen's Nazi Roots," *Der Spiegel*, July 21, 2009.

received much less money: Frei et al., *Flick*, 671, 677, 694.

following his initial donation: Alan Montefiore and David Vines (eds.), *Integrity in the Public and Private Domains* (London: Routledge, 1999), 205 ff.; Frei et al., *Flick*, 762–63.

281 *"total abhorrence"*: Citations in Montefiore and Vines, *Integrity*, 215–16.

could leave him "destitute": Jenni Frazer, "Flick: Payment 'Possible' to Survivors," *Jewish Chronicle*, March 22, 1996.

following an agreement: Osterloh and Wixforth, *Unternehmer*, 379–90; Fulbrook, *Reckonings*, 344–45. For further reading: Spiliotis, *Verantwortung*, 69–179.

"In this way, the German": Fulbrook, *Reckonings*, 345.

Between 2001 and 2006: Facts and figures, EVZ, Dec. 31, 2020, https://www.stiftung-evz.de/eng/the-foundation/facts-and-figures.html; Spiliotis, *Verantwortung*, 181–91; Osterloh and Wixforth, *Unternehmer*, 384–86; Fulbrook, *Reckonings*, 345.

282 *wrote an open letter*: Dagmar Ottmann, "Die Ausstellung Verschieben! Ein offener Brief," *Die Zeit*, August 5, 2004.

donated millions: Ramge, *Flicks*, 12–13; Frei et al., *Flick*, 768–70.

283 *surrounded by bodyguards*: Michael Swersina, "Ingrid Flick im Gespräch mit den Unterkärtner Nachrichten," *Unterkärtner Nachrichten*, March 6, 2019.

"Finally, my husband": Paul Sahner, "Jetzt redet die schöne Witwe," *Bunte*, Jan. 7, 2010.

world's youngest billionaires: David de Jong, "The World's Youngest Billionaires Are Shadowed by a WWII Weapons Fortune," *Bloomberg News*, May 3, 2018.

"I help wherever": Swersina, "Ingrid," *Unterkärtner*, March 6, 2019.

"a very substantial amount": Major Gift for Tel Aviv Museum of Art from Ingrid Flick," *Artnet News*, May 22, 2014.

284 *Ingrid's "main concern"*: Friedrich Flick Förderungsstiftung Gremien, https://www.flickfoerderungsstiftung.de/gremien/.

purposes of whitewashing: Tim Schanetzky, *Regierungsunternehmer* (Göttingen: Wallstein, 2015), 8–9.

Ingrid Flick took over: Friedrich Flick Förderungsstiftung Geschichte und Förderungszweck, https://www.flickfoerderungsstiftung.de/geschichte-und-foerderungszweck/.

Flick's name was removed: Thilo Schmidt, "Der Mann der Kreuztal nicht zur Ruhe kommen lässt," *Deutschlandfunk*, March 20, 2017; see also https://www.flick-ist-kein-vorbild.de/.

Since 2015, the Friedrich: Statement provided by Goethe University spokesman Olaf Kaltenborn, July 19, 2021.

German student scholarship: Deutschlandstipendium sponsors, Goethe University, 2016, https://www.uni-frankfurt.de/61624067/Unsere_F%C3%B6rderer_2016.

285 *The Flick money:* "Barry Eichengreen Appointed Visiting Professor for Financial History 2019," Goethe University, Oct. 4, 2018, aktuelles.uni-frankfurt.de/englisch/barry -eichengreen-appointed-visiting-professor-for-financial-history-2019/.

has earned a seat: Goethe University's foundation board of trustees, March 2, 2021, uni-frankfurt.de/51849455/Mitglieder_des_Stiftungskuratoriums_der_Goethe _Universität.

"Adolf Messer is in no way": "Zur Geschichte der Messer-Werke im NS," Feb. 28, 2018, https://forschungsstelle.files.wordpress.com/2018/03/adolf_messer-kritik_gutachten __akten-maerz2018.pdf.

lounge was renamed: Daniel Majic, "Umstrittene Lounge in Goethe-Uni wird umbenannt," *Frankfurter Rundschau,* Feb. 15, 2019.

rechristened its foundation: The foundation is now named for Adolf Messer's son, Hans Messer. http://dr-hans-messer-stiftung.de/.

are more transparent: Alfried Krupp Stiftung, https://www.krupp-stiftung.de/alfried -krupp/; Fritz Thyssen Stiftung history, https://www.fritz-thyssen-stiftung.de/en/ about-us/general-information/history/.

"The kids have to learn": Sahner, "Jetzt," *Bunte,* Jan. 7, 2010.

286 *are the Quandts:* Eric Friedler, "Das Schweigen der Quandts," ARD/NDR, Sept. 30, 2007, Youtube video, 59:26, https://www.youtube.com/watch?v=FpQpgd_EeWY.

dark part of the Quandts' history: Susanne and Stefan Quandt did comment in the biography on other things: see Jungbluth, *Quandts* (2002), 350 ff. Two of Harald's daughters did comment in it about their father and their grandmother Magda in relation to the Nazi era: Jungbluth, *Quandts* (2002), 275, 334–36.

"Whenever I dream": Friedler, "Schweigen," ARD/NDR, Sept. 30, 2007.

"Since we recognize": Cited in Jungbluth, *Quandts* (2002), 344.

"They reacted harshly": Friedler, "Schweigen," ARD/NDR, Sept. 30, 2007.

Varta eventually did: Jungbluth, *Quandts* (2002), 343.

287 *"We must try to forget":* Friedler, "Schweigen," ARD/NDR, Sept. 30, 2007.

"to treat our history": Cited in Eric Friedler, "Das Schweigen der Quandts" ARD/ NDR, Nov. 22, 2007, Youtube video, 1:29:45, https://www.youtube.com/watch?v= l9hNjmJxc0U.

"an almost pathological": "Nach Kräften Mies," *Der Spiegel,* Dec. 8, 1974.

288 *"in a climate of fear":* Speech, Stefan Quandt, Herbert Quandt Medien-Preis, June 22, 2008, https://www.johanna-quandt-stiftung.de/medien-preis/2008/rede-stefan -quandt.

he could have left: Quandt and Quandt, *Günther,* 245–46.

from a sordid affair: Jungbluth, *Quandts* (2015), 331–41.

289 *"A light has been cast":* Lorenz Wagner, "Susanne Klatten — Die Unbekannte," *Financial Times Deutschland,* Nov. 21, 2008.

"inseparably" linked: Scholtyseck, *Aufstieg,* 763.

"left no room for": Scholtyseck, *Aufstieg,* 849.

"The family patriarch": Scholtyseck, *Aufstieg,* 843.

"lightheartedly and shamefully": Scholtyseck, *Aufstieg*, 314.

"Doubts about the legitimacy": Scholtyseck, *Aufstieg*, 406, 537.

"There can be no doubt": Scholtyseck, *Aufstieg*, 766

290 *"It hurts. Günther Quandt"*: Rüdiger Jungbluth and Giovanni di Lorenzo, "NS-Vergangenheit der Quandts: Man fühlt sich grauenvoll und schämt sich," *Die Zeit*, Sept. 22, 2011.

291 *more than five million:* M. Backhaus and B. Uhlenbroich, "Die Quandt Familien brechen ihr Schweigen," *Bild am Sonntag*, Nov. 6, 2011.

"I don't see any": Jungbluth and di Lorenzo, "NS-Vergangenheit," *Die Zeit*.

292 *"As with other important"*: Biografie Herbert Quandt, https://www.johanna-quandt -stiftung.de/medien-preis. (Last accessed this version of the biography on Monday, October 25, 2021. The biography was replaced on the website between October 26 and October 29, 2021.)

In mid-October 2013: Rüdiger Jungbluth and Anne Kunze, "August Oetker: 'Mein Vater war Nationalsozialist,'" *Die Zeit*, Oct. 17, 2013.

293 *had been denied access:* Jungbluth, *Oetkers*, 388–91.

individual billionaires: David de Jong, "Nazi-Forged Fortune Creates Hidden German Billionaires," *Bloomberg News*, Feb. 3, 2014.

prompted the Oetkers: Finger et al., *Dr. Oetker*, 17; "Wie geht Oetker kommunikativ mit seiner NS-Vergangenheit um, Herr Schillinger?" *Pressesprecher*, Dec. 17, 2013.

"Kaselowsky, and with him": Finger et al., *Dr. Oetker*, 415.

294 *"My father was"*: Jungbluth and Kunze, "Mein Vater."

"We have always agreed": "Oetker-Witwe kritisiert Historiker der Nazi-Studie," *Neue Westfälische*, Oct. 22, 2013.

a power struggle: Simon Hage and Michael Machatschke, "Schiedsgericht soll Machtkampf bei Oetker entschärfen," *Manager Magazin*, Jan. 23, 2014.

The dispute revolved around: Maria Marquart, "Pizza, Pudding, Beef," *Der Spiegel*, March 16, 2019.

295 *nightmare came true:* Dr. August Oetker KG, "Oetker Group to Be Split," July 22, 2021.

"reinforcing its commitment": "Porsche Creates the Ferry Porsche Foundation," Porsche AG, May 16, 2018, https://newsroom.porsche.com/en/company/porsche -ferry-porsche-foundation-social-responsibility-education-social-issues-youth -development-foundation-funding-15487.html.

"Dealing with one's own": "Ferry Porsche Foundation Endows First Professorship for Corporate History in Germany," University of Stuttgart, March 8, 2019, https:// www.uni-stuttgart.de/en/university/news/all/Ferry-Porsche-Foundation-endows -first-professorship-for-corporate-history-in-Germany/.

296 *"As bad as these"*: Porsche and Molter, *Ferry*, 192.

"if you are made": Porsche and Molter, *Ferry*, 124.

indeed voluntarily applied: Pyta et al., *Porsche*, 307–8, 458 n16; Westemeier, *Krieger*, 540-541.

"exposing the denial": Pyta et al., *Porsche*, 308.

funded by the company: Pyta et al., *Porsche*, 15.

became a full subsidiary: Gywn Topham, "Volkswagen Swallows Porsche," *The Guardian,* July 5, 2012.

$250 billion in sales: Volkswagen Group's annual report, 2020, March 16, 2021, https://annualreport2020.volkswagenag.com/.

grown to $21 billion: Christoph Neßhöver, "Knapp 80 Milliarden mehr für die reichsten Zehn," *Manager Magazin,* Sept. 30, 2021.

In fact, the reason: "Ferry Porsche Foundation Endows," University of Stuttgart, March 8, 2019.

297   *a documentary about:* Reuß, "Rosenberger," ARD/SWR, June 24, 2019.

"there was no hesitation": Pyta et al., *Porsche,* 313.

"one cannot shake off": Pyta et al., *Porsche,* 131.

298   *more than $9 billion:* Bloomberg Billionaires Index, Nov. 28, 2021.

assets are said to include: Anna Jikhareva, Jan Jirat, and Kaspar Surber, "Eine schrecklich rechte Familie," *Die Wochenzeitung,* Nov. 29, 2018.

299   *oddball thriftiness:* Roman Deininger, Andreas Glas, and Klaus Ott, "Der Frontmann des Herrn Baron," *Süddeutsche Zeitung,* March 26, 2021.

"To the right of Gustl": "Milliardär in Vaters Schatten," *Der Spiegel,* July 4, 1993.

convicted for tax evasion: Berthold Neff, "Der Freie Bürger und sein Edelmann," *Süddeutsche Zeitung,* Oct. 10, 2002.

300   *All other donations:* Kassian Stroh, "Spendables Imperium," *Süddeutsche Zeitung,* Jan. 30, 2009.

coalition parties successfully: "Große Geschenke erhalten die Freundschaft," *Der Spiegel,* Jan. 17, 2010.

"Mövenpick party": "Hohn und Spott für die Mövenpick Partei," *Der Spiegel,* Jan. 19, 2010.

he donated millions: Christian Ricken, "Der geheime Finanzier," *Manager Magazin,* Dec. 14, 2005.

is based at the von Finck: Ludwig von Mises Institute Deutschland, https://www.misesde.org/impressum/.

the trademark rights: Simone Boehringer, "Recycling der edlen Sorte," *Süddeutsche Zeitung,* Nov. 11, 2011; https://www.degussa-goldhandel.de/en/frequently-asked-questions-faq/.

SS became one of its: Peter Hayes, *From Cooperation to Complicity* (Cambridge, UK: Cambridge University Press, 2004), 175–94, 272–300.

301   *Degussa gold and silver:* List of Degussa shop locations, https://www.degussa-goldhandel.de/en/location/.

the "engine room": Jakob Blume, "Chef von Goldhändler Degussa wettert gegen EZB," *Handelsblatt,* Nov. 9, 2019.

speculated in a memo: Nico Lange and Theresa Saetzler, "Die neue Partei "Alternative für Deutschland," Konrad-Adenauer-Stiftung, April 16, 2013.

published immediately: Political party financing above 50,000 euros, July 2002–currently, https://www.bundestag.de/parlament/praesidium/parteienfinanzierung/fundstellen50000; Germany's political party financing law, https://www.gesetze-im-internet.de/partg/__25.html.

302 *followed the money trail:* Melanie Amann, Sven Becker, and Sven Röbel, "A Billionaire Backer and the Murky Finances of the AfD," *Der Spiegel,* Nov. 30, 2018.

303 *designed by Goal:* Sven Becker and Sven Röbel, "Die Swiss-Connection der AfD," *Der Spiegel,* Sept. 10, 2016.

to be Goal's address: Friederike Haupt, "Internationale Solidarität für die AfD," *Frankfurter Allgemeine Zeitung,* April 24, 2017.

campaigns are notorious: Guy Chazan, "The Advertising Guru Harnessing Europe's Immigration Fears," *Financial Times,* Dec. 30, 2016.

Segert's modern villa: Christian Fuchs and Paul Middelhoff, *Das Netzwerk der Neuen Rechten* (Hamburg: Rowohlt, 2019), 222–23.

"There's danger ahead": Cited in Amann, Becker, and Röbel, "Billionaire."

304 *Bendels has claimed:* Fuchs and Middelhoff, *Netzwerk,* 217–21.

fined more than 400,000 euros: Sven Röbel, "AfD muss 400.000 Euro Strafe Zahlen," *Der Spiegel,* April 16, 2019.

the AfD's national treasurer: Ann-Katrin Müller and Sven Röbel, "Staatsanwaltschaft ermittelt gegen AfD-Schatzmeister," *Der Spiegel,* April 19, 2019.

investigation is still ongoing: Markus Becker, Sven Röbel, and Severin Weiland, "Staatsanwaltschaft beantragt Aufhebung der Immunität von AfD-Chef Meuthen," June 23, 2021.

almost a million euros: List of confirmed AfD fines provided by LobbyControl, July 21, 2021.

"Hitler and the Nazis": "AfD's Gauland Plays Down Nazi Era as a 'Bird Shit' in German History," *Deutsche Welle,* June 2, 2016.

rising in Germany: Frank Jordan and David Rising, "German Officials Say Far-Right Crime Rising as Police Arrest Alleged Neo-Nazi," Associated Press, May 4, 2021.

305 *had recently joined:* Susanne Lettenbauer, "Symbolpolitik im Bayerischen Wald," *Deutschlandfunk,* Jan. 22, 2020.

legal "consulting fees": Deininger, Glas, and Ott, "Frontmann."

306 *"often given some":* This and following quotes from Katrin Bennhold, "Nazis Killed Her Father. Then She Fell in Love with One," *New York Times,* June 14, 2019.

307 *is transparent about:* The Story of the Alfred Landecker Foundation, https://www .alfredlandecker.org/en/article/the-story-of-the-alfred-landecker-foundation.

The magazine estimated: Neßhöver, "Reichsten Deutschen."

siblings control about: BMW Group report 2020, March 17, 2021, 181.

"Our potential stems": Dietmar Student and Martin Noe, "Wer würde denn mit uns tauschen wollen?" *Manager Magazin,* June 20, 2019.

308 *"We don't spend all day":* Jungbluth and di Lorenzo, "NS-Vergangenheit."

"Protect Private Property!": Stefan Quandt, "Schützt das Privateigentum!" *Frankfurter Allgemeine Zeitung,* June 22, 2019; Rede Stefan Quandt, 2019, https://www.johanna -quandt-stiftung.de/medien-preis/2019/rede-stefan-quandt.

joined the newspaper's: "Solide in die Digitale Zukunft," *Frankfurter Allgemeine Zeitung,* June 29, 2019.

309 *of which thirty million:* Financial assets, https://www.bmw-foundation.org/en/ funding/.

"responsible leadership": Our mission, https://www.bmw-foundation.org/en/mission
-responsible-leadership/.

"secured the independence": Statement of BMW Herbert Quandt foundation to author,
July 20, 2021; Foundation, https://www.bmw-foundation.org/en/foundation/.

"profited from the Nazi": Julian Raff, "Offenes Geheimnis," *Süddeutsche Zeitung,* March
26, 2021.

PHOTO CREDITS

INDEX

Page numbers in *italics* refer to illustrations.

Abs, Hermann Josef, 78, 242–43, 247, 250, 265
Accumulatoren-Fabrik AG. *See* AFA
Adenauer, Konrad, 218, 242, 253
AFA (Accumulatoren-Fabrik AG). *See also* Pertrix; Varta
  Abs on supervisory board, 78
  Allied approach and occupation, 188–90
  Aryanizations, 139–40, 215, 244
  bombing raids, 174–75
  company magazine, 144
  corporate coup attempt, 63–65
  forced and slave labor, 156–58, 173, 188–89, 286
  military sales, 23, 76, 79, 131, 157
  Nazi occupation (1933), 63
  Nazi Party, donations to, 61
  Pavel and, 104–5, 175, 190
  postwar situation, 190, 202–3, 243, 244
  Quandt (Günther) takeover, 23–24
  Quandt (Herbert) and, 66, 104–5, 139, 188, 201–3, 245
  relocation to Bissendorf, 189–90
  World War I, 23
AfD (Alternative für Deutschland), 298, 300, 301–4, 309
Agricola (Tacitus), vii
Alfred Landecker Foundation, 306–7
Allianz
  postwar situation, 195, 197, 251–52
  reckoning with Nazi past, 280, 282
  supervisory board, 117, 195
  von Finck and, 40, 41, 60, 251–52
Altana (company), 270, 271. *See also* Byk Gulden

Alternative für Deutschland (AfD), 298, 300, 301–4, 309
Anschluss, 115–16
anti-Semitism, 64, 84, 107, 276, 304
Anton Kohn (bank), 117
Arlosoroff, Victor Chaim, 19, 65
Army Weapons Agency (HWA), 79, 80, 82–85, 161
Aryanizations
  fictitious tax method, 126, 128
  Flick family, 101, 105–12, 117, 125–28, 146, 207, 250, 265
  Oetker family, 96, 100–101, 201
  Porsche-Piëch family, 91–93, 101, 121, 212, 260, 296, 297–98
  postwar restitution, 196–98, 206, 220, 226, 243–44, 265
  Quandt family, 101, 103–4, 139–41, 190, 206, 215, 217, 243–44, 250, 289
  von Finck family, 101, 112–19, 194, 196–97, 220–22, 250
Association for the Preservation of the Rule of Law and Citizen Freedoms, 302–4
Association of Merchants and Industrialists (Berlin), 64
ATG (company), 81
Attlee, Clement, 193
Aufhäuser, Martin, 112–14
Auschwitz concentration camp, 156, 163, 165, 172–73, 191, 264
Austria, annexation of, 111, 115–16
Austro-Daimler, 163
Auwi, Prince, 34

Baarová, Lida, 99, 123, 124, 139
Bahlsen, Verena, 6–7, 12

Bahlsen company, 6–7, 12
Barclays, 269, 298
BASF (chemicals company), 248
Battle for Berlin (J. Goebbels), 48
Beer Hall Putsch, 235
Behrend, Auguste, 17–21, 35, 50
Belgian women, slave labor, 173–74
Belzec extermination camp, 305
Bendels, David, 303, 304
Bergen-Belsen concentration camp, 9, 164, 165, 188
Berlin
    forced labor documentation center, 291
    Soviet approach and capture, 153, 184
Berlin-Erfurter Maschinenwerken, 103–4
Bhagwan Shree Rajneesh, 269
Black Lair (Himmler's command post), 166
Blomberg, Werner von, 78, 82–83
Blut und Boden (blood and soil), 88, 102
BMW
    charitable arm, 309
    forced and slave labor, 10, 156
    modern era, 10, 248, 270, 271, 282, 307, 309
    postwar restructuring plan, 10, 247–48
    Quandt family control, 10, 248, 270, 271, 307
    reckoning with Nazi past, 10, 282
Bochum steel factory, 8
Bosch, Robert, 101
Brauchitsch, Eberhard von, xv, 266–68, *267*
Braun, Eva, 89, 184
Braun, Wernher von, 192
Buchenwald concentration camp, 264
Buddenbrooks (Mann), 200
Buffett, Warren, 279
Bürckel, Josef, 116
Busch-Jaeger Dürener, 245, 248
Byk Gulden (company), 76, 243. *See also* Altana

CDU (Christian Democratic Union), 267, 301, 305
Cegielski weapons complex, 137, 170–71
Central Office for Jewish Emigration, 116
Chaplin, Charlie, 75
Charlottenhütte (steel firm), 27
Chelmno extermination camp, 104, 136
Christian Democratic Union (CDU), 267, 301, 305
Christian Social Union (CSU), 255, 267, 300

Chrysler Building, New York, 271
Churchill, Winston, 142, 143
CIC (US Counter Intelligence Corps), 192, 199, 202
Clay, Lucius D., 213
coerced labor. *See* forced and slave labor
Commerzbank, 77, 87, 154
Communism
    postwar threat of, 11, 213
    prewar Germany, 35, 36, 38, 66
    Russia, 2
concentration camps. *See also* extermination camps
    Auschwitz, 156, 163, 165, 172–73, 191, 264
    Bergen-Belsen, 9, 164, 165, 188
    Buchenwald, 264
    Dachau, 89–90, 113, 156, 168, 191, 207, 214
    Flossenbürg, 191
    Fort VII, 171
    Gross-Rosen, 175, 264
    Gusen, 191
    Jews threatened with, 107, 114
    Kislau, 93
    liberation, 198
    Mauthausen, 191
    as memorial sites, 286–87
    Neuengamme, 156–58, 164–65, 173, 198, 286–87
    Oetker (Rudolf-August) on, 96
    Peugeot employees, 211, 224
    Ravensbrück, 156, 173
    Sachsenhausen, 90, 156, 161, 164–65, 173
    Salzwedel, 198
Counter Intelligence Corps, US (CIC), 192, 199, 202
Crete, German invasion, 141–44
CSU (Christian Social Union), 255, 267, 300

Dachau concentration camp, 89–90, 113, 156, 168, 191, 207, 214
DAF (German Labor Front), 119, 121, 129
Daimler-Benz
    Deutsche Bank, 247, 266
    Flick family, 238, 246, 266
    forced and slave labor, 156
    Hitler's car, repair of, 59–60
    International Motor Show, 69
    Porsche (Ferdinand), career, 58, 59–60
    postwar tank production, 254–55

Quandt family, 78, 243, 245–47, 261–62
    reckoning with Nazi past, 280, 282
death camps. *See* concentration camps; exter-
    mination camps
"degenerate art" exhibition, 102
Degussa (German Gold and Silver Separation
    Institute), 300–301
Degussa (gold-trading firm), 300–302
de Jong, David, 7–9, 276
Delbrück Schickler (bank), Berlin, 4
denazification courts, 214–22, 226–27, 277
Deutsche Bank
    Aryanizations, 117
    Daimler-Benz, 247, 266
    DWM expansion plans, 154–55
    Flick conglomerate, purchase of, 268,
        282
    Jewish Claims Conference, 268
    postwar leadership, 242
    reckoning with Nazi past, 280
    supervisory board, 62, 78, 195
    Third Reich, financing of, 77
Deutsche Waffen- und Munitionsfabriken.
    See DWM
Dietrich, Hugo, 125–26
Dix, Rudolf, 230–33
Döhlen steel plant, 161
Donauwörth (arms firm), 83–84
Dr. Oetker (food company)
    Aryanizations, 96, 100–101, 201
    forced and slave labor, 156, 167–68
    Kaselowsky's management, 87–89, 96,
        201
    as model company, 96
    neo-Nazis and, 259
    Oetker (Rudolf-August) and, 87–88, 94,
        176, 223–24, 249–50, 293
    Phrix joint venture, 167–68
    postwar situation, 201, 223–24, 249–50
    products, *167*, 295
    succession dispute, 294–95
    World War II business, 166
Dresdner Bank, 77, 87, 100, 154, 195
Dreyfus, Willy, xvii, 114–15, 194, 197–98,
    220, 222–23
Dreyfus bank, 114–15, 194, 197, 220
Dreyfus sheet-metal business, 140
Dulles, John Foster, 109–10
Duralumin (product), 80–81
Dürener (DWM subsidiary), 80–81, 97–98,
    243

DWM (Deutsche Waffen- und Munitions-
    fabriken)
    arms complex, 79–80
    Aryanizations, 103–4
    Cegielski weapons complex, 137, 170
    Dürener subsidiary, 80–81, 97–98, 243
    forced and slave labor, 155, 205
    IWK subsidiary, 243, 245, 253–55
    Krupp comparisons, 171
    Lübeck facility, 80
    Mauser subsidiary, 80, 243, 245, 253
    postwar situation, 243
    Quandt (Günther) and, 24–25, 32, 79–80,
        205
    supervisory board, 78
    World War I arms sales, 24
    World War II arms production, 76, 131,
        154–55, 170, 214
Dynamit Nobel, 264–65, 268

Eagle's Nest, 94
East Germany, 218, 242
Eduard von Nicolai bank, 118
Eichmann, Adolf, 116
Einsatzgruppen, 149–51, 208
Eisenhower administration, 253
Eisner, Fritz, 244
election (1930), 34–35, 38
election (1932), 53, 54
election (1933), 3–5, 61
EVZ (Remembrance, Responsibility, and the
    Future), 281–83
extermination camps. *See also* concentration
    camps
    Belzec, 305
    Chelmno, 104, 136
    looting of corpses, 300–301
    Poland, 153
    Sobibor, 8, 305
    Zyklon B, 300

Faulhaber, Ulrich, 149
FDP (political party), 300
Federal Republic of Germany. *See* West Ger-
    many
Fella firm, 192
Ferry Porsche Foundation, 295–97
"Final Solution to the Jewish Question,"
    149–50
Fischer, Otto Christian, 114, 119
Flick, Dagmar, xv, 191, 266, 280, 282

Flick, Friedrich
  Aryanizations, 101, 105–12, 117, 125–28,
    207, 250
  Aryanizations, postwar restitution, 265
  asset value, 160
  ATG, 81
  Berlin, move to (1923), 25
  birth and family background, 26
  BMW, 247
  in cast of characters, xv
  character traits, 25–26, 27, 81
  Daimler-Benz investment, 238, 246–47
  death and memorial service, 264, 265–66
  Donauwörth lease, 83–84
  Dresdner Bank supervisory board, 87, 195
  Dynamit Nobel, 264
  with family, 145, 263
  Fella firm, 192
  financial troubles (1932), 51–52
  fleeing Berlin, 190–91
  forced and slave labor, 85, 156, 160–61,
    209, 228, 232, 264–65, 283
  Friedrich Flick Foundation, 284
  Gelsenberg (mining firm), 28, 51–54
  as Germany's wealthiest man, 238, 256,
    257–58, 264
  Göring and, 98, 109–11, 118, 146, 161
  Gröditz weapons plant, 191, 232
  Harpener and Essener mining, 81, 128
  Haus der Deutschen Kunst donations, 101
  Himmler's Circle of Friends, 85–87,
    89–90, 108, 165–66, 208, 231, 234, 235
  Hindenburg's reelection campaign, 53
  Hitler meetings, 1–5, 52–53, 54, 60–61,
    229
  Krauss-Maffei, 254–55
  Leopard tank contract, 254–55
  Lübeck blast furnaces, 106–7, 112
  Maxhütte (steel firm), 191, 237
  Montan (shell company), 83–84
  Nazi Party, 54, 60–61, 62, 86–87
  Order of Merit, 284
  Petschek conglomerates, 107–12, 125–28,
    231, 265
  portrait, 26
  postwar arrest and trial, 192–93, 207–9,
    228–37, 229
  postwar restructuring of empire, 236,
    237–38
  PR campaign, 160
  rearmament era, 81–85

  Rombach steelworks, 161–62, 235
  Simson negotiations, 84–85
  sixtieth birthday, 159–60
  steel empire, 26–28, 51, 81, 130
  Steinbrinck as right-hand man, 52–55,
    81–85, 105, 107–10, 125, 129–30
  succession plans, 130, 144–46, 161, 262–64
  Südwestfalen (steel firm), 252
  Thyssen (August), pact with, 27
  Tölzer program, 192
  Ukraine, reports from, 148–49
Flick, Friedrich Karl, 267
  in cast of characters, xv
  character traits, 264, 266
  childhood, 26
  death, 282–83
  Deutsche Bank, sale to, 266, 282
  with family, 145, 263
  family succession conflict, 263–64
  Flick affair (corruption scandal), 268
  Flick conglomerate control, 266, 280
  in Flick succession plans, 144, 146,
    263–64, 266
  forced and slave labor, 268, 283
  heirs, 283
  immigration to Austria, 270
Flick, Ingrid, xv, 283, 283–85, 311–12
Flick, Marie, 25, 237, 262–64, 263
Flick, Mick, xv, 263, 266, 280, 282
Flick, Muck, xv, 263, 266, 280–81
Flick, Otto-Ernst
  in cast of characters, xv
  character traits, 144–45, 262
  childhood, 25, 26
  Daimler-Benz, 247
  death, 266
  with family, 145, 263
  fleeing France, 191
  Flick (Friedrich)'s Nuremberg trial, 232
  in Flick succession plans, 130, 144–46,
    161, 262–64
  forced and slave labor, 162–63, 208
  Gröditz weapons plant, 191
  management failures, 161–63, 190–91
  Maxhütte reorganization, 193–94
  Maxhütte (steel firm), 191–92
  postwar arrest and interrogation, 194,
    207–8
  Rombach steelworks, 146, 161–63, 208,
    232
  Steinbrinck and, 130

Flick, Rudolf, 25, 26, 144–46, *145*
Flick conglomerate
    bribery scandal, 267–68, 281
    dissolution, 268
    holdings, 264
    neo-Nazis and, 259
    sold to Deutsche Bank, 268, 282
    succession conflict, 262–64
Flick family, *145, 263. See also* Daimler-Benz
    Aryanizations, 101, 105–12, 117, 125–28,
        146, 207, 250, 265
    cast of characters, xv
    family tree, 314
    forced and slave labor, 85, 156, 160–63,
        191–92, 208, 209, 228, 232, 264–65,
        268, 281, 283–84
    modern day holdings, 191
    Quandt family and, 247
    reckoning with Nazi past, 280–85
    tax exemptions, 266–67
Flossenbürg concentration camp, 191
flu pandemic (1918), 15, 17
forced and slave labor
    abuses, 157–58, 163, 165, 171, 173, 174,
        191–92, 277
    AFA, 15, 156–58, 173, 188–89, 286
    author's family, 8
    Bahlsen company, 6–7
    BMW, 10, 156
    child labor, 160–61, 165, 171
    compensation, 268, 279–82, 307
    Daimler-Benz, 156
    death marches, 188, 192
    deaths, 156, 158, 163, 171, 188–89, 192
    documentation center, 291
    Dr. Oetker, 156, 167–68
    DWM, 155, 205
    expansion, 155–56
    Flick family, 85, 156, 160–63, 191–92,
        208, 209, 228, 232, 264–65, 268, 281,
        283–84
    Gröditz weapons plant, 191
    IG Farben, 156
    injuries, 158, 192
    JAB, 276, 307
    Kapos, 157–58
    Krupp, 156
    liberation, 198
    living and working conditions, 147–48,
        156, 162–63, 165, 170–71, 173–74,
        191–92

Maxhütte, 191–92
    mine conversion to arms factory,
        172–73
    Oetker family, 156, 167–68
    Opel, 225
    overview, 6–7
    Pertrix, 173–75, 219, 291
    Porsche-Piëch family, 147–48, 156,
        164–65, 172–73, 199, 211
    Quandt family, 155–58, 170–71, 173–75,
        187–89, 205, 219, 286–91
    Reimann family, 276, 277, 306, 307
    Rombach steelworks, 162–63
    Siemens, 156
    Volkswagen, 147–48, 156, 164–65,
        172–73, 198, 199, 211
Ford, Henry, 31, 70, 121
Fort VII (prison and concentration camp),
    171
France, Quandt Aryanizations, 139–41
Frank, Hans, 112, 136
Friedländer, Auguste, 17–21, 35, 50
Friedländer, Magda. *See* Goebbels, Magda
Friedländer, Richard, 19
Friedrich Flick Foundation, 284–85
Funk, Walther
    Aryanizations and, 126, 137
    in cast of characters, xvi
    Flick (Friedrich) and, 52–53, 54
    Hitler meetings with businessmen, 2–5,
        39, 41–42, 52–53, 60
    as NSDAP's economic newsletter edi-
        tor, 52
    Nuremberg trial and sentence, 209
    Quandt (Günther) and, 23–24, 75–76,
        137
    as Reichsbank president and minister of
        economic affairs, 75, 116
    Society for the Study of Fascism, 38

Ganz, Josef, 69
Garbo, Greta, 75
Gardelegen, Germany, 189
Gauland, Alexander, 304
Gelsenberg (mining firm), 28, 51–54
German Democratic Republic (East Ger-
    many), 218, 242
German Gold and Silver Separation Institute
    (Degussa), 300–301
German Labor Front (DAF), 119, 121, 129
German National People's Party, 4–5

Gestapo
  abuse of forced and slave laborers, 163
  arrest of fleeing Jews, 8
  Landecker arrest, 305
  Loeffellad arrest, 83–84
  Milch investigation, 97
  Nebuschka arrest, 171
  Rosenberger arrest, 91, 93, 260
  Rosenberger's citizenship revoked, 122
Goal (PR firm), 303, 304
Goebbels, Heidrun, 124, *143,* 181–82, 185, 186
Goebbels, Helga, 71, 99, *143,* 181–82, 185, 186
Goebbels, Helmut, 71, *143,* 181–82, 185, 186
Goebbels, Hilde, 71, *143,* 181–82, 185, 186
Goebbels, Joseph
  affair with Baarová, 99, 123, 124, 139
  appearance, 35
  art collection, 102
  Battle for Berlin, 48
  in cast of characters, xvi
  Christmas (1940), 138–39
  death, 181–85, 257
  "degenerate art" exhibition, 102
  education, 34
  election campaign (1930), 34–35, 38
  election campaign fund (1933), 5
  eradication of Jews, 136, 149–50, 153–54
  gift for rhetoric and bombast, 34, 35
  on Göring, 178
  "The Great German Art Exhibition," 101–2
  Hitler, slavish devotion to, 34
  Magda, courtship, 42–46, *45*
  Magda, first meeting, 35–36
  Magda, wedding, 48–50, *49*
  Magda's miscarriage, 55–56
  marital difficulties, 98–99, 123–24, 135
  as Nazi chief of propaganda, 35, 36
  Nazi Party, rise through ranks, 34–35
  Nazi Party meetings, 49, 99
  Nebuschka and, 171
  Oetker (Rudolf-August) and, 96
  Poland, survey of (1939), 136
  Quandt custody battles, 50–51, 55, 70–72
  Quandt (Günther), arrest, 64–65
  Quandt (Günther), jealousy, 56
  Quandt (Günther), Nazi Party member-ship, 62, 217
  Quandt (Günther), opinion of, 47–48

Quandt (Günther), "peace at any cost" stance, 159
Quandt (Günther), postwar lies about, 202, 203, 215, 217
Quandt (Günther), sixtieth birthday party, 76–77
Quandt (Harald), childhood, 44, *45,* 55–56
Quandt (Harald), final letter to, 183–84
Quandt (Harald), goals for, 138
Quandt (Harald), Luftwaffe service, 135–36, 141, 143, *143,* 152–53, 169–70, 177–78
on Quandt (Herbert), 51, 139
on Quandt (Werner), 51
as Reich minister of public enlightenment and propaganda, 61
Das Reich (newspaper), 76
Reich Press Chamber, 100
on Ribbentrop (Joachim von), 151
sixtieth-birthday party, 144
"Total War" speech, 153, *154*
Volkswagen, opinion of, 102–3
Volkswagen car, 129
Goebbels, Magda (Ritschel/Friedlander/Quandt), *21*
  affairs, 32, 34, 77, 98–99, 124, 248
  art collection, 102
  in cast of characters, xv
  complicity in atrocities, admission of, 186
  death, 181–86, 257
  Goebbels, courtship, 42–46, *45*
  Goebbels, first meeting, 35–36
  Goebbels, marital difficulties, 98–99, 123–24, 135
  Goebbels, wedding, 48–50, *49*
  Hitler and, 9, 35, 42–43, 46
  miscarriage, 55–56
  murder of her children, 185–86, 257
  Nazi Party, 31–32, 34–37
  Nebuschka and, 171
  New York trip, 31–32
  Nordic Ring, 34
  Quandt, courtship, 17–19
  Quandt, divorce, 32–33
  Quandt, marital difficulties, 20–21, 30–32
  Quandt, "peace at any cost" stance, 159
  Quandt, relationship with, after divorce, 36, 135

Quandt, wedding, 19–20, 50
Quandt custody conflict, 50–51, 55, 70–72, 137
Quandt (Ello) and, 185–87
Quandt (Harald), actress girlfriend, 138
Quandt (Harald), final letter to, 181–83, 184
Quandt (Harald), Luftwaffe service, 143, *143*, 152, 169, 177–78
Quandt (Harald), Poland visit, 137
Quandt (Hellmut), death of, 30
religious views, 19
Severin estate, 33, 45, 48–49
Winter (Emil) and, 194–95
Goethe University, Frankfurt, 97, 284–85
Göring, Herbert, 87, 108–9, 112, 217
Göring, Hermann
    Aero Club, Berlin, 89
    Aryanizations, 109–11, 116–18, 126, 127, 146
    aviation sector spending, 80
    bestowing awards, 76, 98, 178
    bribery, 118
    in cast of characters, xvi
    favorite restaurant, 33
    Flick (Friedrich) and, 98, 109–11, 118, 146, 161
    Four Year Plan, 109, 126
    Goebbelses and, 43, 72
    Hitler's meeting with businessmen, 1–5, 60
    Milch and, 97
    Nazi economy, 66, 86
    Nuremberg trial, 209
    obesity, 75
    Oetker (Rudolf-August) and, 96
    Quandt (Günther) and, 64, 75–76, 98
    rearmament and, 78
    Society for the Study of Fascism, 38
    suicide, 209
    Ukraine expropriations, 149
    Volkswagen cars, 93–94, 129
Goudstikker, Jacques, 77
Granzow, Walter, 30, 45, 48–50
Great Depression, 38, 53–54
"The Great German Art Exhibition," 101–2
Greece, German invasion, 141–44
Greiser, Arthur, 104, 171
Gröditz weapons plant, 191, 192, 232
Gross-Rosen concentration camp, 175, 264
Gundlach (publisher), 100

Gusen concentration camp, 191
Gutterer, Leopold, 77

H. Aufhäuser (bank), 112–14
Hackinger, Corbin, 140
Hahn family, xvii, 106–7, 265
Halle synagogue shooting, 304–5
Hamburg Süd, 249
Hamel, Paul, 24, 25, 38, 47
Hanau shooting spree, 304
Hanke, Karl, 77, 124
Hanstein, Fritz Huschke von, 249
Harald Quandt Holding, 9
Harf, Peter, xvii, 277–79, 306
Harpener and Essener mining, 81, 128
Haus der Deutschen Kunst, 67–69, *68*, 101–2, 112, *113*, 194, 220–21
Hayes, Peter, 300
Heine, Fritz, xvii, 103–4
Heine, Johanna, xvii, 103–4
Heldern, Kurt, 96
Helldorf, Count, 124
Henkell (wine producer), 151, 250, 251
Hennigsdorf steel factory, 161
Henry Pels (company), 103–4
Herbert Quandt Foundation, 309
Herbert Quandt Media Prize, 287–88, 292, 308, 309
Herf, Julius, 214–22
Herrmann, Josef, 163–64
Hess, Hans, 67
Heydrich, Reinhard, 149–50
Himmler, Heinrich
    Blut und Boden (blood and soil), 88
    in cast of characters, xvi
    concentration camp tours, 89–90
    driver, 249
    Flick (Friedrich) and, 54, 85
    forced and slave labor, 164–65
    as Holocaust architect, 86, 149
    Lebensborn (human-breeding association), 90
    Nazi Party convention, 86
    as poultry farmer, 54, 88
    Reimann and, 277
    as SS leader, 54, 86
    Volkswagen Schwimmwagen (swimming car), 146–48, *147*
Himmler's Circle of Friends
    Aryanizations, 108, 109
    Black Lair visit, 165–66

Himmler's Circle of Friends (*cont.*)
  business opportunities, 166–67
  concentration camp tours, 89–90
  formation of, 86–87
  importance to Kaselowsky, 176–77
  meetings, 89
  members, 87, 96, 156
  Nuremberg trials, 231, 234, 235
  postwar situation, 208
Hindenburg, Paul von, 1, 53, 56
Hirschfeld sheet-metal factory, 140
Hitler, Adolf
  annexation of Austria, 111
  annexation of Sudetenland, 108, 123–24,
    127
  appointed as chancellor, 1, 56
  Beer Hall Putsch, 235
  business tycoons' view of, 38
  in cast of characters, xvi
  Dr. Oetker (company) and, 100
  election (1933), 3
  Flick (Friedrich) and, 52–53, 160
  forced and slave labor, 155
  in Führerbunker with Goebbelses, 181–83
  Goebbelses' marriage and, 46, *49*, 50, 71,
    99, 123–24
  Goebbels (Magda) and, 42–43, 46, 55–56,
    181–82
  Goebbels promoted to Berlin *Gauleiter,* 34
  Haus der Deutschen Kunst, *67*–69, *68*,
    101–2, *113*, 194
  International Motor Show, 59, 69
  Iron Cross First Class, 94
  Keppler Circle, 54–55
  on Krupp as model for German indus-
    try, 229
  Labor Day speech (1933), 61
  labor unions banned, 61
  Lebensraum (living space) concept, 88
  Luftwaffe budget, 97
  marriage to Braun, 184
  meetings with businessmen, 1–5, 38–41,
    60–61, 229
  Mein Kampf, 35, 88, 206, 235
  murder of Jews, 161
  Nazi Party, ban on membership, 61–62
  Nazi Party meetings, 49
  Night of the Long Knives massacre, 71
  nonaggression pact, 135
  Nuremberg Race Laws, 112
  Operation Barbarossa, 75

Porsche (Ferdinand) and, 59–60, 69–70, 91
private fortune, 196
Quandt (Günther) and, 47, 64
Quandt (Harald) and, 42–44, 55–56, 143,
  178
on Quandt (Werner), 51
rearmament policy, 64
Reich minister of economic affairs, 66
Severin estate, weekends at, 45
on Versailles Treaty, 79
Volkswagen project, 60, 70, 91, 93–94,
  119–21, *120*, 128–29
Volkswagen Schwimmwagen (swimming
  car), 146–48, *147*
von Finck's devotion to, 67, 115, 195–96
Hochtief (construction business), 298
Hofgarten Arcades, Munich, 102
Holocaust, 86, 149–51. *See also* concentration
  camps; extermination camps
HWA (Army Weapons Agency), 79, 80,
  82–85, 161

IG Farben
  forced and slave labor, 156
  Hitler meeting, 1–5
  Nazi Party election fund, 5, 61
  Nuremberg trial, 228
  Petschek coal interests, 108, 109, 112
  postwar use by OMGUS, 193
  threat to American subsidiaries, 111
Ignaz Petschek conglomerate, 107–12,
  125–28, 231, 265
IMT (International Military Tribunal), 193
Industriewerke Karlsruhe (IWK), 243, 245,
  253–55. *See also* DWM
influenza pandemic (1918), 15, 17
International Military Tribunal (IMT), 193
International Motor Show, 59, 69
IWK (Industriewerke Karlsruhe), 243, 245,
  253–55. *See also* DWM

J. Dreyfus (bank), 114–15
JAB (company), 275–76, 278, 279, 306, 307
Jackson, Robert H., 192–93, 208, 210
Jäger, Karl, 150–51
Jewish Claims Conference, 264, 265, 268
Jews. *See also* Aryanizations; concentration
  camps; extermination camps; Holo-
  caust
  "alibi Jews," 204
  art looted from, 77

author's family, 8–9
blamed for Great Depression, 38
businesses expropriated, 10, 84–85, 127
Einsatzgruppen massacres, 149, 150–51,
  208
exemption list, 163–64
"flight tax," 97, 104, 114
immigration to Palestine, 65
Kristallnacht, 113
Lodz ghetto, 136
Nuremberg Race Laws, 85, 97, 103, 112,
  115
Quandt (Günther) and, 64
Star of David, 77
Joh. A. Benckiser. See JAB
Johnson, Philip, 259
Julius Petschek conglomerate, 107–12, 126,
  231, 265
Jungbluth, Rüdiger, 290, 293–94

Kaletsch, Konrad, 228–35
Kaselowsky, Ida Oetker, 87, 89, 94, 95, 150,
  175, 295
Kaselowsky, Richard
  Aryanizations, 96, 100, 101, 201
  in cast of characters, xvi
  death, 175
  Dr. Oetker (food company), 87–89, 100,
    201
  foundation named for, 295
  Himmler's Circle of Friends, 87, 89–90,
    96, 165–67, 176–77, 201
  Hitler, zeal for, 88
  horse-racing stable, 96
  museum named for, 259
  Nazi Party, 87–89, 88, 89, 95, 100
  Oetker (Rudolf-August) and, 87–88, 94,
    96, 176
Kaufmann, Julius, 114–15
Kempka, Erich, 249
Keppler, Wilhelm
  Aryanizations and, 104, 107–8
  in cast of characters, xvii
  Himmler's Circle of Friends, 86
  as Hitler's economic adviser, 54–55, 85,
    86
  postwar ministries trial and sentence,
    228
Keppler Circle (Hitler's economic council),
  54–55, 86
Kyiv, massacre of Jews, 149

Kislau concentration camp, 93
Klatten, Susanne Quandt
  affair and blackmail, 288
  BMW, 270, 271, 307
  in cast of characters, xv
  inheritance, 270, 307–8
  office, 271, 309
  philanthropy, 309
  reckoning with family's Nazi past, 288–89,
    291
Kohl, Helmut, 267
Kohn, Anton, 117
Koolhaas, Rem, 282
Korean War, 241, 253
Kranefuss, Fritz, xvii, 54–55, 86–87, 89–90,
  176
Kransberg Castle (Allied detention center),
  192–93, 199
Krauss-Maffei, 254–55
Kristallnacht, 113
Krupp, Alfried, 228, 236, 285
Krupp, Gustav, 1–5, 101, 228
Krupp (company), 24, 156, 171, 229,
  282
Kuka (firm), 245
Kunz, Helmut, 185
Kuwaiti Investment Authority, 261–62

Laagberg camp, 173
labor, forced. See forced and slave labor
Labor Day (1933), 61
labor shortage, 155
labor unions, 61, 119
Lambsdorff, Otto von, 267–68, 281
Lampe (bank), 249–51
Landecker, Alfred, 305
Landecker, Emily, 305–6
land mines, 255
Laval, Léon, 215, 217
Lebensborn (human-breeding association),
  90
Lebensraum (living space) concept, 88
Leopard tanks, 253–55
Ley, Robert, 119, 209
Liebknecht, Karl, 38
Liese, Kurt, 83, 84
Lipmanns (Jewish couple), 96
Lodz, Poland, 136
Loeffellad, Emil, 83
Lübeck, Germany, 80, 106–7, 112
Lüdecke, Kurt, 31–32, 34, 98–99

Luxemburg, Rosa, 38
Lynch, George, 189

Malmedy massacre (1944), 249, 250
Mann, Thomas, 200
Marcu, Josif, 208–9
Marshall, George C., 213
Marshall Plan, 213
"master race" breeding program, 90
Mauser (DWM subsidiary), 80, 243, 245, 253
Mauthausen concentration camp, 191
Max Franck (underwear producer), 190
Maxhütte (steel firm), 81, 191–94, 237
McCloy, John J., xvii, 236–37, 265
Mein Kampf (Hitler), 35, 88, 206, 235
Mercedes, 59–60, 69
Merck Finck (bank)
    Aryanizations, 114–19, 197, 220
    assets, 118
    Nazi accounts, 112, 196
    postwar situation, 195, 197, 251, 258, 269
    sale to Barclays, 269, 298
    von Finck and, 40, 251, 258, 269
Merkel, Angela, 301, 302, 305
Messer, Adolf, 285
Meyer, Alfred, *150*
Milch, Erhard, 78, 80, 97, 98
Misch, Rochus, 185
Mises, Ludwig von, 300
Mittelstahl (steel firm), 81
Montan (shell company), 83–84
Morgan, J. P., 125
Mouse (supertank prototype), 164
Mövenpick (hotel chain), 298, 300
Munich Re, 40, 194, 195, 197, 251–52
Murnane, George, 110–12
Mussolini, Benito, 37, 129, 159

Nacher, Ignatz, 100–101, 191
National Socialist German Workers' Party. *See*
    Nazi Party
NATO, 253, 255
Naumann, Werner, 248
Nazi Party
    agrarian aspects, 88–89
    annual conventions, 86–89, 99
    Bahlsen family membership, 7
    business tycoons' view of, 38
    cast of characters, xvi
    elections, 3–5, 34–35, 38, 54

financial difficulties, 4, 48
Haus der Deutschen Kunst, 101
membership numbers, 61–62
in New York, 31
Quandt (Günther) and, 31–32, 48, 62–63
Severin estate meetings, 49
Nebuschka, Reinhardt, 171
neo-Nazis, 259
Netherlands, 8, 9, 77
Neuengamme concentration camp, 156–58,
    164–65, 173, 198, 286–87
New York, Occupy Wall Street movement,
    7–8
New York Stock Exchange, collapse of, 38, 51
Nicolai, Eduard von, 118
Night of the Long Knives massacre, 71
Nordhoff, Heinrich, 225
Nordic Ring, 34
NSDAP. *See* Nazi Party
Nuremberg Race Laws (1935), 85, 97, 103,
    112, 115
Nuremberg trials. *See also* denazification
    courts
    American-led trials, 228–335
    executions, 209, 250
    first trial, 209
    Flick trial, 228–36, *229*
    forced and slave labor, 171
    International Military Tribunal, 193
    Jackson as chief US prosecutor, 193
    McCloy's acts of clemency, 236–37
    trial of industrialists (considered), 193,
        202, 209–10

Occupy Wall Street movement, 7–8
Oetker, August (grandfather), 87
Oetker, August (grandson), 293–94
Oetker, Ida (Kaselowsky), 87, 89, 94, 95, *150*,
    175, 295
Oetker, Maja, 294
Oetker, Rudolf-August, *95*
    in cast of characters, xvi
    on concentration camps, 96, 168
    death, 293
    death of his family, 175–76
    Dr. August Oetker, leadership prepara-
        tion, 87–88, 94
    Dr. Oetker, leadership of, 176, 223–24,
        249–50
    Dr. Oetker-Phrix venture, 168

estate, 293
Göring and, 96
hiring former Nazis, 250–51, 259
horseback riding, 94–95
Kaselowsky and, 87–88, 94, 96, 176
Kaselowsky museum and, 259
Kranefuss and, 176
life of privilege, 94–96
Nazi Party membership, 95
neo-Nazis and, 259
paralysis and recovery, 200–201
postwar arrest and denazification,
    200–201, 223
postwar investments, 249–51
postwar wealth, 257–58
Reiter-SA (paramilitary organization),
    94–95
son kidnapped, 269
Spoiled by Luck (memoir), 293
SS veterans, support for, 250, 259
in Waffen-SS, 151, 168, 175–76, 200, 201,
    223
Wehrmacht's catering service, 149–51,
    150
Oetker, Susi, 200–201, 259
Oetker family
    cast of characters, xvi
    companies, 11, 101
    family tree, 315
    forced and slave labor, 156, 167–68
    generational rift, 294–95
    reckoning with Nazi past, 282, 292–95
    succession dispute, 294–95
Office of Military Government for Germany,
    US (OMGUS), 193, 202, 209, 213
Office of Strategic Services (OSS), 187–88,
    192, 199
Ohlendorf, Otto, 208
Oldewage, Walther, 106–7
Olympic Games (1936), 98
OMGUS (Office of Military Government for
    Germany, US), 193, 202, 209, 213
Opel (car company), 225
Operation Barbarossa, 75, 144, 146, 148–49,
    152–53
Operation Citadel, 164
Operation Mercury, 141–44
The Order of the Day (Vuillard), 1
Organization Todt, 175
Oskar Fischer (publishing house), 100

OSS (Office of Strategic Services), 187–88,
    192, 199
Ostarbeiter. *See* forced and slave labor

Pabst, Waldemar, 37–38
Pavel, Horst
    AFA, 104–5, 175, 190
    Aryanizations, 139, 140
    in cast of characters, xv
    fleeing Berlin, 189–90
    forced and slave labor, 175
    Quandt (Günther) and, 104–5, 139, 243
    Quandt (Herbert) and, 104–5, 139, 140,
        175
Peiper, Joachim, 249, 250
Pels, Henry, 103–4
Persilscheine (Persil tickets)
    defined, 203
    Flick (Friedrich), 232
    Oetker (Rudolf-August), 223
    Porsche (Ferdinand), 227
    Quandt (Günther), 203–5, 216
    Reimann family, 277
    von Finck's, 221
Pertrix (AFA subsidiary), 104–5, 139–41,
    173–75, 219, 291
Petschek, Ignaz, xvii. *See also* Ignaz Petschek
    conglomerate
Petschek, Julius, xvii. *See also* Julius Petschek
    conglomerate
Petschek, Karl, 125, 128
Petschek conglomerates, 107–12, 125–28,
    231, 265
Pettibon, Raymond, 311
Peugeot (car company), 210–11, 224
Peugeot family, 279
Phrix (chemical fiber firm), 167–68
Piëch, Anton
    Aryanizations, 91–93, 226, 296, 297–98
    Aryanizations, postwar restitution, 226
    in cast of characters, xvi
    death, 254
    fleeing to Austria, 198
    forced and slave labor, 164–65, 172–73,
        199, 211
    Nazi Party membership, 122
    Porsche (company), control of, 91
    Porsche (company), founding, 57
    Porsche (company), postwar, 225
    postwar arrests and trial, 199, 210–11, 224

Piëch, Anton (*cont.*)
    Renault collaboration, 210
    Rosenberger and, 91–93, 122, 212, 226,
        260–61, 296, 297–98
    as SS member, 122
    Volkswagen, 129, 147, 164–65, 198, 199,
        225
Piëch, Ferdinand, 280
Piëch, Louise
    in cast of characters, xvi
    children, 225
    fleeing Germany, 172
    Rosenberger and, 212
    saving family business, 211, 212, 224
    Volkswagen and, 225
Piëch family. *See* Porsche-Piëch family
Pleiger, Paul, 126–28, 149, 228
Pohl, Oswald, 156, 166–68, 176, 208
Poland
    extermination camps, 153
    forced and slave labor in Germany, 7,
        147–48, 155, 173–74
    German invasion, 131, 135
    German war crimes, 135–36
    Goebbels's survey, 136
    Sobibor (extermination camp), 8
Porsche, Dodo, 172
Porsche, Ferdinand
    Allied questioning of, 198–99
    ambitions, 121
    Aryanizations, 91–93, 296, 297–98
    Aryanizations, postwar restitution, 226
    career history, 57–59
    in cast of characters, xvi
    character traits, 58
    citizenship, 70
    death, 254
    fleeing Germany, 172
    forced and slave labor, 156, 199, 211
    Ford and, 121
    Göring and, 98
    Herrmann and, 163–64
    Hitler and, 59–60, 69–70
    Nazi Party, membership, 62
    Porsche (company), control of, 91
    Porsche (company), founding, 57, 58
    portrait, *92*
    postwar arrests and denazification, 199,
        210–12, 224, 226–27
    race-car design, 57, 60
    Renault collaboration, 210, 211

Rosenberger and, 91–93, 122, 226,
        260–61, 296, 297–98
    as tank commission head, 147, 164, *164*
    Volkswagen, 69–70, 90–91, 93–94, 102–3,
        119–21, 128–29, 146, 156, 224–25
Porsche, Ferry
    amphibious car design, 255
    car design, 212, 226, 227
    in cast of characters, xvi
    death, 296
    fleeing Germany, 172
    forced and slave labor, 172, 211
    foundation named for, 295–97
    hiring former SS officers, 248–49
    Hitler and, 121, 146–47, *147*
    Leopard tank contract, 254–55
    Porsche company (postwar), 248–49
    Porsche design office, 121, 147
    portrait, *92*
    postwar arrests and denazification, 199,
        210–11, 227
    Renault collaboration, 210
    revisionist history, 260–61
    Rosenberger and, 91–93, 121, 212,
        260–61, 296
    saving family business, 211, 212, 224
    as SS officer, 148, 295, 296
    tank production, 254–55
    Volkswagen factory and, 121, 129
    Volkswagen Schwimmwagen, 146–48, *147*
    We at Porsche (autobiography), 260–61
Porsche, Louise. *See* Piëch, Louise
Porsche 356 (car), 212, 226, 227, 248
Porsche (company)
    Allied investigation, 198–99
    as Allied target, 172
    Aryanizations, 91–93, 121, 212, 260, 296,
        297–98
    financial problems (1933), 57, 59
    forced and slave labor, 172
    founding, 57, 58, 297
    hiring former SS officers, 248–49
    Leopard tank contract, 254–55
    Prinzing as commercial director, 227
    profitability (1935), 91
    Rosenberger as financial backer, 57
    saved by Louise Piëch and Ferry Porsche,
        211–12, 224, 225–26
    tank production, 254–55
    Volkswagen design and development,
        93–94

Porsche-Piëch family
  Aryanizations, 91–93, 101, 121, 212, 260, 296, 297–98
  cast of characters, xvi
  companies (*See* Porsche; Volkswagen)
  family tree, 315
  fleeing Germany, 172
  forced and slave labor, 147–48, 156, 164–65, 172–73, 199, 211
  postwar wealth, 225
  reckoning with Nazi past, 282, 295–98
  sex scandals and infighting, 268–69
Potsdam Conference, 193
Pret A Manger (company), 275–76
Prinzing, Albert, 227, 248–49
prisoners of war
  cannibalism, 149
  executions, 149, 249, 250
  forced and slave labor, 148, 162
  Quandt (Harald) as, 177–78, 181–84, 204, 216
  slave labor, 148, 162, 174
Pritzkoleit, Kurt, 244–45
The Protestant Ethic and the Spirit of Capitalism (M. Weber), 218
Puhl, Emil, 116
Pump, Johannes, 158, 173
Pyta, Wolfram, 297–98

Quandt, Colleen-Bettina, 272
Quandt, Ello, xv, 51, 65, 139, 185–87, 203–4
Quandt, Emil (Günther's father), 16
Quandt, Gabriele, xv, 290, 311
Quandt, Günther
  AFA, factory (Hannover), 156–57, 188
  AFA, forced and slave labor, 173
  AFA, military sales, 76, 79, 131
  AFA, Pavel's role, 104–5
  AFA, postwar, 190, 202–3, 243
  AFA, takeover, 23–24
  AFA, takeover targets, 139
  anti-Semitism, 64
  arrest (1933), 62–65
  art collection, 77
  Aryanizations, 101, 103–4, 139–40, 206, 215, 217, 243–44, 250, 289
  Aryanizations, postwar restitution, 206, 243–44
  birth and childhood, 15–16
  business legacy, 244–46
  Byk Gulden takeover, 76

Cegielski weapons complex, 137, 170
character traits, 20, 29, 218, 244–45
Daimler-Benz, 78, 243
death and memorial service, 238, 242–43, 245
Deutsche Bank supervisory board, 62, 78, 195
Dürener, 80–81, 97–98, 243
DWM, arms production, 76, 131, 214
DWM, Cegielski trusteeship, 137, 170–71
DWM, expansion financing, 154–55
DWM, interwar period, 79–80
DWM, postwar assets, 243
DWM, postwar lies concerning, 214
DWM, takeover, 24–25, 32, 76
Egyptian holiday, 238
estate, 245
fleeing Berlin, 187
forced and slave labor, 156, 170–71, 173, 187, 219, 290–91
French takeover targets, 139–40
Goebbels, jealous of Quandt, 56
Goebbels, opinion of, 47–48
Goebbels, postwar lies about, 202, 203, 215, 217
Goebbels, Quandt custody battles and, 50–51, 55, 70–72
Goebbels, Quandt's arrest and, 64–65
Goebbels, Quandt's Nazi Party membership and, 62, 217
Goebbels, Quandt's "peace at any cost" stance, 159
Goebbels, Quandt's sixtieth birthday party, 76–77
Göring and, 76, 98
health problems, 238
Henry Pels (company), 103–4
Hitler meetings, 1–5, 38, 41–42, 46–47, 60–61, 229
investment partners, 24, 25
Magda, courtship, 17–19
Magda, custody agreement, 32–33
Magda, custody conflict, 50–51, 55, 70–72, 137
Magda, divorce, 32–33
Magda, marital difficulties, 20–21, 30–32
Magda, offer to save her children, 186
Magda, Quandt's "peace at any cost" stance, 159
Magda, relationship with, after divorce, 36, 135

Quandt, Günther (*cont.*)
  Magda, wedding, 19–20, 50
  Magda as Nazi Party advocate, 36–37
  Magda's marriage to Goebbels, 46, 50–51
  Mauser, 243
  memoir (1946), 25, 33, 64, 205–6
  Montan financing, 84
  Nazi Party, 31–32, 48, 61, 62, 63, 217
  Neubabelsberg mansion, 16
  OSS memo on, 187–88
  Pavel and, 104–5
  portrait, *20*
  postwar arrest and denazification, 201–7,
    213–19, 230
  postwar assets, 206, 243
  Quandt (Hellmut)'s death, impact on,
    29–30
  on race, 105
  rearmament era, 79–81
  remarriage, rumors about, 72
  Sachs and, 97–98, 204–5
  Severin estate, 30, 33, 45, 48–49, *49*
  sixtieth birthday party, 75–78, 98,
    242–43
  Society for the Study of Fascism, 37–38
  stock market speculation, 22–23
  succession plans, 104–5, 141, 245
  textile factories, 76
  Third Reich involvement, 10
  Toni, death of, 17
  Toni, marriage to, 16
  war crimes, 188
  Winter (Emil) and, 194–95
  Wintershall investment, 23, 29, 243
  as workaholic, 17, 19–21, 238
  on World War II, 131, 144, 158–59
Quandt, Harald
  amphibious car design, 255
  birth, 20–21
  BMW, 247
  Busch-Jaeger Dürener, 245, 248
  in cast of characters, xv
  Cegielski internship, 137
  character traits, 256–57
  children, 256
  custody conflicts over, 32–33, 50–51, 55,
    70–72, 137
  Daimler-Benz, 246–47
  death, 256, 261
  death of his family, 181–85, 256–57
  father's remarriage, rumors about, 72

  Goebbels and, during childhood, 44, *45*,
    49, 50, 55–56
  Goebbels and, during Luftwaffe service,
    135–36, 141, 143, *143*, 152–53,
    169–70, 177–78
  Goebbels's final letter to, 183–84
  Goebbels's goals for, 138
  heirs, 271–72, 287
  hiring former Nazis, 248
  Hitler and, 42–43, 44, 55–56
  inheritance, 245
  IWK, 245, 253–54, 255
  labor service in Poland, 135–36
  Leopard tank contract, 253–55
  Luftwaffe, discussing war with family,
    158–59
  Luftwaffe, Goebbels and, 135–36, 141,
    143, *143*, 152–53, 169–70, 177–78
  Luftwaffe, as prisoner of war, 177–78,
    181–84, 204, 216
  Luftwaffe awards, 143, 178
  Luftwaffe deployments, 141–44, 152–53,
    159, 168–70, 177
  Luftwaffe training, 138, 141
  Luftwaffe uniform, *143*
  mechanical engineering, 77, 216, 245, 253
  Nazi youth organizations, failure in,
    137–38
  portrait by Warhol, 271
  postwar arms production, 255
  postwar employment, 216
  postwar wealth, 256
  Quandt (Ello) and, 203, 204
  Quandt (Günther)'s denazification trial,
    216
  role in Quandt industrial empire, 245–46
Quandt, Hellmut, 16–17, 29–30
Quandt, Herbert
  AFA, 66, 104–5, 139, 188, 201–3, 245
  Aryanizations, 139, 140–41, 190, 215, 289
  BMW restructuring, 10, 247–48
  British surveillance, 190
  in cast of characters, xv
  character traits, 30
  childhood, 16, 17
  children, 256
  on Communist threat to Germany, 66
  Daimler-Benz, 245, 246–47, 261
  death, 270
  education and travels, 65–66
  estate, 270

fleeing Berlin, 189–90
forced and slave labor, 173–75, 219, 289,
    291
France, trip to (1940), 139
Goebbels's opinion of, 51, 139
heirs, 270–72, 286, 287–88
Hirschfeld sheet-metal factory, 140
inheritance, 245
on Magda Quandt/Goebbels, 33, 37
marriages, 66, 138, 139, 256
Nazi Party membership, 139
Niewerle estate, 174
Pavel and, 104–5, 139, 140
Pertrix, 138–41, 173–74, 219
portrait, 271
postwar investigations and denazification,
    202–3, 216, 219
postwar wealth, 257–58
Quandt family separation of assets,
    261
Quandt (Günther)'s denazification trial,
    216
role in Quandt industrial empire,
    245–46
Severin estate purchased for, 30, 49
as SS member, 66
street named for, 309
Third Reich involvement, 10
visual disability, 30, 49
Wintershall, 245, 248
World War II family discussions, 131,
    158–59
Quandt, Inge, 256, 261, 271
Quandt, Johanna, 270, 291
Quandt, Silvia, 138
Quandt, Stefan, 308
    Altana, 271
    BMW, 270, 271, 307
    in cast of characters, xv
    Herbert Quandt Media Prize, 308, 309
    inheritance, 270, 307–8
    office, 271, 309
    philanthropy, 309
    reckoning with family's Nazi past, 288,
        290–92
    wealth, 307
Quandt, Susanne. See Klatten, Susanne
Quandt, Sven, 287, 291
Quandt, Toni, xv, 16–17, 30
Quandt, Ursula, 66, 138–39
Quandt, Werner, 51, 203–4

Quandt family
    Aryanizations, 101, 103–4, 139–41, 190,
        206, 215, 217, 243–44, 250, 289
    Brandenburg textile factories, 15
    cast of characters, xv
    companies (See AFA; Altana; BMW;
        Busch-Jaeger Dürener; Daimler-Benz;
        Dürener; DWM; Harald Quandt
        Holding; IWK; Kuka (firm); Mauser;
        Varta; Wintershall)
    Daimler-Benz, 261–62
    disharmony, 261
    family tree, 313
    Flick family and, 247
    forced and slave labor, 155–58, 170–71,
        173–75, 187–89, 205, 219, 286–91
    as Germany's second-wealthiest family,
        307
    as Germany's wealthiest family, 270
    harmony, 245–46, 261
    holding companies, use of, 245
    political donations, 301
    reckoning with Nazi past, 10, 282, 286–92
    separation of assets, 261, 270–72
    The Silence of the Quandts (documentary),
        286–87
    World War I, 15

Rathenau, Walter, 22
Ratzmann, Hugo, 117, 250
Ravensbrück concentration camp, 156, 173
rearmament (Nazi Germany), 78–85
Reckitt Benckiser (company), 278
Red Cross, 177
Reich Association of German Industry, 3
Reich Association of the German Automotive
    Industry, 90–91
Reich minister of public enlightenment and
    propaganda, 61
Reich Ministry of Economic Affairs, 66–67,
    107, 117–18
Reich Ministry of Transport, 69
Reichstag, burned down, 61
Reichswerke Hermann Göring, 126–28, 149,
    265
Reimann, Albert, xvii, 275–77, 305–6
Reimann, Else, 276–77
Reimann, Wolfgang, xvii, 306
Reimann family, xvii, 275–79, 282, 305–7
Reiter-SA (paramilitary organization), 94–95
Reitsch, Hanna, 182, 184

Remembrance, Responsibility, and the Future (EVZ), 281–83
Renault (car company), 210–11
Ribbentrop, Joachim von (father), 151, 209, 250
Ribbentrop, Rudolf von (son), xvi, 151, 250, 259
Riefenstahl, Leni, 89
Ritschel, Magda. *See* Goebbels, Magda
Ritschel, Oskar, 18–19
Ritter, Edmund von, 118, 119
Ritter, Egon von, 112, 118, 119
Robert, Alan. *See* Rosenberger, Adolf
Rohde, Paul, 25, 38, 47
Röhm, Ernst, 71
Rombach steelworks, 146, 161–63, 208, 232, 235
Rommel, Erwin, 146
Rosenberg, Alfred, 35, 98
Rosenberger, Adolf
    arrested by Gestapo, 91, 93, 260–61
    in cast of characters, xvii
    citizenship revoked, 122
    death, 259–60
    immigration to America, 212
    Piëch and, 91–93, 122, 212
    Porsche (company), buyout terms, 91–93, 297–98
    Porsche (company), financial backing for, 57
    Porsche (company), as foreign representative, 57, 93, 121–22, 212, 260
    Porsche (company), founding, 57, 297
    Porsche (company), restitution battle, 226, 297
    Porsche (Ferry) and, 91–93, 121, 212, 260–61, 296
    portrait, 58
    race-car design, 57, 60
    racing career, 57
Rosenblat, Michael, 272
Rothschild, Louis von, xvii, 116, 118, 196
Rothschild bank, 116–18, 194, 196, 220–22
Rzhev, Soviet Union, 152–53

SA. *See* Sturmabteilung
Sachs, Georg, 97–98, 204–5
Sachsenhausen concentration camp, 90, 156, 161, 164–65, 173
Sagan, Germany, 174–75

Salzwedel concentration camp, 198
Sauckel, Fritz, 84–85, 155, 209
Schacht, Hjalmar
    in cast of characters, xvi
    Hitler meeting, 2–5, 60
    Nazi Party election fund, 4
    postwar detention and trial, 192, 209–10, 230
    as Reich minister of economic affairs, 67
    as Reichsbank president, 78–79, 82
    Society for the Study of Fascism, 38
Schmidt-Polex, Hans, 67, 195–96
Schmitt, Kurt, xvi, 1–5, 41, 60, 66–67, 87, 195
Scholtyseck, Joachim, 289, 292
Schröder, Kurt von, 56, 90
Schuss, Marie. *See* Flick, Marie
Schwägermann, Günther, 185
Segert, Alexander, 303, 304
Seyss-Inquart, Arthur, 136
Sgarbi, Helg, 288
SGS (company), 298
Siemens, Carl Friedrich von, 101
Siemens (company), 156, 282
The Silence of the Quandts (documentary), 286–87
Silent Help (Stille Hilfe), 250, 259
Simon Hirschland (bank), 117
Simson, Arthur, 84–85
Simson (machine-gun factory), 84–85
Six, Franz, 249
slave labor. *See* forced and slave labor
S.M. von Rothschild (bank), 116–18, 194, 196, 220–22
Sobibor extermination camp, 8, 305
Society for the Study of Fascism, 37–38
Söder, Markus, 305
Soerensen, Carl-Adolf, 286
Soviet prisoners of war, 148, 149, 162
Soviet Union, 135, 153, 155, 175, 184. *See also* Operation Barbarossa; Operation Citadel
Spanish flu. *See* flu pandemic (1918)
Speer, Albert, 155, 164, 185, 192, 209
Spoiled by Luck (Rudolf-August Oetker memoir), 293
SS
    Aryanizations, 116–17
    Bahlsen family donations, 7
    Braunschweig march (1931), 44
    execution of forced laborers, 189, 192

extermination camp murders, 300
Flick (Friedrich) donations to, 54
forced and slave laborers, abuse of, 163, 173–74
Himmler as leader of, 86
Himmler's Circle of Friends, 86–87
ideological training, 168
Malmedy massacre (1944), 249, 250
Nuremberg trials, 234
Piëch as member, 122
Porsche (Ferry) as officer, 148
postwar hiring by Porsche, 248–49
Quandt (Herbert) as member, 66
Stille Hilfe (Silent Help), 250, 259
Waffen-SS, 151, 164
SS Economic and Administrative Organization (SS-WHVA), 156, 157, 166–68
Stahl, Ernst Knut, xvi, 299, 302, 303
Stalin, Joseph, 59, 135, 193
Stalingrad, German surrender, 153
Staumühle (British-led internment camp), 200
Steinbrinck, Otto
    anti-Semitism, 107
    Aryanizations, 105, 107–10, 125
    in cast of characters, xv
    as Flick (Friedrich)'s right-hand man, 52–55, 81–85, 105, 107–10, 125, 129–30
    Himmler's Circle of Friends, 85–87, 89–90, 234, 235
    Keppler Circle, 55
    Nazi Party convention, 86–87
    Nuremberg trial and sentence, 228–35
    professional ambition, 130
    in SS, 52, 82, 234
    Thyssen steel empire, 130
    World War I service, 52
Steyr Automobiles, 57–58
Stille Hilfe (Silent Help), 250, 259
stock market collapse, 38, 51
Storch, Beatrix von, 300
Strathallan, Viscount, 111
Strauss, Franz Josef, 255
Student, Kurt, 142
Stumpfegger, Ludwig, 185
Sturmabteilung (SA)
    Braunschweig march (1931), 44
    Flick (Friedrich) donations to, 54
    funding for, 39–42

Goebbels wedding, 50
Night of the Long Knives massacre, 71
parade celebrating Hitler as chancellor, 56
Sudetenland, Hitler's annexation, 123–24, 127
Südwestfalen (steel firm), 252
Summer Olympics (1936), 98

Tacitus (Roman historian), vii
Tata-Daimler factory, India, 254
Tata family, 254
Taylor, Telford, xvii, 208–10, 213, 228–37
Tel Aviv Museum of Art, 284, 311–12
3G (Brazilian investment firm), 279
Thyssen, August, 27, 53, 285
Thyssen, Fritz, 38, 130
"total war," 153, 154
trade unions, 61, 119
Traitor (movie), 99
Treaty of Versailles, 22, 79
Trott, Byron, 279
Truman, Harry, 193, 213, 236, 237, 241
Tudor (battery business), 215, 217

U-boat submarines, 157
UCC (United Continental Corporation), 109–12
Uexküll, Edgar von, 67
Ukraine, 7, 148–49, 174
uniforms, Quandt family production, 15, 76
United Continental Corporation (UCC), 109–12
University of Stuttgart, 295–97
US Counter Intelligence Corps (CIC), 192, 199, 202
US Justice Department's Economic Warfare Section, 196
US Office of Military Government for Germany (OMGUS), 193, 202, 209, 213

V-1 flying bomb, 172
Varėna, Lithuania, 149–51
Varta (battery company), 270, 286–87. See also AFA
Vereinigte Stahlwerke (VSt), 28, 51
Versailles Treaty, 22, 79
Veyder-Malberg, Hans von, 57, 91, 93, 121–22, 260–61
Volkswagen. See also Porsche-Piëch family
    "beetle" nickname, 121
    factory, 119–21, 120, 129, 198

Volkswagen (*cont.*)
  first car, 128–29
  forced and slave labor, 147–48, 156,
    164–65, 172–73, 198, 199, 211
  Goebbels on, 102–3
  as Hitler's prestige project, 60, 119
  Kübelwagen (bucket car), 146, 164
  military conversions, 146–48, *147*
  name, 120–21
  Piëch as chief, 147, 164–65
  Porsche (Ferdinand)'s design and develop-
    ment, 60, 69, 90–91, 93–94
  postwar situation, 198, 224–25
  production numbers, 129
  reckoning with Nazi past, 280, 282
  Schwimmwagen (swimming car), 146–48,
    147
  test cars, 93–94
Volkswagen Group, 296
Voluntary Donations for the Promotion of
  National Labor, 63
von Finck, August, Jr. "Gustl," xvi, 269, 270,
  298–305, *299*
von Finck, August, Sr.
  Allianz, 40, 66, 117, 194, 251–52
  Aryanizations, 101, 112–19, 194, 196–97,
    220–22, 250
  Aryanizations, postwar restitution,
    196–98, 220, 222–23
  in cast of characters, xvi
  children, 269
  death, 269
  divorce, 194
  elimination of Jewish rivals, 112–14
  frugality, 41, 60, 67, 87, 118, 195, 258–59
  Göring (Hermann) and, 116–18
  Haus der Deutschen Kunst, 67–69, *68,*
    101–2, 112, *113,* 194, 220–21
  Hitler, devotion to, 67, 115, 195–96
  Hitler meetings, 1–5, 39–40, 41, 60–61,
    229
  Merck Finck, 40, 112, 114–18, 194, 195,
    251, 258, 269
  Munich Re, 40, 194, 195, 251–52
  Nazi Party membership, 61
  postwar arrest and denazification, 195–96,
    198, 219–22
  postwar revenge plans, 251–52
  postwar wealth, 257–58, 269
  real estate (1970s), 258, 269
  Schmitt and, 66
  Der Spiegel interviews, 251–52,
    257–59
  succession, 269
  Südwestfalen (steel firm), 252
  Winter mining firm, 194–95
  World War I, 40, 222
von Finck, Francine, 298
von Finck, Gerhard, 269
von Finck, Helmut, 269–70
von Finck, Wilhelm, 40, 269, 270
von Finck family
  Aryanizations, 101, 112–19, 194, 196–97,
    220–22, 250
  cast of characters, xvi
  companies (*See* Allianz; Hochtief; Merck
    Finck; Mövenpick; Munich Re; SGS;
    von Roll)
  family tree, 314
von Papen, Franz, 56, 209
von Roll (insulation maker), 298
VSt (Vereinigte Stahlwerke), 28, 51
Vuillard, Éric, 1

Waffen-SS, 151, 164
Wagener, Otto
  in cast of characters, xvi
  Hitler and Magda Quandt/Goebbels, 43,
    46
  Hitler meetings, 2–5, 39, 41
  as Hitler's economic adviser, 66
  Quandt (Günther) and, 47
Wallich, Paul, 114–15, 197, 220
Warhol, Andy, 271
Warsaw, Poland, 136
We at Porsche (Ferry Porsche autobiography),
  260–61
Weber, Christian, 112
Weber, Max, 218
Weiss, Bernhard, 233, 234–35
West Germany
  1950s as dawn of new era, 241–42
  creation of, 218
  culture of silence, 242
  four wealthiest businessmen (1970),
    257–58
  Ministry of Finance, 266–67
  rearmament, 253–54
Wilhelm II (German emperor), 75
Wilson, Woodrow, 37

Winter, Emil, 194–95
Wintershall (potash company)
    Himmler's Circle of Friends, 87, 109
    Hitler meetings, 1–5, 42
    Petschek coal interests, 108–12
    Quandt (Günther)'s investment in, 23,
        29, 243
    Quandt (Herbert) and, 245, 248
Wöbbelin (Neuengamme subcamp), 198
Wolfs (Jewish family), 121

Wolf 's Lair, 146
World War I
    ceasefire, 37
    Charlottenhütte (steel firm), 27
    German arms industry, 23, 24
    Quandt family, 15
    Versailles Treaty, 22, 79
    von Finck's service, 40

Zyklon B, 300

ABOUT THE AUTHOR

David de Jong is a journalist who previously covered European banking and finance from Amsterdam and hidden wealth and billionaire fortunes from New York for *Bloomberg News*. His work has also appeared in *Bloomberg Businessweek*, the *Wall Street Journal*, and the Dutch *Financial Daily*. A native of the Netherlands, de Jong currently lives in Tel Aviv. He spent four years reporting from Berlin while researching and writing this book.